# Erotic Utopia

# Erotic Utopia

## The Decadent Imagination in Russia's Fin de Siècle

Olga Matich



The University of Wisconsin Press

The University of Wisconsin Press
1930 Monroe Street
Madison, Wisconsin 53711

www.wisc.edu/wisconsinpress/

3 Henrietta Street
London WC2E 8LU, England



5 4 3 2 1

Printed in the United States of America

Library of Congress Cataloging-in-Publication Data
Matich, Olga.
Erotic utopia : the decadent imagination in Russia's fin de siècle / Olga Matich.
p. cm.
Includes bibliographical references and index.
ISBN 0-299-20880-X (cloth : alk. paper)
1. Decadence (Literary movement)—Russia 2. Decadence (Literary movement)—Soviet Union. 3. Authors, Russian—19th century—Attitudes. 4. Authors, Russian—20th century—Attitudes. 5. Sex in literature. 6. Russian literature—19th century—History and criticism. 7. Russian literature—20th century—History and criticism. I. Title.
PG3020.5.D43M38 2005
891.709'11—dc22 2004024547

In memory of Charlie

# Contents

# Illustrations

# Preface

This book has been a long time in the writing. The first impetus came at a Russian literature conference held in Berkeley in 1987 ("From the Golden Age to the Silver Age"), where my claim that symbolist life creation emerged in part from Chernyshevsky's *What Is to Be Done?* was well received by colleagues. The paper on Zinaida Gippius, with whom I have had a lifelong scholarly relationship, and her unacknowledged link to the nihilist 1860s marked the beginning of my efforts to revise our view of Russian symbolist culture. I suggested that below the utopian surface of symbolist life creation was a hidden layer that had as yet not been recovered. Further examination of the historical and cultural context of the turn of the twentieth century has led me to recognize other unexpected layers in early Russian modernism, among them European degeneration theory. In rethinking some of the scholarly assumptions about decadence, symbolism, and their predecessors, I have concluded that early modernist writing in Russia, like elsewhere in Europe, was imbricated with the fin-de-siècle medical myth of degeneration. I hope that this claim, as well as the juxtaposition of the later Tolstoy and the apocalyptic visionaries, will receive favorable support from my readers.

Over the years, I have received very generous support from colleagues, friends, students, and academic institutions to whom I express my sincere gratitude. I am indebted to Carol Emerson, Robert Hughes, Hugh McClean, Irina Paperno, Harsha Ram, Yuri Slezkine, Sven Spieker, Viktor Zhivov, and Alexander Zholkovsky, who read individual chapters of this book or the whole manuscript. The book has profited from their valuable comments and criticisms. I would also like to thank my students and colleagues for engaging with me in timely discussions of the different aspects of early modernist culture that I explore here. I am especially grateful to Evgeny Bershtein, John Bowlt, Boris Gasparov, Beth Holmgren, Marsha Kinder, Aleksandr Lavrov, Eric Naiman, Anne Nesbet, William Nickell, Margarita Pavlova, Roman Timenchik, and Yuri Tsivian. I would like to single out two colleagues in Russia—Alexander Sobolev and Nikolai Bogomolov—who have generously shared both their knowledge of the period and archival materials with me.

I don't know how to acknowledge adequately the role of Charles Bernheimer, scholar of French and comparative literature who shared my fascination with the fin de siècle and who read those chapters that were written before his untimely death. When we met in the early nineties, we were both beginning to write books on the fin de siècle in our respective literatures of choice. The conception of *Erotic Utopia* owes a great deal to our frequent discussions, especially of decadence, which expanded my European perspective on Russian literature at the turn of the twentieth century. These discussions were an irritant to thought in the best meaning of the phrase. I only wish that Charlie were here to see the publication of his book and of mine.

I also wish to thank my research assistants Polina Barskova, Aleksei Dmitrenko (in Petersburg), Mike Kunichika, Jonathan Stone, and especially Jeff Karlsen, whose careful work, including editorial revisions and translations from Russian, has made this a better book.

Last but not least, I am indebted to the John Simon Guggenheim Memorial Foundation, the International Research and Exchanges Board, the Woodrow Wilson Center of International Studies, the University of Southern California, and the University of California, Berkeley, including the Institute of Slavic, East European, and Eurasian Studies, for major financial support. They funded both the research and the writing stages of this project. Without the necessary time off from teaching, I could not have written this book.

# A Note on Transliteration and Abbreviations

Transliteration of Russian names and words follows a modified version of the Library of Congress system, with *-ii* and *-oi* in personal names rendered as *-y* and *-oy*, respectively, except in instances where a different spelling has been accepted in English. Unless indicated otherwise in the notes, translations from Russian are the author's.

Below is a list of acronyms—referring to archives in Russia—that appear in the book:

| | |
|---|---|
| GLM | Gosudarstvennyi literaturnyi muzei (State Literary Museum, Moscow) |
| IRLI | Institut russkoi literatury (Institute of Russian Literature, St. Petersburg) |
| RGALI | Rossiiskii gosudarstvennyi arkhiv literatury i iskusstva (Russian State Archive of Literature and Art, Moscow) |
| RGB | Rossiiskaia gosudarstvennaia biblioteka (Russian State Library, Moscow) |
| RPB | Rossiiskaia publichnaia biblioteka (Russian Public Library, St. Petersburg) |

# Erotic Utopia

# Introduction

In 1921 the symbolist poet Viacheslav Ivanov described decadence posthumously as "the sense both oppressive and exalting of being the last of a series."[1] He was referring to a sensibility prevalent among early Russian modernists, who, like their European counterparts of the last decades of the nineteenth century, had a keen sense of the end. In Russia the feeling of doom was accompanied by utopian, millennial hopes to an extent unknown in Europe. This utopian orientation was expressed variously in political, social, and apocalyptic terms and may have been the only common denominator linking otherwise diverse circles of the intelligentsia engaged in transforming Russian life at the turn of the twentieth century. Such groups included visionary thinkers and messianic writers awaiting apocalyptic transfiguration as well as proponents of revolutionary movements that culminated in the revolutions of 1905 and 1917.

*Erotic Utopia: The Decadent Imagination in Russia's Fin de Siècle* examines what has come to be known as the "Russian spiritual renaissance," in which a cohort of apocalyptic visionaries set out to transfigure life.[2] Products of the fin de siècle, which in Russia spilled over into the twentieth century, these men and women filtered their decadent fears and utopian hopes through an apocalyptic lens. They were inspired by various mystical and religious teachings, especially by the book of Revelation. Steeped simultaneously in religious idealism and a decadent ethos, they espoused a sensibility that I propose to call "decadent utopianism," a designation that suggests a causal relation between their sense of doom and utopian dreams. This sensibility, consisting of innovative artistic and life practices, emerged out of their individual attempts to transcend the epochal crisis that Ivanov encapsulated in his memorable phrase rendering the world-view of his contemporaries, whom he dubbed "the last of a series."

Ensconced in an ethos that accentuated physical decline, the subjects of this study sought an economy of desire that would overcome what became known in European medicine as degeneration. Most importantly, they sought to immortalize love's body by defeating death: mortality was not only a decadent but also a utopian obsession of the fin-de-siècle generation in Russia.[3] Its most radical members, uniquely committed to the interrogation of sex and the meaning of love, believed that they could conquer death by resisting nature's procreative imperative and rejecting traditional notions of gender. Death, in their view, was the inexorable product of birth in nature, which inscribes the hour of death into the hour of birth. I will argue that the decadent utopians rejected the responsibility of procreation by choosing as their goal the transcendence of mortality, to be accomplished through a paradoxical erotic economy.

Their utopian project was affiliated with the zeitgeist of the fin de siècle in Russia, where, because of the country's sociopolitical backwardness, it began later than in Europe, approximately in the 1890s, and lasted longer, till the beginning of the First World War. This characteristic Russian time lag resulted in a cultural sensibility of belatedness, which gave rise to some unexpected consequences. According to Viktor Shklovsky, for instance, the late development of the Russian novel produced a genre that instead of imitating established literary tradition parodied West European prose fiction, resulting in a renewal of the novelistic genre.[4] I will claim that one of the striking consequences of Russia's belated fin de siècle was the fusion of decadent and utopian thinking into one.

The Russian "erotic utopia," a term that I borrow from Evgenii Trubetskoy,[5] had as its fundamental premise the conviction that only love can overcome death and immortalize the body. Considered in relation to Freud's better known concept of the death instinct, the erotic utopia presented a different view of the problematic relationship of eros and thanatos. But the Russians flouted not only nature's dictum of biology as destiny, they also posed a radical challenge to the ways individuals experience erotic love. The program for erotic revolution as it was understood by the decadent utopians aimed at overcoming the pan-European crisis of sexuality, as well as creating new forms of love and corresponding life practices that would transform the family and even the body itself.[6] The most controversial "real-life" dilemma posed by this utopia was the belief that the transfiguration of life could be accomplished only in an economy of desire that proscribed coitus.

An interrogation of the life practices of the decadent utopians reveals a fundamental difference between Russian and Western views of sexuality. Instead of locating the sex drive in the individual unconscious, as did Freud and most European psychoanalysts, they introduced a theory of erotic love that transcended the individual and focused on collectivity beyond the family unit. The virtual absence of bourgeois individualism in Russian culture may help explain the different approaches to individual and family in the fin de siècle. This in no way confutes the Russian novel's intense exploration of interiority. What it suggests is a difference in subjectivity, whose examination in the nineteenth-century Russian novel was not defined by bourgeois individualism and, in many instances, the biological family.

The key difference between the Russian erotic utopia and Freud's theory, however, is its grounding in a profoundly religious as well as utopian vision of life instead of individual psychology. Rejecting the nineteenth-century positivist tradition, the decadent utopians elevated eros to the metaphysical sphere. The greater importance of religion in Russia and the religious revival among some of the cultural elites at the turn of the century explain their turn to metaphysics at the expense of psychology. So does their disavowal of progress in favor of utopian idealism, which offered these men and women a way out of a national history characterized by social, economic, and political backwardness. Russia's visionary thinkers and poets embedded the erotic utopia in a fin-de-siècle historiosophy, defined by the goal of bringing history to an end. Their theories of sexuality became intertwined with the intelligentsia's conflicted view of Russian identity and the nation's place in history. And even though the Bolshevik revolution was firmly grounded in a social philosophy of history, its subtext was also related to utopian thinking and a concern with Russia's role in history.

The cornerstone of *Erotic Utopia* is the specifically Russian challenge to individualism, procreation, and genealogy. Leo Tolstoy (1828–1910), Russian literature's greatest family novelist, was the first to throw down the gauntlet to sex and the family, eventually representing sex even with procreative intentions as immoral and unnatural. Traditional accounts of Russian literary history consider later Tolstoy separately from those writers whom I have labeled decadent utopians, but as I show in chapter 1, he was a transitional figure between realism and early Russian modernism as it was shaped by Vladimir Solov'ev and his symbolist followers. It is after all Pozdnyshev, the degenerate hero of Tolstoy's controversial novel *The Kreutzer Sonata* (1889), who claims that in an ideal world the human race will come to an end.

At the heart of the antiprocreative challenge to society was the religious philosophy of Vladimir Solov'ev (1853–1900), whose extravagant ideas on love laid the foundation for the subsequent activity of several key modernists: the married symbolist poets Zinaida Gippius (1869–1945) and Dmitrii Merezhkovsky (1865–1941), whose theories and experimental life practices constituted one of the epoch's most extensive antiprocreative utopian programs; the symbolist poet Alexander Blok (1880–1921), whose celebrated poetry coexisted with a mystical cult surrounding his virtually celibate marriage to Liubov' Dmitrievna Mendeleeva; and the philosopher, critic, and journalist Vasilii Rozanov (1856–1919), whose writings on sex, religion, and race, along with his innovative prose, presented his contemporaries with a new and shocking mutation of a patriarchal sensibility tinged by decadence.

What is especially remarkable about the writers and philosophers whom I examine in this study is their effort to put their ideas into practice. Many of them, mostly symbolists, carried forward their apocalyptic dreams, not limiting themselves to the printed page and inscribing them into their personal lives. Quite uniquely, they sought a merging of writing and life practice, which became known as "life creation" (*zhiznetvorchestvo*). Besides creating art, the Russian symbolists participated in a grand project of making a utopian *Gesamtkunstwerk* of their lives.[7] The younger poet Vladislav Khodasevich, writing about symbolism a decade after the 1917 revolution, identified life creation as its fundamental quality: "Symbolism did not want to be merely an artistic school, a literary movement. It always strove to become a life-creating method, and in this was its most profound, perhaps unembodiable truth. Its entire history was in essence spent in pursuing that truth. It was a series of attempts, at times truly heroic, to find a fusion of life and art, as it were, the philosopher's stone of art."[8]

Because the practice of life creation is so central to the utopian project of this study, I treat the biographies of its authors as inseparable from their works; indeed, the biographies of Solov'ev, Blok, and Gippius became an integral part of their literary creation. In chapter 2, I examine the successes and failures of Solov'ev's mystical vision, and its conflation of sex and metaphysics, through the prism of the construction of a celibate public persona. In chapter 3, I consider the story of Blok's marriage to Liubov' Dmitrievna Mendeleeva (daughter of the famed chemist Dmitrii Mendeleev) and its perception by his circle as "a world historical task": Blok's marriage was expected to instantiate a utopian transfiguration of life. In chapter 4, I discuss Blok's vision of history as a palimpsest and its inseparability from the failure of his world-historical marriage. In chapters 5 and 6, I turn to the preemigration biography of Gippius. Drawing on her diaries and personal letters (largely unpublished), I focus on the alternatives to patriarchal institutions—heterosexual sex, monogamous marriage, and the procreative family—that she proposed and actively sought to initiate within her private circle. In forging experimental intimate groupings based on a Solov'evian concept of erotic celibacy, Gippius sought to bring about transfiguration in the here and now.

## Erotic Celibacy

Erotic celibacy, considered a prerequisite for abolishing death and immortalizing the body, is an oxymoronic sexual practice.[9] Not only does it erase nature's reproductive dictum and celebrate unconsummated erotic desire, it also reflects the radical idea that sexual renunciation is the agent of change. In step with the general climate of sexual liberation at the turn of the century, the subjects of my book endorsed the primacy of sex in their lives, elevating it to the realm of the divine. Yet most of them found heterosexual union, with its connotations of procreation, historically regressive; they believed that it would delay the wished for end of history. In promoting celibacy, Solov'ev resembled the later Tolstoy, but in contrast to Tolstoy, who drew on the moral tradition of Christian asceticism, the philosopher and his symbolist followers professed erotic desire as a necessary component of transfigurative celibacy.

One can make sense of this paradoxical economy of desire by considering it a two-stage process, even though its participants never represented it in such terms: in the first stage, located in history, the practitioners of erotic celibacy would store their libidinal energy in their mortal bodies; in the second stage, marking the transition to time after history, the accumulated erotic energy would be expended collectively—in a grand orgasm, so to speak, whose release of energy would immortalize the body. Describing erotic celibacy in familiar psychological terms, we could say that sexual desire would be sublimated until the collective union took place, but not completely, since the practice of celibacy was contingent on erotic desire. In other words, the practitioners of celibacy were expected to experience erotic arousal—after all, in the words of Solov'ev, erotic love was the sole trace of divinity in the here and now—but without the culminating moment of sexual consummation.

Even though its proponents claimed that erotic love was divine, celibacy as defined by Solov'ev represented a repressive practice, certainly for those partners whose desire was heterosexual, not to speak of the fact that the interlacing of abstinence and a heightened state of sexual arousal (without consummation) is virtually untenable, except in the locus of cerebral, or decadent, sexuality. An erotic agenda premised on the postponement of coitus until the realized utopia seems not only untenable but also phantasmic. What is so extraordinary about this practice is that it was considered sexually liberating. In actual fact instead of releasing the body from patriarchal strictures and promoting erotic love, the decadent utopian project demanded the very asceticism it proscribed. It enlisted the body to perform its own repression, to police itself.

Given the gender-bending climate of the time, the prescription of erotic celibacy, because coitus would compromise the immortalization project—by bringing a new child into the world—may be interpreted as favoring same-sex desire. Homosexuality displaced nature's law of perpetuating the species and subverted patriarchal gender restrictions. Distinguishing between an erotic economy that feeds the natural cycle and one that has the potential for transfiguring the mortal body, Solov'ev and his followers did not specify any gender restrictions on erotic love. Solov'ev seemed to suggest that homosexuality is an ontological condition, not a perversion. Such an opinion surfaced on occasion in the views of other Russian modernists of the turn of the century, with Rozanov, the main proponent of procreation in the Russian fin de siècle, giving the ontological meaning of same-sex love its fullest expression. Michel Foucault would later explain this ambiguity as the product of a whole series of discourses on homosexuality that developed in the European fin de siècle with the purpose of advancing stricter "social controls into this area of 'perversity,' [which, according to him] made possible the formation of a 'reverse' discourse: homosexuality began to speak in its own behalf, to demand that its legitimacy or 'naturality' be acknowledged, often in the same vocabulary, using the same categories by which it was medically disqualified."[10]

The emergence of a simultaneously repressive and legitimizing agenda on same-sex love expressed itself in Russia in an ambiguous discourse in the sphere of gender. The most striking instance of such ambiguity was the theory of universal bisexuality, proposed by Solov'ev and some of his followers. Its master trope was the figure of the androgyne—an image of plenitude appropriated by Solov'ev from ancient myth for his ideal gender of the future. In the discourse of the European fin de siècle, however, the androgyne was a euphemistic substitute for the homosexual. This double meaning would surround Solov'ev's future male-female gender with an aura of sexual ambiguity. Such an aura extended to other interpretations of the androgyne's sexuality: considered the epoch's artistic sex par excellence, the androgyne was regarded as having strictly cerebral desire, so that, like Solov'ev's ideal, it would experience erotic desire without having sexual intercourse.[11] Like all utopian plans of transfiguration, Solov'ev's apocalyptic vision was suggestive rather than specific; it was limited to the page and the sphere of metaphoric discourse.

## History

Since the "erotic utopia" was meant to bring history to an end, let's try to envision how its proponents conceptualized history. Instead of developing an abstract historiosophy, the decadent utopians superimposed a utopian teleology on an organicist model of history, which is premised on the idea that every culture passes through the stages of growth, stagnation, and death. This paradigm makes sense if we think of history as part of nature, which the decadent utopians intended to overcome. Rejecting the progressive model, their view of history resembles instead a pre-Spenglerian eschatology, which in fact was articulated in Russia before Otto Spengler's *The Decline of the West* (1918–22). Konstantin Leont'ev, an influential conservative thinker and writer of the Russian fin de siècle whose ideas are virtually unknown outside Russia, proposed an organicist historical paradigm in 1875 consisting of three stages: "primitive simplicity," "exuberant growth and complexity," and "secondary simplification," which represented the stage of decline and decay.[12] Rejecting progress, Leont'ev, who was a student of the natural sciences and a medical doctor by training, considered himself a pathologist of contemporary society. He applied to history the laws of biological organisms, thus conflating history and nature.

Living in the stage of historical decline, the early Russian modernists grafted onto it apocalyptic rupture, which would mark the end of cyclical history, a theoretical model that supposedly replicated reproductive nature. They imagined the end by invoking familiar eschatological cultural paradigms, among which were the coming of Christ in the book of Revelation and the divine androgyne, which they borrowed from Plato's *Symposium,* an influential text for early Russian modernism. Some also informed their visions of the end with ideas borrowed from positivist science, especially the theory of degeneration, despite their ostensible disavowal of nineteenth-century positivism. So even though essentially apocalyptic, the decadent utopians were in fact embedded in a scientific world view.

Some Western thinkers of the turn of the twenty-first century have also speculated about the end of history, proffering ideas that are reminiscent of the turn-of-the-twentieth-century Russian dream of transfiguring the body in the here and now. The potentialities of a genetically engineered body have both inspired and threatened our sense of the future; even though the transfigured body of Russia's utopians was the product of a phantasmic theory, it was perceived in similar terms as is biogenetic manipulation today. If we project, for instance, Slavoj Žižek's interpretation of messianic time, which he affiliates with biogenetic manipulation and a universal crisis of ideology, back to the 1890s and 1900s in Russia, we detect certain profound similarities between his view of the end of history and the messianic vision of the decadent utopians. Thinking about the end of history in our time, Žižek writes that messianic time "stands for the intrusion of subjectivity irreducible to the 'objective' historical process, which means that things can take a messianic turn, time can become 'dense,' *at any point.*"[13] It was precisely time's subjective potentiality of becoming "dense"—caused by the subjective experience of its compression—and achieving a state of timelessness that inspired the messianic hopes of the decadent utopians. Such a relationship between time and the timeless transfigurative moment informed their view of history, not to speak of the fact that the desire to bring it to an end was motivated by their profoundly ambivalent view of history in the first place. Living in a backward country whose history in the eyes of its Westernizing intelligentsia was merely "a blank slate"—because Russia had no history in a progressive sense—the decadent utopians were anxious to transcend it at all cost.[14]

## Decadence/*Degeneration*

A question that I examine particularly closely in this study involves the possible sources of the epoch's obsession with physical and moral decline. I look for answers to this question at the intersection of literature and medical science in European cultures of the second half of the nineteenth century.

Baudelaire's *Flowers of Evil* (1857), commonly considered the harbinger of decadence in literature, appeared in the same year as Bénédict Augustin Morel's *Physical, Intellectual, and Moral Degeneracies of the Human Species* (*Traité des dégénérescences physiques, intellectuelles et morales de l'espèce humaine*), which first introduced the term "degeneration" into French medical science. Published at a time when European cultures espoused progress and Darwinian evolution, these two texts revealed a pessimistic view of human development. They uncovered the underside of progress, which Morel called degeneration, and applied symptoms of the disease to individuals and whole nations. In hindsight, the coincidence of Baudelaire's book of poetry and Morel's scientific treatise speaks to the emergence of an important cultural discourse in the second half of the nineteenth century that entwined artistic decadence and the pseudoscientific theory of degeneration.

Nietzsche's *Ecce Homo* (written in 1888 and published in 1908), in which the philosopher called himself "a decadent," opens with a biographical section that resembles a psycho-medical case study of his delicate, morbid nature and physical ailments. *The Case of Wagner* (1888) treats degeneration and decadence as instantiations of a single discourse: "[T]he change of art into histrionics," wrote Nietzsche, "is no less an expression of physiological degeneration (more precisely, a form of hystericism) than every single corruption and infirmity of the art inaugurated by Wagner."[15] He preceded this comment with the claim that Wagner is a decadent, "the modern artist par excellence," embodying modernity's sickness. Calling Wagner a "neurosis," he wrote, "[P]erhaps nothing is better known today, at least nothing has been better studied, than the Protean character of degeneration that here conceals itself in the chrysalis of art and artist."[16]

Following Nietzsche, I treat decadence and degeneration as part of a single discourse. One of my main claims is that early modernism was imbricated with contemporary medical investigations of declining mental and physical health. This was particularly true of literature about sex, gender, and the family. I interpret the Russian debates of the 1890s and early 1900s about marriage and procreation as a response to degeneration's crisis of heredity and to the fear of perverse sexuality. As Foucault wrote in *The History of Sexuality*, degeneration "explained how a heredity that was burdened with various maladies ([. . .] organic, functional, or psychical) ended by producing a sexual pervert."[17] Psychopathology, the science associated with degeneration, considered sexual perversion both degeneration's baneful cause and its consequence.

Psychopathology and its neurological explanatory models developed complex taxonomies of hereditary degeneration as disorders of the central nervous system. Although the taxonomists seemed to derive pleasure from describing degenerate symptoms—as if they were decadent aesthetes themselves—they proposed ways of, if not curing them, then at least containing them.

So the fin-de-siècle expectation of the end of nature and history subsumed not only the desire to memorialize the end in beautiful works of art—and to create what Socrates in the *Symposium* calls "children not of the flesh"—but also the fear of degenerate heredity and of familial extinction. The phantasmic disease of degeneration, whose symptoms included neurasthenia, hysteria, atavism, hereditary syphilis, fetishism, and homosexuality, supposedly infected not only the individual but also the national body. Of the authors whom I examine in *Erotic Utopia,* the writer who experienced the crisis of heredity most keenly was Blok. In the context of the degeneration epidemic, his desire to enter into marriage imagined as a celibate union that heralded apocalyptic transfiguration offers a different perspective: celibacy for him represented a way of escaping the genealogical taint. One way that he inscribed this taint into his poetry was by employing in it images of decadent vampirism, whose blood taint passes from body to body. The vampire served as a symbol of what Blok perceived as his doomed bloodline. The decadent poet Blok, infected by venereal disease, represented himself as a vampire proliferating degeneration. The trope of blood as it is related to familial and racial health as well as to sexual perversion figures prominently in this study.

All my subjects make references to leading European psychopathologists of the second half of the nineteenth century. Tolstoy had Prince Nekhliudov in *Resurrection* (1899) read psychopathological studies by Jean-Martin Charcot, Cesare Lombroso, and Henry Maudsley. Solov'ev devoted a whole section of *The Meaning of Love* (1892–94), the epoch's programmatic treatise on erotic love, to Alfred Binet's essay on fetishism (1887) and Richard von Krafft-Ebing's *Psychopathia Sexualis* (1886), one of the most influential studies in psychiatry before Freud. (Even the clerics at the Religious-Philosophical Meetings made references to Krafft-Ebing's book.) Rozanov published a book titled *People of the Moonlight,* his own version of Krafft-Ebing's compendium of pathological case studies, which can be read as an eccentric study of gender and homosexuality. Andrei Bely wrote in his memoirs that Gippius was reading Krafft-Ebing with great interest in 1906.[18] As Igor Smirnov has shown, Bely later wrote that his youthful book of poetry *Gold in Azure* (*Zoloto v lazuri*, 1904) could only be understood as an expression of hysteria.[19] In 1918 Blok referred derisively to Max Nordau's best-selling critical study *Degeneration* (*Entartung*, 1892–93).[20]

*Degeneration* is an obsessive attack on the artistic production of European modernism, which Nordau labels as a pernicious product of fin-de-siècle pathology, as if he had mistaken art for life and had become the delusional patient himself. Yet the book was unique in its time, being the most comprehensive contemporary response to early modernist art and philosophy. "What is most effective about [Nordau's] book," wrote Robert Thornton, "is that almost all except the opinion is accurate."[21] Even though Thornton overstated the contribution of *Degeneration,* Nordau did exhibit a certain intuition about his time by situating the study at the intersection of contemporary medicine and literature. A journalist trained as a medical doctor, Nordau took degeneration theory out of the psychiatric hospital, where he had worked under the supervision of Charcot, and applied it to the literary and philosophical avant-garde. The older generation of Russian symbolists and those sympathetic to their artistic sensibility first learned about decadence and new trends in literature from the notorious book and from an essay on French symbolism by the critic and translator Zinaida Vengerova published in *The Messenger of Europe* (*Vestnik Evropy*) in 1892.[22] In 1893 she wrote a long review of Nordau's book—calling it "a history of the disease of the century"—in which she polemicized with his medical approach to literature.[23] *Degeneration* was widely discussed in the Russian press, with some critics finding Nordau's perspective enlightened, not just paradoxical or misguided. "The best people," wrote Akim Volynsky in the *Northern Messenger* (*Severnyi vestnik*), the first Russian journal dedicated to modernist literature, "have been embarrassed by his [Nordau's] perceptive analysis of their aesthetic and philosophical tendencies."[24] By "best people" he meant Europe's early modernists.

Though published later than Nordau's massive study indicting modern literature and the other arts, Tolstoy's treatise *What Is Art?* (*Chto takoe iskusstvo?* 1898) was conceptualized by the novelist before the publication of Nordau's book. The essay bears an uncanny resemblance to *Degeneration,* despite the chapter on later Tolstoy as a degenerate artist.

Besides lambasting modernist writing, music, painting, and philosophy from a similar perspective, Tolstoy quoted some of the same authors, even the same French symbolist poems, as did Nordau, attributing to them unhealthy, immoral concerns. Likewise, he was very critical of such modernist figures as Nietzsche, Wagner, and Eduard Manet, who, according to him, strain every nerve to satisfy the public's craving for pleasurable stimulation. Suffering from "erotomania," these artists, wrote Tolstoy, produced an art that is sickly and morally corrosive.[25] Only instead of "degenerate," he deploys the epithets "perverse" (*izvrashchennyi*) and "infectious" (*zarazitel'nyi*) to characterize their art. A total condemnation of European modernism, *What Is Art?* was nonetheless the most comprehensive contemporary Russian study of it, and like *Degeneration,* it was the most comprehensive despite the negative assessment.[26]

The Russian paradoxalist Vasilii Rozanov wrote about degeneration more than the other authors examined in *Erotic Utopia,* depicting its symptoms with disapprobation as well as sympathy. Like those who espoused a patriarchal view of sexuality, Rozanov was obsessed with images of healthy blood, in contrast to Blok's fascination with its sickly, degenerate aspect. Rozanov's imagery was linked to the blood of sex, especially as celebrated in Judaism's blood rituals. He extolled Judaism and the blood ritual of circumcision because of its life-affirming power and denounced Christianity as a degenerate religion, one that privileges celibacy over procreative marriage. This was Rozanov's position in his philo-Semitic writings, but he also scripted incendiary anti-Semitic feuilletons, which abound in vicious representations of the degenerate trope of blood as specifically Jewish.

Russian anti-Semitic paranoia reached a high pitch in the second decade of the twentieth century, especially on the eve of the war. One of its most outrageous manifestations was the Beilis case in 1911, in which a Jewish factory shop assistant in Kiev was accused of blood libel. The Beilis case prompted Rozanov's most malevolent anti-Semitic journalism, in which he figured Jews as decadent carriers of infection and vampires sucking the blood of their victims, thus undermining the health of the Russian nation. I examine the Beilis case, the Russian counterpart of France's notorious Dreyfus affair, in which a Jewish French officer was convicted of high treason (1894), through the prism of degeneration paranoia in society, as it was manifested in an obsession with blood taint and racial decline. As Sander Gilman wrote in *Difference and Pathology:*

*Stereotypes of Sexuality, Race, and Madness,* anti-Semitism was one of the most malevolent aspects of European degeneration politics.[27] Its most pernicious trope was the blood fetish, displayed most famously in Russian writing by Rozanov.

An unexpected consequence of my focus on the link between early Russian modernism and degeneration theory is the recovery of the discourse of degeneration in the criticism of contemporary Russian opponents of modernist literature, many of whom modeled their responses on Nordau's *Degeneration.* They have been largely neglected by serious non-Soviet literary historians, even though at the turn of the century they outnumbered those critics sympathetic to the new trends in literature.[28] Most contemporary critics whose political and literary ideologies were either liberal or progressive viewed the first modernists as victims of neurasthenic degeneration. The populist B. B. Glinsky, for instance, in his 1896 essay "Illness or Advertisement," described the generation of the 1880s, from whose pens came the first examples of Russian modernism, in diagnostic terms: "The acute ailment of neurasthenia first struck two, three mentally and spiritually anemic representatives of the 1880s. . . . The twilight of society's social consciousness offered favorable circumstances for nervous infection; . . . Mr. Merezhkovsky, his wife, Mrs. Gippius, [and others] got sick in the epidemic. . . . There were so many sick people that they needed a kind of 'Ward No. 6'."[29]

Using Nordau's *Degeneration* as his starting point, Glinsky identified the Russian symbolists as pathological subjects, suggesting that their writing was "the patrimony of psychiatric literature."[30] He depicted Gippius as "a sick writer with a ruined nervous system" whose recovery was unlikely;[31] the poet Konstantin Bal'mont and Merezhkovsky as writers with "sickly thoughts and ruined nervous systems" as well;[32] elsewhere Glinsky referred to Merezhkovsky as "a patient of Mrs. Gurevich's ward" and author of "a sickly, convulsive essay" on Pushkin.[33] A similar approach continued into the next century: exemplary is the 1908 essay by Iurii Steklov, the Marxist critic and future editor of the Bolshevik newspaper *Izvestiia,* in which he made extensive use of medical vocabulary to diagnose the pathology of modernist literary production. Its practitioners, wrote Steklov, borrowed their discourse "from courses on sexual psychopathology," translating "textbooks on sexual psychopathology [an apparent reference to Krafft-Ebing's *Psychopathia Sexualis*] into the language of belles-lettres."[34] As in the case of Nordau's observations, Steklov's were misguided. He treated modernist literature as if it merely reflected a clinical phenomenon and remained deaf to its aesthetic innovation.[35] Yet his comment reveals an aspect of modernist writing that the authors themselves and their sympathetic critics either overlooked or repressed.

Most serious scholars continue to ignore the intersection of Russian symbolism and degeneration. They have circumvented the pathological subtext of symbolist writing as if degeneration were indeed a shameful disease. Sensing the link between decadence and degeneration, "symbolists" such as Merezhkovsky insisted on distinguishing themselves from the "decadents." Merezhkovsky described the difference between them thus: "The decadents [are] those who are perishing and driving the refined cultivation of the decrepit world to the brink of disease, insanity, bad taste; the symbolists . . . [are in the process of] being reborn, prophesying . . . the coming of a New World."[36] They resemble those writers whom I call decadent utopians.

## The Poetics of Utopia and Degeneration

If fin-de-siècle sexual and racial anxiety and tension between diseased genealogies and their utopian cures comprise an important line of analysis in my book, so do the aesthetic practices of its subjects. In representing my heroines and heroes as if they were subjects of "case studies" seeking cures for their maladies in collective and individual utopian projects, I also consider the poetics of their literary production, especially as they reveal the ethos of utopia and degeneration. One way that I approach their works is to apply to them Charles Bernheimer's description of decadence as "a stimulant that causes a restless movement between perspectives, the goal being the attainment of a position outside decadence."[37] I would go further and call the decadence that united the authors discussed in *Erotic Utopia* an irritant to the senses and to thought, resulting in a new relationship to language.

Among the aesthetic consequences of interlacing artistic decadence and degeneration is the perception of imaginative language as the product of a heightened stimulation of the nervous system, with synesthesia as one of the consequences. Linked to Baudelaire's programmatic poem "Correspondances," synesthesia became one of symbolism's key poetic strategies designed to express referred physical sensations by means of metaphors that fuse sensual perception—for instance, color, sound, and texture—into one. Symbolism's obsession with the acoustic aspect of language could be seen in terms of the trancelike condition of heightened suggestibility that Charcot's hysterical patients experienced as part of their treatment at the Salpêtrière clinic.

Without using the term, Nordau interpreted symbolist synesthesia as a pathological addiction: the degenerate, according to him, "demands more intense stimulus, and hopes for it in spectacles, where different arts strive in new combinations to affect all the senses at once. Poets and artists strain every nerve incessantly to satisfy this craving."[38] Elsewhere in *Degeneration,* he claimed that "the [degenerate] mind mingles the perceptions attained through the different senses, and transforms them one into another. . . . [But] to raise the . . . confusion of the perceptions of sound and sight to the rank of a principle of art, to see futurity in this principle, is to designate as progress the return from the consciousness of man to that of the oyster."[39] In other words, synesthesia, according to Nordau, is atavistic. As in other cases, he supported his arrogation of the commingling of the senses to pathology by referring to medical authority, for instance, the authority of Binet, who considered the fusion of the senses a "stigmata" (Nordau's term) of hysteria.[40]

Perhaps the first Russian critic to note the "thirst for [such] unknown [nervous] sensations" and the "desire to create a new language" to express them was Zinaida Vengerova, who wrote about this in the year of the first symbolist manifesto (*On the Reasons for the Decline . . . of Russian Literature,* 1892), composed by Merezhkovsky. Vengerova would soon become affiliated with the first group of writers and critics interested in the new trends in literature.

The aesthetic device of decadent poetics that I consider most closely in *Erotic Utopia* is rhetorical fragmentation. "Decadence in literature," wrote Naomi Schor, "signifies a disintegration of the textual whole, the increasing autonomy of its parts, and in the end a generalized synecdoche."[41] Nietzsche described "literary decadence" in *The Case of Wagner* as "life no longer liv[ing] in the whole. The word becomes sovereign and leaps out of the sentence, the sentence reaches out and obscures the meaning of the page, the page gains life at the expense of the whole and—the whole is no longer whole. . . . The whole no longer lives at all: it is a composite, calculated, artificial, and artifact."[42] The most passionate practitioner of this rhetorical strategy in nineteenth-century Russian literature was Tolstoy, Nietzsche's older contemporary, who frequently deployed the literary fragmentation of the body, a rhetorical practice that originated in the positivist trope of anatomical dissection. Suppressing its positivist connotations, the trope became a hallmark of modernist aesthetics. Its immediate genealogy included the metalanguage of degeneration theory revealing an obsessive fascination with the decomposing individual and national body and its breakdown into separate parts.

Nietzsche suggested that decadence is the revolt of the part against the whole, a revolt that disperses and displaces it. Although the Russian decadent utopians had their own apocalyptic teleologies, like Nietzsche and their older European counterparts they saturated their work with the dissolution of society's and nature's whole. Yet, even if without much hope, they also longed for its reconstitution. We could say then that these early modernists infused the severed part with a fetishizing, mystical aura, while indulging their nostalgia for the whole. The obsession with dispersal typically took the form of a rhetorical fragmentation, or dismemberment, of the body—a discursive practice that at the turn of the century was closely associated with the tropes of blood, castration, and fetishism. I would suggest that in the fin de siècle sex and blood became unrelentingly synechdocal, despite the epoch's nostalgia for investing the whole body with erotic power.

Foucault wrote in *The History of Sexuality* that fetishism, governed by "the interplay of whole and part," became "the model perversion" in the fin de siècle, serving "as the guiding thread for analyzing all other deviations."[43] It was first identified as a sexual pathology in an 1887 essay by Alfred Binet titled "Le fètichisme dans l'amour" (to which Solov'ev referred in *The Meaning of Love*). Like Freud more than a decade later, Binet described homosexuality as a form of fetishism: instead of reconstituting the whole in procreation, the fetish, wrote Binet, displaces procreative sexuality.[44] While Freud's initial conception of fetishism (*Three Essays on the Theory of Sexuality*, 1905) resembled that of the French psychiatrist, he later developed his own theory, which reflected more closely the crisis of masculinity across the turn of the century. Imbricating it in his thoroughly decadent castration theory, he viewed the fetish both as a surrogate for the simultaneously imagined and castrated maternal phallus and as a "screen memory" for the phantasm of male castration.[45]

My deployment of the psychoanalytic theories of fetishism and castration is merely discursive.[46] I treat them as a consequence of their time, as culturally, not psychically, determined. In representing fetishizing fragmentation and displacement in Russian discourse, I view them as tropes articulating the epoch's subversion of procreative sexuality.[47] Emending Nietzsche's definition of decadence as the revolt of the part against the whole, I would add that decadence infused the part with a fetishizing aura.

## Artifice/Gender

Russia's decadent utopians fetishized the part at the expense of the whole as a battle against the biological order of things. In creating and mythologizing fetish substitutes for objects of desire, they invoked the superiority of artifice to nature and of beautiful works of art to realistic representation. One of the areas where the European decadent generation fought this battle was on the front of gender difference, conceiving an indeterminate and emancipatory sphere situated between male and female. Among the emblematic figures of gender fluidity that the decadence celebrated were the male dandy or homosexual, on one hand, and the masculinized, castrating woman, on the other. The figure of the dandy, described by Charles Baudelaire as an artful self-construction, displaced and sublimated heterosexual masculine identity, whereas the masculinized femme fatale emancipated from nature's procreative demands enacted her superiority to the "ordinary" woman.[48] A construction of the epoch's crisis of masculinity, the castrating female was frequently figured as the artfully bejeweled Salome, who conceals an imaginary phallus behind symbolic veils. Critics using a psychoanalytic approach have described her veil as a screen memory that protects the male spectator from the phantasm of castration, with the veil screening the desired part that is hidden and repressed.[49]

A question that arises in relation to the fetishization of the part and to gender uncertainty, as I suggested earlier, is the locus of the androgyne in decadence. An "unnatural" union of male and female, the androgyne, who served as a stand-in for the homosexual in the fin de siècle, represents a decadent ideal: it embodies its preference for artifice over nature while also satisfying the epoch's nostalgia for the whole. It is as if decadence displaced the nostalgic longing for the whole onto a figure of artifice, which served to transcend nature instead of perpetuating life in it. An artificial gender that resides beyond the organic whole and beyond history, the phantasm of the androgyne had the power to erase the attraction between the sexes that culminates in coitus and, as a consequence, the perpetuation of the species. As an instantiation of an artificial whole, it became at once an aestheticized fetish object and the single gender that recovered the whole and immortalized the body after the end of nature and history. It embodied a multiplicity of meanings, all of which were premised on gender fluidity. In the context of the epoch's obsession with pathology, however, the androgyne—a trope of homosexuality—represented a degenerate, unnatural gender. But in the context of a universal theory of bisexuality, the androgyne was that whole which reunited the fragmentation of gender into male and female.

## Celibacy versus Marriage

My study is not limited to the epoch's antiprocreationist utopia. To continue the delineation of the book's chapters, chapter 6 presents both sides of the procreation question as it was heatedly debated during the controversial Religious-Philosophical Meetings in 1901–3 in St. Petersburg. A unique, virtually unstudied forum for discussion, these meetings involved prominent members of the religiously inclined intelligentsia and the educated Russian Orthodox clergy. The brainchild of Gippius, they represented a confrontation of decadent utopianism, institutional Russian Orthodoxy, and Rozanov's shocking procreative religion. They served as a platform for Rozanov, who defended marital sex at the meetings by deploying what his opponents perceived as pornography. Faced with Rozanov's subversive references to religious asceticism as sublimation of same-sex love, the monastic clergy must have experienced great discomfort and anxiety. It is remarkable that they were willing to participate in these semipublic discussions at all.

This book opens with an examination of Tolstoy and closes with one of Rozanov, figures who both initiated and straddled the procreation debate. Even though I focus on the moralistic Tolstoy (chapter 1), whose condemnation of sexual desire resonated with the decadent utopians' fascination with celibacy, I also represent him as Russian literature's towering defendant of patriarchal values. Chapter 7 is an interrogation of Rozanov, the archprocreationist in symbolist circles whose unconventional writings sanctified sex, the procreative family, and its genealogical function. In the 1890s, Rozanov was an enthusiastic admirer of Tolstoy's earlier depictions of family and childbirth, as exemplified by the famed synecdoche of the diaper with the yellow stain in the epilogue of *War and Peace.* A product of a procreative economy, the diaper—in contrast to the later use of synecdoche in the fin de siècle—reconstitutes nature's whole, affirming the reproductive cycle. A champion of family and childbirth, Rozanov was nonetheless not a moralist. Quite the contrary! He could easily have undersigned Nietzsche's self-description as "the first immoralist," writing slippery, discontinuous texts that rejected Christian morality as decadent.[50] According to him, Christianity gave preference to decadence and female sterility over the childbearing female body.

Rozanov remains the most controversial and aesthetically most radical of the authors whom I examine. A symbolist fellow traveler, he bared their discursive sexual agendas and fears and shocked their sensibilities, comparing celibacy, for instance, to constipation. More vocally than anyone else, Rozanov emphasized the divinity of sex, representing it, however, in explicitly physical terms. He privileged the everyday, not symbolist abstraction. Instead of veiling sex with abstract images and discourses, as did his symbolist contemporaries, he delighted in representing images of secreting genitalia, female breasts, and pregnant stomachs in his works. He treated them as fetish objects in the religious and sexual senses. More than anything else, he promoted heterosexual copulation, which he believed was the only true sign of God in the everyday. On the front of literary innovation, however, Rozanov fetishized narrative fragmentation and stylistic heterogeneity, creating, as the formalist critic Viktor Shklovsky later pointed out, a new literary genre.[51]

## Russian Precursors

Besides contextualizing the erotic utopia of the Russian fin de siècle in the European decadence, I examine it as the product of specifically Russian cultural and literary circumstances. Perhaps the most radical philosophical theory of antiprocreationism was articulated by Nikolai Fedorov in his posthumously published *The Philosophy of the Common Task* (1906–7). It proposed a utopia no less remarkable, not to say delusional, than that suggested by Solov'ev and his followers. The utopia consisted of a "common task" whose goal was the collective resurrection of all ancestors. As Irene Masing-Delic put it, Fedorov "offer[ed] the most detailed program for a victorious campaign against death in Russian nineteenth-century philosophy," bringing together the rhetorical projects of "materialist scientism" and Russian Orthodoxy.[52] A marginal and virtually unknown figure in his time, Fedorov (1829?–1903) worked all his life as a librarian in Moscow; an ascetic religious thinker and fantast, he had a profound impact on his contemporaries, especially Tolstoy,

Dostoevsky, and Solov'ev, as well as on subsequent Russian cultural figures, including Konstantin Tsiolkovsky, frequently called "the father of Soviet rocketry science."

Fedorov's plan of immortalizing the body through the revivification of the dead was the first in a series of Russian projects that challenged the power of nature in a totalizing way. He sounded the first salvo against nature's death-dealing self-replenishment. Earlier than Solov'ev, whose ideas were formed within the antinature sensibility of decadence, Fedorov believed that the eternal cycle of birth and death could be vanquished by means of a collective inversion of libidinal energy, which instead of giving birth to new life would restore the dead. The implication was that Fedorov's resurrected bodies would lack reproductive organs, suggesting that the path to resurrection involved castration—a figuration of the sundered body that later appeared in the decadent imagination. The resurrected would be transfigured by erotic means but would be liberated from desire, proffering a future community of immortal eunuchs.

Fedorov's road to collective resurrection, rooted theologically in Revelation and scientifically in 1860s positivism, openly prescribed abstinence. In moments of sexual arousal, heterosexual partners would redirect their desire from coitus to the rebirth of their dead forebears. The Solov'evian erotic utopia had a similar goal: erasing nature and thereby death by storing individual sexual energy until the big transfigurative explosion would expend the energetic excess, thereby inaugurating a *vita nuova.*

A search for less obvious roots of the modernist erotic utopia in the Russian literary past uncovers them in the radical 1860s and 1870s, which were defined by an ideology of scientific positivism and socioeconomic progress in the socialist vein. It is a commonplace of literary history that the new men and new women of the turn of the twentieth century wanted to make a total break with the positivist, utilitarian heritage of the 1860s and 1870s. They replaced their predecessors' views with decadent aestheticism and apocalyptic transfiguration. I contend, however, that the life practices of the 1860s radicals, especially as formulated in Nikolai Chernyshevsky's highly influential radical novel *What Is to Be Done?* (1863), prefigured antiprocreative life creation at the turn of the century.[53] Even though the antiprocreative message of the novel had gone virtually unnoticed, Chernyshevsky's contemporaries the poet Afanasii Fet and the critic Vasilii Botkin titled their critique of the novel "Are Children Expected?" in which they exposed the novel's hidden antiprocreative agenda.[54]

Despite the first modernist generation's vituperative criticism of Chernyshevsky and other utilitarian writers, some of its members, perhaps unconsciously, inherited their "fathers'" utopian desire to extend social transformation to the corporeal realm. These parallels would be trite if it weren't for some astonishing similarities between the programmatic life practices of Chernyshevsky and his radical characters and some of the life creators of the turn of the century. The most striking example is the case of Gippius, elements of whose life uncannily echoed that of the characters of *What Is to Be Done?* I have in mind Gippius's celibate marriage to Dmitrii Merezhkovsky, a highly influential writer of the time, and their sexually unconsummated *marriage à trois* with Dmitrii Filosofov, a journalist and critic. A homosexual, he was the son of the well-known feminist Anna Filosofova. In linking the experimental triple union to an overarching goal of transfiguration, I suggest that Gippius appropriated Chernyshevsky, who had proposed a similar extramarital structure, with its power to harness erotic energy, as a tool for radical social change.[55]

Rozanov, a virulent opponent of socialist revolution and positivist utilitarianism, wrote more extensively about Chernyshevsky than did any of his symbolist contemporaries. Predictably, he treated Chernyshevsky ironically and with a certain distaste. Yet he regularly commented with great interest on Chernyshevsky's proclivity for what Eve Kosofsky Sedgwick, in *Between Men,* a study of English literature, termed "homosocial desire," which she described as the product of erotic triangulation involving two men with a woman in between.[56] Rozanov discovered in *What Is to Be Done?* traces of male homosocial desire that resonated more powerfully in the fin de siècle than in the earlier 1860s. In his review of the 1905 publication of the formerly censored novel, he ascribed to it degenerate psychopathology, a condition normally not associated with the progressive radical Chernyshevsky. Rozanov claimed that, without knowing it, Chernyshevsky deployed triangulated desire as love "between men," which psychopathologists considered a symptom of degeneration. "The desire to possess the one who is already possessed" in Chernyshevsky, wrote Rozanov, reveals erotic desire between husbands and their wives' lovers.[57] In *People of the Moonlight* (1911), Rozanov's pseudoscientific history of the displacement of heterosexual desire by ascetic practices and same-sex love, he went so far as to claim that in the 1860s, especially in the case of Chernyshevsky, "the storm of the time emerged out of the glass of homosexuality."[58] The "storm" refers to 1860s sexual politics, to which Rozanov ascribed a degenerate substratum; the glass refers to the positivist retort.

Thus beneath Gippius's and Rozanov's polemics against positivism and the social utilitarianism of the fathers lay hidden a Chernyshevskian layer, serving cultural continuity, not rupture. These overlapping ideological and chronological layers can be described as a palimpsest, a trope that renders particularly well the epoch's conflicted decadent sensibility. A metaphor of storing suppressed cultural memory, the palimpsest represents a vision of history in which the past is hidden or veiled but never erased. In the words of Renate Lachman, the palimpsest represents the "shifts between forgetting and remembering as the inner motion of a culture."[59] It allows the reader to indulge in a thicker reading of texts, based on multiple, frequently contradictory, unexpected subtexts. Freud suggested the "mystical writing pad," consisting of a wax layer covered by a sheet of transparent celluloid, as a metaphor of memory. Based on the model of a palimpsest, it preserves what is written by storing the text in the wax layer after its erasure from the celluloid sheet, which has been lifted from the wax pad beneath.[60] The recovery of the lower layer in Gippius's personal palimpsest, for instance, allows us to discover the surprising common ground shared by the decadent and positivist visions of transfiguring life. In the case of Rozanov, we observe the opposite—his discovery in an older text traces of a sensibility that would be elaborated by subsequent generations.

## Approaches

Scholars of Russian modernism have often insisted on clear boundaries between decadents, symbolists, and naturalists that were never there. Reflecting a scholarly emphasis on literary taxonomies, on one hand, they privileged the symbolists, on the other, perhaps because the symbolist generation had been discredited in the Soviet era unlike some of their more fortunate contemporaries. This produced artificial boundaries that have become increasingly less firm as a result of the shift in literary politics, especially since the end of the Soviet Union.

My examination of Russian modernism problematizes historical rupture by considering more closely questions of literary continuity and of the lingering presence of overlapping cultural concerns lying just below the surface of change and difference. The main contribution of *Erotic*

*Utopia* to literary studies is its examination of early Russian modernism in conjunction with degeneration theory. It treats sexuality in the Russian fin de siècle as a complex negotiation of the epoch's anxieties, especially those lodged in the body, and their reflection in contemporary aesthetic practices.[61] Its approach to Russian theories of sexuality is fundamentally indebted to Foucault's view according to which "sex was [. . .] constrained to lead a discursive existence" in European cultures since the eighteenth century.[62] Even though Foucault's claim regarding the transformation of sex into discourse is at times too all-encompassing and reductive, it sheds light on the creation of love's body by the men and women whom I call decadent utopians. Their view of eros—based on a phantasm—was almost exclusively discursive. I suggest that the discursiveness of the Russian erotic utopia was more totalizing than even Freud's theory and practice of psychoanalysis, which also reflected the epoch's sexual anxieties, but in a bourgeois, not utopian, ambience. If we articulate the creation of love's body in the Russian fin de siècle by means of an inverted Christian symbol, we could say that "flesh became word," subsuming the New Testament symbol of the "word becoming flesh."

My attempt to particularize the discourse of the antiprocreative utopia of Russia's fin de siècle involves an examination of its master tropes. Besides the palimpsest, the tropes that I have mentioned so far are fetishism, dissection, castration, blood, vampirism, the androgyne, and veiled women; some others are decollation and triangular desire, all of which I consider in historical perspective. In doing so I demonstrate that magisterial tropes acquire new layers of meaning in new cultural contexts while suppressing others, having the effect of expanding and contracting the metaphor's repertory of references. The accretion of layers forms a palimpsest, in which, as in ancient manuscripts, the older strata are submerged by overwriting. But as I show, they exist just below the surface, waiting to be retrieved and deciphered by a reader inclined to perceive cultural development not just as rupture but also as continuity. In this I follow Shklovsky, according to whom the principle of cultural layering informs all literary history. He described it as a process in which the vanquished literary line "can be resurrected again, being an eternal pretender to the throne."[63]

This does not mean that the subjects of this study perceived their utopian project in terms of cultural continuity. Quite the opposite! Like Russia's revolutionaries and literary radicals such as Shklovsky, they expected rupture of the historical cycle. Sharing with Bolsheviks and others a radical vision of "remaking man" and "conquering nature," the decadent utopians and their followers wanted radical change. This shared vision helps explain why those among them who were alive during the 1905 revolution welcomed it; some initially welcomed the Bolshevik revolution, considering it an apocalyptic event.

The realized utopia of the Bolsheviks revealed magnificent, delusional, and repressive dreams and practices. We can only speculate regarding the repressive possibilities of the realized erotic utopia, although in my discussion of it, I have already suggested some of its repressive and delusional aspects. Erotic celibacy, without which transfiguration could not take place, was meant as a totalizing sexual practice, displacing the consummation of erotic desire with cerebral sexual play. But as an exemplar of modernism, the symbolist and presymbolist life-creation project is Russian literature's truly dazzling commingling of life and art.

# 1

# Lev Tolstoy as Early Modernist

## Fragmenting and Dissecting the Body

Viktor Shklovsky, the formalist critic who derived his theory of defamiliarization from Tolstoy's fiction, began his 1963 biography of the author with a chapter titled "About the Green Sofa which Was Later Upholstered in Black Oilcloth." The centerpiece of the chapter is a Moroccan leather sofa dotted by little gilt nailheads, with three drawers at the bottom and sliding book rests on both sides. This sofa in Tolstoy's study in Iasnaia Poliana, where it still stands today, assumes a life of its own in Shklovsky's biographical study. It is this object, rather than Tolstoy's gentry family or his fiction, that Shklovsky presented as the agent of generation and writing.

The sofa, reported Shklovsky, was the site of the birth of Russian literature's great patriarch and is the only surviving relic of the house in which that birth took place; it also saw the birth of most of Tolstoy's thirteen children. When asked where he was born, Tolstoy would answer: "'In Iasnaia Poliana, on the leather sofa.' . . . Of all the things in the house, Tolstoy was probably fondest of this leather sofa," wrote Shklovsky. "He wanted it to be the raft on which he would sail through life, from birth till death."[1]

Shklovsky claimed that the sofa was also Tolstoy's literary repository, not just his birthplace: "In the drawers of the sofa he kept those manuscripts which he wished to protect from being leafed through and scrutinized" by his anxiously inquisitive family members.[2] For Shklovsky, who was interested in multipurpose constructivist furniture of the 1920s, the sofa seems to represent a bed-desk as the locus of procreation cum writing.[3] His discussion of Tolstoy's bed suggests a conflation of

Green sofa reupholstered in black oilcloth in Iasnaia Poliana (2002)

writing and procreation. When the later Tolstoy began to disavow the procreative family ideal, however, the sofa became a safe haven for the "illegitimate children" of Tolstoy's pen. Instead of children of the flesh, who would perpetuate his family line, this progeny was cerebral, as were Plato's favored children not of the flesh.[4]

Shklovsky focused on Tolstoy's bed because of his reputation as one of literature's greatest family novelists. *War and Peace* stands as the nineteenth century's unsurpassed monument to procreation and nature's vital force, in the same way as the green sofa in Iasnaia Poliana stood as the emblem of Tolstoy's family lineage. In *War and Peace,* which marks the high point of Tolstoy's celebration of the body as the object of novelistic representation, family and genealogy are identified with biological continuity. The championship of family in this novel, as well as in *Anna Karenina,* reflects the author's lifelong preoccupation with the relationship of the invisible, natural whole and its visible parts.

In figuring the green sofa as a raft that would carry Tolstoy from birth to death, Shklovsky evoked the patriarchal image of dying in the family bed. A rebel who rejected the family at the end, including marriage and procreation, Tolstoy died in a strange bed at the Ostapovo train station after fleeing from the familial estate. Like Christ's apostles and their followers, Tolstoy had left behind his worldly attachments and belongings in search of a more righteous life, just as he had abandoned his view of nature as an organic whole. Unlike the green sofa, made of oak wood and standing on eight wooden legs, Tolstoy's accidental deathbed was made of metal. Photographs of it reveal an ascetic metal cot.

In his growing asceticism and demonization of sexual desire, Tolstoy was influenced by the fin-de-siècle concern with degeneration. Although he had been obsessed with sexual desire throughout his life, in his later years he became increasingly disturbed by sex in all its forms and considered even procreative sex deviant, if not depraved. But unlike many psychopathologists of that period, who ascribed depravity to tainted heredity, Tolstoy saw its root in immorality. Despite this crucial difference, Tolstoy's views on sex echoed those of the psychopathologists: in representing the body, he typically deployed a discourse informed by obsessive repetition and fetishism, one of the objects of psychopathological concern. Of particular interest in this respect is his choice of words to express the power of art, which he described using medical discourse. I have in mind the well-known essay *What Is Art?* (*Chto takoe iskusstvo?* 1897–98), in which he affiliated its power with infection (*zarazhat'*) and contagion (*zarazitel'nost'*). Although he ascribed positive meaning to these words, the unconscious medicalization of both "good" and "bad" art reveals the epoch's preoccupation with medical pathology.

I suggest that Tolstoy's treatise on aesthetics, in fact, reveals the influence of degeneration theory. It intersects in profound ways with Max Nordau's *Degeneration* (1892), which pathologized early modernist art, including Tolstoy's writing. Ironically, however, like Nordau's book, his essay served as an introduction to early European modernism for Russian readers, offering them perhaps the most extensive contemporary discussion of modernism in Russian, including the quotation of whole poems by Charles Baudelaire, Paul Verlaine, and Stéphane Mallarmé.

Nordau criticized Tolstoy's realism for its excessive use of detail, which he considered exemplary of degenerate "stigmata."[5] In *What Is Art?* Tolstoy himself arrogated the excess of descriptive detail to what he called "bad art"; he was particularly critical of "realistic" detail that roots the narrative in a particular time and place.[6] Yet his major fiction is characterized precisely by what some have called the "superfluous detail," whose primary purpose is conjuring up the body as a whole. This mimetic device has the opposite function as well, with severed body parts standing only for themselves. Rather than synecdoches evoking a larger whole, lips, eyes, jaws, hands, legs, and other body parts become fetish objects, as I will demonstrate in this chapter. For Tolstoy these fetishes were not so much objects of worship or of displaced sexual desire, as the Freudian view of the fetish holds; rather, they functioned as agents of dispersal, reflecting Tolstoy's growing reservations about nature, which linked him to the fin-de-siècle suspicion of life contaminated by nature's pullulation. Reflecting a tendency toward bodily renunciation, the rhetorical strategy of severing parts of the body came to serve his growing desire to eradicate sexual desire.

This chapter focuses on Tolstoy as a transitional figure in the history of late nineteenth-century literature. More than the work of any other nineteenth-century Russian writer, his fiction represents the transition from a traditional world-view based on the procreative family and organic nature, associated by Shklovsky with the green sofa, to one that reveals a fear of degeneration, not only of society but also of the body. Justified by an ascetic moral position, Tolstoy's ideology shifted resolutely from one that celebrated the family and childbirth to one that problematized procreation. In this chapter we shall see that it may also be viewed as an instantiation of the decadent displacement of the whole by a fetish object as an instrument for controlling bodily excess and that beneath Tolstoy's condemnation of sex lay the fear of pathology and physiological decay.

## *Young Tolstoy*

Tolstoy's earliest attacks on the body took the form of prescribing bodily renunciation by rigid rules that he applied to his personal life. His early diaries are filled with abject self-recriminations and detailed plans for self-improvement that reveal an optimistic view of the relationship between the deleterious part and the healthy, salubrious whole. In his very first diary entry, written March 17, 1847, in the Kazan' University clinic, he discussed the part-whole relationship by examining his feelings of self-recrimination in response to his life of sexual debauchery. "I got gonorrhea, it goes without saying, the way it is usually gotten," wrote Tolstoy in that entry. His private parts had been infected in the brothels of Kazan', a condition he associated with "youthful debauchery of the soul."[7] According to a close friend, he stood by the bed of the prostitute after his first sexual encounter in the brothel and cried.[8]

Tolstoy recorded that he was alone in the hospital, deprived of all social stimuli, including those provided by servants. This situation allowed him to explore his relation to the universe, which he proceeded to do in what Boris Eikhenbaum in *Young Tolstoy* described as a deliberate and logical eighteenth-century manner that indicates faith in reason.[9] Tolstoy offered a Cartesian disquisition on individual reason as part of the organic whole, contrasting it to society, which, like his private parts, he considered unhealthy because it lacked wholeness. He concluded his discourse with the optimistic idea that despite the great difficulty of controlling behavior, one's reason can be trained to merge with the whole felicitously: "The reason of a single man is part of all existence, and a part is incapable of upsetting the order of the whole. Rather, it is the whole that is capable of killing the part. Thus you must arrange your reason so that it conforms with the whole, with the source of everything, and not with the part, with human society; then your reason will merge with this whole, while society, as part, will no longer have an influence on you."[10]

Instead of having fetishist power, the part is subsumed by the whole. Otherwise it would need to be plucked out like the eye that offendeth!

The moral lesson is that one should not mistake the part—the social world—for cosmic unity, which Tolstoy associated in this passage with nature's divinely reasoned kingdom. The implied subtext of the moral prescription is also sexual desire: instead of allowing his private parts to lead their own immoral, and clearly unhygienic, life, he essayed to merge them with the organic moral whole.

After his sexual encounters and resultant feelings of self-disgust, he longed for a return to nature, which, according to this passage, embodies reason as a moral force. Nature for Tolstoy was proof that beyond the world of artificial social convention there exists a "real" life. After returning home from the clinic, Tolstoy wrote on April 17: "[A]ll within her [nature] is constantly developing . . . each component part unconsciously facilitates the development of the other parts." Since human beings are part of nature, endowed with reason, they must make a conscious effort to contribute to the further development of organic unity.[11] Needless to say, this reflects a view of nature that is very different from the vision of the experimental scientist who considers nature a cold, dead corpse to be dissected on the anatomist's table.

The entries following Tolstoy's first experience with venereal disease are emblematic of the many subsequent diary entries in which he developed a complex, logical argument that culminated in a set of rules that would prevent him from succumbing to uncontrolled sexual desire. The rules consisted of very detailed checklists and charts whose purpose was to purge the body of all excess and train his personal moral reason to pursue an orderly life. What he didn't consider at this point was the contemporary view that excess is part of nature, a view held by naturalists as well as decadents. In fact, he didn't seem to understand that a "fresh child" is part of nature's excess.

Eikhenbaum argued in a formalist vein that despite Tolstoy's moral concerns and feelings of anguish, these diary entries were first and foremost literary experiments: the future author was developing an analytical method of "anatomizing" complex philosophical and psychological problems, a method that he would later use in his fiction.[12] This is certainly true, but the behavioral prescriptions must also be taken at face value. They reveal Tolstoy's lifelong preoccupation with the unresolvable conflict between desire and moral reason. Rejecting the value of desire, he never wrote in his diaries about the pleasure derived from sex. The emphasis was always on loss of self-control. He only wrote of the before and after—of his unsuccessful efforts to abstain followed by self-castigation and renewed plans for self-improvement.

## Metonymic Representation of the Body

The early symbolist Dmitrii Merezhkovsky called Tolstoy the "seer of the flesh" (*tainovidets ploti*) in his classic study *L. Tolstoy and Dostoevsky: Life, Work, and Religion* (1901–2). Perhaps Tolstoy's most original, though failed, representation of the bodily is the depiction of childbirth in *Anna Karenina,* which offers an abundance of obstetrical and other female bodily details as perceived through a man's eyes. This is how a contemporary feminist reader most likely would see the novel's birthing scene, despite Tolstoy's apparent desire to access female experience in the corresponding chapters. Tolstoy's contemporary the poet Afanasii Fet wrote him that "no one since the beginning of time [had] done" anything so bold aesthetically.[13]

In trying to assess the scene from Tolstoy's perspective, Merezhkovsky—who predictably failed to notice the absence of Kitty's body—wrote that the author was critical of Levin's response to the birth of his son. According to the critic, Tolstoy represented the response as the mere production of language with no lasting embodiments. Unlike his cerebral male protagonists, who endlessly "philosophize," Tolstoy's procreating heroines puncture the sphere of language—in Merezhkovsky's words—by offering "a silent and irrefutable argument, the bringing into the world of a fresh child."[14] The birth of a child shatters the continuous flow of "unnatural" language. Contrary to Plato's vision in the *Symposium,* in which preference is given to philosophical and poetic children, Tolstoy celebrated childbirth in the flesh. In using the epithet "silent" to characterize it, Merezhkovsky underscored Tolstoy's vision of the superiority of nature: its self-expression without the artificial filter of language.

The birth of Mitia in *Anna Karenina* severs the son from the mother. As such, it symbolizes the Tolstoyan metonym that evokes and reconstitutes nature's whole. Yet when Levin first sees his newborn son, he is disgusted because he can only visualize him as a red quivering piece of flesh. Only Kitty, Tolstoy's subject of wordless childbirth, is capable of experiencing the organic relationship between part and whole without the mediating power of language. Levin attains this understanding by means of philosophical epiphany; he is inspired by the *idea* of procreation and nature's cycle of birth and death, not by the organic body of his newborn son. Like Tolstoy and his intellectual heroes, Levin cannot appreciate the physical experience without distancing himself from it discursively—with words.[15]

The suggestion is that Mitia is nature's mainspring of embodiment and continuity. This example of metonymic embodiment is emblematic of Tolstoyan representation that restores the natural whole. Despite the child's physical severance from the mother's womb, it is an act of nature's replenishment, not of dismemberment, in contrast to some of the other uses of discursive severance in Tolstoy's fiction.

In the epilogue of *War and Peace,* Tolstoy distributed the ability to grasp organic connections between part and whole along similar gender lines. Natasha, now a mother, famously displays the diaper with the yellow stain, while her husband Pierre produces rational language. Natasha's youthful, feminine subjectivity, in which language had played a prominent role, has been transformed into an ego-less site of reproductive nature. As Merezhkovsky disapprovingly commented, she has come to represent sex in nature, which dissolves all that is individual into the faceless, natural process of reproduction. He compared her to a statue crowning "one of the greatest edifices ever built by mankind," over which Tolstoy raised the "victorious banner" of the "diaper with the yellow stain."[16] Merezhkovsky's architectural metaphor of Tolstoy's novel conjures up nurseries with dirty diapers and sprawling familial spaces for bodies that multiply. The metonymic diaper of the epilogue serves its author in making whole the novelistic edifice of *War and Peace,* which resembles the family home that housed Tolstoy's favorite green sofa. Searching in *War and Peace* for male equivalents of the maternal bodies of Kitty and Natasha, Merezhkovsky predictably selected the body of the peasant Platon Karataev, who embodies the harmonious relation between part and the whole of life: "He does not exist independently: he is only part of the Whole, a drop in the ocean of nationwide, all-human, universal life. And he reproduces this life with his personality, or lack thereof, in the same way that a drop of water, in its perfect *roundness,* reproduces the earthly sphere."[17]

Merezhkovsky interpreted Tolstoy's representation of Platon (Plato) as consisting simultaneously of visible parts and invisible unity: not a universe unto himself, he is its perfect microcosm. His body, despite its incorporeal representation, is inextricable from the natural cycle. One possible explanation for this oxymoron of disembodied nature is Tolstoy's budding but still covert desire to disincarnate the natural by castrating the male sex. Since the desire is covert, if not unconscious, and without decadent overtones, Platon experiences the inexorable repetition of birth and death as a true natural man, whose decomposing corpse, unbeknown to him, will replenish nature.

Besides discussing the organic wholeness of such characters as Kitty, Natasha, and Platon Karataev and Tolstoy's anatomical precision in representing the human body, Merezhkovsky also examined another trademark of Tolstoy's fiction: the obsessive repetition of a singular bodily detail, such as the mustachioed short upper lip of the "little Princess" and Speransky's soft white hand, both in *War and Peace.* Although Merezhkovsky wrote that the recurrent detail creates the harmonious and expressive physical universe of Tolstoy's novels, he also perceived its violent disjunctive potential: "Finally, this white hand begins to pursue one like a specter: like the young princess's upper lip, it becomes as if severed from the rest of the body. It acts independently and lives its own individual, strange, almost supernatural life, resembling a fantastic face, as in Gogol's 'Nose.'"[18]

Merezhkovsky's introduction of gothic horror into Tolstoy's novelistic world offers a grotesque blowup of the recurrent detail. By comparing the representational technique to supernatural dismemberment, Merezhkovsky implied that Tolstoy's strategy in these instances disperses the whole instead of restoring it. Deploying this device in conjunction with his spiritually deficient or negative characters, Tolstoy disintegrated their bodily unity. The Tolstoyan metonymic detail in such instances becomes not a token of the whole, but a fetish with its own narrative momentum, as in Gogol's fantastic yet realist story, in which a civil servant's nose displaces the body from which it has been severed. Likewise, Lise's short upper lip becomes independent of her body. It is safe to say that most readers of the novel remember her physical presence primarily in terms of this grotesque detail, a synecdoche that gets out of control. To reiterate Naomi Schor's observation: "[A] disintegration of the textual whole, the increasing autonomy of its parts, and in the end a generalized synecdoche" characterize the nonmimetic, realistic detail, especially as it was transformed in the late nineteenth century. "Decadence," suggested Schor, "is a pathology of the detail."[19]

Tolstoy used the grotesque, fetishistic detail not only to dismember the body but also to dissolve higher meaning. In the case of Lise, the fetishized upper lip reflects her lack of access to the deeper meaning of life; a similar conclusion can be drawn regarding Speransky's white hand. The fetishized detail then is not merely a substitute: in contrast to the psychoanalytic fetish, which displaces the fear of castration, the Tolstoyan severed body part puts up a screen to life's meaning, representing the character's inability to access nature's moral truth.

## Vivisecting/Dissecting

In the introduction to *Young Tolstoy*, Eikhenbaum described the negative reception of formalism by his contemporaries: "It was held that studying the work itself meant to dissect it, and this, as everyone knows, entails killing a living creature. We were constantly reproached for this crime." It appears from this observation that he made no distinction between dissection and vivisection, which refers to cutting up a living body. Defending the formalist method—and by extension his approach in *Young Tolstoy*—he claimed that it is applied only to the past, which "had been killed by time itself."[20] Without examining the reasons for Eikhenbaum's disclaimer and desire to distance himself from the charge of critical dissection or vivisection, we can state with confidence that he examined Tolstoy's rhetorical strategies both as they anatomize the body and as precedents for the formalist approach to literature.

Was Tolstoy a practitioner of literary vivisection and/or dissection? Considering his fascination with the dismembered body and with the slippery relation of part and whole, I offer a qualified "yes." Even though Tolstoy opposed positivism, he appropriated its emblematic metaphor of dissecting the body. The image of nature's corpse on the dissecting table went against his belief in nature as a developing, organic whole, but as a man whose world-view was rooted in the eighteenth century, he was fascinated by the procedure of anatomizing, applying it not only to psychological and moral processes but also to its original object of study in eighteenth-century science—human anatomy.

In one of his most daring early stories, "Sevastopol in December" (1855), he represented the body at war by dismembering it before our eyes. Besides its persuasive indictment of war, "Sevastopol in December" also implicates the reader in acts of violence by means of the rarely used second-person narrative, drawing "you, the reader" into the text. Staging the reader as a tourist in the besieged town of Sevastopol, the narrator guides us through its various spaces. Instead of being voyeurs located outside the frame, we are forced inside it to bear witness. In the words of Gary Saul Morson, the story "does not so much have an 'implied' reader as an implicated one."[21]

Whereas dismemberment connotes violence and mutilation, vivisection is an experimental procedure whose goal is new knowledge. If we consider "Sevastopol in December" not only as a moral statement but also as experimental fiction, the surgical amputations that we witness function as metaphors of rhetorical vivisection. Appropriately, instead of the battlefield, the site of the experiment is the military hospital, which the reader enters together with the narrator-guide: "Don't be ashamed that you came as though to *look* at the sufferers," the narrator tells the reader as he invites her to enter the narrative site, which is inhabited by the recurrent, horrible detail or fragment, not the whole. He exhibits to the reader the disturbing sight of limbs just amputated or awaiting severance from the rest of the body:

> Now, if your nerves are strong, go through the door to the left; in that room they bandage and operate. You will see doctors with arms red with blood up to the elbows and pale, gloomy faces, busy at a bed on which a wounded man lies under chloroform. His eyes are open and he utters, as if in delirium, incoherent but sometimes simple and touching words. The doctors are engaged in the horrible but beneficent work of amputation. You will see the sharp curved knife enter healthy white flesh; you will see the wounded man regain consciousness suddenly with terrible, heart-rending screams and curses. You will see the doctor's assistant toss the amputated arm into a corner. . . . [Y]ou will see war . . . in its real aspect of blood, suffering, and death.[22]

The hospital ward houses dismembered bodies: the first soldier we see has lost his leg above the knee, although he continues to have physical sensations in the body part blown off on the battlefield; an older soldier "has no arm at all: it has been removed at the shoulder"; the wife of a sailor has her leg amputated, also above the knee; the arms of the surgeon are covered with blood up to his elbows, blending his body into the hospital space, which evokes the image of the anatomical theater. It houses body parts. The white arm that the surgeon's assistant throws into the corner prefigures the metonymic image of Speransky's autotelic white hand. The delirious patient whose arm will be lopped off shortly utters fragments of speech, not coherent sentences. The function of medicine in this hospital is not to make the body whole but to dismember it, just as war disjoins the organic meaning of life. The narrator's cold, methodical voice is that of a moralizing vivisectionist whose experiment in fiction rips the body apart rhetorically in order to make a moral statement about the horror of the severing aspect of war. Underlying the moral message, however, is fascination with the process itself.

Tolstoy's obsession with the dismembering effect of war and with surgical amputation continued in his later writings. In *War and Peace*, it underlies Prince Andrei's experience at the battle of Borodino: as Andrei lies in the field hospital after being mortally wounded, he watches the amputation of Anatole Kuragin's leg, which is represented in almost the same terms as was amputation in the Sevastopol story:

> On the other table, round which many people were crowding, a tall, well-fed man lay on his back with his head thrown back. . . . One large, white, plump leg twitched rapidly all the time with a feverish tremor. The man was sobbing and choking convulsively. Two doctors . . . were silently doing something to this man's other, gory leg. . . . "Show it to me. . . . Oh, ooh . . . Oh! Oh, ooh!" his frightened moans could be heard. . . . The wounded man was shown his amputated leg stained with clotted blood and with the boot still on. . . . In the miserable, sobbing, enfeebled man whose leg had just been amputated, he recognized Anatole Kuragin. . . . "Yes, it is he! Yes, that man is somehow closely and painfully connected with me," thought Prince Andrew, not yet clearly grasping what he saw before him.[23]

Anatole is the handsome, debauched aristocrat who aroused young Natasha's desire, thereby symbolically violating her body and making it impossible for Andrei, scion of a great patriarchal family, to marry her. This dissolves Andrei's plans for a new family that would, he had hoped, give him access to the unreasoned, organic life of which Natasha is a natural extension. In his symbolic castration—he loses his leg—Anatole is punished for cutting Andrei off from nature's whole.[24] Yet Andrei takes no pleasure in this vengeance, feeling only compassion and love for Anatole as they both lie in the makeshift field hospital. Although his response suggests forgiveness, it also effectively equates physical amputation with the larger loss of meaning that so troubles Andrei, as it did Tolstoy.

The most powerful example of Tolstoy's morally motivated vivisection is in a late polemical essay promoting the vegetarian ideal. As part of his growing asceticism and renunciation of the body, Tolstoy became a vegetarian in 1885 on moral grounds, associating vegetarianism with sexual continence. He intended the essay "First Step" ("Pervaia stupen'") as a preface to the Russian edition of Howard Williams's *The Ethics of Diet* (1883), a book on vegetarianism. The essay first appeared in *Questions of Philosophy and Psychology* (*Voprosy filosofii i psikhologii*) in 1892. It preaches the "moral life," characterized by abstinence from gluttony, sloth, and sex. Like his youthful diaries, "First Step" emphasizes a totally good life (a good life cannot be partial!), which requires absolute self-control, consistency in all things, and a regimented plan for achieving perfection. The first step in this process is fasting.

The high point of Tolstoy's sermon is a painfully long description of the Tula slaughterhouse (Tula was the closest city to Iasnaia Poliana). The purpose of the passage was to destroy the reader's pleasure in eating meat. Tolstoy created a feeling of horror by accretion, depicting the butchery of many animals, one after another. He applied the metaphor of the "first step" on the ladder of self-improvement—one thing leads to another—to vegetarianism, linking animal slaughter to gastronomic pleasure and subsequent sexual excess.

The technique is reminiscent of "Sevastopol in December," characterized by terse, almost aphoristic, depictions of human dismemberment. But in "First Step," terseness is replaced by expansive, detailed portrayals of violence that the author observed from the doorways of slaughter chambers. Without using the narrative technique of the *Du-Erzählung* in the Crimean story, he still implicated the reader in the slaughter by making her bear witness. We enter the scene with him step by step. First, Tolstoy depicted the butchery of a pig in a village. After learning that the biggest slaughter took place in Tula on Fridays, he went there on a Friday but arrived too late; the butchers, covered in blood, showed him around the building and described their work. Next, he went on the Friday before Pentecost (June 6, 1891), at which time he became a true observer. The Trinitarian feast of Pentecost (*Troitsa* in Russian also means "Trinity"), which celebrates the descent of the Holy Ghost on Christ's apostles fifty days after Easter, is symbolized by the three main scenes of animal slaughter, although the actual number of killings that Tolstoy watched—and the reader with him, if he hasn't stopped reading—is five. (The printed text is approximately five pages.) Appropriately, the last animal was a lamb, the symbol of Christ and, in this scene, of the crucifixion. It was placed on a table, which the author compared to a bed symbolizing Christ's cross (it is like the bed of nails that resembles the bed of Chernyshevsky's revolutionary Rakhmetov, who despite his asceticism eats only rare meat, in *What Is to Be Done?*).

The theological implications and didactic message of this scene are self-evident. The slaughtered animals suggest Christ's Passion. We are expected to reject animal slaughter because killing innocent animals for food is evil; Tolstoy rejected it because it serves the natural cycle, which feeds the human animal with meat so that it can continue its natural, procreative function in the organic chain. Tolstoy, who by this time opposed procreation even in the context of the lawful family, associated the ingestion of meat with carnal passion; one thing led to the other.

Even though he deployed Christian symbolism to make his moral point, the rhetorical strategies and some of the essay's images are naturalistic: the Tula slaughterhouse becomes an amphitheater in which butchers perform a kind of vivisection on cattle and sheep, a procedure that Tolstoy endowed with moral significance. But if we bear witness to the hidden meaning of the passage, we also discover the displaced sexual subtext of Tolstoy's representation of animal slaughter. As I will show later, Tolstoy saw the sex act itself as resembling slaughter that moral men must eschew.

Tolstoy's unhinged sexual morality aside, one wonders how he could have been so blind to the violent language that came out of the narrator's mouth and only be concerned with what went into it? How could he rationalize his rhetorical strategies, which are so gruesomely violent, as moral?

> Through the door opposite the one at which I was standing, a big, red, well-fed ox was led in. Two men were dragging it, and just as they managed to bring him in I saw a butcher raise a dagger above its neck and stab it. The ox, as if all four legs had suddenly given way, fell heavily on its belly, immediately turned over on one side, and began to work its legs and all its hindquarters. Another butcher at once threw himself on the ox from the side opposite to the twitching legs, grabbed its horns, and twisted its head down to the ground, while another butcher cut its throat with a knife. From beneath the head there flowed a stream of blackish red blood, which a besmeared boy caught in a tin basin. All the time this was going on the ox kept incessantly twitching its head as if trying to get up, and waved all its four legs in the air. The basin was quickly filling, but the ox still lived, and its stomach heaving heavily, both hind and forelegs worked so violently that the butchers stood aside. When one basin was full the boy carried it away on his head to the albumen factory, while another boy placed a fresh basin, and this one began to fill up. But still the ox heaved its body and worked its hind legs. When the blood ceased to flow the butcher raised the animal's head and began to skin it. The ox continued to writhe. The head, stripped of its skin, showed red with white veins, and took the position given it by the butchers; the skin hung on both sides. The animal did not cease to writhe. Then another butcher caught hold of one of the legs, broke it, and cut it off. In the remaining legs and the stomach the convulsions still continued. The other legs were cut off and thrown aside, together with those of other oxen belonging to the same owner. Then the carcass was dragged to the hoist and crucified, and the convulsions were over.[25]

Even though Tolstoy evoked the crucifixion and conveyed the animal's suffering, what is most striking about this passage is the narrator's rhetorical pleasure in skinning the animals alive and vivisecting them himself. Tolstoy was fascinated by the process of bloody, naturalistic dismemberment, including its effect on the central nervous system, which may have served as a subtext for his favorite literary techniques of repetition and recurrent detail. Sadistically severed from the whole, the body parts—the twitching legs and the head of the ox—evoke horror and assume a gruesome life of their own as if ready to embody the synecdoche, rhetorically poised on the cusp between naturalist and decadent writing. The streaming blood, while naturalistic, also prefigures the trope of blood in decadence, as employed, for instance, by Rozanov in his anti-Semitic prose.

We can safely say then that the Tolstoyan recurrent detail becomes pathological, as if it were a tainted fetish object. But what then do these body parts displace? If we consider them in relation to the author's late nineteenth-century punitive desire to castrate the human male, the dismembered parts displace the phallus. Yet instead of only fearing castration, Tolstoy, like the Russian radical sect of self-castrators (*skoptsy*), also worshiped it, as if suggesting that only through castration can one achieve the ideal state of sexual continence.[26] In the words of Christ according to Matthew (5:30), loss of an offensive body part is preferable to the danger that it will infect the rest of the body: "And if your right hand is your undoing, cut it off and fling it away; it is better for you to lose one part of your body than for the whole of it to go to hell." This is precisely the response of Father Sergius in Tolstoy's eponymous story of 1898; his behavior serves as an illustration to this verse from Matthew. Yet as we know from the story's message, the castrated male is here not Tolstoy's ideal. So despite his growing punitive moral message at the end of the century, he maintained a level of ambivalence in his writing till the end.

What we can conclude about the Tula narrative is that it represents the body's irreversible dismemberment. Unlike "Sevastopol in December," the culmination of Tolstoy's interest in dismemberment, "The First Step," lacks a humanistic message. The viciously sundered parts only serve the appetites of sexually active men and women with the purpose of engaging in the immoral pursuit of replenishing nature's procreative power. It is this link in the food chain that the Tolstoy of the 1890s hoped to break.

## Sex on the Dissecting Table

While sex is linked with unmentionable body parts in Tolstoy's early diaries, war subsumes the sexual connotations of dismemberment in "Sevastopol in December" and *War and Peace.* This is not the case in *Anna Karenina,* in which war and its dismembering consequences loom outside the text and only at the end of the novel. We suspect that Vronsky will die, or at least lose a limb, in the Balkans, where he is heading at the end. Yet earlier in the novel, Vronsky himself is the agent of dispersal, sundering the gentry family and its hallowed genealogy.

The battle site is the body of Anna, prefigured in the terrible accident at the train station where the future lovers meet: a watchman is cut in two by the train. A well-known scene right after the lovers consummate their adulterous passion depicts Anna's body cut into pieces. Just as in the diaries that refer to his own sexual adventures, Tolstoy made no mention of Anna's and Vronsky's experience of pleasure. The scene represents only their feelings of pathological guilt. Anna's postcoital broken body lying at Vronsky's feet and his pathological response to the sex act as a kind of ax murder dominate the scene: "He felt what a murderer must feel when looking at the body he has deprived of life. . . . But in spite of the murderer's horror of the body of his victim, that body must be cut in pieces and hidden away, and he must make use of what he has obtained by the murder. Then, as the murderer desperately throws himself on the body, as though with passion, and drags it and hacks it, so Vronsky covered her face and shoulders with kisses" (135–36).

Even though Tolstoy did not ascribe these "magnificently ferocious" feelings, to borrow Sergei Eisenstein's epithet, to Vronsky directly, he did inscribe the sex-murder analogy into Vronsky's consciousness.[27] Tolstoy transmitted the discourse of punitive dismemberment to him, making Vronsky his pathological co-conspirator and revealing his authorial penchant for bodily fragmentation. I find it difficult to imagine Vronsky, a well-adjusted member of aristocratic society, who has waited so long for this encounter, experiencing the moment right after coitus as if he were an obsessive, paranoid murderer who hacks the desired body into pieces. Despite his limitations, Vronsky is a man of honor who stands by Anna till the very end. After all, following Anna's suicide, he goes off to seek the mutilation of his own body. What the murder analogy accomplishes, however, is the permanent sundering of the whole; Anna's body—and her family—from this moment can only be dispersed, never to be reassembled.

Tolstoy's criminalization of the sex act would have fascinated Richard von Krafft-Ebing, the author of *Psychopathia Sexualis,* which opens with words affirming the power of the procreative impulse as mediated by moral law.[28] Some of Krafft-Ebing's case studies of sexual degeneration resemble Tolstoy's evocation of sexual violence in *Anna Karenina,* perhaps based on his own punitive sexual fantasy displaced by Old Testament vengeance. The case study in *Psychopathia Sexualis* that could be seen as a grotesquely hyperbolic counterpart to Vronsky's behavior is that of Andreas Bichel, who violated girls, killed them, then *dissected* and buried them.[29] The first edition of *Psychopathia Sexualis* appeared in 1886, the first Russian translation in 1887, that is, shortly before Tolstoy's own psychopathological case study, *The Kreutzer Sonata,* a work consumed by the violent representation of the sex act.

The mutilation of Anna by Vronsky marks a shift in her representation. Although the reader's gaze typically dismembers the object of vision, Tolstoy frequently countered this effect with his magical conjuring metonym. If before the fall the recurrent, individual physical details of Anna's magnificent body facilitate her incarnation right before our eyes, the unlawful sex act problematizes the joyful emergence of her body from its parts. As Vronsky approaches Anna on the veranda the next time the reader sees them together, his only thought is that "he would see her immediately, not merely in fancy, but alive, all of her—as she was in reality."[30] And he does! Vronsky's desire to see all of her alive is rhetorical, as if he were a practitioner of reconstitutive metonymic representation like his author. Together with Vronsky, we get a particularly luxurious sense of Anna's physical presence in the first part of this scene—before her son interrupts their meeting—but the effect does not last. She is no longer alive and whole in the same way as before: adulterous passion has begun to fragment Anna.

Thus Anna's dismemberment in the sexual sense is the direct consequence of transgressing God's law. Tolstoy completed the dismemberment of Anna in her suicide, representing her mutilated body through Vronsky's eyes once again: he remembers it at the train station on his way to the Balkans. Overflowing with vitality, Anna's body has dominated the Moscow station in part 1; now it occupies the station in death. Vronsky remembers how "on a table, stretched shamelessly before the eyes of strangers, lay her mangled body still warm with recent life. The head, left intact . . . was thrown back; and on the lovely face with its half-open red lips . . . [and] fixed open eyes was frozen an expression—pitiful . . . and horrible" (707).

The fixed open eyes bring to mind one of the dead bulls in the slaughterhouse scene in "First Step": Tolstoy described the bull's fixed eyes as shining with such a beautiful light only five minutes before its death. Right after recollecting Anna's dismembered body in the railway shed, Vronsky tries to remember its joyful wholeness when he first met her, also at the train station. He is unable to do so, as if, together with his author, he could conjure up, not the magical, reconstitutive metonymic detail, but only the one that fragments her.

The image of Anna's dead body on display in a railway shed evokes the anatomical theater exhibiting the archetypal figure of the female corpse. Although placed in a different context, Tolstoy's representation of the female corpse resembles Turgenev's eroticized medical fantasy in *Fathers and Sons,* in which Bazarov imagines Odintsova's beautiful body in the anatomical theater: "What a magnificent body," says Bazarov to his friend. "Perfect for the dissecting-table."[31] Sof'ia Andreevna wrote in her diary that Tolstoy's decision to have Anna commit suicide by throwing herself under a train was influenced by a similar occurrence near Iasnaia Poliana. Anna S. Zykova, the jilted common-law wife of a neighboring landlord, A. N. Bibikov, jumped under a train at Iasenki in 1871. "Then she was dissected," wrote Sof'ia Andreevna. "Lev Nikolaevich saw her in the Iasenkov barracks, completely undressed and slit open, with her skull bared. It made a horrible impression on him and affected him profoundly."[32] The obvious question is why Tolstoy went there to have a look. I would attribute it to his prurient fascination with the dissected body and cadavers on display.

Shklovsky also considered the suicide of Zykova a source for *Anna Karenina.* Shklovsky's description of the woman's corpse as "spread-eagled" (*rasplastannaia*) and "dissected" invokes the nihilist trope of the spread-eagled frog, which Dmitrii Pisarev deployed as a symbol of the salvation and renewal of the Russian people.[33] The epithet "spread-eagled" was used in the 1860s and 1870s in reference to the positivist practice of dissecting frogs and to its symbolic meaning. In building his case for the novel's nihilist subtext, Shklovsky wrote that the landlord in question, like the nihilists, did not respect the family and the permanence of sexual commitment.[34] Both Eikhenbaum and Shklovsky proposed nihilism and Tolstoy's opposition to it as a cultural subtext of the novel. Shklovsky made the point that the decision of Levin's brother

Nikolai to take a fallen woman as his common-law wife reveals Tolstoy's criticism of the cooperative workshop for prostitutes organized by Vera Pavlovna in *What Is to Be Done*.[35] His criticism of nihilism notwithstanding, the nihilist locus of the anatomical theater occupies a prominent place in *Anna Karenina*—onto which Tolstoy superimposed a sadistic punitive layer.

The representation of Anna's corpse as an anatomized dead body underscores Tolstoy's adherence to the realist/naturalist method, whose ideological sources were positivism and its emblematic tropes. "No image for the literary stance of the realist or naturalist writer in France was more widespread than that of the anatomist dissecting a cadaver," wrote Charles Bernheimer. As an example, he referred to the 1869 caricature by Lemot, which pictures Flaubert, magnifying glass in hand, extracting organs from Emma Bovary's dead body.[36] Waxing metaphorical, Émile Zola told writers to "put on the white apron of the anatomist and dissect, fiber by fiber, the human beast laid out completely naked on the marble slab of the amphitheater."[37] In the preface to *Thérèse Raquin* (1867), he wrote that he had chosen to depict "persons completely dominated by their nerves and blood, . . . led into every act of their lives by the fatalities of their flesh." Zola "performed on two living bodies [those of Thérèse and Raquin] the sort of analytical operations that surgeons perform on cadavers."[38]

Konstantin Leont'ev was perhaps the first critic to point out the naturalistic surgical subtext of Tolstoy's literary method. Having served in the Crimean War as a military surgeon and being an adherent of a kind of "aesthetic positivism," he viewed society and history through the eyes of a pathologist and anatomist. In his 1890 essay, *Analysis, Style, Trend: About the Novels of Ct. L. N. Tolstoy,* Leont'ev compared Tolstoy to a graphic scientist-artist in an anatomical theater, who while drawing a part of the body visible to the naked eye—for example, the skin on the hand—suddenly decides to depict it severed in several places and to insert into the incisions, or wounds, the tiniest cells and thinnest fibers normally visible only through the strongest microscope.[39] Leont'ev's description of Tolstoy's literary method borrows its images from naturalist vocabulary. The images refer to Tolstoy's minute, at times excessive, analysis of human feelings and behavior and to his love of the magnification effect, as if he were describing the world through a microscope. It also sheds light on Tolstoy's fascination with bodily mutilation and his penchant for voyeurism, what Leont'ev called "excessive peeping" (*izlishnee podgliadyvanie*), both of which are gruesomely staged in "First

Step."[40] He insinuated into Tolstoy's surgical method the dispersion of the whole and loss of faith in the organic universe, traditionally considered hallmarks of Tolstoy's novelistic universe.

Leont'ev, who was an admirer of Tolstoy, considered *Anna Karenina* the apogee of Russian naturalism, whose "sickly" offspring was decadence. Although his 1890 essay on Tolstoy does not represent Tolstoy as a decadent, Leont'ev's theory of cultural "blossoming" and subsequent "degeneration" could be considered an analogue of the naturalism/decadence relationship—in the sense that naturalism represents the overripe fruit marking the onset of degeneration and decadent literature. (Leont'ev's organicist historical model consisted of three stages: "primitive simplicity," "exuberant growth and complexity," and "secondary simplification," with the last representing the stage of decline and decay.)[41] Vasilii Rozanov, in his review of Leont'ev's essay, offered a sensuous, anatomical metaphor in treating Leont'ev's view of Tolstoy's novels; he wrote that Tolstoy overloaded his works with "sinewy" detail, as if for its own sake ("Ding an sich").[42] This was also Merezhkovsky's perspective, according to whom the novelist's truly magical *"insight into the flesh* . . . [sometimes drew] him into excess."[43] Excess was in fact Nordau's reason for designating Tolstoy a victim of degeneration.

## Sexual Continence

Tolstoy's best known and most controversial disquisition on sexual continence is *The Kreutzer Sonata* (1889), a bitter attack on carnal desire, marriage, and procreation, as well as contraception, prurient doctors (especially gynecologists), sexual intercourse during pregnancy and nursing, divorce, and feminism. Pozdnyshev, the unhinged hero of *The Kreutzer Sonata,* after having been exonerated of murdering his wife, tells a casual travel companion on a train the story of his marriage with the purpose of "infecting" him, to use Tolstoy's metaphor. The novel was his best-known work abroad, creating for him an international reputation as an author who treated degeneration. Censorship prohibited publication of the novel in Russia, but it was widely discussed and reviewed in the press, symbolically marking the beginning of the debate of the "sexual question" in the Russian fin de siècle. After Sofia Andreevna's personal appeal to Alexander III, permission was granted to publish the novel, but only as part of the author's collected works.

Reading *The Kreutzer Sonata* in light of Tolstoy's green leather sofa, we quickly realize that the emblematic sofa of procreation and genealogy

Leo Tolstoi.

Die Kreuzersonate.

Deutsch von Th. v. Galetzki.

Illustriert von Hans Volkert

Book cover of German edition of *The Kreutzer Sonata*

has been banished from his fiction. The family bed in the novel's household is the site of sexual depravity and of female hysteria, attributed by Pozdnyshev to the purposeless, immoral life of his class and the weak nervous system of women. The bed is the site of sexual desire, which Tolstoy, like his hero, considered sordid, even when it results in childbirth. The perverse message is that children, conceived in the sex act, are also morally tainted; Tolstoy seems to have taken the taint of degenerate heredity and incorporated it into the moral sphere. In describing his wife's attack of hysteria, Pozdnyshev refers ironically to Jean-Martin Charcot, pioneer of the study of hysteria as a degenerate disorder, revealing Tolstoy's familiarity with psychopathological literature.

Tolstoy suggested that the husband's jealousy of his wife, a contemporary woman of the leisure class, leads to murder. The title, taken from a Beethoven piece, refers to Pozdnyshev's heightened sensitivity to music, which excites his nerves and agitates his paranoid mind. This extreme response is the product of his pathological excitability and exhausted nerves, symptomatic of degeneration: "This sonata," says Pozdnyshev, "is a terrifying thing. . . . [M]usic is a terrifying thing. . . . They say, music elevates the soul,—nonsense, falsehood! . . . It neither elevates, nor degrades, but rather irritates the soul."[44] The passage in fact resembles Tolstoy's description in *What Is Art?* of the impact of Wagner's music on the nervous system: "If you sit in the dark in the opera and submit your brain [and] auditory nerves to the strongest possible impact of sounds calculated to produce the most irritating effect, you will probably also enter an abnormal psychological state."[45] Like Nordau in *Degeneration,* which has a whole chapter on Wagner, Tolstoy rejected his music precisely because it produces in the listener a state of unstable excitement. He considered the *Gesamtkunstwerk,* without using the term, bad though infectious art, comparing it to the power of opium, alcohol, and hypnosis. In *The Kreutzer Sonata,* however, bad music is not only the "infectious" cause of nervous disorder; its pathological impact is also the product of the listener's unstable nervous system. Bad music according to Tolstoy "cuts both ways," to use Dostoevsky's famed metaphor from *The Brothers Karamazov.*

Pozdnyshev imagines that the sonata, played as a duet by his wife and the violinist Trukhachevsky, has an erotic effect on them, resulting in adultery. The husband's sexual fantasy, stimulated by music, leads to their adulterous behavior in his paranoid imagination and to his violent behavior in reality. Since we hear the story exclusively from the point of view of Pozdnyshev, whose obsessive sexual fantasies have been stimulated by music, we never learn if the adultery actually took place. Clearly, Tolstoy was no longer interested in distinguishing between thought and action, having become preoccupied with eradicating carnal desire itself.

The most radical aspect of Tolstoy's message in *The Kreutzer Sonata* is its totalizing asceticism, which subverts the family and reproductive nature. It is in this context that he quoted Matthew 5:28, which also serves as the epigraph to the novel: "But I say unto you that everyone whosoever looketh on a woman to lust after her hath committed adultery with her already in his heart." Pozdnyshev's extremist interpretation of Christ's admonishment includes one's own wife. Even though the interpretation belongs to Pozdnyshev, Tolstoy didn't contradict it. The procurator of the Holy Synod Konstantin Pobedonostsev, who identified Pozdnyshev with the author, attacked Tolstoy's interpretation, as did other representatives of the church. In 1890 Archbishop Nikanor of Odessa and Kherson accused Tolstoy in "A Conversation on Christian Marriage" of misreading Matthew: "Your narrow and superficial interpretation sounds in the ears of the Christian world for the first time in the nineteen hundred years it has existed. Before you, no one among the thousands of interpreters of the Gospel, not even the most ascetic, has had the idea that these words from Holy Writ should bear the meaning ascribed to them by your arrogant sophistry."[46] The controversy surrounding the church's preference for celibacy or marriage was taken up several years later at the Religious-Philosophical Meetings (see chapter 6).

The obvious differences notwithstanding, Tolstoy's antiprocreative, antifamily ideology had certain points of contact with the utopian project of early Russian modernism. Instead of aspiring to the immortalization of the body, however, Tolstoy preached the moral evolution of men and women in the here and now, both in *The Kreutzer Sonata* and in the *Afterword to The Kreutzer Sonata.* Despite this, some of his claims bear an uncanny resemblance to those of Dostoevsky's Kirillov (*The Possessed*), who is perhaps Russian literature's most memorable utopian nihilist concerned with bodily transfiguration and the end of procreation. Although Pozdnyshev's philosophical sources may be different from Kirillov's, his discourse is remarkably similar. I am, of course, referring to Pozdnyshev's controversial dictum that "life ought to come to an end when the goal is reached," which according to him is transcendence of carnal passion. He speaks of a time when "the prophesies will be fulfilled, people will be united, the goal of mankind will be attained, and there will be no reason for it to live."[47] These words are almost identical to Kirillov's statement that "man should stop giving birth. Why children, why development, if the goal has been achieved? It's said in the Gospel that in the *Resurrection* there will be no birth, but people will be like God's angels."[48]

What differentiates Kirillov from Pozdnyshev is Tolstoy's morbid pessimism. The end for Tolstoy, who did not believe in an afterlife, is death, not personal or collective resurrection. Neither did he believe in Darwinian progressive evolution, based on the survival of the fittest. In the words of Pozdnyshev, "the highest breed of animals, the human race, in order to maintain itself in the struggle with other animals must unite into one whole like a swarm of bees, and not breed infinitely; it should bring up sexless members as the bees do; . . . it should strive toward abstinence and not toward inflaming lust."[49]

Considered against the earlier quoted passage (when "the prophecies will be fulfilled, there will be no more reason for living"), Pozdnyshev's notion of the survival of the fittest could be read in apocalyptic terms, even though the metaphor of the beehive in *The Kreutzer Sonata* reduces humankind to the animal level. Instead of God's asexual angels, Pozdnyshev compares future man to sexless bees, making the point that procreation is superfluous in a world informed by reproductive excess.

The beehive is Pozdnyshev's answer to the criticism of his chance traveling companions that his half-baked morality leads to the end of the human race. Intended by him as a metaphor for a nonbreeding collective, he claims that the end of the whole is just as inevitable as individual death. Commenting on the logical connection between abstinence and humanity's extinction in the *Afterword,* Tolstoy wrote that "chastity is not a rule or prescription, but an ideal . . . one of its conditions. And an ideal is an ideal only when its realization is possible only as an idea, in thought, when it appears possible only in infinity and when because of this the possibility of coming closer to it is infinite."[50] What this suggests is a discursive ideal, but an ideal nevertheless.

Pozdnyshev, Tolstoy's murderous alter ego, claims that the inevitability of the end is taught not only by the church but also by contemporary scientific theory. To illustrate the idea that the practice of total chastity will result in the end of human life, Tolstoy offered in the *Afterword* the analogy of heat death (cooling of the sun), a contemporary scientific theory of the end. The populist critic Alexander Skabichevsky in a negative review of *The Kreutzer Sonata* referred the reader to the theory of heat death: tongue-in-cheek, he wrote that it serves as the scientific justification of Tolstoy's prediction of the end of the human race.[51]

In Tolstoy's puritan ethics, striving for celibacy without the reward of immortality is life's highest ideal. The reward is an unsullied life. This position is based on Paul's teaching in the First Epistle to the Corinthians, according to which only the few can achieve complete celibacy. Whereas Paul prescribed marriage for those who fail at celibacy, Tolstoy went further, writing that the married couple should always strive to live in a chaste fraternal union. In 1890 in a private letter to a family tutor, whom he advised to live with his wife "as brother and sister," Tolstoy wrote that "the struggle against sexuality . . . is life itself . . . and a duty."[52]

I suggested earlier that *The Kreutzer Sonata* is a blowup of the postcoital scene in *Anna Karenina,* in which Vronsky experiences himself as a murderer who disperses Anna's body. Even the physical detail that typifies Vronsky's feelings of torment in that scene—the trembling jaw—travels to *The Kreutzer Sonata,* characterizing Pozdnyshev's physical demeanor just before the murder. Tolstoy represented both couples as criminal collaborators, with the difference that Vronsky's crime is metaphoric; Pozdnyshev also compares the sex act to murder, telling his traveling companion that he killed his wife long before the actual murderous act. As in *Anna Karenina,* in which the sex act resembles rape, rape is imputed into Pozdnyshev's murder of his wife, with the enraged husband plunging a crooked damascene dagger into her side right under the breast: "I heard and remember the momentary resistance of the corset and of something else," reveals Pozdnyshev, "and then the immersion of the knife into something soft."[53]

Intended by Tolstoy as a moral sermon, Pozdnyshev's confession instead resembles a psychopathological case history from *Psychopathia Sexualis,* even more than does Vronsky's experience of the sex act as prescribed by Tolstoy. The discourse of psychopathology, as I suggested earlier, informs Pozdnyshev's uncertain confession, which is lacking in unambiguous feelings of guilt. Like Krafft-Ebing's criminal exhibitionists, he details his deranged condition to a captive listener, whom he hopes to *infect* in accordance with his author's subsequent prescription in *What Is Art?* Attributing atavistic physical characteristics to his imagined rival, Trukhachevsky, Pozdnyshev describes him as a feminized male, with damp almond eyes, red lips, and "especially protruding buttocks, like a woman's, like a Hottentot's"; in nineteenth-century Europe,

Hottentot women were considered exemplars of atavism, a particular kind of degenerative condition.[54] Even though Pozdnyshev does not use either the term "psychopathology" or "degeneration," their discourse informs his confession. In addition to exhaustion, hysteria, and effeminacy, he makes numerous other references to degenerate symptoms: irritability, facial twitching, hypersensitivity to sound and light, masturbation, prostitution, mannishness in women, venereal disease, uncontrollable utterance of strange sounds, and uncontrollable desire to speak. And like the contemporary psychopathologist who tries to be scientific, Pozdnyshev overwhelms his listener with statistics as corroborations of his rather wild observations.

The neo-Slavophile critic Rtsy (I. F. Romanov), who reviewed *The Kreutzer Sonata,* wrote that "had Tolstoy wanted to dig in forensic medical literature, he could have found plenty of factual material proving that uncontrolled vice really leads to murder[, . . . that] a hand that has just caressed its victim, reaches out for the neck to strangle it." Had he done so, continued Rtsy, he would have produced a "psychopathological drama."[55] I suggest that he did.

Tolstoy was familiar with psychopathological literature. As early as 1860, he read an article by Alfred Mori in *Revue de deux Mondes* titled "The Degeneration of the Human Race: The Beginning Consequences of Idiocy."[56] It was written shortly after the term "degeneration" first appeared in medical literature in B.-A. Morel's *Treatise on Physical, Intellectual, and Moral Degenerative Disease in the Human Species* (1857). Tolstoy was a reader of the *Russian Archive of Psychiatry, Neurology and Forensic Psychopathology,* edited by the noted psychiatrist Pavel I. Kovalevsky, professor at Kharkov University, with whom Tolstoy corresponded.[57] He noted in his diary of 1884 that he was reading the case study of a landowner who had sexual relations with his servants, which appeared in Kovalevsky's essay "On the Study of Pathological Affects: Two Forensic Psychiatric Cases" ("K ucheniiu o patologicheskikh affektakh: Dva sudebno-psikhiatricheskikh sluchaia").[58] In 1890 he read the psychopathologist Auguste Forel on the subject of alcoholism among students. In his last novel, *Resurrection* (*Voskresenie,* 1899), he incorporated the vocabulary of degeneration into the forensic discourse of the assistant public prosecutor at Katiusha Maslova's trial for murder. Recapitulating the prosecutor's presentation of the case, the narrator refers ironically to his deployment of the forensic theory of the famed Italian criminologist and psychopathologist Cesare Lombroso, commingling it with decadent discourse. Like other degeneration theorists, Lombroso considered flawed heredity to be the cause of criminal behavior. Tolstoy, like Nordau before him, linked degeneration and decadence. The novel's main male character, Prince Nekhliudov—in an attempt to make sense of criminal degeneration—reads, besides Lombroso, the French psychopathologist Gabriel Tarde, the English Henry Maudsley, and the Italian Enrico Ferri. Needless to say, none of them offers him the kind of morally persuasive answer that he is seeking.[59]

Tolstoy mentioned Nordau's *Degeneration* (1892) in a diary entry in 1893, without, however, referring to the vitriolic attack on his own fiction in it. Instead, he spoke positively about Nordau's criticism of contemporary fiction as degenerate.[60] Nordau devoted what can be described as a delirious chapter to Tolstoy in his book, calling "Tolstoism a mental aberration, . . . a phenomenon of degeneration."[61] Despite the chapter's frenzied discussion of Tolstoy, it contains some perceptive observations, including the first references to the "degenerate" aspect of Tolstoy's writing. Discussing what he views as Tolstoy's excessive use of detail in representing reality—which Merezhkovsky and Rozanov will suggest later—Nordau considered it the source of his degeneration as a writer. He compared Tolstoy's literary strategies to the thought processes of a "mystical degenerate," whose focus, according to Nordau, is diffuse because of his uncontrolled "hyperemotionalism." He likens Tolstoy to a degenerate whose nervous system is dominated by the morbid excitability of its sexual centers, resulting in a pathological obsession with women that Tolstoy transmitted to Pozdnyshev like a disease. If we may borrow Tolstoy's own medicalized literary discourse to describe the relationship between the author and his hero in *The Kreutzer Sonata,* the former "infects" the latter.

According to Nordau, Tolstoy's international reputation was based on *The Kreutzer Sonata,* not on his greater earlier works, which fell on deaf ears. He implied that Tolstoy's fin-de-siècle readership made his reputation abroad, suggesting that contemporary readers were ready for the degenerate Tolstoy. He concluded his analysis of *The Kreutzer Sonata* by dubbing Pozdnyshev, as well as his author, unconscious *skoptsy,* members of the Russian sect of self-mutilators, whom Nordau described as "degenerates."[62]

The underlying cause of Tolstoy's degeneration, according to Nordau, was his rejection of science and the scientific method. Citing *Le roman russe* (1886), the first influential European study of Russian literature, by Eugene-Melchior Vicomte de Vogué (1848–1910), Nordau questioned the author's description of Tolstoy's fiction as a "scientific study of the phenomena of life."[63] Instead, he compared Tolstoy's writings to those of Flaubert's *Bouvard and Pecuchet*, whom he called "Flaubert's two idiots, who, completely ignorant, without teacher or guides, skim through a number of books indiscriminately, and fancy themselves in this sportive manner to have gained positive knowledge . . . and then believe themselves justified sneering at science."[64] Although a misguided comparison, it reveals Nordau's view of the Tolstoyan detail as a severed and fetishistic one whose reconstitutive function has been lost.

When asked about *The Kreutzer Sonata*, Zola told a critic that the novel is like "a nightmare, the fruit of a sick imagination."[65] The Russian liberal and populist critics Nikolai Mikhailovsky, Alexander Skabichevsky, and Leonid Obolensky, whose ideological positions were formed in the positivist 1860s, also applied the discourse of psychopathology to *The Kreutzer Sonata*.[66] Criticizing Tolstoy's pessimism and antifeminist ideology, they offered progressive antidotes, as did Nordau. For instance, they proposed gender equality and women's rights to education and professional careers as a cure for the depraved relations between men and women in Russian society as described by Tolstoy.[67]

Tolstoy himself did not draw explicitly psychopathological conclusions about the causes of Pozdnyshev's unhinged murderous behavior, even if he seemed to represent his confession as a case history. Especially mystifying is the absence of an articulated condemnation of Pozdnyshev's psychopathic behavior. It is difficult to imagine that Tolstoy, a firm believer in individual moral responsibility, put all the blame on society, even though Pozdnyshev seems to attribute his condition to the depraved state of contemporary family relations. Yet Tolstoy shared Pozdnyshev's radical moral solution of universal abstinence, just as he expressed his own view of sex through Vronsky's consummation of love as an act of a demented murderer.

The "most enthusiastic apologist of the family and of childbirth in world literature . . . who had crowned the epic tale of the great war with a portrayal of children's diapers, who had created an apotheosis of motherhood in the image of Kitty's birth" came to claim that the family was evil and childbirth the result of moral imperfection.[68] This observation, offered at the Religous-Philosophical Meetings in 1903 by the early Russian symbolist Nikolai Minsky, aptly summarizes Tolstoy's passage from an ideology defined by family, genealogy, and nature to one espousing an "unnatural" ascetic ideal. Tolstoy's shift coincided with his growing sense of the impossibility of fitting the world into an orderly causal pattern, resulting in a moral extremism that contributed to the final and irrevocable dissolution of the whole.

Tolstoy's personal struggle with these questions is well known, and we could simply interpret it as a private affair. But if we place the proverbial green sofa of the Tolstoy family and his accidental deathbed into the larger context of nineteenth-century Russian cultural history, we get a thicker description of the transformations in Tolstoy's life. Tolstoy was virtually alone among his contemporaries in championing the procreative family. This can be attributed in part to his class affiliation and personal history. Unlike, for instance, Turgenev and Goncharov, also of the gentry, Tolstoy married into his class and had a traditional gentry family with many children. Although Dostoevsky did not reject the procreative family—on the contrary—he frequently represented relations between biological parents and children in negative terms. Instead of the biological family, which is fraught with difficulties in his novelistic world, he offered some positive images of what he called the "accidental family" as an alternative form of filiation.[69]

Edward Said described modernism as the "transition from a failed idea or possibility of filiation to a kind of compensatory order . . . that provides men and women with a new form of relationship," marking the transition from human bonds grounded in nature to those based on culture.[70] In this respect, Dostoevsky's alternative form of community reveals his affinity for modernism, which is not the case with Tolstoy. However, Tolstoy's representation of the body and of modernity's assault on bodily integrity make him an important precursor of modernist discourse.

If we consider Tolstoy's growing rejection of sex and the family against the larger context of Russian utopian ideologies, first articulated in the 1860s, we may conclude that ultimately he was swept away by the utopian tide that yearned to transcend both nature and history. Despite his distrust of positivist science, he was certainly seduced by the scientist's procedure of penetrating and anatomizing the body, from which he learned some of his rhetorical strategies, as did the subsequent symbolists, whose rejection of positivism was also vituperative. Yet unlike the new men and new women of the 1860s, and of the 1890s and early 1900s, Tolstoy engaged dissection and vivisection as a punitive measure or to create a gothic effect, not to construct an immortal body. Beginning with the 1860s, the goal of the radical utopians was to give birth to themselves and to the "new word"; the goal of the most radical among them—especially Nikolai Fedorov—was to transform the body, including the collective one. In Tolstoy's battle with nature, the focus was always on the moral life: Pozdnyshev cancels nature rhetorically, claiming that sex, unlike eating, is unnatural. As proof, he adduces the feelings of shame and fear of sex, especially in children and innocent young women. Whatever Tolstoy's reasons for writing *The Kreutzer Sonata,* the novella fired the first salvo in the turn-of-the-century Russian debate regarding the "sexual question." The novel's privileging of celibacy became one of the debate's key issues.

Unlike most of the writers whom I discuss in this book, Tolstoy rejected life beyond death and the project of transforming life; however, his views of the end in some of his late writings do have apocalyptic connotations. Most importantly, he shared the antiprocreative chaste ideal of Vladimir Solov'ev and his followers, with the significant difference that he was a puritan extremist. Unlike them, Tolstoy appropriated the apocalyptic notion of chastity in this life as a "historical" ideal. For that matter, if we look closely at Solov'ev's utopian project, it also proposes sexual abstinence in this life—as a strategy of defeating the power of nature and replacing it with the artifice of androgyny, which is beyond gender. Solov'ev's profound ambivalence about the meaning of sex—shared by Tolstoy—arose in part from the fear that contemporary psychopathology had instilled in him.

Tolstoy, of course, was no decadent. But as a man living at the end of the century, like Solov'ev, he was brushed by decadence, which in its birthplace (France) emerged from under naturalism's overcoat. This is especially true of the way he used the recurrent detail in fragmenting the whole and enhancing the autonomy of its parts. I would go so far as to suggest that fetishism of the part in his early writings already marked a slippage of his procreative ideal, which contributed to the divisive fragmentation of his poetics.[71]

# 2

# The Meaning of *The Meaning of Love*

## What Is Erotic about Vladimir Solov'ev's Utopia?

The future Russian philosopher Vladimir S. Solov'ev arrived in Cairo on November 11, 1875, having abandoned his studies of the kabala and Gnosticism at the British Museum in London. We learn from a letter to his mother that he visited the standard tourist sites in and around Cairo, including "a real Sphinx" and local mosques. The reason for his trip, wrote Solov'ev, was to study Arabic.

What was Solov'ev doing in Egypt, and why did he suddenly abandon his studies? Contrary to what he wrote his mother, he told M. M. Kovalevsky that a spirit directed him to visit a secret kabalist society in Egypt.[1] (Kovalevsky was a well-known legal scholar and sociologist with whom he became friends in London.) Eugene-Melchior Vicomte de Vogué, a versatile writer and author of the first influential European study of Russian literature (*Le roman russe*, 1886) and onetime diplomat in Petersburg, described meeting Solov'ev in Cairo in the home of another Frenchman:

> [His was] one of those faces that, once seen, is never forgotten: handsome, beautiful regular features on a thin, pale face that was buried in long, curly hair and taken over by large, wonderful, penetrating, and mystical eyes. . . . [He seemed] the very model that inspired the ancient monk icon-painters who tried to represent the Slavic Christ on the icons—loving, meditative,

> mournful. In the heat of the Egyptian summer, this Christ wore a long black raincoat and a top hat. He artlessly told us of setting off alone, dressed this way, to the Bedouins of the Suez desert; he was searching for a tribe whose members, he had been told, had preserved certain kabalist secrets and Masonic traditions passed down to this tribe directly from King Solomon. The Bedouins did not provide him any clarification regarding this matter, but they stole his watch and ruined his top hat.[2]

On November 25, Solov'ev wrote his mother that he was going on foot to the "uncivilized" desert of Thebais in upper Egypt, about two hundred versts away. Two days later, he wrote another letter, telling her that he had almost been killed by Bedouins about twenty versts from Cairo and that he had abandoned his trip to Thebais. "The Bedouins . . . in the night took me for the devil. I had to spend the night on the bare earth [in the presence of jackals], as a result of which I went back."[3] Describing his sojourn in the desert many years later in the poem *Three Meetings* (*Tri svidaniia*, 1898), he remarked how funny he must have looked in his coat and London top hat. V. A. Pypina-Liatskaia, the daughter of the populist critic and historian A. N. Pypin, told another version of Solov'ev's story about his desert journey. She claimed that he visited the desert fathers, Christian ascetics living like hermits in the Egyptian desert. According to Pypina, Solov'ev told her that he tried without success to induce Christ's vision of the Transfiguration on Mount Tabor, imitating the local hermits.[4] Whatever its factual basis, Pypina's memoir is the only evidence we have of Solov'ev's going so far into the desert.

Even though Solov'ev did not refer to Sophia, his mystical lodestar throughout his life, as the primary reason for the trip, he went to Egypt to meet his divine mistress, who represented the emanation of divine light and wisdom in Gnostic mysticism. Solov'ev's female ideal, she supposedly had appeared to him in the British Museum and arranged a kind of supernatural rendezvous in the Egyptian desert. The presumed visitation in Egypt occurred between November 25 and 27, which corresponds to the dates of his desert sojourn. In all likelihood, the "meeting" took place in the area where he was attacked by the Bedouins. This was Solov'ev's last meeting with Sophia, as recorded in *Three Meetings.*

Vladimir Solov'ev (1852–1900), Russia's most important academic philosopher, was also the most influential utopian visionary of his generation; his writings—influenced by the Christian, Gnostic, and Neoplatonic traditions—helped shape the core of the apocalyptic symbolist ethos. Situated generationally between the positivist 1860s and the symbolist early 1900s, his utopian project represents an amalgam of paradoxical ideas borrowed from a variety of mystical, scientific, and aesthetic traditions and sensibilities. A fin-de-siècle metaphor that represents his philosophical syncretism best is the palimpsest, a figure of overwriting and cultural layering that reflects the time's eclecticism and its fascination with old and exotic cultures. The anecdote of Solov'ev wearing a European top hat in the Egyptian desert in search of Sophia or the desert fathers certainly presents an eccentric physical and cultural palimpsest.

The catalyst of Solov'ev's utopia was erotic love, which he viewed paradoxically, describing it both as the source and the transcendence of sexual desire. His most important philosophical statement about erotic love is *The Meaning of Love* (*Smysl liubvi,* 1892–94), the focus of my discussion in this chapter and the looking glass in which Alexander Blok, Andrei Bely, and Sergei Solov'ev, the philosopher's nephew, as well as Zinaida Gippius, Dmitrii Merezhkovsky, and Dmitrii Filosofov discovered their anxious erotic reflections. Polemically, it was directed at Tolstoy's *Kreutzer Sonata,* whose private reading Solov'ev apparently attended in 1889 in the salon of the widow of Solov'ev's favorite poet, Aleksei Tolstoy.[5]

Both Tolstoy and Solov'ev were concerned with sex and the problematic relationship between the philosophical meaning of love and the physical consummation of sexual desire. The dilemma presented by Solov'ev's erotic paradox in the debate about sex and marriage initiated by *The Kreutzer Sonata* in the 1890s concerned the economy of desire. The unresolved question for Solov'ev was whether men and women should expend their sexual energy now or save it, storing it till the end of history, at which point the energy would be released collectively in a big bang that would transfigure the world. Like the later Tolstoy, who banned the sex act even from marriage, Solov'ev rejected procreation in a retreat from nature and generation, but his position, especially in *The Meaning of Love,* was paradoxical, not pessimistically moralistic. He could not accept Tolstoy's moralizing asceticism, basing his own advocacy of the celibate ideal on a view of erotic love that problematizes sex without stigmatizing it.

Like Tolstoy, Solov'ev was also preoccupied with death and its contingency on the natural cycle, rejecting, however, Tolstoy's acquiescence to nature. The birth of a fresh child overcomes death in his novelistic universe, as demonstrated in *Anna Karenina* by Levin's justification of his brother's death by the birth of his son. Solov'ev disavowed the naturalist justification of death, advocating the termination of coitus and childbirth as its surplus, with the purpose of ending nature's cycle. An apocalyptic thinker, he sought to overcome death by transfiguring the body. In the words of his nephew Sergei, he "felt revulsion to the physical aspect of childbirth."[6]

It is Solov'ev's "immortalization myth," to use Irene Masing-Delic's apt phrase, that unveils the paradox of his erotic philosophy.[7] Like Nikolai Fedorov, who developed the fantastic theory of resurrecting the fathers, he proscribed the sex act because it feeds the natural cycle that results in death yet celebrated erotic love because only it possesses the necessary libidinal power to vanquish the grim reaper. Although he called for abstinence and the end of nature, he refused to privilege heavenly Aphrodite over the earthly one, as did Plato in the *Symposium*, instead insisting on the equal value of the ideal and the real, or spirit and flesh, while also revealing an uncertain relation to the physical body. Unlike Tolstoy, Solov'ev was a theorizing mystic, not a realist writer whose point of reference is the empirical world, which is not to suggest, however, that he was not also attached to the body. The representation of the physical body in the uncertain utopian future concerned him all his life. Using the term I advance in the introduction, I suggest that Solov'ev was the harbinger of "decadent utopianism," which characterized the *Zeitgeist* of Russia at the turn of the century.

Solov'ev's views regarding the inseparability of eros and thanatos and the idea of channeling the sex drive toward the abolition of death in nature offers a uniquely Russian alternative to Freud's later concept of "the death instinct." The fundamental difference between the two is Solov'ev's utopian desire to overcome death instead of grappling with its psychological power over the individual. In recent years, we have learned that Freud's theory of the death drive was in fact influenced by a young Russian psychoanalyst: Sabina Spielrein introduced the notion in a 1912 paper titled "Destruction as Cause of Coming into Being." Her approach to the relationship of life and death, including the idea that they are two sides of one coin, may very well have been influenced by Solov'ev's *The Meaning of Love* written ten years earlier;[8] Spielrein was an educated woman, and Solov'ev's essay was common reading for young educated Russians at the turn of the century. We find corroboration of this in Boris Pasternak's *Doctor Zhivago*, whose young heroes read

*The Kreutzer Sonata* and *The Meaning of Love* in tandem in the early 1900s and whose mentor Nikolai Nikolaevich Vedeniapin presents a theory of history premised on abolishing death.

Solov'ev's views were formed not only by his utopian dreams but also by the time in which he lived. True, his utopian optimism was Christian, Gnostic, and Neoplatonic in origin. But living in the 1880s and 1890s, when cultural discourse was permeated by pessimistic theories of psychobiological degeneration, introduced a sense of pessimism into his faith regarding the transfiguration of human life. Solov'ev's obsession with the coming end was influenced by the epoch's growing uncertainty about nature's ability to maintain the health of the race no less than by the philosophical and theological traditions which he embraced. Hence the affixture of decadent to his utopianism.

The premise of Solov'ev's theory of transfiguring human life was the reconstitution of the originary whole, sundered since the beginning of time. Despite his apparent belief in originary wholeness, he was, like Tolstoy, uncertain about the relationship between the whole and its parts. Many in the European fin-de-siècle generation were torn between a melancholy nostalgia for the whole and an obsession with the fragment, or the synecdoche, the trope of fetishism. Haunted by degeneration and fetishist desire, the men and women of the time still sought to recover the whole, typically located only in the imagination. Solov'ev's imaginary whole was the figure of the divine androgyne, borrowed from Plato's *Symposium* and the Neoplatonic tradition.

Solov'ev's "erotic utopia," a term first applied to his writing on love by Evgenii Trubetskoy, is eclectic, consisting of divergent elements.[9] It unites Darwin's theory of evolution with Christian eschatology. Considered in the fin-de-siècle context, it represents a hybridization of decadence and mystical philosophies that combines elements of Christian mysticism, Neoplatonism, Gnosticism, and other forms of the occult. We might see Solov'ev as a kind of alchemist mixing together in his utopian retort the figures of the androgyne, Christ, and Sophia, the Gnostic incarnation of God's female other, whose revival was central to his immortalization project. This chapter considers Solov'ev's strange brew—his paradoxical interlacing of erotic love and celibacy, religion and positivism, part and whole, ideal and parody. It addresses Solov'ev's ambiguity and slippages in the erotic sphere by considering the theory of degeneration as the unexamined subtext of his utopian writings.

## Darwinist, Occultist, Christian

Solov'ev came from a liberal academic family. His father, Sergei M. Solov'ev, was an eminent Russian historian and rector of Moscow University. As a teenager of the mid-1860s, Vladimir, like Turgenev's Bazarov, grew his hair long so that he would look like a nihilist, although these tresses, which he kept till the end of his life, also marked him as a poet and romantic. The father was neither a romantic of the 1840s nor a man of the 1860s, even though he respected Chernyshevsky, whom he had met; the historian was upset by the judicial conviction of the radical ideologue for subversive political activity in 1864, considering the decision unjustified.[10] Under the influence of the positivist ethos, young Solov'ev studied botany and comparative anatomy, which explains his knowledge of the natural sciences as reflected in his philosophical writings. Lev Lopatin, a philosopher and friend, wrote: "[T]here was a time in his life when he was a total materialist. . . . I never met a materialist whose convictions were more passionate. This was a typical nihilist of the 1860s. He believed that a new truth has emerged from the basic precepts of materialism, one which must replace and supplant all previous beliefs, overturn all human ideals, create a completely new happy and rational life. . . . [An] expert on Darwin's writings, he believed with all his soul that by means of this famous naturalist's theory not only all teleology but also all theology and prejudices would be brought to an end."[11]

Solov'ev never fully abandoned the natural sciences, appropriating in particular Darwin's theory of evolution for his utopian enterprise of the 1890s. He developed his own fantastic theory of evolution that fused Darwinian theory, the Christian resurrection, and an occult view of the body with the goal of immortalizing humankind.

Solov'ev early on criticized the positivist methods of studying nature. As a student of the natural sciences, he wrote to his cousin Ekaterina Romanova on March 26, 1872: "People look into microscopes, cut up suffering animals, boil some kind of rubbish in chemistry retorts, and imagine that they are studying nature."[12] Two years later, Solov'ev's *Crisis of Western Philosophy* (*Krizis zapadnoi filosofii*, 1874) presented a fully developed theoretical attack on positivism, including what he considered its unwarranted claim to absolute knowledge and arrogant dismissal of all other epistemological approaches. Yet elsewhere Solov'ev deployed, albeit ambivalently, the discourse of positivist practice for nonscientific purposes. As an example we can take his analysis of one of Pushkin's best-known poems "The Prophet" ("Prorok"), in which, in the words of Solov'ev, an angel performs literal and figurative *surgery* on the living body of the poet. He interpreted the poem by metaphorically applying to it the experimental technique of vivisection, associated with the experimental natural sciences. Comparing the angel to an "experienced surgeon" who penetrates the body of the poet, he created a metaphoric palimpsest, superimposing surgical intervention over metaphysical transfiguration. He then went on to liken the brutal angel to a "red-skinned Indian," incorporating barbaric violence into the dissection metaphor and thereby tainting both the positivist and the metaphysical tropes of radical transformation.[13]

In the context of his own philosophical development, Solov'ev's rejection of positivism resulted from his decadent utopian project of annihilating death by transforming nature. In many respects, it resembled Fedorov's pseudo-scientific "Common Task," which espoused the feasibility of applying nature's laws to revivifying the dead. In *Lectures on Godmanhood* (1878), Solov'ev typically spoke of the "real world" in metaphoric terms—as fallen, selfish, and fragmented. He applied to it Newtonian mechanics: "Each individual being, each element excludes and repulses all others resisting this external action, occupies a certain fixed place, which it strives to keep exclusively for itself, demonstrating the force of inertia and impenetrability."[14] His weapon of choice against Newton's law of impenetrability—forcing mortal bodies to relinquish the space they occupy for subsequent generations—was the power of love, which he pitted against nature in *The Meaning of Love.*[15] In the words of Evgenii Trubetskoy, "one feeling is displaced by another. Two beloved people cannot simultaneously fit in one human heart, just as two bodies cannot temporarily occupy the same locus in space."[16] Trubetskoy's point suggests that there is no space for the child in Solov'ev's view of love.

Even though he abandoned the study of nature and positivist methodology in favor of idealist philosophy and mysticism, Solov'ev remained a materialist of sorts. He did not want to give up the material body in exchange for pure spirit and a purely abstract philosophy. A member of the fin-de-siècle generation, he wanted to recover the sexual body from the bourgeois closet to which it had been relegated in the nineteenth century. In his philosophy, this recovery took the form of Sophia, a Gnostic embodiment of the feminine principle, representing Christ's body as well as the human collective.

Solov'ev's philosophical interests lay in the liminal space between mind and body. This space was typically the province of the occult, with which he was engaged throughout his life. Although occult practices were condemned by both positivist science and the Christian church, Solov'ev, like the ancients and some of his contemporaries, believed in the reconciliation of science and religion in the occult. Trubetskoy disapprovingly described Solov'ev's chiliastic kingdom of God as the site of an immortalized love affair, suggesting that the kingdom resides in the space of the occult.[17] Trubetskoy implied that Solov'ev believed that the kingdom's population of lovers could be spirited out of their intermediate state between embodiment and disembodiment by a medium. We can certainly agree with his assessment of Solov'ev's project, but this is not the point. What is important for our argument is that Solov'ev did indeed attempt to embody the spiritual, as we see in particular in his quite personal love for Sophia and his desire to materialize her in ways that would influence some of his symbolist followers.

Striving to transcend the limitations of the empirical world and positivist thinking, Solov'ev's postpositivist generation imitated ancient occult practices by combining science and religion with the intention of accessing extrasensory experience. Many in the 1870s–90s dabbled in parapsychology and investigated paranormal phenomena. The best-known neurologists and psychiatrists of the time—Charcot in Paris, Lombroso in Rome, Krafft-Ebing in Vienna—made the paranormal the object of intense study. In fashionable salons in European capitals, men and women practiced spiritism, believing that it facilitated the physical revival of the dead body recycled into organic nature, calling it forth from beyond this life. Solov'ev frequented spiritist séances in the early 1870s at the home of the Orientalist Ivan O. Lapshin in Petersburg, then in his apartment in London in 1875, and later at the estate of the widow of Aleksei Tolstoy. If we are to believe Kovalevsky and the explanation that Solov'ev gave him, an apparition at a London séance initiated Solov'ev's trip to Egypt. Mochul'sky wrote that Solov'ev was a talented medium, with an extraordinary power of telepathy.[18] His manuscripts, especially in the 1870s, before and after his trip to the Egyptian desert, show evidence of spiritist automatic writing. The messages, mostly in French and in an altered handwriting, are from his mystical lover, Sophia.[19]

Although parapsychology is not considered a science, at the end of the nineteenth century its quasi-scientific status was considerably higher than it is today. Solov'ev's theory of evolution, premised on Christ's resurrection and the miraculous transfiguration of humankind as the end of evolution and of history, was even further from the scientific norm. Yet his fantastic visions of the future retained vestiges of scientific theory. In *Beauty in Nature* (*Krasota v prirode,* 1889) and later in *The Meaning of Love,* Solov'ev rehearsed the standard stages of Darwinian evolution. It begins with the birth of organic life in inorganic matter, followed by the evolution of the species from the simplest form of organic life to complex human life, and ends with the development of human consciousness, whose primary concern is battle with death. *The Spiritual Foundations of Life* (*Dukhovnye osnovy zhizni,* 1882–84) represents life in nature as a violent, even cannibalistic, struggle. Solov'ev's Darwinian view perceived nature's struggle as one of who will devour whom. But he veered away from Darwin in the course of anthropomorphizing the question: will nature devour man or vice versa? His view that if man devours nature, he will end up murdering living organisms in order then to commit suicide through procreation, was totally beyond Darwin. Both nature's and humankind's victories, wrote Solov'ev, are death-dealing activities that can be overcome only by transforming nature's body into the body of the God-man.

In an Easter letter titled "Christ Has Risen!" published in the newspaper *Russia* (*Rus'*) in 1897, Solov'ev described nature as a "multicolored bright shroud covering her continuously decomposing corpse," revealing his typically decadent image making.[20] He repeated once again in the letter the textbook version of natural history, portrayed by him in this instance as a joyful record of nature's and humankind's progress. He punctuated the narrative by shifting from a scientific perspective to a Christian one, capping it with the miraculous story of Christ's resurrection:

> Just as the appearance of the first living organism in the midst of inorganic nature [was a miracle] and just as, following that, the appearance of the first rational being in the kingdom of the dumb was a miracle, so the appearance of the first person who was completely spiritual, and therefore not subject to death—the firstborn of the dead [*pervenets ot mertvykh*]—was a miracle. . . . But what *presents* itself as a miracle is *understood* by us as a perfectly natural, necessary occurrence. The truth of Christ's resurrection is the complete truth, the full truth—not only the truth of faith, but also the truth of reason. If Christ had not risen, . . . the world would have been senseless, the kingdom of evil, deceit, and death. . . . If Christ had not risen, who then could rise? Christ has risen![21]

The letter begins dramatically with the statement that the resurrection was "the first conclusive victory of life over death" and ends with the assertion that the battle will be won when the process of man's disintegration into "disembodied spirit" and "rotting matter" will cease.[22] The happy end will come when man acquires Christ's body, which Solov'ev, following the Gospel of Luke (24:36–43), described in anatomical terms: as a material body with limbs and a digestive tract.

So the paradox that informs Solov'ev's optimistic story of evolution is that it combines scientific theory with Christian miracle, as if the latter followed the former naturally. Solov'ev seems to slip seamlessly from natural history into the supernatural, as did Fedorov. Instead of presenting creationism from a Christian perspective, he appropriated the scientific theory of evolution, incorporating it into his own miraculous prophecy of nature's transfiguration.

If we once again juxtapose Solov'ev's faith in the victory of life over death to Freud's theory of the life and death instincts, we are struck by the profoundly Christian imagination of the former. They help to explain the anti-psychological approach to subjectivity in the writings of Russian religious thinkers at the turn of the twentieth century. I would suggest that the substitution in Russia of metaphysics for psychology—in the sexual sphere—is the most substantive difference between Western and Russian theories of sexuality: divinity and religious teleology are given precedence over the grounding of desire in the individual unconscious.

## Painting Solov'ev's Portrait

Solov'ev was a colorful figure, eccentric in behavior and in appearance. His image was that of a homeless wanderer wearing odd items of clothing: a black top hat in the Egyptian desert, a batlike cape, an Orthodox priest's fur hat. According to his contemporaries, he had an amorous disposition, yet went on periodic retreats to Sergiev Posad, an ancient monastery near Moscow, where he lived the life of a hermit. He was known to have fallen in love many times, usually without reciprocation. His first recorded unfulfilled infatuation was at the age of nine: "I didn't sleep all night, got up late, and had great difficulty putting on my socks," wrote the young boy in his diary after the object of his love abandoned him for another boy.[23] Although he advocated the celibate ideal, he proposed marriage to several women, usually already married, only to be turned down in every case. His most important romantic involvements were with Sofia P. Khitrovo, the married niece of Aleksei Tolstoy's widow, and Sofia M. Martynova, also married and the subject of some of his most inspired love poetry to Sophia, his occult mistress. The relationship with Martynova was passionate and brief (1891–92); it coincided with the period of writing *The Meaning of Love.* He was in love with Khitrovo most of his life, especially during the decade between 1877 and 1887. Solov'ev never married and had no children, which marked the end of his immediate bloodline. The same was true of his sister Poliksena, who displayed her lesbian sexuality by wearing male attire.

The portrait of Solov'ev that we find in memoirs conflates several images: Christ, nihilist, and decadent. The long hair, which initially may have been an emblem of Solov'ev's nihilist affiliation, quickly acquired another meaning, that of an iconographic poet cum Christ figure. In a typical gesture of the time, Solov'ev and his contemporaries staged his body as the site of a fin-de-siècle palimpsest, superimposing a spiritual look onto an outmoded nihilist fashion. A friend of Lev Tolstoy, N. V. Davydov wrote that Solov'ev resembled the figure of John the Baptist from the painting by Alexander Ivanov.[24] According to the nephew of Aleksei Tolstoy, D. M. Tsertelev, Solov'ev's portrait served as an icon for his little daughter: "When my daughter was two years old, no sooner would she see Solov'ev's portrait, than she would reach for it as toward an icon, wanting to kiss it, and with reverence utter, 'God.'"[25] Boys on the street regularly called him God ("Bozhen'ka") or priest.

Although the descriptions of Solov'ev emphasize his Christlike appearance, they also conjure up a hybrid image that contains hermaphroditic, corpselike, and bestial, even vampiric elements, reminiscent of decadent representation, for instance, by the Dutch artist Jan Toorop. In a stylized verbal portrait (1874), M. D. Muretov, professor of the Moscow Theological Academy, described him as bestial, androgynous, and corpselike: "Long black hair resembling a horsetail or a horse's mane. A face . . . of feminine youthfulness, pale, with a bluish hue, and large, very dark eyes with clearly defined black eyebrows, but devoid of life and expression, somehow standing upright, not blinking, staring off into the distance. A withered, thin, long, and pale neck. An equally thin and long back. Long, thin hands with pale, corpselike, limp, long fingers. . . . Finally, long legs in narrow, threadbare black cloth trousers. . . . Something long, thin, dark, withdrawn, and perhaps enigmatic."[26]

Considered in the context of decadence, the portrait reveals a typical degenerate, with a bestial head of horsehair framing a pale girlish face and an anemic, unusually elongated, corpselike body. It prefigures, so to speak, the physical appearance of the future fictional cult figure of the European decadence Des Esseintes, the hero of Joris-Karl Huysmans's

John the Baptist, fragment of Alexander Ivanov's *Christ Appears to the People* (Tretyakov Gallery in Moscow)

programmatic decadent novel *Against Nature* (*A rebours,* 1884). Des Esseintes is the last scion of an old family whose degeneration resulted in male offspring that were "progressively less manly." Of the family portraits preserved in the Chateau de Lourps, Des Esseintes resembles the ancestor who is pale, drawn, with rouge on his cheeks and a thin, painted neck. He himself is "frail, . . . highly strung, with hollow cheeks,

Vladimir Solov'ev in 1881

cold eyes of steely blue . . . and thin papery hands."[27] I am not suggesting that Muretov implied that Solov'ev was afflicted by degeneration, but some of its standard physical stigmata are incorporated, probably unwittingly, into Muretov's portrait of the eccentric philosopher, making his appearance stereotypically decadent.

One of the typifying features of decadence is hybrid morphology.

Hybrid forms frequently replace the "natural" body. The more expansive verbal portraits of Solov'ev engage some of the most common decadent hybrids that bring together in an "unnatural" union the living and the dead, male and female, animal and human: vampire, androgyne, and Sphinx.[28] Another such portrait was given by Elizaveta M. Polivanova, with whom the young philosopher was in love and who attended his lectures on Greek philosophy at the Higher Women's Courses (a woman's university) in the mid-1870s. She recorded the strong impression that Solov'ev's lectures on Plato, especially about *Phaedrus,* made on her. In her notebook, she described Solov'ev's face, which she compared to that of a Christian martyr. To this Christlike description, however, she added a vampiric detail: a bright red mouth set off by a deathly pale face.[29] The portrait is a typically decadent fusion of mystical Christian purity and beastliness.

The most striking example of a hybrid depiction of Solov'ev is by Andrei Bely, well known for his grotesque, stylized, sometimes vicious verbal portraits, which I cite in later chapters of this book. This portrait appeared in 1911 in *Arabesques* (*Arabeski*), eleven years after the occasion he described. The setting was a reading by Solov'ev of his last work, the apocalyptic "Short Tale of Antichrist," at the home of his brother Mikhail, in 1900. Like Polivanova's, Bely's description emphasized the mouth. He portrayed "a large as if torn mouth with a protruding lip," evoking the image of a mouth dripping blood, its own or someone else's, which brings to mind the late Victorian fiend Dracula.[30] The other detail that he repeated is the philosopher's famous raucous, demonic laugh. An avatar of decadent incongruity, the description—aside from vampirism—suggests a fleshy, oracular mouth giving birth to the "words of a prophet." Instead of giving birth to life in the flesh, however, the mouth gives birth to ideas, in accordance with Plato's metaphor of "birth in beauty." Besides the bloody mouth, Bely depicted Solov'ev's incongruous body: a giant with a small torso, long legs, and lifeless, bony hands; a child with a lion's mane and seraphic eyes. Bely concluded that Solov'ev was simultaneously a prophet and a wicked devil.

While these saintly yet vampiric portraits of Solov'ev certainly reflect the iconographic practices of the time, they also reveal much about Solov'ev's public image, which, like his philosophy, consisted of a juxtaposition of incompatible characteristics. The saintly look affiliated him with Christ, the effeminate characteristics, with the androgyne. And in broader terms, the verbal portraits linked him to decadence, a sensibility that combined synecdochal fragments from various representational practices. They also substantiated the decadent aspect of his utopian life-creation project.

## Does the Androgyne Abstain?

Solov'ev's androgynous ideal reflects the syncretism of his utopian philosophy. Its Gnostic and Neoplatonic aspect (Neoplatonism resurfaced at the end of the century throughout Europe) mirrors the epoch's obsession with origins, nostalgia for the whole, and conflicted view of gender. In Gnostic cosmogony, divine unity was splintered by its fall into nature at the beginning of time, scattering unity's dismembered parts. The Gnostics, like Solov'ev, perceived unity as lacking sexual difference, whose creation resulted from the Fall. On the face of it, Solov'ev viewed life's task as reassembling the sundered body into a whole by reuniting male and female in a collective gender that is beyond sexual difference, a state that he affiliated with the figure of the androgyne. He wrote in *The Meaning of Love* that the cause of disintegration was the splitting of the primal ancestor into biological men and women, who represent mortal parts of an immortal whole. The underlying as well as overt message of each of the five lectures of the essay is the coming recovery of the originary whole, the unrelenting goal of the personal and collective life journey.

Yet transfigurative love according to Solov'ev requires erotic arousal, not the transcendence of desire by means of a higher spiritual indifference. It is premised on the sexual difference of the lovers, which must be maintained as the source of the libidinal energy necessary for their androgynous union. What Solov'ev prohibits is coitus, without, however, pathologizing sex. This is the paradoxical meaning of his erotic utopia and one of the fundamental causes of its unrealizability.

Solov'ev's Gnostic schema of history was influenced in part by Origen, an Alexandrian Christian mystic of the third century. Origen "interpreted 'the end or consummation' of all things as a rotation back to their primal unity. 'For the end is always like the beginning,' and in the coming world 'that dispersion and separation from the one beginning will undergo' a process of restoration to one and the same end and likeness."[31] While appropriating Origen's cyclical history, Solov'ev added a new dimension to it: he embodied the "rotation back" to divine totality-unity by giving it the shape of an eroticized androgyne.

Solov'ev formulated his erotic utopia by borrowing from various cosmogonies; we already know that from Christianity he appropriated the

Vladimir Solov'ev in 1900

resurrection and revelation, and from modern science, the Darwinian theory of evolution. In all the ancient mythologies from which he borrowed, he stigmatized the sexual split—partition—that initiated life in nature, the cause of death. Death is the source of nature's power, wrote Solov'ev repeatedly, and he offered instead an eschatology that is death defying.

The division into male and female in the Judeo-Christian tradition has its origin in the biblical Fall and the expulsion of Adam and Eve from Eden. In *The Meaning of Love,* Solov'ev described the creation of man in terms of the verse from Genesis (1:27): "So God created man in his own image, in the image of God he created him; male and female created he them." His reading of this verse is Neoplatonic, that is, it emphasizes the androgynous essence of the creator and of created humankind. To the Neoplatonic interpretation of the Judeo-Christian creation myth, he affixed Gnostic Sophia, his personified ideal who adds a crucial feminine dimension to the cosmogonic blend. According to the Gnostic myth, nature came into existence when Sophia acquired a physical body and, like Eve, was thereby split off from her divine spiritual consort. When Solov'ev's cosmogony leans toward its Judeo-Christian origins, Sophia exchanges places with the androgynous figure of Adam, reflecting the philosopher's sense of gender uncertainty and penchant for substitution. Thus it doesn't really matter if the cosmogony is gendered male or female, since the two were not clearly differentiated in the fin de siècle and were therefore mutually interchangeable.

The accretions to Solov'ev's ideal synthetic body do not end here. Onto androgynous Adam and his feminine Gnostic counterpart, Sophia, Solov'ev grafted the figure of the Platonic androgyne from the myth of Aristophanes, a figure whose uncertain gender titillated the decadent imagination: was the fin-de-siècle androgyne a homosexual, simply a feminized male, or an anatomical hermaphrodite?[32] One may also ask whether the interchangeability of the androgyne and Sophia ever entered Solov'ev's self-conscious writerly practice. There is no evidence of it on the textual surface, but we can say with some degree of certainty that his idealization of the androgyne reveals an affinity for decadence, not just a quest for originary wholeness. Linking wholeness with the "unnatural" body of the androgyne, which exists in the imaginary, Solov'ev replaced the "natural" whole with an artificial one. In this he revealed his unambiguous preference for artifice over nature, one of the cornerstones of decadent utopianism.

The other Platonic subtext of *The Meaning of Love* is the philosophy of eros articulated by Socrates in the *Symposium,* whose vision of ideal love originates in unconsummated erotic desire. He gave absolute preference to erotic, not procreative, love, proclaiming "birth in beauty" superior to childbirth in nature: "[T]he partnership between [those whose progeny is spiritual] will be far closer and the bond of affection far stronger than between ordinary parents, because the children that they share surpass human children by being immortal as well as more beautiful. Everyone would prefer children such as these to children after the flesh."[33]

Solov'ev certainly subscribed to Plato's erotic ideal. He differed from the ancient philosopher, however, in his turn-of-the-century Russian utopianism, which envisaged love as an active force in life creation. Love's goal was to bring history, associated with the irrevocable natural cycle, to an end and to immortalize the body. Dissatisfied with Plato's idea of erotic transcendence as mere abstraction, Solov'ev believed that erotic love has the active potential for transfiguring life in nature.[34] The Christian subtext of his concept of transfiguration and faith in the attainment of an immortal body was, of course, Christ's resurrection, which served as the basis and symbolic precedent for the epoch's utopian life creation.

The question still remains, however, whether Solov'ev's androgyne abstained sexually. Certainly Solov'ev believed that the best among historical men and women must, maintaining all the while a high degree of erotic desire in the expectation of apocalyptic transfiguration. The philosopher concluded *The Meaning of Love* with a series of fantastic images heralding the immortalization of humankind by means of a larger-than-life sex act at the end of history. So sexual gratification must be deferred till the collective coupling of one and all. Quite a remarkable repressive fantasy if one tries to imagine it literally!

Besides androgyny these concluding passages evoke Fedorov's utopian project of resurrecting the ancestors by including past generations in a "syzygial coupling" of all individuals. This polymorphous coupling, figured as a union that embraces the cosmos, resembles Fedorov's intertwinement of fantastic science and eros in his project of resurrecting the ancestors. It is not irrelevant in this context that Solov'ev knew Fedorov personally and corresponded with him for several years. An astronomical term that denotes the alignment of three bodies in the solar system, the syzygy is a key image in Gnostic mysticism.[35] In Solov'ev's usage, "the idea of the universal syzygy . . . produces or frees up real spiritual-bodily currents [*dukhovno-telesnye toki*], which gradually gain control of the material environment . . . and incarnate in it . . . living and eternal likenesses of absolute humanity."[36] In other words, the powerful orgasmic release of the universal sex act will produce the necessary physical energy to transfigure the human body.

Solov'ev implied throughout *The Meaning of Love* that individual couplings of men and women cannot by themselves release enough sexual energy to transform the world; instead they result in a fresh child, which brings with it the inevitability of death. Transfiguration can be accomplished only by humankind's participation as a whole in a universal coupling that will transcend biology as destiny.[37] Yet immediately following the reference to syzygial coupling, Solov'ev presented an image that seems to contradict the idea of universal coupling: "The power of this spiritual-material creativity in man is only the transformation or the *turning inward* of the creative power that in nature, being turned outward, produces the flawed infinity of the physical reproduction of organisms."[38] This image again evokes Fedorov, who proposed the internalization of sexual energy—sexual inversion—as an antidote to procreative sex.

Both thinkers sought an alternative to the procreative sex act, in which the phallus directs its seed outward—into the female womb. Solov'ev seems to propose as the final act of history the penetration by the phallus of its own body in an act of self-love and self-impregnation. If we consider this form of consummation in the context of the fin de siècle, it suggests either sexual inversion, a euphemism for homosexuality, or autoeroticism.

The conflicted description of death-defying, life-creating copulation clearly demands that we reexamine the role of sex in Solov'ev's utopia. The collective syzygial coupling of *all* men and women, living and dead, in the grand finale of *The Meaning of Love* evokes the prophetic last act of the Christian drama of history in Revelation, which links redemption and divine marriage. The book of Revelation entwines the figures of Christ as redeemer and Christ as bridegroom, whose bride is the New Jerusalem, but the apocalyptic conflation nowhere suggests symbolic erotic inversion.

The question that remains unresolved in the finale of *The Meaning of Love* is the presence in it of erotic union. How can it be considered a union between two individuals if the transfigurative sexual moment is "the turning inward of creative power?" Solov'ev's image of erotic inversion connotes solitary erotic experience, not fusion with another. When considered against the background of decadent eroticism—especially in the terms articulated by Freud—the inverted phallus suggests the epochal fear of castration and of male lack, not phallic power.

This makes the discussion of the place of sex in Solov'ev's eschatology by Trubetskoy, a contemporary Moscow philosopher, especially noteworthy; as I pointed out, he was the first to use the term "erotic utopia" in reference to Solov'ev's ideology of love. Trubetskoy began his analysis with Solov'ev's statement that "men and women are not immortal separately, only the *androgyne*," a figure whom Solov'ev described as "the combination of the two representatives of both sexes in *one* individuality," is immortal.[39] Trubetskoy proceeded to censure Solov'ev's view of androgyny for its indeterminacy, writing that it offers neither a spiritual ideal nor a real-life model. His main criticism is that androgyny, premised on abstinence, is "unnatural in all respects. . . . Such an understanding of love," in the words of Trubetskoy, "cannot be considered healthy from any point of view."[40]

As someone whose world-view was defined by the power of procreation and genealogy, Trubetskoy denied Solov'ev the stance of paradoxicalist. He concluded that Solov'ev's "attempt to sacrifice love to salvation so completely [made] it barren in this life and impart[ed] to it the *likeness of castrated love*" (emphasis mine). Trubetskoy's reference to castration is in all likelihood an allusion to Solov'ev's reputation as a Russian Origen. It was widely believed that Origen, perhaps the most influential Christian theologian before Augustine, had castrated himself as part of his radical ascetic project of purifying the body.[41] In the context of the fin de siècle, however, the allusion conjures up not Origen but the figure of the castrated male and the image of inverted, or castrated, eros at the end of *The Meaning of Love,* which Trubetskoy may have incorporated into his allusion to castration. He could not accept an erotic philosophy that castrates the male, especially one that sacrifices the present generation to the future. He considered unsubstantiated the idea of reconstituting the whole, whether in the figure of the Platonic androgyne or that of the Christlike God-man.[42] As a "naturalist" who privileged nature over artifice, Trubetskoy rejected Solov'ev's propagation of celibacy as an instrument for elevating lovers out of nature into life beyond death. Taking Trubetskoy's criticism a step further, it is as if Solov'ev granted immortality only to "freaks" and excluded those who replenish nature with healthy offspring from the heavenly kingdom.

If, following Trubetskoy, we judge Solov'ev's erotic utopia from the perspective of real life, it is indeed profoundly subversive, bringing life as we know it to an end (as does Pozdnyshev's fantasy, only for very different reasons). The project, despite Solov'ev's ambitions, remained strictly rhetorical. So we judge it not by its practical consequences but by its imaginary power and radical utopian vision. We consent to it as a symbolic system contingent on the utopian culture of the fin de siècle, not as a life practice that we must consider literally. In doing so, however, we refuse to take it seriously.

Abstinence has been the subversive subtext of all utopian projects whose goal is immortality in this world. When addressing the question regarding the outcome of his teaching, Solov'ev gave conflicting answers. In *The Meaning of Love,* he said facetiously that if procreation is the cause of death, abstinence is the logical expedient for "abolishing death." But as everyone knows, wrote Solov'ev in an obvious barb against *The Kreutzer Sonata,* abstinence hasn't saved anyone from dying.[43] Solov'ev's problem with Tolstoy was not his advocacy of celibacy, but the moralistic discourse in which Tolstoy wrapped it.

We can only conclude that Solov'ev either never really worked out his erotic philosophy or that it was simply unrealizable because of its utopian ambition. We must also recognize that his philosophy of love would slip on occasion from the Platonic realm of ideas and the Christian realm of the spirit into decadent fantasy. Although androgyny is represented as a spiritual ideal in his writing, the image of the decadent androgyne, which subverts gender difference by occupying the "perverse" space between male and female, lurks in the shadows of Solov'ev's Platonic universe. Whether the androgyne abstains or not remains a mystery, although the question really pertains to living men and women in search of transfiguration. Are they expected to abstain until the crowning sex act that will inaugurate the transcendence of sexual difference, marking the end of history? If they are, then Solov'ev's view of sex seems not only repressive but also perverse, revealing an erotic economy in which sexual pleasure is deferred until the end: in the meantime erotic desire would be stimulated and then stored, with the expenditure of erotic energy in the here and now remaining strictly cerebral. The prohibition would only heighten the intensity of perverse pleasure.

## Virgin or Eunuch?

From the perspective of some of his contemporaries and Alexander Blok's symbolist generation, one of the keys to the Solov'ev myth is his image of "knight-monk," to borrow Blok's description.[44] Solov'ev's virginal reputation was promoted by his brother Mikhail and nephew Sergei; the latter would later become an active member of the Blok cult. Emphasizing the paradoxical aspect of Solov'ev's ideology and behavior, Mochul'sky described him as an erotic ascetic who fell in and out of love many times. I. Ianzhul's wife, who watched over him during his stay in London in 1875, was struck by his ascetic appearance.

Expressing the epoch's psychopathological anxiety, she noted his weakness and sickliness: because his mind developed too quickly, he was destined to go mad.[45]

Shortly after the first installment of *The Meaning of Love,* the journal *Pilgrim* (*Strannik*) described it as "the analysis of a contemporary Origen."[46] There was even a study of the philosopher titled *Russian Origen of the Nineteenth-Century: Vladimir Solov'ev.*[47] Solov'ev authored the entry on the theologian in the Russian version of the encyclopedia of Brockhaus and Efron, writing that according to church history, Origen had himself castrated "to avoid temptation from the side of the numerous female students" in his school. Yet he expressed doubt that Origen became a castrate.[48]

According to Max Nordau, self-castration is one of the "stigmata" of psychopathology. What strikes today's reader of Nordau's *Degeneration* (1892) is the author's obliteration of the difference between the epoch's fear of castration, what Freud would later call the castration complex, and physical castration. This lack of distinction is most clearly revealed in Nordau's discussion of the Russian religious sect of the *skoptsy* (self-castrators), whom he labeled "degenerates" and "sexual psychopaths" who practice castration "as the only effective treatment to escape the devil and be saved."[49] By claiming that the *skoptsy* suffer from castration anxiety in the fin-de-siècle sense, he conflated the actual mutilation of the body and the discursive fear of castration without considering the important difference between them. Such an intentional conflation of the literal and the phantasmic may have served as a subtext of the comparison of Solov'ev to Origen by his contemporaries, especially since there is absolutely no evidence that Solov'ev had himself castrated.

The twin myths of Solov'ev's virginity and of his self-castration were exploded by the publication in 1993 of an exchange of letters from the 1890s between Solov'ev and Sergei N. Trubetskoy (a close friend and the brother of Evgenii).[50] Sergei was also a philosopher, a specialist on Plato whose lectures Andrei Bely attended at Moscow University. Besides contradicting Solov'ev's reputed virginity by referring to his sexual encounters, the letters offer examples of his obscene verse.

The letters contain what their publishers call Solov'ev's "Barkoviana," after the eighteenth-century Ivan Barkov, considered to be the founder of the tradition of obscene verse in Russia. Solov'ev, the Trubetskoy brothers, L. M. Lopatin, and Nikolai Grot, all members of the Moscow philosophical circle, regularly exchanged letters containing obscene verse. According to the publishers of the letters, the members of Solov'ev's family most likely destroyed most of his obscene writing after his death. His nephew Sergei, one of the editors of the 1911 collection of Solov'ev's works, even tried to exclude his parodic poetry, finding it at odds with Solov'ev's saintly persona. Sergei Solov'ev's biography of his uncle reflects the same desire to sanitize the philosopher's image.

A letter to Sergei Trubetskoy dated December 27, 1894, includes both a sample of Solov'ev's writing on asceticism and obscene poems in which he spoke of his sexual frustrations and revealed a lifelong lusting for the "cunt," no less powerful, I would suggest, than was Tolstoy's. ("I've committed many sins, terrible ones too, / a l'endroit du con," wrote Solov'ev in one of them.) The letter was written soon after the publication of the final installment of *The Meaning of Love.* What makes this typically male exchange characteristic of Solov'ev's rhetorical practice is the ironic juxtaposition of high and low. The combination of high-minded asceticism and male "cunt talk" deconstructs his erotic idealism. The best known published example of Solov'ev's penchant for converging high and low was his blasphemous poetry about Sophia, which shocked his contemporaries.

The first poem is an obscene, witty response to Trubetskoy's earlier letter, in which he apparently wrote that Solov'ev had been canonized and declared *tselkomudrennyi* (virgin-wise), clearly referring to the *Pilgrim* article about *The Meaning of Love.* The neologism *tselkomudrennyi* is a play on the Russian compound adjective *tselomudrennyi,* made up of the words for "whole" and "wise" and meaning "virtuous." The insertion of a *k* into *tselyi* ("whole") produces *tselka,* a vulgar word for virgin. The pun is appropriately ambiguous, connoting both virginity and knowledge of virgins. Solov'ev accepted the sobriquet but expressed doubt about his canonization:

For three and a half years now
My c—ck has seen no work
Useless fuss and bother
With a useless machine.

I was compared in the journal *Pilgrim*
With Origen himself.
Why don't I just drop my underdrawers
Before a tall mirror?

I will furnish myself with a sharp blade—
Snip! Deftly through the b—lls,
And I'm forever liberated
From my weakness for the c—nt.

Уж три года с половиною
Нет работы для х—я
С бесполезною машиною
Бесползная возня.

Был сравнен в журнале «Страннике»
С Оригеном я самим.
Уж не снять ли мне подштанники
Перед зеркалом большим?

Бритвой острою снабжуся я—
Чик! Ловчее сквозь м—де,
И навек освобожуся я
От пристрастия к п—де[51]

Solov'ev began the first stanza with the comment that he had not had sex for the past three and a half years and had only practiced masturbation. The time frame apparently refers to his last encounter with Sof'ia Martynova, the last great love of his life. Known as Sappho in the aristocratic circles of the Sollogubs and Trubetskoys, she was the embodiment of Sophia in Solov'ev's poetry of the time. Martynova was married; they carried on their sexual affair, among other places, in hotels near railroad stations.[52] So in private, he was no virgin, even though publicly he promoted abstinence.

The comparison to Origen evoked in the philosopher the obscene fantasy of narcissistic self-castration—to be performed in front of a large mirror—which resonates with the image of the phallus turned inward at the end of *The Meaning of Love*. Solov'ev concluded that only such an act would have the benefit of freeing him from his obsession with female genitalia. The other poem depicts him lusting after unattainable women, again undercutting his celibate reputation. And in relation to *The Meaning of Love,* it debases quite self-consciously Solov'ev's romantic idealization of unrequited love in yet another conflation of high and low.[53]

This is certainly not the letter of a knight or a monk, but of a man obsessed with sex, one who makes light of his celibate reputation and advocacy of sexual renunciation. Yet the comparison with Origen and the fantasy of taking a razor to his private parts suggest something more than a grotesque parody of the purification of the male body with the purpose of making it a receptive vessel for the divine spirit, something more than a Tolstoyan desire to rid himself of lust forever. It is not simply a spoof of Origen and Tolstoy's fictional ascetic Father Sergius from an eponymous story or a humorous spoof of castration anxiety.

I would suggest that Solov'ev's castration fantasy is also a parody of the androgynous ideal, which, as we know, looms high in the philosopher's teleology. Unlike the androgyne, a figure of plenitude that reunites man with his female half, thereby neutralizing sexual difference, the castrated male was imbued with the epochal fear of male lack. This phantasmic eunuch, whose penis had been stolen from him by the phallic woman, was the stereotype of emasculation, or feminization, in decadence. In imagining himself as a eunuch, Solov'ev revealed his affiliation with decadent discourse, reducing the androgyne to a eunuch or a monstrous hermaphrodite. And even if only in private, he parodied his androgynous Gnostic and Platonic utopia.

Because castration was probably the most common trope of decadence, the link that Solov'ev presented between the androgynous ideal and his grotesque castration fantasy resonates with some of the deep-seated fears of the time. Castration certainly is the originary myth in Freud's psychoanalytic project. In Freud's castration theory, all children share the sense of anatomical sexual sameness, according to which both men and women have a penis. A child's knowledge of sexual difference and the ability to differentiate between genders come later, after the castration anxiety has been fixed in the child's unconscious.[54] In other words, Freud's original ancestor is male, although in the turn-of-the-century hothouse dominated by the figure of the phallic woman, the male felt himself castrated: he felt like a woman. He possessed a phallus in mythical time but lost it after his fall into degeneration. Solov'ev, who, unlike Freud, had no apparent stake in claiming the male sex as primary, postulated the androgyne as an ideal according to which humankind's creative energy, or phallus, has been "turned inward." I suggested in the preceding section that this inversion is in fact an image of castration. I would add here that in longing for the erasure of sexual difference, Solov'ev may have been trying to overcome his own real-life desire.

## Fetishist?

In *The Meaning of Love,* Solov'ev, like Tolstoy, rejected the Darwinian "tyranny of the species over the individual," because it perpetuates the organic world. His fantasy of a transfigurative collective sex act at the end of history rejects nature. His vision of the end also reflects contemporary ideas about degenerate physiology and heredity. To borrow Nordau's punning term, it is informed by fear of the *"fin de race."*[55] The end of the race was felt in Russia, both from without—by the assimilation of the anxieties of the West into its culture—and from within. Although the apocalypse was a state of mind, the fear of the "end of the race" was also a demographic concern, especially in France, where there was a panic over the decline of the birthrate during the last two decades of the century. Caused principally by the massive deaths of young men in war in 1870, the decline was also attributed to syphilis and to degeneration, with the consequent belief in the sterility of family lines. Solov'ev expressed a similar set of concerns in one of his "Sunday Letters" published in Russia in 1897, titled "Russia in a Hundred Years" ("Rossiia cherez sto let"). The feuilleton is ostensibly about patriotism, but its real concern seems to be demographic. According to recent statistics, wrote Solov'ev, the Russian population had been declining since the 1880s. The increase shown by the census in 1897 revealed the growth of non-Russian or mixed populations on the margins of the empire, but not of ethnic Russians. Even the population of Moscow stopped growing during the 1890s. Not known as a Russian nationalist, Solov'ev expressed concern over the population decline of ethnic Russians and attributed it to an "organic cause," on which he did not elaborate.[56]

The similarity between the French anxiety about a dwindling population and Solov'ev's is striking, including its medical subtext. Although objective factors helped explain the apparent decline of ethnic Russians—such as increasing ethnic intermarriage in the cities—the fear was also shaped by contemporary medical research on sexual pathology. The product was genealogical anxiety related to racial decline, which, in the instance of early modernists such as Solov'ev, was projected onto a decadent view of procreation, making the discourses of medical psychopathology and decadent literature virtually indistinguishable.[57]

Thus Solov'ev's dual view of the end in *The Meaning of Love* engaged not only his utopian vision but also the anxiety of his generation. The utopian in him looked forward to the "chemical fusion [that] can render possible (both in the natural and the spiritual order) the creation of a new man, the actual realization of the true human individuality," which will bring procreation to an end.[58] The Solov'ev grounded in decadence and psychopathology, however, was less optimistic, concerned not so much with alchemical transfiguration as with the effect of the declining birthrate on Russia's national vitality. Even though *The Meaning of Love* is known primarily as a philosophical text, it also speaks to the issue of genealogy. Discussing it in the Old Testament context (part I.3), Solov'ev asserted the superiority of erotic over procreative love because the former has no relation to the quality of offspring and therefore cannot be tainted by their potential defects. Solov'ev was trying to escape "genetic continuity" as he sought a means to bodily transfiguration, a project reflecting the feelings of a generation that considered itself biologically tainted; this generation, the "last in a series," I call decadent utopians.[59] What I am suggesting is that the fear of degeneration, which was linked to the epoch's crisis of masculinity and anxiety around reproductive fertility, fueled Solov'ev's antiprocreative utopia. Yet we must also acknowledge Solov'ev's implicitly positive view of degeneration: genetic exhaustion by implication has the beneficial effect of erasing the biological tyranny of the species over the individual.

The *Meaning of Love* devotes several pages to contemporary degenerate ailments, especially fetishism, later viewed by Freud as a defense mechanism against castration and homosexuality. Writing about fetishism in *The Meaning of Love,* Solov'ev referred to the work of two well-known psychiatrists: Richard von Krafft-Ebing, the author of *Psychopathia Sexualis* (1886) and the teacher of Freud, who later, in the 1890s, identified sadism and masochism as sexual perversions; and Alfred Binet, Charcot's student who first identified fetishism as a sexual perversion in "Le fétichisme dans l'amour" (1887). Krafft-Ebing's case study was translated into Russian in 1887, almost immediately after the first German edition appeared. Both Krafft-Ebing and Binet influenced contemporary medical and general cultural discourse in Europe as well as in Russia. Following the two European psychiatrists, Solov'ev listed the most common fetishes as women's hair, hands, feet, aprons, shoes, and handkerchiefs, without addressing the more complex homosexual fetishist model, which identifies the fetish with the phallus. Like Krafft-Ebing and Binet, however, he considered the fixation on the part instead of the whole to be almost exclusively a male issue.

The example that attracted Solov'ev's attention and sympathy was case (observation) no. 17 in the first edition of *Psychopathia Sexualis.* It is the story of an apron fetishist "of a badly tainted family; of small mental development; deformed skull. At fifteen his attention was attracted by an apron hung out to dry. He put it on and masturbated behind the fence. From that time on he could not see aprons without repeating the act. . . . He sought to free himself of his weakness by a sojourn of several years with the Trappists," but was unsuccessful.[60] The source of this example, according to Krafft-Ebing, is Charcot-Magnan (1882). In Solov'ev's version, which is much shorter and omits the reference to masturbation, the apron is "hanging on the clothesline, just washed and not yet dry."[61] Implied but not named, masturbation figures in the description of the apron fetishist, whose full story was readily available in the recently published Russian edition of *Psychopathia Sexualis.*

What becomes clear in these pages of *The Meaning of Love* is that the object of criticism is not fetishism but current therapeutic practices of treating it. Although there is no evidence in *Psychopathia Sexualis* of therapies that use pornographic pictures of naked women, Solov'ev accused psychopathologists, like Krafft-Ebing and Binet, of using such tools to "cure" what they considered to be deviations from the norm:

> Partly through persistent medical advice, primarily through hypnotic suggestion, the patient is forced to occupy his mind with the image of a naked female body or with other pictures of a *normal* sexual character [*sic*]. The cure is then considered successful and the recovery complete if, under the influence of this artificial excitation, the patient begins willingly, frequently, and successfully to visit *lupanaria* [brothels]. . . . It is incredible that these honorable scientists were not given pause, if only by the simple consideration that the more successful this kind of therapy becomes, the more likely that the patient will need to turn his attention from one medical specialty to another, and that the psychiatrist's triumph might cause the dermatologist considerable trouble.[62]

Like Tolstoy, who claimed in *The Kreutzer Sonata* that contemporary medicine sent "boys to brothels" only to treat them for syphilis, Solov'ev condemned brothel going because of its link to venereal disease.[63] Taking Tolstoy's attack on prostitution further, he compared prostitution to necrophilia and the body of the prostitute to "a corpse," images that resemble nineteenth-century representations of the prostitute as the diseased part of society irrevocably severed from it.[64] More importantly, however, in comparing fetishism and prostitution, Solov'ev gave preference to the former because in his words it is more "normal," not merely more hygienic. In doing so he censured the psychiatrists' definition of sexual normalcy as heterosexual desire based on chronic brothel going. It is in the slippage from hygienic to normative thinking that Solov'ev's assertion regarding the normalcy of fetishism becomes opaque. His explanation seems to rest on the claim that prostitution is a form of fetishism: the prostitute's body is a fetish object, wrote Solov'ev, only, unlike the apron, it is infected. Solov'ev went so far as to suggest that most forms of male coitus—not just in the brothel—are fetishistic, erasing female subjectivity, especially its spiritual aspect.[65] What then can we conclude about his erotic economy and its normalization of fetishism?

Offering the standard definition of fetishism as the "part displacing the whole," Solov'ev qualified it as "affiliation instead of essence."[66] "Essence" in the Solov'evian context refers to the union of male and female—mere fragments of the whole—in a single androgynous gender, marking the end of nature and history and the beginning of the *real* erotic utopia, beyond death. In the meantime, fetishism in the form of an affiliated metonymic clean apron remains for Solov'ev preferable to the fetishized naked female body. It precludes syphilis as well as tainted heredity, legitimizing Solov'ev's own fetishist sensibility and worship of the fragment.

Implying that fetishism is a model perversion, Solov'ev anticipated by almost a whole century Foucault's oft-quoted statement to that effect.[67] Opaque in its own terms, Foucault's post-Freudian claim that fetishism is the master perversion of the fin de siècle is perhaps more transparent than Solov'ev's. Fully cognizant of the primary function of displacement in perverse sexual behavior, he saw what Solov'ev did not have to articulate or perhaps could not fully appreciate in his time: that late nineteenth-century fetishism served as the model of all perverse behavior.

In a letter to the widow of Aleksei Tolstoy, Solov'ev revealed his own fetishist preferences. He wrote her that her niece, Sof'ia Khitrovo, the main love of his life, had not given him "a sacred relic [memento], although she [had] promised . . . so that the main object of [his] worship remain[ed], as before, a photograph [of her] with her head torn off."[68] The head had been severed from the body, just like the penis in Freud's castration fantasy, and Solov'ev found it inadequate, thus implying that it lacked full fetishistic power. Not so in the case of the bootee that he supposedly carried close to his chest. According to his sister M. S. Bezobrazova, Solov'ev carried a knit bootee of one of Khitrovo's children in a waistcoat pocket: "From time to time, he took it out, admiring it, he looked at it with a smile, sometimes kissed it and carefully hid it again," revealing a penchant for shoe fetishism about which he had read in Binet and Krafft-Ebing.[69] A Freudian reading of the bootee would very likely make something of the fact that it linked Khitrovo back to the image of the phallic mother. In Solov'evian terms, however, fetishism as a solitary sexual practice reinforces abstinence and the celibate ideal.

Taking Solov'ev's exploration of fetishism out of the personal and contemporary psychiatric realms and placing it in the context of turn-of-the century decadent discourse, we can view it as an expression of the epoch's general struggle with the relationship of part and whole. He seems to have longed for the whole, as he wrote to Sof'ia Khitrovo's aunt, while also worshiping the synecdochal fragment—the headless body in the case of the photograph. In the more philosophical sense, the fetish became the epoch's fragment of choice, which if viewed in later Freudian terms brings us to the fear of castration and the triumph of the fetish, which screens the castrated penis from the subject's memory.[70] In more formal literary terms, the severed fetish informs fragmented narrative, modernism's key rhetorical strategy.

A celebrated fetish of turn-of-the-century art and literature was the severed head of John the Baptist, whom a contemporary compared to Solov'ev and whose head will figure prominently in the subsequent chapters devoted to Blok. As a Christian devotional object, the Baptist's fetishized head underscored the epoch's decadent fusion of sexual desire and religious worship. Because of its metonymic character rhetorically, the fetish also reified the conflicted desire of the age: it had the potential to restore the whole, thus reconstituting the sundered body, yet serve the epoch's displacement of desire from the genitals to a substitute love object. In the latter function, the fetish became the phantasmic fragment that assumes an aesthetic power of its own, whether in the shape of a body part, a piece of clothing, or an ornament. From this we can conclude that it is not so much the metonymic tension between part and whole that informs the fetishist's solitary sexual experience as the fetish's role as substitute for something he both desires and fears. At least this was how Freud articulated the sexual anxiety of the time.

The contemporary reader is struck by Solov'ev's disavowal of psychology at the expense of a radical utopian vision. While we may be more interested in the unconscious, hidden meanings of love, Solov'ev's Russian contemporaries focused on its philosophical substance. In considering Solov'ev's views, they were especially concerned with the place of the procreative family in his vision of eros and conception of evolution from inorganic life to the kingdom of God on earth. The "Moscow philosophers," the Trubetskoys and Grot, were particularly critical of his depreciation of the family, which was perhaps most strikingly reflected in the following statement about maternal love:[71] "Maternal [love], in both strength of feeling and the concreteness of its object, approaches sexual love, but for different reasons cannot have an equal meaning for human individuality. It is conditioned by the fact of procreation and the law of generational change."[72]

The public response to *The Meaning of Love* and *Justification of the Good* (1897), in which Solov'ev continued the discussion of procreation, became part of the general polemic about sex and marriage initiated by *The Kreutzer Sonata* in 1890.[73] Like Tolstoy in the afterword to *The Kreutzer Sonata,* Solov'ev mocked the concerns of those who fear that his propagation of the celibate ideal will bring about the end of the race: "To propose that even the most energetic and successful advocacy of sexual abstinence could *prematurely* halt the physical procreation of the human race and lead to its demise is an opinion so absurd that fairness compels one to doubt its sincerity."[74] Solov'ev stated emphatically that until the time when all living and dead join in a collective syzygial coupling, "the cessation of childbirth in the name of chastity" made no sense. Revealing his awareness of the discursive nature of the utopian project, he wrote that until such a time procreation would continue and the miracle of childbirth would continue to atone for what he described as man's "carnal sin."[75]

Although he spoke of the sex act as carnal sin, Solov'ev's mockery of his generation's fear was not moral but philosophical. His position was not that of Tolstoy, whose saw humankind as simply too weak to abstain from sex permanently. Unlike Pozdnyshev in *The Kreutzer Sonata,* who associates shame with the sex act itself, Solov'ev's philosophical discourse linked sexual shame with man's failure to vanquish nature by perpetuating the power of death.[76] Like Nietzsche, he believed that man is unfinished and must be surpassed, except that Solov'ev replaced the man-god with the God-man. Nietzsche's superman overcomes the fear of death; Solov'ev's God-man, who is not merely an isolated individual, overcomes death itself in a totalizing project of transforming the world.

What till now has remained virtually unexplored are the ways that Solov'ev subverted his own erotic utopia. Its most subversive aspect—because of its impracticability as well as covert repressive intentions—is the prescription to historical men and women that they defer erotic gratification till the realized utopia, suggesting in the meantime cerebral sexuality reminiscent of decadent eros. Commingling celibacy and eros in an age characterized by gender uncertainty, he also implicitly suggested same-sex and fetishist desire as alternatives to procreative love; these were "decadent," not utopian sexual practices. So if we delve deeper into Solov'ev's erotic palimpsest, we may discover that underlying his transfigurative life-creation project were autoeroticism and same-sex love.

Solov'ev's erotic philosophy informed the life-creation projects of his followers, especially Blok's. Young Blok devoted himself to Solov'ev's ideal woman, Sophia, even marrying her real-life incarnation in the hope of realizing Solov'ev's celibate erotic union. But in visiting *lupanaria,* censured by Solov'ev in *The Meaning of Love,* Blok, like the young Tolstoy, acquired the dreaded venereal disease. As his ideal woman grew darker in visage, he began to transform her into an object of fetishist desire. Blok's conflict between spiritual love and fetishist desire for the demonic femme fatale is the subject of the next two chapters.

# 3

# The Case of Alexander Blok

## Marriage, Genealogy, Degeneration

Alexander Blok and Liubov' Dmitrievna Mendeleeva were married on August 17, 1903, in an eighteenth-century church in Tarakanovo that stood on a green meadow overlooking a ravine near Blok's family estate. Coming from high-ranking Petersburg academic families, young Blok and Liubov' Dmitrievna had known each other since childhood. Blok's maternal grandfather was A. N. Beketov, botanist, rector of Petersburg University, and pioneer of women's higher education; his father, A. L. Blok, was professor of state law at Warsaw University. Liubov' Dmitrievna was the daughter of Russia's foremost chemist, Dmitrii Mendeleev, the author of the table of elements. Their family estates, Shakhmatovo and Boblovo (Klin *uezd*), which Beketov and Mendeleev purchased shortly after the liberation of the serfs (1861), were situated close to each other. The wedding party was to be equally illustrious and intimate.

Blok had invited Andrei Bely (Boris Bugaev), whom he knew only through his poetry and their correspondence, to be his bride's attendant.[1] Bely was the son of the acclaimed Moscow professor of mathematics Nikolai Bugaev, whose death prevented the young admirer of Blok from attending the wedding.[2] Like Blok, Bely had grown up in the academic world, spending his childhood summers about seventeen versts from Shakhmatovo.[3] Blok's best man and maternal second cousin, Sergei Solov'ev, who also spent his summers in the Klin region, was the nephew of the philosopher Vladimir Solov'ev. Even though Bely and Sergei were not related, the latter's family became young Bely's spiritual

Church in Tarakanovo in 1900s (Museum of Alexander Blok in Solnechnogorsk)

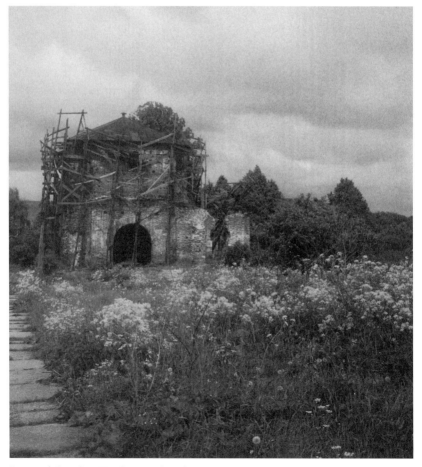

Ruins of church in Tarakanovo (2002)

family; they lived in the same building on the Arbat as the Bugaevs. Children of Russia's academic elite at the turn of the century, the three young men and one woman, whose lives were closely entwined, became involved at the beginning of the century in what can be described as a mystical affair among scions of the academic world.[4]

The wedding ceremony was staged as a stylized Russian Orthodox and folk ritual. In imitation of folk tradition, the mother of the bride did not attend the ceremony. Sergei initiated the first act of the anachronistic epithalamic ritual when he set out to Boblovo to fetch the bride in a troika decorated with ribbons, bringing her a bouquet of pink asters from the Shakhmatovo garden.[5] When the married couple came out of the church, local peasants greeted them with bread and salt and white geese—a folk tradition—that became pets at Shakhmatovo. The bride's old nanny sprinkled the married couple with hops on their arrival back at the family estate. Instead of city silks, the bride wore a white batiste dress and wild orange blossoms in her hair, whereas the bridegroom was dressed in his student frockcoat and carried a sword. During the wedding feast in the Boblovo house, peasant women in holiday costume sang wedding songs in the yard to honor the newlyweds.[6] Inside guests toasted the future of Russian science.[7]

Blok and Bely were mystical poet-brothers engaged in symbolism's most celebrated life-creation project, whose beginning was marked by Blok's "epoch-making wedding" (52). The project was inspired by Vladimir Solov'ev and was based on a symbolic reading of personal and everyday life according to an esoteric utopian blueprint. Although Bely did not attend the wedding, he described it in *Reminiscences about Blok* (*Vospominaniia o Bloke*, 1922), basing his description on Sergei Solov'ev's stories about the festivities.[8] Bely's *Reminiscences*, written right after the untimely death of Russia's premier symbolist poet in 1921, offers the most extensive and complex representation of the mystical love story of the handsome young poet and his beautiful wife, whose appropriately emblematic name, Liubov', means "love" in Russian.

Liubov' Dmitrievna had become for the poet the real-life incarnation of Solov'ev's mystical bride, Sophia, to whom Blok dedicated much of his youthful love poetry, collected in *Ante Lucem* (1898–1900) and *Poetry about the Beautiful Lady* (*Stikhi o prekrasnoi dame* [1901–2]). Full of presentiments of the end, this poetry staged Blok's apocalyptic hopes of a new beginning as an epiphanetic appearance of a chaste love goddess, typically in the natural surroundings of Shakhmatovo. The future affiliation

Alexander Blok in 1907 (Institute of Russian Literature in Petersburg)

of apocalyptic revelation with a female apparition also reflects Blok's early childhood: abandoned by his father in infancy, he grew up in the company of loving and cultivated women who had left on him their profound imprint.

As someone whose initial adoration of his spiritual brother and his life-creating power turned to resentment, Bely questioned the relia-

Liubov' Dmitrievna Blok in 1905 or 1906 (Andrei Bely Museum in Moscow)

bility of his memoirs in *Reminiscences.* He admitted to the habit of scrambling facts, yet insisted on his unique memory of Blok's gestural language, its symbolic nuances, and the special atmosphere of his poetic universe (87–88). Unlike Bely's later memoirs, *Reminiscences* idealizes Blok and glosses over the acrimony that emerged between them as their life-creating love for Liubov' Dmitrievna turned into a nasty triangular entanglement.[9]

Bely was willing to cast the story as a symbolist fairy tale because of the poet's untimely death. An architect of the esoteric Blok cult, whose most extensive public document is *Reminiscences,* Bely propagandized Blok's ideas to the Argonauts, a loosely organized circle of mystically inclined Moscow students, even before the poet-twins had met.[10] The Argonauts, who had emerged out of Bely and Sergei Solov'ev's friendship, developed a keen though rather adolescent sense of the fin de siècle, and this stimulated their life-creation hopes modeled on the examples of Nietzsche and Solov'ev.

Like the Argonauts, who saw signs of the coming end in common occurrences and mythologized their personal relations, Blok imbibed not only Solov'ev's apocalyptic prophecies but his playfulness as well. Apocalyptic games became one of the hidden layers in Bely's and Blok's

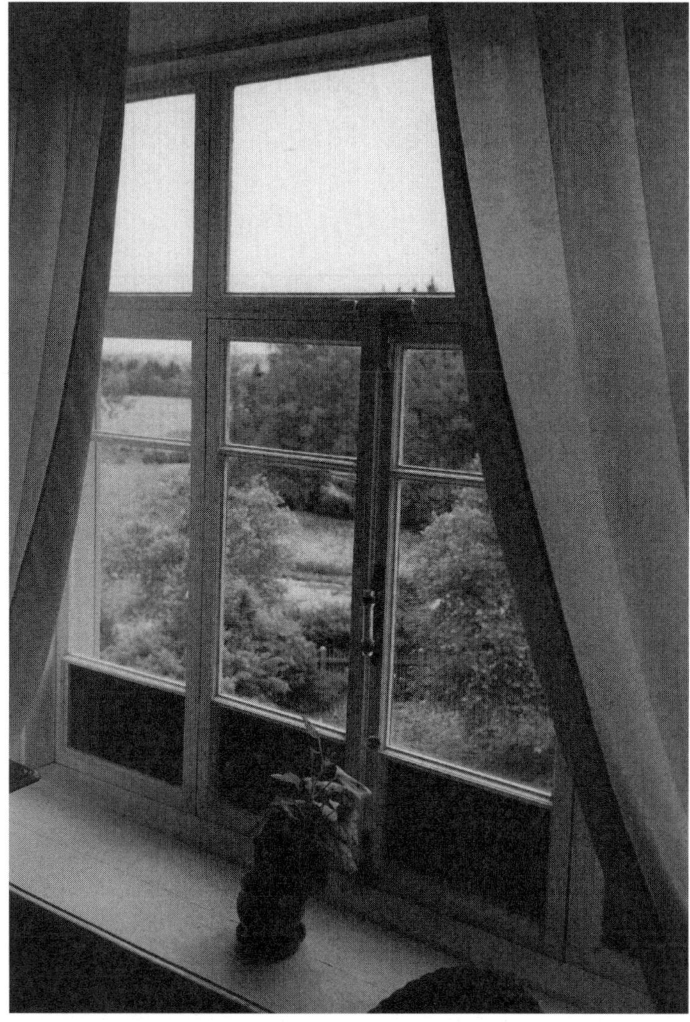

View from Blok's study in Shakhmatovo (2002)

symbolism: "We were playing a game called the end of the world," wrote Bely, in reference to the early period of their relationship.[11] Staging himself as Blok's poet-twin, Bely believed that together they would hasten the "coming dawn" of the end, predicted by Solov'ev in his apocalyptic vision of Sophia, the embodied eternal feminine. Blok's death offered Bely the opportunity to revisit the poetic myth of their youth and inscribe it into Russian cultural history as the single most important narrative of symbolist life creation.

In this chapter I consider the Blok circle in Shakhmatovo through the prism of Bely's confessional memoir, which came to define both the idealistic and the dark aspects of the Blokian legacy. The centerpiece of the Shakhmatovo drama was Blok's marriage to Liubov' Dmitrievna, to which the members of the Blok cult ascribed Solov'evian apocalyptic meaning. In *Reminiscences,* Bely also locates the marriage within the history of life-creating love by including it in the great "love stories" of the past.

I also examine Blok's conflicted views on sex, marriage, procreation, and genealogy, as well as Liubov' Dmitrievna's demythologizing story of their love and of Blok's fear of degeneration. More than his immediate predecessors and contemporaries, he sensed the degenerate underside of his commitment to a Solov'evian erotic utopia; he was truly a decadent utopian. Even though Blok derided Max Nordau's *Degeneration* and his views on European modernism, he could have undersigned his prophecy of *fin de race.*[12] In his public and private writings, Blok interrogated the same degenerate stigmata as Nordau—nervous exhaustion, vampirism, venereal disease, and tainted genealogy—which underlie the top layer of his erotic and poetic palimpsest associated with the heavenly goddess Sophia, who bears the name Beautiful Lady. The transformation of his muse into a castrating woman of the fin de siècle is the subject of the next chapter.

## An Epoch-Making Marriage

Bely wrote that the atmosphere of the wedding fused the participants into a mystical union. He described nature as "radiant," (*luchezarnyi*), a term associated with Solov'ev's mystical encounters with Sophia that informed Blok's and Bely's discourse of those years: it connoted otherworldliness and transfiguration. Sergei, according to Bely, believed that the marriage was going to usher in a Solov'evian theocracy in which the bride and groom would play key roles. Despite the element of irony in Bely's account of the wedding—after all, many difficult years had passed since their youthful idealism and childish games—its representation by him as "epoch making," despite the quotation marks, attaches to it a significance beyond the real-life event.

Formed in Shakhmatovo in the summer of 1904, a year after the wedding, the Blokist commune, consisting of the young married couple, Bely, and Sergei Solov'ev, was the ideological consequence of the marriage. Bely and Sergei considered themselves a "syzigial" extension of the apocalyptic marital union. The figure of the syzygy, an astronomical term, comes from Solov'ev's *Meaning of Love*, in which it represents transfiguration through erotic love (see chapter 2, "Does the Androgyne Abstain?").

The Blokists, as I will refer to the members of the Blok cult, superimposed Solov'ev's supposed celibate image onto Blok.[13] They felt that their poet, "in love with Eternity," simply could not marry an "empirical young woman." "If [his bride] is Beatrice—one doesn't marry Beatrice," wrote Bely. "If she is simply a young woman, marriage [to her] is a betrayal of the way." Sergei told Bely that LDM, Liubov' Dmitrievna's mystical acronym in the Blok sect, was an extraordinary woman who understood the "double meaning" and "ambiguity of her position: becoming Blok's bride [required newness and] daring to set out on the radiant way" (52). The reference to a double meaning suggests that Liubov' Dmitrievna accepted Solov'evian marital celibacy and did not have the expectations of an ordinary young wife—sexual relations with her husband and a family.

The Blokists' refusal to reconcile the bard's celibate image of the ethereal Beautiful Lady with patriarchal marriage reflects Solov'ev's view of spiritual marriage in *Justification of the Good* (*Opravdanie dobra*). In it Solov'ev described marriage as the union either of Christ and the church, the emblem of Christ's body, or of Christ as Logos and the eternal feminine as Cosmos. Bely discussed *Justification of the Good* in *Sacred Colors* (*Sviashchennye tsveta*), which he wrote in 1903, the same year as Blok's wedding. Like Solov'ev, he claimed in the essay that apocalyptic marriage is the emblem of embodiment: "Symbolism comes to an end, incarnation begins. We must incarnate Christ, just as Christ was incarnated."[14] He concluded in the essay that marriage represents "a world historical task," meaning that it will instantiate the transfiguration of life.[15] It was this task, premised on unconsummated erotic love—stored till the requisite expenditure of erotic energy—that the Blokists ascribed to Blok's marriage. This must have been an extraordinary challenge to a young couple in love.

The Blokists were not alone in pondering the dilemma of Blok's marital celibacy. Shortly before his wedding, Blok wrote his father: "[Zinaida Gippius], along with all her partisans, disapproves of my marriage and finds in it a 'disharmony' with poetry. I find this somewhat strange, because it is difficult to grasp the completely rational theories that the Merezhkovskys rigorously carry out, to the point of negating the reality of two incontrovertible facts: marriage and poetry (as if either of these were not real!). I am censured chiefly for allegedly 'not feeling the end,' which (in their opinion) follows from the present circumstances of my life."[16]

Gippius's position was that procreative marriage subverts apocalyptic poetry in the same way that procreation subverts the end of history. Her view of Blok's marriage suggests that she expected the poet and his wife to have children, which in symbolist life creation would undermine the creation of Platonic offspring not of the flesh. Blok referred to this when writing Bely about Gippius's theory of marriage shortly before their first meeting; he wrote that Gippius considered the life of a poet and that of a married man incompatible. He went on to say that she tried to convince him of it on a beautiful spring night; "but at that moment I loved the spring night more; I didn't grasp the theory, and understood only that it was difficult. I got married—and I am again writing poetry."[17]

Solov'ev's and the Blokists' discourse of ideal marriage, its representation as a "mystery" and as a "universal historical task," echoes the book of Revelation. The Apocalypse, which informed their vision of the future, is the last act in the drama of history, featuring the figure of Christ as bridegroom and the New Jerusalem as his bride. In their apocalyptic imaginary, Bely and Sergei viewed the young couple as enacting, or preenacting, the spiritual marriage of Revelation. Imitating Christ and his bride by joining in marriage, Blok and Liubov' Dmitrievna would mark the end of history and usher in the transfiguration of life.[18]

Such was the fantasy of the young Blokists, whose favorite activities were hunting for esoteric meaning in everyday life and representing real-life occurrences as mystical signs of the end of history: they read into Blok's marriage an entwined Christian, Neoplatonic, and revolutionary meaning. Mystical young alchemists, playing a game called "the end of the world," they transformed a real-life young woman into a "New Goddess in whose light this world would be transfigured." "We willed [*volili*] transfiguration," wrote Bely, using one of his favorite Nietzschean neologisms *volit'*, from *volia* (will) (52). What an extraordinary burden for a young wife with a different set of expectations.

"Everything drew us to one another," claimed Bely in *Between Two Revolutions* (*Mezhdu dvukh revoliutsii*, 1934); "S. M. Solov'ev at one time even dreamed of establishing a collective commune, there were the communes of Tolstoyans; Michel Bakunin dreamed of a commune made up of brothers and sisters."[19] The reference to the Bakunin estate, which was located not far from Shakhmatovo, evokes the gentry hothouse of

1820s and 1830s Russian romanticism characterized by an ideal view of erotic love.

Although the Blokists were critical of the sect that Gippius formed around her marriage, their secret union had something in common with the commune of their older Petersburg contemporaries. Functioning as an inner sanctum, the Shakhmatovo quasi cell resembled that of the Merezhkovskys, who considered themselves and Dmitrii Filosofov the secret nucleus of their religion of the Third Testament (see chapter 5). Just like them, the Blokists held their own secret communion mass with church wine on January 14, 1904.

Quoting Solov'ev's poem "The Beautiful Lady" ("Prekrasnaia dama"), Bely described Liubov' Dmitrievna as the "eye in the triangle," which fuses its participants into a whole (91). The Blokists endowed the Masonic symbol with Solov'evian erotic meaning. Each of the young men had a function in the triangle: Blok was the clairvoyant poet; Bely, the philosopher; Sergei, the theologian, who perceived the union as "the first world council" of their sectarian church. Invoking the New Testament, Bely declared that each embodied an aspect of Christ's disciples: he compared Blok to John, Sergei to Peter, and himself to Paul (64). Like the Bakunin conspiratorial commune (Mikhail Bakunin became an internationally known anarchist, whose popularity even Marx envied), the Blokist one also had a political dimension: the inauguration of Russia's future theocracy. Modeled on the official slogan of Orthodoxy, autocracy, and nationalism, their triadic motto consisted of Sophia, theocracy, and the folk (*narod*) (65).

The historical drama was enacted in the summer of 1904 on the countryside stage around Shakhmatovo. It was as if they expected the "revolution"—or transfiguration—to take place in nature, not in the city. In the essay "Green Meadow" ("Lug zelenyi," 1905), Bely described Russia as a big meadow, invoking simultaneously Blok's and Tolstoy's estates. All four Blokists spent the summer of 1904 at Shakhmatovo, acting out their fantasy. Blok and Liubov' Dmitrievna played the roles of Russian folk prince and princess, living in a pastoral little house overgrown with roses. Like the celibate married couple Vera Pavlovna and Dmitrii Sergeevich Lopukhov in Chernyshevsky's *What Is to Be Done?* they had separate bedrooms and a common room.[20] Blok's maternal aunt, Maria A. Beketova, described the couple's Shakhmatovo house as an Old Russian *terem,* an idealized fairy-tale image. Bely compared Blok, who wore peasant-style shirts on which Liubov' Dmitrievna had embroidered red swans, to Ivan Tsarevich, the hero of Russian fairy

Blok and Liubov' Dmitrievna in Shakhmatovo, caricature by Alexander Blok

tales; he likened Blok's young wife in her flowing pink dress to Botticelli's Flora (128–30). Blok himself superimposed the image of his bride on the Virgin Addolorata by the Italian mannerist Sassoferrato, whose reproduction had stood on his desk since 1902.[21] The 1904 photograph of Bely and Sergei, taken shortly after their summer in Shakhmatovo, represents Liubov' Dmitrievna as a visual icon. Dressed in evening wear and

Andrei Bely and Sergei Solov'ev with photographs of L. D. Blok-Mendeleeva and V. Solov'ev (1904)

looking dead serious, they sit at a table with a Bible on it; on either side of the Bible are photographs of Vladimir Solov'ev and Liubov' Dmitrievna Mendeleeva-Blok, who functions as pure representation in this photo within a photo.

Even though the three young men imagined themselves as courtly fraternal knights and Liubov' Dmitrievna as their pure sister, they all fell in love with her. As she acknowledged in her memoirs, she enjoyed her role "between men." The Blokists' attempt to embody Solov'ev's syzygial union, which was based on an unconsummated triangulated erotic subtext, proved disastrous. The explosion took place in Shakhmatovo during the summer of the 1905 revolution; Bely's and Liubov' Dmitrievna's mutual attraction threatened the Blok marriage, provoking histrionics such as Bely's challenge of Blok to a duel. Liubov' Dmitrievna, who was considering leaving her husband, couldn't make up her mind to do so. She suggested a ménage à trois, to which the impassive Blok may have agreed, but Bely, who was passionately in love with Liubov' Dmitrievna, could not. The year 1906 was a particularly difficult one in Bely's life.[22] In the context of their life-creation project, he declared Blok a traitor to Solov'ev and to symbolist ideals. The mystical romantic triangle degenerated from theurgy into a confused, angry threesome, changing the life of the symbolist foursome forever. According to Bely, Sergei responded to the collapse of their commune with the comment that he disdained Blok's "psychopathology and if he was not the chosen poet, then he wished upon him a child from the Lady."[23]

Returning to Blok's marriage, the question that we must ask concerns Blok's feelings for Liubov' Dmitrievna. It was no secret that Blok did not honor the rules of marital fidelity, even publicly. The young couple's teenage flirtation, fraught with exaltation and anxiety from the beginning, turned to mutual passionate love in the fall of 1902, when they would meet secretly in Petersburg's Kazan cathedral and a furnished room that Blok, a university student then, rented for their trysts. He wrote his most passionate letters to his future bride from the German spa Bad Nauheim, to which he had accompanied his mother for a cure shortly before the wedding. Although written in an overwrought Solov'evian discourse, the letters reveal not only adoration of the Beautiful Lady but also sexual desire for the real Liubov' Dmitrievna.

Blok seems to have had profound anxieties about having sexual relations with the woman he loved, especially if she belonged to his class. Just as importantly, he feared offspring, considering himself a member of a degenerate bloodline. Recording his anxieties just before the wedding, he wrote of his feelings about family and genealogy in his diary, using vocabulary such as "breed" (*poroda*) and "multiply" (*rasplodit'sia* from *plod* ["fruit"], which in Russian suggests nature's fecundity). This discourse was emphatically biological, not apocalyptic. On July 16, 1903, a month before his wedding, he offered a list of members of the

"Blok breed that still intend[ed] to multiply." The entry concludes, however, with a Platonic assertion privileging art over biology: "[I]f I have a child, it will be inferior to my poems. . . . If Liuba finally understands the point, nothing will happen [meaning that they will not have children]. . . . I am a *degenerate* [emphasis mine] from the Blok family." Two weeks later, after a conversation with his bride—in all likelihood, it was the prenuptial talk about children to which Liubov' Dmitrievna referred in her memoir—he recorded in his notebook that "it would be better for the child [conceived in marriage] to die."[24] These are not the thoughts of a man entering marriage with healthy feelings about sexual love, nor are they the feelings of a utopian youth committed to the transfiguration of life through an apocalyptic marriage.

A year before his wedding, Blok offered a long disquisition on mythology in a diary entry, in which he revealed his conflicted feelings about sex and marriage. He compared marriage to the threshold to the truth, whose crossing he described as the two becoming one flesh, symbolizing "resurrected spirit," or "new body," not sexual union. Elaborating the threshold metaphor, he figured the bride as a mysterious "door to ecstasy," which again suggests something other than sexual consummation. He concluded the passage on epithalamic symbols by paraphrasing the end of Revelation, in which the Spirit and his bride beckon others to partake of apocalyptic prophesy. The implication is that he not only rejected the sexual connotations of marriage, but by evoking the union of Christ and his bride, he envisioned marriage to Liubov' Dmitrievna as the last act of Christian history.

Yet the same diary entry reveals Blok's more explicitly articulated fear of sex, reflected in his rather confused thoughts on the relationship between castrated flesh and "phallic sexuality," which, as he noted, permeates nature. In this instance privileging the latter, he described desexed nature as perverse. The example that he adduced is the figure of a castrated animal: "'The earth' without phallicism is no more desirable than an animal without sex organs," wrote Blok. "Both . . . are anomalous. It is better to look phallicism straight in the eye than to shut one's eyes to perversion."[25] The conclusion suggests a variety of possible interpretations, most importantly an epochal fear of castration, which characterized his later poetry dedicated to his dark muse (see chapter 4). About a month later, he wrote in his diary that he was reading Merezhkovsky, which caused him to feel the need to "care for his body. Soon it will come in handy," remarked Blok enigmatically.[26] We can only guess whether he was referring to sex in marriage, but it is likely.

In a diary entry adjacent to the one about castrated flesh and written in response to his visiting Liubov' Dmitrievna in Boblovo, Blok revealed conflicted feelings about physical love by parodying Gippius's Nietzschean "I want" (most clearly expressed in her best-known poem, "A Song" ["Pesnia"]. Blok gave Gippius's poem about the unattainability of desire for that "which does not exist in this world" a decidedly erotic interpretation, writing that "what I want [*khochu*] are *not* embraces: because embraces (sudden union) are only a momentary shock. After that comes *'habit'*—putrid monstrosity." He followed it with an enigmatic cryptic remark in Latin: the body cannot act in the sphere where it is absent ("Corpus ibi agere non potest, ubi non est!"). Since the remark appears directly after the entry in which he discussed castration as perverse, in all likelihood, it suggests castration as well, in this instance inspired directly by the physical presence of the beloved. He continued, however, in a more positive vein by lifting erotic desire into the apocalyptic sphere: "I want superwords and superembraces. I WANT THAT WHICH WILL BE." Then he hesitated again, describing female desire with misogynist disdain, revealing his fear of women: "[M]any unfortunate women think they are disappointed because what happened was not what they had wanted: they wanted nothing at all." Yet he ended the entry with the assertion: "[T]hat which I want will come to pass."[27]

What becomes amply clear from his prenuptial notes is Blok's crisis of masculinity, which he veiled with apocalyptic discourse and the belief that his relationship with Liubov' Dmitrievna was more than an earthly union. As we know, this resulted in great sadness for the young woman, who must have felt the terrible burden of marrying Russia's premier poet, designated by his friends as the great apocalyptic hope of their generation.

## Liubov' Dmitrievna's Self-Representation

Liubov' Dmitrievna's memoir *Facts and Fables: About Blok and Myself* (*I byl', i nebylitsy: O Bloke i o sebe*), finished in 1929, is not that of a poet's widow promoting the romantic myth of her poet-husband. Instead, it deconstructs the legend of their fairytale marriage without being acrimonious or disloyal. Liubov' Dmitrievna wrote with affection about her husband, yet her goal was to reveal the problematic aspects of their relationship. Her purpose was to liberate herself from the ethereal Galatea image of the Beautiful Lady and to emphasize that, contrary to the myth, she was a sensual woman, that this Beautiful Lady was more body than

L. D. Blok-Mendeleeva room in Shakhmatovo house (2002)

spirit. Living since 1907 in what today would be called an open marriage, Liubov' Dmitrievna did not write an exposé, even though it was clearly intended for public consumption. She focused on her own story and self-representation. She bared her body to the future reader in two striking tableaus. In the first, set in her father's house, she admires her nude body in a standing mirror, one that resembles the mirror that stands in the Shakhmatovo house today. In the second, staged in a seedy hotel room where she stayed while on tour with Meyerhold's theater, she poses nude before an adoring lover.[28]

Tall and large-boned, not at all the ethereal Beautiful Lady of Blok's youthful poems, Liubov' Dmitrievna paid attention to her looks. Written many years after the event, the scene of the young woman as Venus before the mirror, in which she unabashedly compares herself to a Giorgione nude, is a celebration of her beautiful, naked body. Besides the Renaissance painting, she invokes the figure of the popular barefoot dancer Isadora Duncan, whose transparent tunic symbolized the same obsession with veiling and unveiling, as would Blok's later poetry dedicated to his dark muse. (Many years later, Liubov' Dmitrievna would write admiringly about Duncan in her book about ballet.)[29] The American's dance, however, was inspired by the naked body in ancient Greece. Liubov' Dmitrievna's description of her own nudity, which focuses on her velvety, sensuous white skin, the "blossoming of her little breasts," and her body as an "intoxicating hothouse flower," resembles fin-de-siècle erotic prose. These descriptions bring to mind Fedor Sologub's representation of the beautiful, self-intoxicated Liudmila in his widely read novel *Petty Demon* (*Melkii bes*, 1907), especially phrases such as "blossoming flesh" that characterize the awakening of her and Sasha's youthful desire. "This is how I was in the spring of 1901 [before her romance with Blok]," wrote Liubov' Dmitrievna about her very young self at the conclusion of the mirror scene. "I was waiting for something to happen, was in love with my body, and was already demanding an answer from life."[30] What a terrible disappointment she must have experienced after her fairy-tale wedding. It is remarkable, in fact, that her memoirs do not express more resentment of Blok and his friends, who had cast her in a role she did not want to play.

The second *tableau vivant*, which takes place after she had begun taking lovers, stages the male gaze and Liubov' Dmitrievna as a work of art. Recreating the tableau, she described how she asked her lover to look away while she arranged her nude body and golden hair on the sheets of the bed. She didn't hesitate to inform the reader that she took into consideration the way the ceiling lamp lit her unblemished, youthful skin. When she invites the young man to look at her, he gazes at her framed body with adoration as if indeed she were a Giorgione nude.[31] Implicitly, she wants us to do the same from outside the frame, which we, of course, do. Liubov' Dmitrievna reveled not only in her physical beauty but also in her masterful staging of the gaze.

Rejected sexually by her husband—his love for Liubov' Dmitrievna appears to have been asexual—she set out to prove her sexual desirability in her memoirs. Although she complained of the artificial literariness of Blok's love for her, claiming that he saw her as an ideal, not as a living woman, she described her own sexuality in a stylized way. She seems to have objected less to objectification than to the role in which Blok cast her in his symbolist drama: the passive role of Beautiful Lady, which placed her on a pedestal that stood in the shadow of her husband and deprived her of physical love. Liubov' Dmitrievna was a strong woman in her own right who longed for something more than the passive role between the Blokist men as well as between the poet and his adoring mother.

## Venereal Disease and Fear of Degeneration

Liubov' Dmitrievna wrote that young Blok contracted venereal disease around 1898 while frequenting Petersburg brothels. This claim is substantiated in Blok's diary entry from 1918 in which he reconstructed his past and spoke of an unmentionable illness that he contracted in 1898. He went on to say that in the summer of 1899, he was not allowed to go to Boblovo on horseback because of his recent illness.[32] His aunt, Maria Beketova, wrote in her diary on November 9, 1902: "Sashura is again ill with that dreadful disease, again he is bedridden, and with all that a marriage remains childless. Alia [Blok's mother] is utterly crushed."[33]

According to Liubov' Dmitrievna, "physical closeness with a woman for Blok since his high school years meant paid love. . . . It was not his idolized beloved who introduced him to life, but a chance, impersonal [woman] bought for a few minutes [who brought him] humiliating, tormenting suffering."[34] During a meeting with Bely in a seedy Petersburg pub in 1912, Blok appears to have told him about a recent bout with venereal disease. Blok's disappearance into the Petersburg fog from which a prostitute beckoned to him brought the scene in the pub to an end (391). Bely followed it with descriptions of Blok's chance sexual encounters, references to brothels, and passages from letters to his mother, his closest confidante. According to Nikolai Valentinov, Bely gossiped about Blok's dissipated life but never spoke publicly about it.[35]

Venereal disease, very likely syphilis, one of the symptoms of the fin-de-siècle condition of degeneration, was Liubov' Dmitrievna's explanation for her essentially celibate marriage. In other words, it was not simply the high-minded idea of celibate marriage that made Blok question his right to marry in the ordinary sense and have children but also the fact of venereal disease. There is no evidence that Liubov' Dmitrievna knew about Blok's condition before the wedding, but she claimed in her memoir that she understood unconsciously that he suffered from something that one did not discuss with young women, adding also that she was extraordinarily naive in matters of sex. After the wedding, Blok theorized that they should not consummate their marriage because sex expressed the dark power of Astarte, not the spiritual power of divine Sophia. Liubov' Dmitrievna disclosed that when she expressed sexual desire after they were married, he would say that a relationship based on sex never lasts. Underlying this view was his experience of sex with prostitutes, which helps explain his misogynist descriptions of physical love in his diary. And underlying his personal experience was the misogynist myth of decadence based on the equation of female sexuality with prostitution and decomposing, infected nature. Certainly this was Huysmans's view in *Against Nature (A rebours)*, a copy of which was in Blok's library.

In the fall of 1904, more than a year after their wedding, Liubov' Dmitrievna seduced Blok, consummating the marriage in what was a brief, unsatisfying sexual encounter. She wrote that "the encounters that followed were infrequent, brief, and characterized by masculine selfishness." They came to an end in the spring of 1906, at a time when their marriage was already in serious trouble. Liubov' Dmitrievna added that she was so naive about sex that she did not know that it could be otherwise.[36] According to Avril Pyman, "early experience determined [Blok's] feeling that to have physical intercourse with a woman was necessarily to humiliate her and was essentially the expression of a drive to self-destruction, . . . which became a kind of pre-condition to passion."[37] When visiting Bad Nauheim again in 1907, the site of his first love in 1897 for Ksen'ia M. Sadovskaia, a woman twice his age, Blok remembered the feelings of "sweet revulsion for the sex act." "It is impossible," wrote Blok in his notebook, "to have intercourse with a very beautiful woman; for that one should choose women who are unattractive."[38] According to Liubov' Dmitrievna, Blok's fear of sex with women he knew persisted until his love affair in 1914 with the actress Liubov' Del'mas, the prototype of the exotic Carmen of his later poetry. Only Del'mas was able to "conquer his trauma," wrote his widow, "and only with her did Blok learn the desired synthesis of the two kinds of love."[39] The unexpurgated diaries and notebooks from the period of his relationship with Del'mas describe regular sexual encounters with her, frequently in the Blok apartment.[40]

From these statements and Blok's dark poetry, we can conclude that Blok suffered from a form of erotophobia; sexual passion tainted spiritual love. Many of Blok's male contemporaries shared his fear of sex,

Liubov' Delmas as Carmen in 1913 (Museum of Alexander Blok in Solnechnogorsk)

either because it degraded their love for a "beautiful lady" or because it threatened to corrupt Platonic same-sex desire, which emerged as an alternative to heterosexual love at the turn of the century. Blok's poetic passion is pointedly heterosexual, albeit sadistically so; yet his intense triangulated relationship with Bely during the early years can be considered in light of Eve Kosofsky Sedgwick's persuasive theory of homosocial desire put forth in *Between Men: English Literature and Male Homosocial Desire.* According to Kosofsky Sedgwick, the classic erotic triangle of two men and one woman has a homoerotic subtext.[41] Certainly Bely's feelings toward his poet-twin were eroticized discursively, but such a discourse was common between men at the turn of the twentieth century. I suggest that the triangular model may also have served as a solution to Blok's venereal predicament, offering him an alternative to sexual relations with his wife.

The prudishness of Russian biographical scholarship in the Soviet period and the cultural tradition of deifying poets may explain why so little is known about Blok's illness. Except for his widow and the British biographer Avril Pyman, Blok scholars have shrouded in silence his venereal disease, which was in all likelihood syphilis.[42] As a result, the relationship between Blok's idealization of the feminine and his illness has remained virtually unstudied, as if it did not belong in scholarly discourse. M. M. Shcherba's and L. A. Baturina's article "The Story of Blok's Illness," astonishingly, makes absolutely no mention of it. Instead it contains detailed information about his colds, nervous exhaustion (neurasthenia in the discourse of psychopathology), and depression. The authors' interest in protecting the poet's pristine image is clear; except for one oblique reference, there is also no mention of Blok's heavy drinking.[43]

Blok's venereal disease and fear of degeneration shed a different light on his life-creation project. A sensitive young man of good family infected with gonorrhea or worse must have experienced enormous anxiety about marriage to a woman of his family circle, especially if she represented the embodiment of his feminine ideal. Looking at the problem from the perspective of Blok's worship of the Beautiful Lady and related cults of chastity and celibate marriage, we can conclude that marriage to *Her* offered a way out of a real-life predicament. I suggest that it was precisely the chaste ideal that alleviated, if only somewhat, his fear and guilt, which may have been reinforced by his bride's admission to him of her abhorrence of motherhood. It was in this context that Blok probably told her in a prenuptial conversation that they would never have children.[44] Medical science of the time maintained that venereal disease was hereditary and that it precluded healthy offspring. Congenital syphilis was called "syphilis of the innocents" in Victorian England.[45] In his autobiography of 1918, Blok wrote that his illness contributed to the ethereal image of the Beautiful Lady.[46]

As a man of the fin de siècle, obsessed by degenerate heredity, Blok was concerned about his bloodline early on. He liked to declaim in the last years of the nineteenth century a poem about degeneration ("Madman" ["Sumasshedshii," 1890]) by the fin-de-siècle poet Aleksei Apukhtin.[47] Constructed as a monologue by a madman committed to a psychiatric institution, it contains the following lines:

> But why? What is our crime? . . .
> That my grandfather was ill and my father also,
> That they used this phantom from childhood to frighten me,—
> So what can I conclude? I could after all,
> Not be the heir of this damned inheritance!

Но все-таки . . . за что? В чем наше преступленье? . . .
Что дед мой болен был, что болен был отец,
Что этим призраком меня пугали с детства,—
Так что-ж из этого? Я мог же, наконец,
Не получить проклятого наследства![48]

Portrait of Blok by Constantine Somov (1907; Tretyakov Gallery in Moscow)

Blok wrote in 1918 that his illness was reflected in his early poetry: in a 1902 poem from the cycle devoted to the Beautiful Lady ("A Silent Phantom in the Tower" ["Bezmolvnyi prizrak v teremu"]), the poet described himself as "the black slave of a damned bloodline."[49] He sent a copy of the poem to Liubov' Dmitrievna in a letter dated November 10, 1902.[50] On one of his walks with Bely at Shakhmatovo in the summer of

1904, a year after his wedding, Blok spoke about the end of the human race. He told Bely that "inertia, blood, and heredity play a key role in a man's life, . . . he felt these hereditary forces at work in himself"; they were the source of his darkness.[51]

Dmitrii Blagoi described Blok as the offspring of a degenerate family.[52] His father was psychologically unstable; according to his two wives, he was also physically abusive. Blok's paternal grandfather died in a mental institution. His mother suffered from a variety of nervous disorders, especially hysteria and neurasthenia, a psychopathological term for hereditary nervous disease. Blok's own psychic history was punctuated by frequent bouts of neurasthenia and depression. In her memoirs, Liubov' Dmitrievna wrote that physical and psychopathological illness characterized her husband's genealogy on both sides. Using fin-de-siècle medical discourse, she associated this with "gentry degeneration and impoverishment of the blood [line]." After listing several examples of tainted heredity on Blok's side and pointing out that contemporary psychiatry would describe his genealogical tree as exhibiting extreme "marginality," she proudly referred to her own healthy family. It was her fundamental health, claimed Liubov' Dmitrievna, that attracted Blok to her.[53] This may very well have been true in light of Blok's outline of the unfinished narrative poem *Retribution* (*Vozmezdie*); it features a healthy young woman who is to give birth to the poet's child, revivifying his degenerate family line.

## Genealogy and Vampirism

Blok read Bram Stoker's popular fin-de-siècle novel *Dracula* (1897) in Russian translation in 1908. We learn from a letter to his friend Evgenii Ivanov dated September, 3, 1908, that it made a big impression on him: "I read it over the course of two nights and was beside myself with terror. Afterward I came to understand its profundity as well, apart from its literariness, etc. I have written a jubilee article on Tolstoy for the 'Fleece' [*Golden Fleece*] under the influence of this story. It is a remarkable, stupendous piece; thank you for compelling me finally to read it."[54]

Inspired by Stoker's novel, Blok's jubilee essay for Tolstoy's eightieth birthday (1908) deployed the figure of the vampire as a metaphor for official Russia, whose main embodiment, according to him, was the dead yet "undead" bloodsucker Konstantin Pobedonostsev, the former procurator of the Holy Synod, which had excommunicated Tolstoy from the Russian Orthodox Church in 1901. Pobedonostsev's "dead

Caricature of Konstantin Pobedonostsev (1905)

and vigilant eye, the subterranean, sepulchral eye of the vampire" continued to watch over Iasnaia Poliana, wrote Blok. (The vampiric procurator reappears in *Retribution,* which I discuss later in this chapter.) He attributed vampiric desire not only to Pobedonostsev but also to other reactionaries, such as the ascetic monk M. A. Konstantinovsky, who, in the words of Blok, "sucked the dying Gogol's blood."[55] Several years later, in 1913, he again referred to *Dracula,* this time in a diary entry, describing the response of one of the sisters of Mikhail I. Tereshchenko to Stoker's novel.[56] The sister, according to Blok, was haunted by Dracula and sought various ways to unspook herself, including creams advertised in the newspaper.[57]

Vampiric self-representations appear even in his early letters to his bride. During the most passionate period of their correspondence in the spring of 1903, he wrote her: "I have pierced your life and am drinking it."[58] In *Terrible World* (*Strashnyi mir,* 1909–16), a year after he had read *Dracula,* he figured his poetic persona as a vampire in two 1909 poems: "Song of Hell" ("Pesn' ada"), which in manuscript form bore the subtitle "Vampire," and "Finally I Conquered Her!" ("Ia ee pobedil nakonets!"). They come from the cycle *Black Blood* (*Chernaia krov'*), which foregrounds the decadent trope of blood in its very title. Both poems depict a male vampire who kills his beautiful female victim in a sadistic sexual encounter in which he drinks her blood. In the first, the poet's double, a feminized, pale, vampiric youth, plunges a pointed amethyst ring into a woman's white shoulder and drinks her blood.[59] "Song of Hell," especially its imagery of the displaced sex act, suggests vampiric defloration. Commenting on the poem, Blok wrote that it was an attempt to represent "'infernality' (Dostoevsky's term), the 'vampirism' of [their] time," as if to suggest that Dante's *Inferno,* which figures prominently in the poem, had become inhabited by vampires in the fin de siècle.[60] In "Finally I Conquered Her," the poem's subject drinks the blood of a woman ("And the charred mouth bleeds" [*I obuglennyi rot v krovi*]). He then places her in a coffin and while doing so imagines her blood singing in him, as if it had revived his body ("Your blood will sing in me!"). What makes these two examples of decadent kitsch relevant to my analysis is that Blok expressed in them the sadistic fantasies of his age that were associated with Dracula and the vampiric blood fetish.[61]

Blok's fascination with *Dracula* was not only sexual. It also engaged the epoch's preoccupation with genealogy that assumes particularly monstrous forms in Stoker's novel. An inhabitant of decadence, Count Dracula belongs to an extinct bloodline of which he is proud: "We

Szekelys have a right to be proud, for in our veins flows the blood of many brave races who fought as the lion fights, for lordship."[62] As one of the living dead driven to keep death alive, he drinks the healthy blood of the living in search of what I would describe as decadent immortality—perpetuation of the state on the verge of death. This condition was most clearly articulated by Huysmans in *Against Nature,* in which the liminal state between life and death characterizes the desire of its degenerate hero, Des Esseintes. The vampire's bite, which depletes its victims of physical vitality, transports them into life on the verge of death. The sexual fiend poisons the victim's bloodline, spreading contagious vampirism, which, as critics have shown, was a fin-de-siècle metaphor for syphilis. Stoker himself in all likelihood died from it, as probably did Blok.[63]

Reading Blok's vampiric poems through the filter of heredity infuses them with the bane of degeneration and the feeling of being the last in a series; we know that he was preoccupied with both. To take the example of the diary entry at the beginning of 1912: moral strength, wrote Blok, is a matter of "blood"; it is "*hereditary*" (emphasis mine). He attributed it to those who possess "cultural chosenness," distinguishing his contemporaries who still had "hope" (meaning moral strength) from those who had "degenerated."[64] The latter were the effete gentry obsessed with bloodlines and the "blood taint."

Blok's references to blood during this period must also be read in the context of the notorious Beilis case being tried in Kiev. Mendel Beilis, a Jewish shop assistant in a factory, was accused of ritual murder in 1911, provoking a wave of anti-Semitism among conservatives and reactionaries and moral outrage among the intelligentsia. The accusation invoked the anti-Semitic medieval myth of the use of the blood of Christian children in religious rituals, with the vicious claim that they were bled through incisions made in the body following Jewish kosher law. The reemergence of the myth fed the turn-of-the-century figuration of the Jew as evil vampire and inspired anti-Semitic sexual fantasies.[65]

Blok referred to the Beilis affair as a momentous event in his introduction to the unfinished epic poem *Retribution:* "In Kiev the murder of Andrei Iushchinskii occurred, and the question of the use of Christian blood by Jews was raised."[66] The reference to the blood libel in the introduction to the poem on family genealogy sheds light on Blok's view of the decadent tropes of blood and vampiric desire, suggesting possible anti-Semitic overtones. It may be significant in this context that he spoke of the Beilis trial in a strictly neutral tone—without expressing outrage, even though in 1911 he had signed a petition against the blood libel accusation, which was published in the liberal newspaper *Rech'* (Speech) and was signed by Gorky, Korolenko, and others.[67] True, the introduction was written in 1919, that is, many years later, when the emotions surrounding the affair had subsided. It should be mentioned, however, that rumors persist that Blok was a closet anti-Semite and maybe a closet Jew.[68]

*Retribution* was Blok's most extensive though unfinished statement on origins and genealogy. As Bely wrote after his death, *Retribution* is about "a damned bloodline," which, like the poem "It Was in the Dark Carpathian Mountains" ("Bylo to v temnykh Karpatakh," 1913), is reminiscent of Gogol's "Terrible Vengeance" ("Strashania mest') (415–16). Blok worked on the poem from 1910 till the end of his life. Inspired by the death of his father, a confirmed anti-Semite, in 1909 and the subsequent deaths of Tolstoy, the decadent artist Mikhail Vrubel', and the popular actress Vera Kommisarzhevskaia in 1910, *Retribution* commemorates the end of a family line—the Bloks and the Beketovs—and of a whole era. It also reveals the poet's aspirations during this period to break out of the confines of the lyric voice and personal isolation and become the epic voice of the nation. It was Blok's attempt to write his own *War and Peace,* in which he represented two or three generations of his family—on both sides—against the background of Russian history. But unlike Tolstoy, whom he had recently described as a victim of the epoch's official vampirism, Blok considered his own genealogy tainted. Even though he hoped to transcend the taint poetically by ending the poem with a freshly born child, the product of a chance encounter with a healthy woman of the people, the story of the diaper was never written.

In the introduction to the poem, Blok described *Retribution* as his version of *Les Rougon Macquart,* Emile Zola's twenty-volume series of novels about the genealogy and degeneration of the Rougon Macquart family. The "theme" of the poem, wrote Blok, is the development "of the links in a single family chain."[69] Although each of its members aspires to the highest level of individual development offered by his or her genetic pool, "the universal whirlpool sucks into its funnel almost the whole person; the individual . . . [is] disfigured. . . . [What] remains is wretched flabby flesh."[70] The whirlpool makes the flesh weak, which results in the end of the bloodline. As Bely suggested, the poet had abandoned symbolism's concerns with eternity by returning to a "positivist" concern with biology (416), that is, to Zola's naturalism based on a biological model and the belief that a predisposition to pathology assumes increasingly malevolent forms, both physical and moral, in subsequent generations. Blok's youthful attempt to supplant these notions with a utopian belief in transcending biology was unsuccessful.

Yet Blok's fantasy was also to show the rejuvenation of the bloodline by planting the poet's seed in the womb of a woman not of gentry stock but of the people, a woman who is not even Russian but Polish.[71] The implication is that Blok's imagined son will escape the taint of heredity by having healthy blood flow through his veins. He will be the new man of the future; history as Blok knew it would come to an end. The themes of historical retribution and redemption, which concerned many at the beginning of the twentieth century, acquire a mystical, populist complexion in the poem's planned conclusion. The people, not the intelligentsia, would save Russia from extinction.

While the imagined son could escape degeneration, Blok's lyrical double does not. It is only through the peasant woman's pure milk that the next generation is rescued from the taint of what Blok called in the poem the "vampiric [nineteenth] century." This suggests that Blok himself, the poem's fin-de-siècle scion, was intended as *Retribution's* vampire, although the overt fiend of the poem is the father, who insinuates himself into the maternal side of the lyrical persona's family (the Beketovs). He is described as Mikhail Lermontov's Demon and Lord Byron's sickly brother, who wants to fill his corpse with living blood ("as if he wanted to pour into the corpse / Living playing blood"), conceiving his son in a vampiric coupling, represented metaphorically as vampiric rape:[72]

> (Look: the bird of prey gathers its strength:
> Soon it will spread its ailing wings
> And descend silently upon the meadow,
> To drink the living blood
> Of its victim, who trembles,
> Mad with terror . . .) Such was the love
> Of that vampiric century,
> Capable of crippling
> The honorable title of man!
>
> Be thrice damned, wretched century!

> (Смотри: так хищник силы копит:
> Сейчас—больным крылом взмахнет,
> На луг опустится бесшумно

И будет пить живую кровь
Уже от ужаса—безумной,
Дрожащей жертвы . . .)—Вот—любовь
Того вампирственного века,
Который превратил в калек
Достойных званья человека!

Будь трижды проклят, жалкий век![73]

Blok illustrated this passage in the margins of the manuscript with what appears to be an image of his father figured as a pitiful Jew, although it is he who sucks the blood of the female victim; the caption to the pencil drawing reads "the accused."

Thus sex and genealogy emerge in Blok's poetry as a tainted, bloody affair in contrast to the academic family affair of his early youth. The vampiric images in *Retribution* become even more suggestive of physical degeneration if we consider them against what Blok called the "muscular" structure of the poem.[74] Discussing the background of *Retribution* in 1919, Blok used images of human anatomy to describe the poem's evolving structure, comparing it to the development of muscles: "In systematic manual labor the first muscles to develop are those of the arms, the so-called biceps, and then, gradually, the more delicate, more refined and rare system of muscles in the chest and the back under the shoulder blades. Such a rhythmical and gradual growth of muscles was supposed to [produce] the rhythm of the entire poem. Its underlying idea and theme are also related to this."[75]

Blok's muscle metaphor serves as an antidote to degeneration and the vampirism of the age. It recalls the late nineteenth-century notion of "muscular Christianity," which advocated regular exercise to strengthen the body with the purpose of containing sexual desire.[76] The notion also reflects the epoch's general insistence on sports and body culture for modern men and women. But in literary terms, the metaphor reveals Blok's belated interest in Zola, suggesting naturalism's affiliation of literature and human anatomy.

During the winter of 1910–11, Blok was diagnosed as suffering from neurasthenia or, perhaps worse, from a bout of venereal disease. (Blok referred to *neirasteniia* as a nineteenth-century illness in *Retribution*.) The doctor prescribed injections of *spermin*, a contemporary medicine for impotence and nervous exhaustion, which Blok claimed was for poor blood circulation.[77] He was worried about his health, as reflected in a letter to his mother in the winter of 1911. In it he described his personal focus on body culture and systematic exercise, including muscle building,

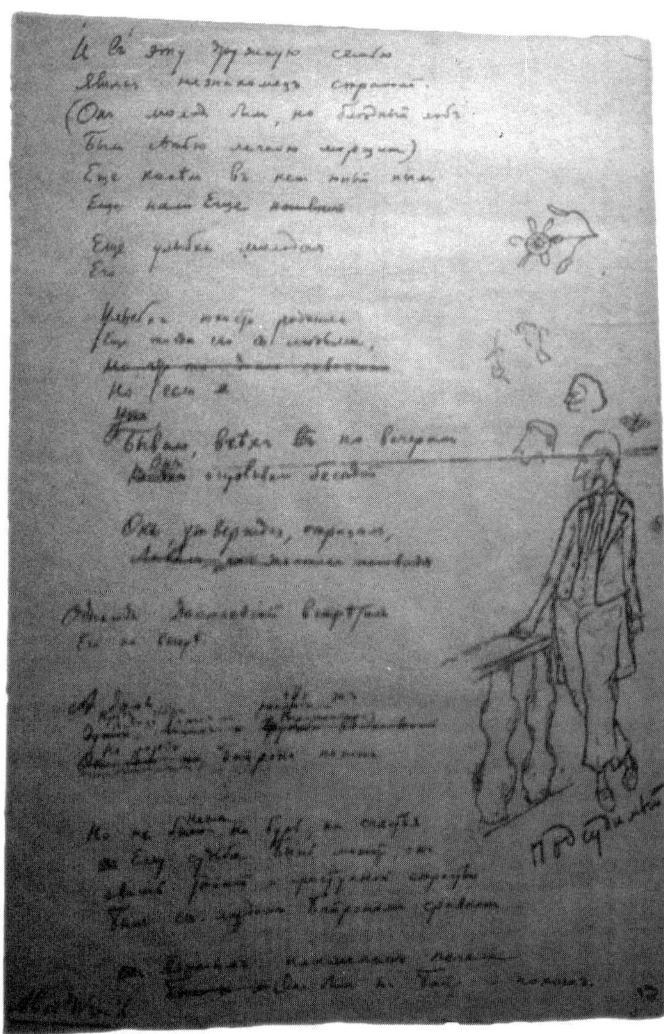

Blok's marginalia in manuscript of *Retribution* (Blok Museum in Shakhmatovo)

gymnastics, massage, and regular attendance of wrestling matches. He also swam and bicycled. As in the introduction to *Retribution*, Blok drew an analogy in the letter between his athletic efforts of physical rejuvenation and writing. He spoke of poetry using the discourse of kinship and degeneration. But instead of *vyrozhdenie* (degeneration), which is what he feared, he described the kinship between poetry and gymnastics using the verb *rodnit'sia* (to be related in the familial sense; note that the two words contain the root *rod*, which refers to genealogy and generation). To acquire form, poetry must acquire a body, a healthy body, wrote Blok, suggesting an anatomical relation between them.[78]

Fear of the blood taint informed Blok's anxieties around 1910. Susceptible to the cultural climate of his time, which prophesied the end of the old order with which Blok felt a blood tie, he was one of its representatives who succumbed to degeneration. He had lost the hereditary moral strength of the traditional gentry intelligentsia and had not acquired the strength of the vigorous new world. Its absence led to the bloodletting and bloodsucking of Blok's "terrible world."

## Shakhmatovo as Premukhino

While Blok's concern with origins was primarily a question of genealogy, Bely's view of them in *Reminiscences about Blok* was broadly cultural, despite his own "hysterical" mother and his personal depressions and neurasthenia. In the memoir, Bely did not conceptualize his own life in relation to the end of the gentry class and estate culture. He seems not to have been obsessed with questions of degeneration and the hereditary taint of blood, even though they dominate *Petersburg* (1916), the crowning achievement of Bely's own literary legacy. In that novel, Nikolai Ableukhov, a classic neurasthenic whose prototypes were both Bely and Blok, represents the end of his family line. Constructing the Blokist myth in *Reminiscences*, Bely, however, staged himself as a *raznochinets* (a person of nonnoble rank) in contrast to Blok's aristocratic image. He described Shakhmatovo as a "gentry estate," alien to the *raznochintsy* (85), who were not defined by hereditary nobility. This distinction as developed by Bely is pure invention and image making, since the poet-twins both came from the academic gentry intelligentsia.

One of symbolism's main mythmakers, Bely interpreted the life of the Blokists in the summers of 1904 and 1905 in relation to the Nietzschean myth of cultural return. He treated them not only as men and women of the apocalypse, enacting the prophesy of Solov'ev, but also as young people reenacting the lives of the members of an earlier generation. Seeking out nineteenth-century predecessors, Bely chose Russia's romantic idealists of the 1830s and 1840s. His retrospectivist reading of the Blokist cult placed at its center the Premukhino idyll, whose locus was the Bakunin family estate in Tver' province. Created in the 1820s as an enlightened, sentimental utopia by Alexander Bakunin, the father of the future anarchist, it became in the 1820s and 1830s the gentry nest, or hothouse, of Russian romanticism. In its second phase, it was defined by the personalities and ideologies of Mikhail Bakunin and his young university friend Nikolai Stankevich, followers of German romantic philosophy.

What links the participants of the Premukhino and Shakhmatovo idylls is their experience of personal life, especially of love and friendship, in relation to abstract ideas and history. Grandiose in their ambitions, the members of the Stankevich circle, mostly children of the landowning class, felt the taint of living in a country that, as Peter Chaadaev famously postulated, lacked history and was therefore destined to imitate ideas developed elsewhere. Yet this notion of Russia as a historical tabula rasa also gave these impressionable and narcissistic young men and women the freedom to view their own lives as momentously important for the future of Russia and even of the world. They imagined themselves to be unconstrained by the past and by tradition. This feeling inspired them to ascribe historical significance to their personal lives, imparting "a grandeur, a lofty and universal meaning, to even the most intimate experiences."[79] Like the Blokists three-quarters of a century later, the members of the Stankevich circle, as well as Alexander Herzen and Nikolai Ogarev, treated their real-life friendships, romances, and marriages as embodying philosophical ideas and as having the potential to bring about the transfiguration of life. Their sisters and the women they loved were perceived as the mediators of their transfigurative projects. They viewed eros as the catalyst of history: "[O]ur love," wrote Ogarev to his bride, Maria, in 1836, "contains in itself the seed of mankind's liberation. . . . [It] will be spoken of from generation to generation, and all who live after us will preserve our memory as something sacred."[80]

Locating a Premukhino substratum in the Blokist palimpsest, Bely thought that their conversations and discourse would require just as much explication by future generations as did the Stankevich circle's endless Hegelian discussions. About himself he remarked ironically that he resembled Repetilov, the loquacious liberal from Alexander Griboedov's play *Woe from Wit* (*Gore ot uma*, 1836), a Russian classic, meaning that he had done time in both Stankevich and symbolist circles. The latter "'symbolized,'" wrote Bely, "in the way that the members of the Stankevich circle had 'Hegelianized.'" He went on to compare his behavior to that of the two other paradigmatic figures of the 1830s: Vissarion Belinsky, the epoch's quintessential *raznochinets* and most important literary critic, and Bakunin. In an obvious case of self-parody, Bely characterized his own behavior as "michel-like" (*mishelisto*), from

Michel, the French version of Bakunin's first name. Like Bakunin, he "Hegelianized" human relationships, wrote Bely, including those of his immediate interlocutors (61). Premukhino, with its romantic Hegelian life creation, had its continuation, according to Bely, in the gentry nest of Shakhmatovo. He considered the Moscow circle of university students under the tutelage of Stankevich the predecessor of the Moscow Argonauts.

Parodying the myth of cultural return, Bely depicted Blok's and Liubov' Dmitrievna's first visit to the Argonauts in 1904 as a series of anachronistic double exposures: Blok found himself simultaneously in a symbolist circle, at Stankevich's, in the 1840s, in Griboedov's comedy, and in the fin de siècle. "At my Sundays," wrote Bely, "Vissarion Belinsky [and] Bakunin met the undying Repetilov and Huysmans's hero" (74), avatar of decadent sensibility. Alexander Lavrov commented that in all likelihood Bely was referring to Des Esseintes from *Against Nature* (523). What is striking about this list is its conspicuous eclecticism and historical incongruity, as if Bely's salon were a meeting place that staged a cluttered and fantastic version of history, fashionable among the decadents.

Bely wrote that the Blokists resembled Stankevich and his friends, who interpreted his love for one of the Bakunin sisters, also named Liubov', as the embodiment of Hegel's idea of history. Yet he set Blok apart from the symbolist reenactment of the Stankevich circle, considering it his own provenance, even though his view of Blok's love for Liubov' Dmitrievna did in fact correspond to the way the inhabitants of Premukhino interpreted the ideal love of Stankevich. Making these half-serious historical analogies, Bely associated the self-possessed, elegant Blok with the Petersburg aristocracy, not with the nervous, democratic Moscow intelligentsia, with its penchant for schematic intellectualizing: "Of course, one would say that A. A. [Blok] did not frequent those salons where Repetilov held forth with Vissarion Belinsky or Michel Bakunin, with whom he was 'friends,' of course. More likely, A. A. would stand for a long time by the Neva and knew the 'Bronze Horseman.' He did not construct symbols [*ne simvoliziroval on*]; symbolic perception was for him a physical fact of existence" (61).

The association of Blok with the imperial figure of the Bronze Horseman links him to Pushkin, the aristocratic Petersburg poet who towered over the golden age of Russian poetry. The implication is that Blok is Russian symbolism's Pushkin. Pushkin may have been on friendly terms with men like Belinsky, but he did not frequent their gatherings. In keeping with his aristocratic manner, Blok, accordingly, was a "natural" symbolist who felt symbols—symbols were his legitimate patrimony—in contrast to Moscow's symbolists, who constructed them artificially (*simvolizirovali*).

Cluttering this fragmented, fetishist representation of their cultural genealogy further, Bely wrote that the Blokists wanted to bring about the fusion of apocalyptic ideas and social justice in accordance with Nikolai Fedorov's and Solov'ev's ideas of immortalizing the body and the social philosophies of Herzen and Petr Lavrov, a populist thinker and journalist (109–10). What he failed to include, however, is the striking similarity between the love stories of Herzen and Blok. Yet one must assume that Bely felt a profound link between them and especially between his own epochal memoirs and Herzen's: he clearly modeled his later three-volume memoirs (*At the Turn of the Century* [*Na rubezhe dvukh stoletii,* 1930]; *The Beginning of the Century* [*Nachalo veka,* 1933]; *Between Two Revolutions* [*Mezhdu dvukh revoliutsii,* 1934]) on Russia's best-known memoirs, Herzen's *My Past and Thoughts* (*Byloe i dumy*). In a letter from 1928, Bely referred to *The Beginning of the Century* as "his 'past and thoughts.'"[81]

This is not the place to speak at length about the friendship of Herzen and Ogarev or the romantic triangle of Herzen, his wife and cousin Nathalie, and the German poet Georg Herwegh, but I would like to suggest some cursory comparisons. The Herzen and Blok circles both gave equal value to passion and friendship, and their members treated one another as brothers and sisters. There is a remarkable resemblance, in fact, between the intense youthful friendship between Herzen and Ogarev and that between Blok and Bely. The former pledged eternal brotherhood whose goal was the world-historical task of transfiguring Russian life. Their pledge, given on Sparrow Hills in Moscow, to carry on the work of the Decembrists, is an emblematic event in Russian cultural history. Herzen's idealistic focus on fraternal affection also influenced his view of erotic love, so that he and his bride for a time entertained the idea of celibate marriage, with Nathalie combining the roles of sister and wife. As in Blok's case later, this had broad cultural implications: "Herzen's love [became] more than a fact in his personal biography; it [was] a fact in the spiritual history of the age," noted Martin Malia.[82]

The literary source of Herzen's and Ogarev's high-minded idea of love was the friendship of Carlos and Marquis Posa in Schiller's *Don Carlos;* Posa was also a participant in the illicit platonic love of Carlos and his young stepmother, the queen. He "communed mystically in the love" of his friend.[83] All three were opposed to the tyranny of the king, who was also father and husband to two of them. Herzen and Ogarev modeled their youthful idealism on Schiller's play, which intertwines friendship, love, and politics, investing them with the power of liberation and change. Herzen's idealization of friendship and his ideal of freedom in erotic love crumbled, however, over the love affair between Herwegh and his wife. Despite his enlightened views, he wasn't able to accept their sexual relations, the product of an ideologically conceived romantic triangle.

Bely evoked the figure of Marquis Posa in describing the very difficult period in his triangulated relationship with Blok and Liubov' Dmitrievna, during which the poet's wife considered leaving her husband. He did so punningly: "dictat[ing] his ultimatum" to a duplicitous Blok "by means of a pose [*poza* in Russian]" and "show[ing] off [to him] by striking a pose" (221). Blok's response to these signs, wrote the memoirist, "was devoid of a pose as [he], Marquis Posa, stood before him" (222). Although Bely's references to the noble Marquis are ironic, they nevertheless allude to Schiller's and Herzen's romantic idealism as well as to Bely's apparent nostalgia for his youth and high-minded dreams of love and friendship. The image of Posa contributes another layer to the generational palimpsest that Bely fashioned to legitimate their youthful dream of life beyond history by connecting them back to the early years of the Russian intelligentsia, its successes and failures. What resulted in a difficult relationship and, especially in Blok's case, a dissipated, or degenerate, life, began with an idealistic friendship and spiritual love that was expected to bring about the transfiguration of life. One way that Bely tried to recover Blok's image as harbinger of apocalyptic transfiguration was to enshrine his life among the mythologized lives of Russia's romantic generation.

In conclusion, I would reiterate that Blok's close identification with gentry culture—what Bely called his aristocratism—led to his obsession with blood and degeneration, an obsession that originated in the romantic generation. That generation also felt genealogically tainted and feared the inevitability of disease. For the romantics it was tuberculosis (Stankevich died of tuberculosis at twenty-seven), for the decadents, syphilis.

Exemplary of Russian antiprocreative life creation, Blok's marriage represents a fin-de-siècle link in the chain of celibate utopias proposed by Chernyshevsky, Fedorov, and Solov'ev. Blok's erotic views typified the

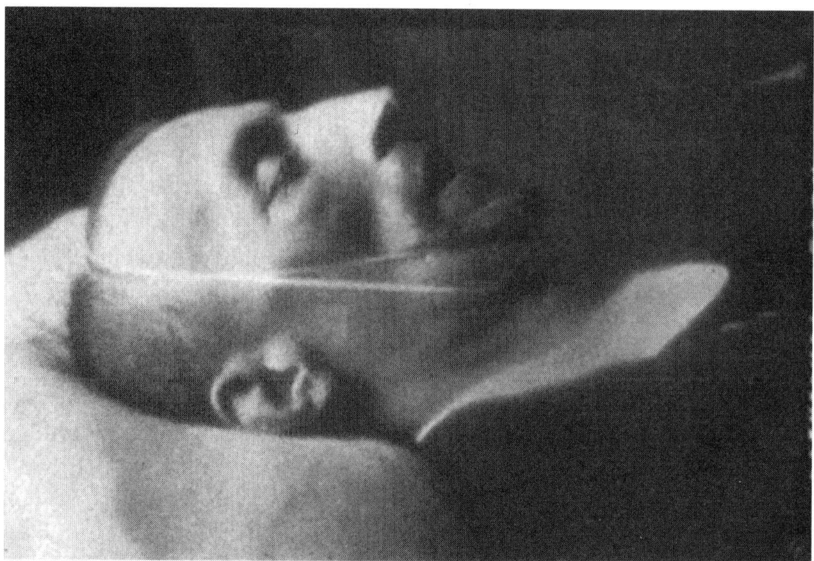

Blok on deathbed (August 8, 1921; Museum of Alexander Blok in Solnechnogorsk)

conflict that his contemporaries experienced with regard to love, sex, and procreation. The paradox of Blok's supposedly celibate marriage and dissipated life of "sexual vampirism" reveals the epoch's profound ambivalence regarding sex, genealogy, and history. On one hand, Blok and the members of the Blokist commune of 1903–4 believed that his marriage to Liubov' Dmitrievna Mendeleeva was apocalyptic: it would inaugurate life beyond history, premised on the cessation of procreative nature. As late as 1921, Blok wrote that the "'human race' is obviously imperfect and must be replaced with a more perfect species."[84]

On the other hand, his hope of transfiguring life through a Solov'evian love that would revoke procreation degenerated into vampiric lust figured in the trope of blood. Interchangeable with semen in the discourse of the decadents, the trope reveals Blok's fascination with rhetorical excess as sexual excess in the vampiric poems. It also reveals his fetishist figuration of poetic language, which I examine in the next chapter, devoted to the fin-de-siècle femme fatale.

On the ideological and biographic levels, however, he mourned the end of his bloodline instead of celebrating apocalyptic transfiguration. The specter of degeneration, which also informed Solov'ev's erotic utopia, was an important component of Blok's utopian idealism. Even though he hoped to overcome biological extinction in moments of inspiration, as in the finale of *Retribution,* it is in the order of things that he never wrote that chapter. As I noted in the introduction, the dual feeling of the end that Blok and his contemporaries experienced at the beginning of the twentieth century was articulated best by Viacheslav Ivanov, who described decadence as "the sense both oppressive and exalting of being the last of a series."[85] For Blok that feeling was physiological, spiritual, and rhetorical.

# 4

# Blok's Femme Fatale

## History as Palimpsest

Giovanni noticed that in the places where Merula scraped off the church letters, new ones appeared, almost imperceptible lines, colorless traces of ancient writing, hollows in the parchment—not letters, only ghosts of letters that had disappeared long ago, pale and gentle.

Dmitrii Merezhkovsky, *Leonardo da Vinci*

One of the originators of the Russian symbolist movement and author of numerous historical novels widely read all over Europe at the beginning of the twentieth century, Dmitrii Merezhkovsky perceived history as a palimpsest. In seeing himself as a writer-archeologist who penetrates the layers below the surface, he reflected his generation's retrospectivist historical sensibility and fundamental objection to the Enlightenment view of history as the chronology of progress. Instead of progress, Merezhkovsky expected the end of history; in the meantime, he studied the previous historical epochs that underlay the culturally impoverished surface of the present. The palimpsest as a fin-de-siècle metaphor was in part the product of the archeological craze of the eighteenth and nineteenth centuries, especially of its fascination with classical antiquity and the desire to recover the aesthetic richness of the past. The metaphor also mirrored the epoch's syncretic eclecticism, entwining such culturally and historically disparate images as Christ and Dionysus, temples and theaters, including anatomical theaters, the New Jerusalem and the Russian peasant commune.

In the first scenes of Merezhkovsky's popular novel *Leonardo da Vinci* (1901), which influenced Freud's psychoanalysis of the artist, an ancient Greek sculpture of Aphrodite—not Roman Venus—buried for centuries, emerges from a grave mound near Florence to inspire the artist.[1] The image reflects the view of history as a graveyard in which a precious "corpse" is recovered by the local lovers of antiquity. The point is that the ancient past lies buried just below the surface and is more valuable than the present. Merezhkovsky made direct reference to the palimpsest in the same chapter, juxtaposing the excavation of the long lost marble statue with the scene described in the passage I have used as an epigraph to this chapter. A Renaissance scholar finds "ghosts of pale and gentle letters" in a church book, "letters that disappeared long ago," which Merezhkovsky projected onto the female body. The emergence of the ancient woman's marble body echoes the recovery of antiquity's traces on parchment, traces that some medieval scribe buried by writing over them. Instead of serving nature's procreative machine, the female body becomes the site of history. Hidden at the bottom of the palimpsest in the old grave mound is an ancient female corpse—in the shape of a beautiful statue—that haunts the inhabitants of Merezhkovsky's novel.

In the same year, 1901, Andre Gide published *The Immoralist*, a novel read with interest in Russian symbolist circles at the beginning of the century.[2] In that novel, the historical palimpsest emerges as an important metaphor that the protagonist Michel deploys to describe his tormented subjectivity. He discovers the symbolic potency of the palimpsest while traveling with his young wife to North Africa on their honeymoon, which also becomes for him a journey to health. Formerly a tool in his scholarly studies of ancient Greek history, the palimpsest now becomes for Michel the emblem of his search for personal authenticity, which he locates in the archeological metaphor's lowest layer. The palimpsest comes to refer to Michel's gradual self-divestiture of his scholarly, bourgeois identity and the discovery of his homosexual subjectivity: "The layers of acquired knowledge peel away from the mind like a cosmetic, says Michel, and reveal, in patches, the naked flesh beneath, the authentic being hidden there. . . . I would compare myself to a palimpsest; I shared the thrill of the scholar who beneath more recent script discovers, on the same paper, an infinitely more precious ancient text."[3]

The precious ancient text is his body, whose artificially constructed top layer has served as a cover for homosexual desire. At the bottom of this palimpsest, Michel discovers not an ancient art object or classical text hidden beneath later historical layers but his own desiring self. His new Orientalized identity erases his former commitment to history and family, which have suppressed his authenticity. A metaphor of personal transformation, the palimpsest in Michel's case represents rupture with the past, historical and genealogical. It figures him as an empty slate on which the reborn, liberated male inscribes his new word.

In the preceding chapter, I focused on Blok's mythologized marriage, whose task was to bring history to an end by proclaiming the new word of apocalyptic transfiguration. I showed how the fin-de-siècle fear of degeneration and tainted heredity both shaped and undermined his apocalyptic project that would herald the birth of new men and women. The focus of this chapter is Blok's symbolic engagement with the historical past and a Eurasian imaginary future, both of which served him as an escape from biology. In his descents into history, he distanced himself from nature's law, either by entering an aestheticized European past or by imagining his place in a Eurasian eschatological future.

Blok's myth of history, I will argue, took the form of a palimpsest and of the femme fatale. Contextualizing her representations in the European arts, including the fin de siècle, I will examine the poet's dark muse as eroticized and historicized art object and as mediator of poetry. The centerpiece of this chapter is Blok's journey to Italy. Evoking Ivan Karamazov's image of Europe as graveyard, Blok discovered in Italy not his authentic self in the manner of Gide but the corpse of history, as did Merezhkovsky before him. He embodied this corpse in the artistic representations of Cleopatra and Salome, emblematic Oriental women of the decadence, who, like the Orient itself, exist outside progressive history. Blok celebrated Italy's preservation of the past, not its modern progress. Instead of finding in himself the necessary energy to make history, he contemplated passively the representations of the past that reside in museums and churches. Gide's hero, on the other hand, discovers bodily health on his journey to North Africa, removing from himself the layers of culture that have inhibited life in the body. For Gide the journey led to the discovery of his homosexual identity; for Blok it was a sojourn into the historical palimpsest—European and Eurasian—in which he found liberation of his poetic voice as well as liberation from his degenerate body.

## Italian Journey

The journey to Italy, in the tradition of the grand tour, was a high point in the cultural history of travel.[4] In the earliest conceptualization of travel as *Bildung*, Italy signified Rome and Roman antiquity almost exclusively. The interest in ancient Greece, associated with the name of the eighteenth-century German archeologist Johann Winckelmann, developed later. Then romanticism shifted the primary focus of the traveler to Italy from antiquity to the Middle Ages and the Renaissance. Canonized by Goethe in the *Italian Journey* (1816–17), the modern journey to Italy also suggested erotic awakening and personal transformation.

As in Europe, travel in Italy became part of the educated Russian's pilgrimage to monuments of Western culture and sites of Western learning. The European journey as cultural practice was initiated in 1697–98 by Peter the First, the original Russian westernizer who traveled to Europe in search of a new identity for Russia.[5] The Russian romantic interest in Italy reached its peak in the middle of the nineteenth century and was revived again by the symbolist generation. Among the many turn-of-the-century Russian travelers who went to Italy with cultural intentions and erotic hopes were Dmitrii Merezhkovsky, his wife, Zinaida Gippius, and Akim Volynsky (see next chapter), and Aleksandr Blok and Liubov' Dmitrievna Mendeleeva.[6]

The Merezhkovskys and the critic Akim Volynsky went to Italy on a joint cultural mission in 1896 and traveled to the sites associated with the life and work of Leonardo da Vinci. The journey had the apparent purpose of solidifying their burgeoning erotic and ideological triple union. Although personally the trip was a failure, it resulted in Merezhkovsky's *Leonardo da Vinci* (1901), Volynsky's biography of Leonardo (1900), and Gippius's unpublished Italian diary.[7]

In May and June of 1909, Aleksandr Blok and his estranged wife, Liubov' Dmitrievna, the erstwhile Beautiful Lady, traveled to Italy, Baedeker in hand. The trip was intended as a second honeymoon during a particularly strained period in their relationship, following the death of Liubov' Dmitrievna's child by another man. The child, whom Blok accepted as his own, perhaps in hope of transcending his tainted genealogy, died almost immediately after birth. Linked in cultural memory to ideal love, especially to Dante's love for Beatrice, Italy was supposed to rekindle the heavenly bond between the Russian poet-knight and his Russian Beatrice. Italy, wrote Blok in his unfinished Italian travelogue, *Lightning Flashes of Art* (*Molnii iskusstva*, 1909), evoked in him the images of Dante and his immortal travel guide, Virgil, with whom he hoped to journey through the circles of the underworld: "Traveling in a country with a rich past and poor present is like descending into Dante's hell. From the depths of the bared ravines of history appear eternally pale images. . . . It's all right if you carry in your soul your own Virgil who says: 'Don't fear, at the end of the road you will see the One Who sent you.'"[8]

"The One Who sent him" did not reveal herself to Blok. During the journey he was unable to replay Solov'ev's phantasmic encounter in the Egyptian desert with divine Sophia some twenty years earlier. Blok had by this time lost touch with "his personal Virgil" and Beautiful Lady; Liubov' Dmitrievna did not even figure in his Italian writings.[9] The only women who revealed themselves in Italy were of ancient provenance, maintaining their power over him in death. Instead of finding celestial Beatrice, Blok discovered that Italy is the space of eroticized Madonnas and fatal women, who resemble not Liubov' Dmitrievna but his dark muse of those years—the actress Natal'ia Volokhova, prototype of Blok's Russian veiled women.

The trip was a failure both as a second honeymoon and as an apocalyptic epiphany. But it was successful as a poetic experience, inspiring Blok's *Italian Verses* (*Ital'ianskie stikhi*, 1909), which contain some of his best poetry. Italy represented for Blok a mesmerizing journey into history and into poetic discourse.

What Blok's Italian journey as presented in his Italian travelogue has in common with Dante's descent into hell is its subterranean downward course. Since Italy, according to Blok, had a rich past but a poor present, he traveled it vertically, not just horizontally. Formerly ravishing and then ravished, Italy beckoned to him with the "subterranean voices of her dead" and the "underground rustling of history."[10] In contrast to Dante's journey into hell, Blok descended into Italy as if it were an ancient graveyard that offered him an alternative to death-defying apocalyptic history. The descriptions of this metaphoric graveyard include women of myth and history—Cleopatra in Florence, Salome in Venice, and the empress Galla Placidia, of the Western Roman empire, in Ravenna—and old burial places and actual physical descents into ancient archeological sites.[11]

Outside Spoleto, Blok climbed into a deep hole in the ground that contained the ruins of a Roman bridge, which he referred to as "the ghost of Rome." He painted a detailed picture of the dead inhabitants of one of the most important Etruscan burial sites located near Perugia—the Hypogeum of the Volumni, discovered in 1840.[12] The dead of this

Natal'ia Volokhova (Museum of Alexander Blok in Solnechnogorsk)

underground necropolis, according to Blok, own and consume everything, even the air: "[T]here is nothing living there, because all the air has been imbibed by them," as if the Etruscan dead were undead, vampirically consuming nature's life forces.[13] Sepulchral Italy had the inviting promise of death, which appealed to Blok much more than the modern industrial world.[14]

Besides prefacing the subterranean journey with cultural references, Blok, like Goethe in *The Italian Journey*, referred to European travel as a mining expedition. Unlike Goethe, however, Blok rejected this metaphor for travel as serving the cause of progress. Modern man, according to him, descends much less willingly into the human past than into the earth's layers that are industrially useful, even though the latter lie further from the surface than the ancient artifacts of culture's past grandeur. Instead of listening to the voices of history, industrial civilization, greedier than the old world, heeds the call of geology, wrote Blok, as if progress promised immortality. Death, however, vanquishes the progressive hopes of modern man. Humankind in *Lightning Flashes of Art* appears to have forgotten that everyone will eventually join the voices beckoning to those walking the earth: "Contemporary culture listens to ore's voice in the bowels of the earth. How then can we not hear that which lies immeasurably closer, right below our feet, buried in the earth or sinking into it miraculously, offering its space to the second and third layers, which in turn are fated to sink, to 'return to their native soil (revertitur in terram suam)?'"[15]

Blok's vision of Italy's undead does not serve progressive change. Instead the undead sink slowly into the earth from the surface, gradually descending into its lower contiguous layers. The vision evokes the already quoted lines from *Lightning Flashes of Art,* in which "eternally pale images" emerge "from the depths of the bared ravines of history." Blok admired Italy's palimpsest in which he represented himself as an archeologist-lover of the dead past. At the bottom of Blok's Italian palimpsest, as at the bottom of Merezhkovsky's Italian novel *Leonardo da Vinci,* is an ancient female corpse that he brings to life as an admiring observer, not as a participant. In contrast to Gide's hero, neither Blok nor Merezhkovsky discovered their reborn, healthy body in the Italian palimpsest by divesting themselves of the past. Unlike Michel's, their goal was not to free themselves from its burden. The Russian travelers existed, after all, on the margins of European culture. While many disliked bourgeois civilization, Russian travelers experienced its existential contradictions less keenly than Europeans and perceived Europe primarily as a testing ground for their own tenuous relationship to the West. Blok found in Europe much to destabilize his European identity—most prominently the Oriental woman, who resembled his dark muse.

## Cleopatra

"The Gaze of the Egyptian Woman," one of the seven essays in *Lightning Flashes of Art,* is set in the Archeological Museum in Florence. It is devoted to a Faiyum portrait of a young Egyptian woman, which, according to Blok, some considered a portrait of Cleopatra. Ravaged by time, the papyrus is cracked, even torn in several places. A postcard reproduction of the image has been preserved in Blok's album, now in the Blok archive.[16] The portrait comes from Alexandria, a site of cultural syncretism and the home of Cleopatra: although Egyptian, the representation is Greek.

The ekphrasis may be Blok's most minutely observed physical representation of a woman, in which, like a fetishist, he described in great detail her jewelry, hair, facial features, and dress. The cheeks seemed to him Mongolian, evoking Blok's Eurasian mythology. "The eyes conquer the face; probably, conquer the whole body and everything around her," wrote Blok.[17] Eyes that mesmerize characterize Faiyum portraits. In Blok's depiction of the portrait in Florence, he singles out the subject's commanding immortal eyes, tireless, unmaternal, joyless, which displaced her body. The decadent Medusa-like stare appealed to him with its dull, insatiable appetite. No one, he imagined—neither Roman emperor and Olympic god nor hyperborean barbarian—had been able to quench Cleopatra's desire. Typifying her Egyptian provenance and Blok's synesthetic poetics, the woman's gaze suggested to him the heady perfume of the lotus flower. Blok brought to the description a personal touch: the eyes enclosed in dark rings resembled those of Volokhova, who had black tormenting eyes with dark circles around them. Such circles were fashionable at the turn of the century, especially among women who wished to project a fatal, corpselike image.[18]

In the essay, the Egyptian woman's eyes stare from one century into the next, traversing one cultural layer after another in the manner of a historian. Like Blok's native femme fatale, whose name is Stranger and whose translucent silks represent layers of history and myth, the young Egyptian lives in both the ancient past and the present. In one of his most celebrated poems—"The Stranger" ("Neznakomka," 1906)—it is, however, the poet who for a brief moment penetrates the past by looking through the mysterious woman's dark veil and finding behind it an "enchanted shoreline and enchanted distances."[19]

The Italian Cleopatra haunts the poet with a gaze that inhabits the centuries, but her fetishized gaze also suggests erotic desire: her eyes seek "that which does not exist in this world," invoking the best-known line of verse by Zinaida Gippius ("A Song" ["Pesnia"]), Petersburg's Cleopatra of Blok's time. As we saw in the last chapter, the poet deployed this line in his diary as an expression of both erotic desire and sexual

Portrait of young woman painted on wood

anxiety, even though the standard reading of the poem emphasizes Gippius's wish for transfiguration (see next chapter). The meaning of the reference in the context of Blok's essay about the Faiyum portrait seems to be erotic as well, especially if we consider Pushkin's Cleopatra from *Egyptian Nights,* whose love brings death: the queen offers one night of love—what we could now call a one-night stand—in exchange for a man's life.

The question arises why an Egyptian woman occupied such an important place in Blok's Italian travelogue. Why was Cleopatra the emblem of the feminine in a country to which she was connected only through Caesar and Mark Anthony? Blok linked her to Italy through the archeological museum, imagining the museum as an artificial receptacle of history created by scholars. The museum is a circumscribed syncretic space, which brings together a variety of national histories from various times. Disconnected geographic locations are made contiguous horizontally in the museum. In Blok's portrait of Cleopatra they are layered vertically as in a palimpsest: below Italy is Rome; below Rome, Hellenistic Greece and Alexandria. Below all these historical layers is the terrifying female body that threatens the anxious male of the fin de siècle. Dreading the female threat, Blok contains it here by means of an ekphrastic representation.

Blok linked his interest in the Faiyum portrait to archeology, even though, unlike Merezhkovsky, he was not one of the scholarly poets or novelists of Russian symbolism. The essay associates archeology with poetry and love: "An archeologist is always a little bit a poet and in love," noted Blok. "Caesar's erotic imprisonment and the shame of Actium is his [the archeologist's] imprisonment and shame. To conceal his armchair shame, he hides in the shadows of the emperor and triumvir," justifying his presence by Caesar's and Mark Anthony's fateful loss of power to Cleopatra's charms.[20] It is ambiguous, however, who feels the "armchair shame": the archeologist who identifies with his subjects and has erotic fantasies about them or the poet who has appropriated the archeologist's task. Hiding in the shadows of the ancient emperor and triumvir, the archeologist and the poet, feeding on the past, become one; the archeologist-poet also becomes one with the historical lovers of Cleopatra. He inhabits the Roman-Egyptian palimpsest with the purpose of escaping the present and the future, suggesting perhaps the real reason for his armchair shame. He remains passive, sitting in his armchair, a disempowered male of the fin de siècle.

Different in genre and mood, Blok's well-known poem "Cleopatra" also locates the Egyptian queen in the space of a museum, in which, as he would later write in *Lightning Flashes of Art*, he hoped "to steal at least one moment of incomparable ecstasy from time."[21] Written before his Italian journey, the 1907 poem was inspired by an effigy of Cleopatra in the Petersburg wax museum established several years earlier at 96 Nevsky Prospect, not far from the Nicholas Railroad Station. The poem's centerpiece is the wax figure of the queen:

St. Petersburg Wax Museum

The sad wax museum has been there
One, two, three years.
Insolent and drunk we rush,
The queen awaits us in her coffin.

She lies in a glass sarcophagus
Neither dead, nor alive,
While people without pause whisper
Shameless words about her.

She sprawls languidly—
Hoping to forget and sleep forever.
Gently, without haste
A serpent stings her waxen breast.

Disgraced and venal,
With dark circles under my eyes,
I also come to gaze at the great profile,
At the wax display.

Everyone scrutinizes you,
But had your coffin not been empty,
I would have heard more than once
The arrogant sigh of decayed lips:

"Burn incense to me. Strew me with flowers.
In immemorial centuries

I was the queen in Egypt,
Now—I am wax, ashes, dust."

"O queen! I am your captive!
In Egypt I was just a slave,
Now fate has made me
Poet and tsar!

Do you see from your coffin
That Russia, like Rome, is intoxicated by you?
That through the centuries
I and Caesar will be equal before fate?"

I grow quiet and look. She doesn't hear.
But her breast moves slightly,
And she breathes behind the transparent veil . . .
And I hear these quiet words:

"Then—I commanded storms.
Now I can evoke better than anyone
The drunken poet's—hot tears,
The drunken prostitute's—laughter."

Открыт паноптикум печальный
Один, другой и третий год.
Толпою пьяной и нахальной
Спешим . . . В гробу царица ждет.

Она лежит в гробу стеклянном,
И не мертва и не жива,
А люди шепчут неустанно
О ней бесстыдные слова,

Она раскинулась лениво—
Навек забыть, навек уснуть . . .
Змея легко, неторопливо
Ей жалит восковую грудь . . .

Я сам, позорный и продажный,
С кругами синими у глаз,
Пришел взглянуть на профиль важный,
На воск, открытый напоказ . . .

Тебя рассматривает каждый,
Но, если б гроб твой не был пуст,
Я услыхал бы не однажды
Надменный вздох истлевших уст:

«Кадите мне. Цветы рассыпьте.
Я в незапамятных веках

Была царцею в Египте.
Теперь—я воск. Я тлен. Я прах»,—

«Царица! Я пленен тобою!
Я был в Египте лишь рабом,
А ныне суждено судьбою
Мне быть поэтом и царем!

Ты видишь ли теперь из гроба,
Что Русь, как Рим, пьяна тобой?
Что я и Цезарь—будем оба
В веках равны перед судьбой?»

Замолк. Смотрю. Она не слышит.
Но грудь колышется едва
И за прозрачной тканью дышит . . .
И слышу тихие слова:

«Тогда я исторгала грозы.
Теперь исторгну жгучей всех
У пьяного поэта—слезы,
У пьяной проститутки—смех».[22]

This archly staged decadent poem celebrates the power and past glory of Cleopatra, who occupies the liminal space between death and life. The site of commemoration is a wax museum: a wax figure covered by a veil and displayed in a glass coffin, the Egyptian queen is being kept alive in death. In placing her in the wax museum, Blok represented history as an aesthetic object—an embalmed female corpse that is brought back to life, like a doll, by a metal spring. Like Nikolai Fedorov, he figured the museum as the locus of revivification. In the words of Fedorov, the museum is "not a *collection of objects but a collective of people;* its function is not in the accumulation of objects, but in restoring to life remnants of that which has become obsolete, in revivifying the dead . . . by means of their works."[23]

The metal spring installed in the wax body of Cleopatra activates the serpent's death-dealing sting of her wax breast, while also serving as a metaphor for the spectator's desiring gaze, which reduplicates the poet's and the crowd's spellbound gaze. Contrary to the Cleopatrine figure in Blok's Faiyum portrait, it is the queen who is the passive subject in the poem. One rainy day, the well-known critic and author Kornei Chukovsky watched Blok in Petersburg's wax museum press the metal spring repeatedly, obsessed by the mechanical gesture that animated Cleopatra.[24]

The image of the poet who joins the crowd that comes to ogle Cleopatra's prostituted body evokes the figure of Baudelaire's *flâneur,* who traverses city space horizontally, although Blok's lyrical persona also plumbs history vertically. The evocation of the *flâneur* marks an early attempt by Blok to transcend lyrical solipsism, which he accomplished here by becoming part of the anonymous crowd. The composite persona also echoes Baudelaire's image of the poet as prostitute, a figure whom the French poet had linked to the *flâneur* in his *Intimate Journals.* But this is not all. Besides *flâneur* and poet-prostitute, Blok's lyrical persona functions as court poet, with all three figurations inhabiting the voice of the nation intoxicated by Cleopatra ("The queen awaits us in her coffin"). The decadent proliferation of the persona's identities continues further. The prostitute-poet assumes another role by becoming the double of Cleopatra, history's prostitute-queen. A mere slave in Egypt, he reveals the ambitious desire to enter history, like Caesar, and become poet-tsar, as had Pushkin.[25] What is so remarkable about the poem's subjectivity is the fragmentation of the persona, which has been dispersed in the space of the city and history.

The poem is a virtual compendium of decadent topoi poached from a variety of cultural discourses. Besides revealing his apparent fascination with the wax figure of Cleopatra on Nevsky, Blok may have borrowed the image of the wax museum as the site of history from the decadent fiction of the popular Polish writer Stanislaw Przybyszewski, whose florid prose he knew well.[26] Considering the wax figure of Cleopatra in relation to Blok's 1910 essay on Russian symbolism in which he places her in the anatomical theater, it also evokes the positivist trope of dissecting the body, a practice that served as a source of one of the master metaphors of realist writing. In the decadence, however, the figure of dissection had become mere artistic representation, having lost its positivist ideological connotations.

Wax female models, called "anatomical Venuses," were used in anatomy lessons in European medical schools, starting in the seventeenth century. European medical museums had some of them on display, lying prone in glass cases. As Ludmila Jordanova observed, these figures were not only anatomical surrogates to be dissected but also erotic art objects penetrated phantasmically by male students.[27] There was such a museum in Florence, in which Blok may have seen some of these wax Venuses. In the poem, as in his 1910 essay on the decline of Russian symbolism, he superimposed a layer of sadistic desire onto the original positivist trope, creating a characteristic fin-de-siècle palimpsest that consists of decadent desire and a submerged trope from an earlier cultural epoch. Representing a vision of history according to which the past can be suppressed but not erased, the palimpsest is a metaphor for preserving cultural memory, which lies submerged below the surface.

In eroticizing the wax museum, Blok followed the characteristically decadent representation of desire as artifice. One of the most bizarre figurations of the wax museum in decadent literature is its simulation in *Monsieur Venus* (1884), the notorious novel by the French writer Rachilde (pseudonym of Marguerite Eymery). Blok knew Rachilde's fiction: he wrote a review of her *Le dessous* (*Underside*) in 1905 and underlined her name in the book review section of his personal 1904 April issue of *Balance* (*Vesy*). The gender-bending heroine of *Monsieur Venus* transfigures the corpse of her feminized lover into a wax mannequin—a classic fetish object. First, she removes the hair, eyelashes, body hair, and nails from the corpse with "scarlet pincers, a velvet-covered cuticle hammer and solid silver scissors." Then she orders them to be transplanted onto a wax replica of her lover encased in transparent rubber. Finally she places the figure on "a shell-shaped couch guarded by a marble Eros," as if for erotic viewing in a wax museum or a funeral parlor. The mannequin has "a spring set inside the lower body . . . connected to the mouth," which the heroine presses every night so that the lips come to life. The novel's final statement speaks of the mannequin as "an anatomical masterpiece," evoking the image of an anatomical Venus.[28]

Rachilde's anatomical metaphor harks back to the prototypical decadent novel *Mademoiselle de Maupin* (1835) by Théophile Gautier, in which dissection is linked directly to sexual knowledge. "I wanted to study man in depth, to dissect him fibre by fibre with an inexorable scalpel and to have him alive and throbbing on my dissection table," says Mademoiselle de Maupin, the novel's transvestite heroine.[29] To invoke again the writing of Przybyszewski, the Polish decadent recycles the sexualized dissection trope in his novella *Requiem aeternum* (1904), a compendium of anatomical discourse and decadent eroticism. The hero of the story associates the sex act with female vampirism and the anatomical theater: "I had the feeling that I experienced frequently when entering . . . the anatomical theater and touching the corpse during an autopsy."[30]

The springs that activate the mouth in *Monsieur Venus* and the serpent's sting in "Cleopatra" superscribe the body over and over again. Janet Beizer has referred to the repeated layering of scars by the heroine of *Monsieur Venus* on her lover's wax body as the creation of a palimpsest.[31] Blok's obsessive reanimation of the spring that wounds Cleopatra as if with a scalpel has a similar rhetorical effect. I have not been able to establish whether Blok had read Rachilde's novel, nor do I want to suggest that it served as a subtext for his poem, but his Cleopatra bears an uncanny resemblance to Rachilde's wax mannequin, and the poet's necrophilic desire similarly resembles that of the novel's heroine, both of which are satisfied by artificial, fetishist means.

The wax figure of Cleopatra reappears in Blok's well-known essay "On the Contemporary State of Russian Symbolism" (1910), in which she represents symbolism's demise and the demise of his Solov'evian muse. Death without transfiguration replaces the poet's earlier apocalyptic vision. Blok wrote that were he painting the demise, he would represent it as "a huge white hearse swinging in the purple dusk of the unembraceable world; on [the hearse would lie] a dead doll with a face vaguely reminiscent of the one that used to be transparent among the heavenly roses."[32] The chaste Beautiful Lady has sunk into a lower layer of Blok's palimpsest. The body of the wax doll is studded with jewels, as if she were a decadent object of fetishist desire. She resembles Flaubert's Salammbô of his eponymous novel, which Blok admired; as in the instance of Flaubert's decadent heroine, the jewels that overwrite the female nature of Blok's doll are alloys of various magical substances: purple dusk, ocean sighs, clouds, golden swords, amethysts, sacred scarabs, and winged eyes.[33]

The question that arises regarding Blok's figuration of Cleopatra in the poem and in the essay on symbolism is who wields the sword: history's femme fatale or the poet? In the poem he shares power with her, although in the biographical episode in the museum the poet strikes the final blow. The erstwhile poet-knight of the essay has turned anatomist in what he describes as an eroticized "anatomical theater" and in the related puppet theater of wax dolls.[34] Both represent the site of a spectacle in which we watch the poet wield the sword. As in the poem, the man-hunting Cleopatra of myth and history has become mere representation or metaphor. The once idealist poet, who worshiped the Beautiful Lady, now brandishes the scalpel of poetry with which he inscribes his words on the queen's dead body. The reanimating yet lethal gesture in "Cleopatra" leaves repeated traces on the queen's breast, triumphing over female nature with the power of poetic discourse.

The anatomizing trope so central to the Russian radicals of the 1860s is here divested of its positivist subtext. Instead it reveals a fetishist relation to the body and by extension to language. If Turgenev used his nihilist hero Bazarov's fantasy of dissecting a beautiful woman's body to evoke his contemporaries' desire to subsume the erotic into the scientific, Blok deployed the anatomical theater both to erotic and to rhetorical ends. I would further suggest that the reference to the scalpel as a metaphor of his fetishistic relation to language ultimately overwrites the surgical instrument's sadistic, erotic function. Like so many decadent writers, Blok seemed to erase the scientific meaning of dissection from the image altogether, though the older Przybyszewski still engaged its nineteenth-century medical connotations. The positivist meaning of the dissection trope remains in the subtext, however, sinking into a lower layer of the Blokian palimpsest that houses the metaphor and is available to the critic's detection.

## Salome

Venice is a city that exhibits its undercoating. The city's damp climate and waters of the flooding lagoon erode the very foundations of the homes and palaces, baring the architectural layers beneath the surface. In Blok's Italian poems, Venice is the city of death, which he associated with Salome. She appears in the middle poem of his Venice triptych, dedicated to his friend Evgenii Ivanov:

A cold wind from the lagoon.
The silent coffins of gondolas.
And I on this night, young and ill,
Lie prostrate by the lion's column.

On top of the tower
The giants strike midnight.
Mark drowns his ornamental iconostasis
In the moonlit lagoon.

In the shadow of the palace arcade,
Barely lit by the moon,
Salome passes stealthily
With my bloody head.

All sleep—palaces, canals, people,
Only the gliding step of the phantom,
Only the head on the black platter
Stares with anguish into the surrounding gloom.

Холодный ветер от лагуны.
Гондол безмолвные гроба.

Я в эту ночь—больной и юный—
Простерт у львиного столба.

На башне, с песнию чугунной.
Гиганты бьют полночный час.
Марк утопил в лагуне лунной
Узорный свой иконостас.

В тени дворцовой галлереи,
Чуть озаренная луной
Таясь, проходит Саломея
С моей кровавой головой.

Все спит—дворцы, каналы, люди,
Лишь призрака ско ьзящий шаг,
Лишь голова на черном блюде
Глядит с тоской в окрестный мрак.[35]

We read in Blok's notebooks that Salome interested him throughout his Italian trip. In the diary entry of May 25, 1909, Blok singled out in the Uffizi a painting by the seventeenth-century artist Carlo Dolci of Salome holding a charger with the head of John the Baptist. On May 28, in the same diary, he referred to her depiction by the Renaissance artist Gianicolo di Paolo in the frescoes in the Collegio del Cambio in Perugia.[36]

As with Cleopatra, one rightfully asks why Blok linked Salome to Italy, especially to Venice. Searching for an answer, one is again struck by his representation of Italy as a mythological Oriental woman immortalized in Western art. European artists have appropriated the Orient for centuries with the purpose of clothing the feminine in the garments of mystery and power. But unlike Cleopatra in the "Gaze of the Egyptian Woman," who has center stage in the text and whose piercing eyes occupy the center of the portrait, the Salome of the Venice poem appears in the textual and spatial margins. She emerges for a fleeting moment in the dark arcade of the Doge's Palace, which delimits the Piazzetta, where the poet lies prostrate. This marks a change in the place the Oriental woman occupies in Blok's poetic landscape. Blok's Cleopatra is the ancient corpse of history as well as the site of poetry: despite the awe she inspires, she is the body on which the poet inscribes his words; he wields the sword.

Blok's Salome dismembers the poet, separating his body from the spirit, only to disappear into the poem's frame. The consideration of the poet's dismemberment steers us toward the epoch's master plot based on the castration paradigm, which suggests loss and consequent lack. The question that underlies this poem, however, is whether the disintegration of the bodily whole does not in effect imply gain, whose consequence produces greater poetic autonomy. What the disintegration of the whole seems to suggest here is an increased autonomy of the part in the form of a generalized synecdoche. Only instead of pathology, as Naomi Schor has suggested, it represents liberation from the body. Escape from the body as seen through the fin-de-siècle lens that emphasizes the crisis of masculinity reveals the taint of degeneration. But in the terms of Blok's own poetic project, it marks the release of the poet's voice. The poem's fetish object—the poet's bloody head—represents the voice of poetry, in whose liberation Salome appears to play a key role. This makes Blok's Oriental woman not only an emblem of history but also the instrument of poetry, which sheds further light on the problematic fin-de-siècle relation of the part to the whole. In contrast to the fetishistic detail in Tolstoy, which can't reconstitute the whole and therefore dissolves higher meaning, the severed head in Blok's Salome poem symbolizes the poet's transcendence, not his failure. It represents the victory of the fragment and its fetishistic relation to language, here represented by male decapitation.

Salome inspired fin-de-siècle European artists and writers more than any other mythological female figure.[37] Blok was no exception. Let me suggest possible sources of his Salome poem. One may have been the celebrated ekphrasis of Gustave Moreau's "Apparition" (1876) in J.-K. Huysmans's *Against Nature* (1884), which Blok had in his library. The Baptist's decollated and illuminated head soars upward and looks with melancholy into the distance in Moreau's painting, as in the last line of Blok's poem. A more immediate inspiration for the Venetian version of Blok's decapitating muse may have been the group of mosaics depicting the life of John the Baptist in the Basilica of San Marco. These exquisite Byzantine mosaics, ordered by Doge Andrea Dandolo between 1343 and 1354 and executed by several Venetian masters, reinforce Blok's Orientalized representation of history. A well-known admirer of San Marco and the foremost midcentury English art critic, John Ruskin, whose writings Blok knew well and to whom he referred in his Italian travelogue, considered them "the most beautiful symbolic design of the Baptist's death."[38] Located in the baptistery, the mosaics occupy an area that apparently was once an open archway between San Marco and the Doge's Palace. Such an archway appears in Blok's poem as Salome carries the bloody head of the poet through the palace arcade. It is as if Salome had left the walls of the baptistery after midnight and walked into the palace arcade. Only instead of the saint's head, she holds the

Gustave Moreau, *The Apparition* (1876)

poet's; instead of occupying a central place, she remains in the shadows. In the next stanza, we don't see her at all; she has become a phantom, a trace. The poet's gaze and ours move to his bloody, severed head, which "stares in anguish into the surrounding gloom," as if from an Odilon Redon painting or drawing.

Redon, a symbolist artist who represented the decapitation of the Baptist by Salome many times, is best known for his disembodied floating heads, whose eyes gaze into space in search of truth. I have not found any references to Redon in Blok's published writing, but the painter was well known in Russian symbolist circles. Valerii Briusov and the Moscow symbolists were fascinated by his work; Bely made references to him in his writings.[39] Briusov dedicated the fourth issue of the symbolist journal *Balance* to Redon in 1904. We know from the markings in

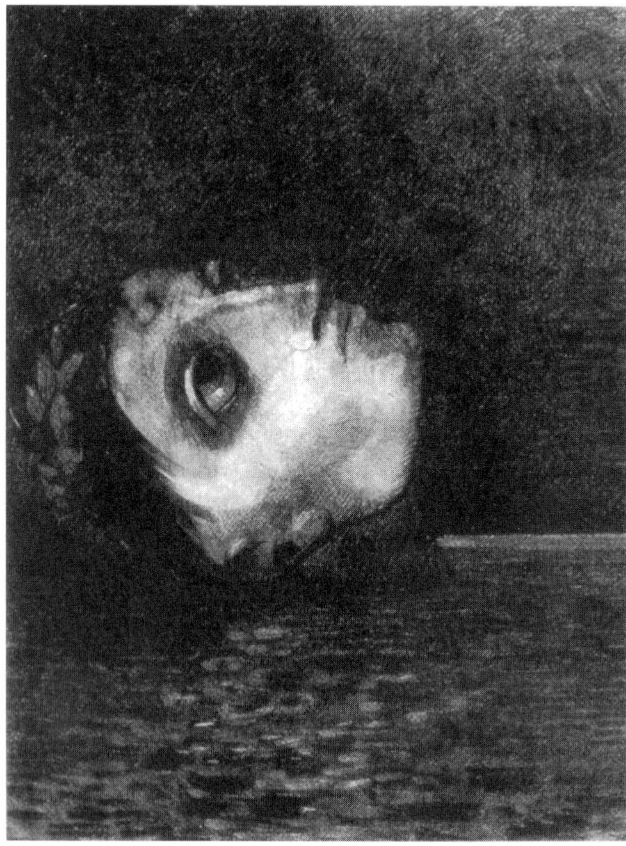

Odilon Redon, *Head of Orpheus Floating on the Waters* (1881)

Baptistery in Basilica of San Marco, Venice

Blok's copy that he had read it.[40] In one of the essays in the issue, Redon's "thoughtful faces . . . with huge, wide-open eyes, glimmering with human thought" are described as rising "over the rounded earth in the black sky, cleft by rays."[41]

To return to the mosaics in San Marco, they are located in two adjacent lunettes that narrate the story in an anachronistic medieval style. The first lunette depicts the story of the Baptist's martyrdom as a whole, starting on the left, with the figure of the beheaded saint with his severed head at his feet; in the middle is Salome's presentation of the head to Herod, with Herodias at his side; on the right is the burial of the Baptist's decapitated body. As is typical in medieval—as well as modernist—narration, pictorial simultaneity coexists with sequential order; time and space are fused into one. The second lunette portrays Herod's banquet. Most striking here is the figure of Salome, treated as an upper-class Venetian woman of the first half of the fourteenth century. She wears a jeweled red and green gown with ermine trim on the sleeves and skirt and stands very erect in a dancing pose, holding the head of the Baptist on a platter over her head. Ruskin compared the pose to that of

Salome in Basilica of San Marco, Venice

a "Greek maid on a Greek vase, bearing a pitcher of water on her head" even though she is a princess.[42] The figure of Salome dancing is to the left of the banquet table laden with food and drink. To the right is a male servant bringing a plate of food to the table. The two figures function as servants delivering delectable dishes to the feast.

What is interesting about the image of decapitation in the first lunette and what may very well have influenced Blok's representation of his own head on the platter is the figure of the saint stepping out of the doorway of the dungeon, sans head, and leaning down toward it as if to pick it up and give it to Salome himself. The supplicating pose is reminiscent of Blok's earlier role as troubadour genuflecting before the inaccessible Beautiful Lady. More importantly, the Venice poem seems to replicate the anachronistic medieval representation of the bifurcated figure in the mosaic, which could be seen as a model for the dispersal of the persona's voice in the poem: the figure of the poet is split in two; weak and ill, his decapitated body lies prostrate at the bottom of the lion column by the lagoon, the site of execution in earlier Venice. The lyrical first person experiences bodily weakness; the severed head, in the third person, stares into the Venetian night. Not only is the poet's body bifurcated, but his voice is also.

Blok first mentioned the decapitation of John the Baptist in an August 1908 essay on the poetry of Nikolai Minsky, who himself had just published an essay on Oscar Wilde's *Salome* in the *Golden Fleece* (*Zolotoe runo*), a symbolist journal. That same August the symbolist theater director Nikolai Evreinov received permission to start producing the play, in which Blok's muse Volokhova was to play the lead. Wilde's Salome was in the air.[43] She left a trace in one of the discarded stanzas of the Venice poem, which contains a reference to an image of Salome in a transparent tunic kissing the decapitated Baptist's head:

I can't escape dark fate—
I must admit to my degradation:
The dancer in a transparent tunic
Kisses my severed head!

Мне не избегнуть доли мрачной—
Свое паденье признаю:
Плясунья в тунике прозрачной
Лобзает голову мою![44]

The discarded stanza corresponds to part of the long erotic monologue that Salome addresses to the Baptist's head late in Wilde's play ("Ah! Thou wouldst not suffer me to kiss thy mouth, Jokanaan. Well! I will kiss it now. I will bite it with my teeth as one bites a ripe fruit. Yes, I will kiss thy mouth, Jokanaan.") and to the corresponding illustration by Aubrey Beardsley ("The Climax"), whose graphic work Blok admired.[45]

But in his essay, Blok seemed more interested in the severed head of the Baptist than in the decapitating femme fatale. One explanation may be that he was disturbed by Wilde's play, in which Salome silences John: from Orphic voice of a new religion, she transforms the saint into a mute aesthetic object. As a poet straddling two centuries and expecting the transfiguration of Russian life, Blok was drawn to the Baptist's position at the juncture of the Old and the New Testament.

Substituting immolation for beheading and Herodias for Salome, as did Stéphane Mallarmé in *Herodiade* (1864), Blok linked writing with the

Aubrey Beardsley, *Climax,* illustration to Oscar Wilde's *Salome*

Baptist's self-sacrifice: the creative act, wrote Blok in the essay about Minsky, is like "a charred soul offered . . . to Herodias on a platter as an exquisite work of art."[46] The femme fatale as aesthetic object is replaced by another "exquisite work of art," the Baptist's head, which is charred instead of bloodied. The image evokes Redon's multiple figurations of the severed head on a platter or floating in space as pure spirit or as emblem of creative autonomy. Herodias, wrote Blok, is unworthy of the poet; he compared her to the satiated, arrogant crowd, which has no artistic appreciation. Instead of the myth of Salome and Herodias as decadent jewels whose beauty is evil, the description celebrates the image of the decapitated Baptist as poet. The image symbolizes the act of writing and poetic commitment—sealed in symbolic blood by the persona's beheading—in relation to which Herodias is a mere bystander. In this configuration of the myth of Herodias/Salome, the Oriental princess cedes her place on the pedestal of art to her victim, who, like the mythical poet Orpheus, also figured by Redon, submits his body to the power of the spirit.

The poet who sacrifices himself to his artistic calling dominates Blok's view of the Salome myth. The powerful visual image of the severed head in the Venetian Salome poem echoes the earlier metaphor of the poet's soul burned to cinder and lying on a platter. In severing his head, the source of prophecy and artistry, from the body, Salome has liberated him from nature and instinctual desire. A castrating muse, she does not disable him, however; she is not a projection of castration fear—the standard representation of Salome in the fin-de-siècle arts. On the contrary, Salome frees his creativity, which can soar upward after the poet's voice is decoupled from his body. A peripheral figure in the poem's cityscape, which resembles a painting, she is a crucial player behind the scene, enabling the poet's creation of "exquisite works of art." If the very erect figure of Salome in San Marco is the prototype, Blok's Salome is phallic, but her masculinization serves the cause of male art, not female power. Instead of the subject, she becomes the mediator of poetry.

In this respect, Blok's Salome bears an uncanny resemblance to Mallarmé's Herodiade in the celebrated short poem "Cantique de Saint Jean" ("The Song of St. John"), the third part of *Herodiade,* begun in 1864. The poem was first published in 1913, many years after Mallarmé's death. In it the decapitating muse liberates the poet's voice: the Baptist's head that has just made a clean break from the body becomes the voice of pure poetry. Herodiade enables poetry by working "against nature," unmanning the poet and releasing his head from his corporeal history. In a well-known essay on writing ("Ballets," 1896), Mallarmé used the figure of Salome to suggest that the process of writing fragments the subject; he wrote that "the dancer is not *a woman who dances,* . . . but a metaphor—sword, cup, flower, etc."[47] Following Mallarmé's lead, I suggest that the blood from the severed head in Blok's Salome poem is not naturalistic blood but a metaphor of poetry, revealing his fetishistic relation to language. The image serves a similar function in his poetry as does the generalized castration trope in the writing and artistic representation of the decadence.

Again I have no evidence of Blok's familiarity with Mallarmé's writing on poetry, but the similarity of their association of Salome-Herodiade with the creation of art is striking. Blok's description of the creative act as "a charred soul offered . . . to Herodias on a platter as an exquisite work of art," which in the poem seems ready to float upward from the charger into the night, certainly resembles Mallarmé's representation of Salome in "The Song of St. John" and in the essay on ballet.[48]

The bifurcation of the poet's voice reappears in the prologue to Blok's unfinished narrative poem *Retribution* (*Vozmezdie*), which, as we know, he began in 1910. Bifurcation is again figured by the poet's severed head lying on Salome's charger which is then placed on a scaffold, an image that also appears in Redon's representations of decapitated heads.[49] As in the Venice poem, the severed head is an emblem of the poet's martyrdom. And as in the Venice poem, Blok rendered the liberation of the poetic voice by speaking of the poet in the first and third persons in the space of a few lines. Visual representation enters the sphere of grammar:

But a song will always remain a song,
In the crowd, someone will still sing.
The dancer brings to the tsar
His head on a platter;
He lays down his head
There, on the black scaffold;
Here, *his poetry* is branded
As shameful . . . But *I sing*,[50]
Yours is not the last judgment,
It is not for you to seal my lips!

Но песня— песнью все пребудет,
В толпе все кто-нибудь поет.
Вот—голову его на блюде
Царю Плясунья подает;
Там—он на эшафоте черном
Слагает голову свою;
Здесь—именем клеймят позорным
Его стихи . . . И я пою,—
И не за вами суд последний,
Не вам замкнуть мои уста! . . .[51]

The poet in *Retribution* transcends his historical isolation by becoming part of the crowd, which echoes his locus in "Cleopatra"; his poetry is described as "shameful," an epithet also characterizing the prostitute-poet of the earlier poem. And as in the Venice poem, the dispersal of the "lyrical I" is affiliated with the figure of Salome, a nameless dancer who severs the part from the whole, delivering the poet's head to the tsar. Even though repressed in the text, trickling down only into the subtext, decollation produces blood, the binding trope of poetic language. The head, which must be bloody, *is* poetry in fact, as we read in the lines "He lays down his head / There, on the black scaffold." The verb *slagat'* (lay down) is used frequently in the collocation *slagat' stikhi,* which means to compose poetry. Rhetorical power is invested in the bloodied part, though the blood is invisible; in contrast to Wilde's Salome, who seals the lips of the prophet, Blok's symbolizes his liberation. The poet's voice is not only dispersed; it has been released, perhaps to become vox populi. The representation of the bifurcated body by means of grammar reflects Blok's desire to inhabit not only the lyrical voice of the poet but also the poetic voice of history. Familial and national history are, after all, the poem's theme.

Contrary to Freud then, decapitation in *Retribution* liberates the poet's imagination, allowing him to transcend his lyrical persona and inhabit his familial past. The poet imagines an alternative genealogy in which, like Nikolai Fedorov, he engenders his parents, inverting the precedence of fathers over sons. "The sons are reflected in their fathers," wrote Blok in the prologue of *Retribution,* as if the trajectory of history were regressive, not progressive.[52] A similar inverted view of genealogy informs the third poem of the Venice triptych. The poet, whose severed head may come to life in the coming century ("will fate really order my eyelids . . . to open at the lion's column?"), imagines his parents as if they were his creation that exist in the future.[53] Progressive historical time, as in Nietzsche's myth of eternal return, is erased: past and future become interchangeable so that the poet can prophecy the past, into which he "regresses," freeing himself from both procreative and apocalyptic obligation.[54]

Describing Blok's study in 1917, a contemporary referred to a reproduction of a Salome painting by the Flemish Renaissance artist Quentin Metsys.[55] In the painting, which Blok had seen in Antwerp in 1911, Salome wears what appears to be a heavy purple and gold dress. An ekphrasis of the painting comes to dominate the city poem "Antwerp" (1914). Just as in some of his Italian poems and prose sketches, a painting becomes the centerpiece of a poem about a city whose museum houses the decapitating Oriental woman. Writing at the beginning of the First World War, the poet addresses the city as the war rages. He suggests to Antwerp that it gaze into its history, as into a mirror, located in the city museum where Salome reigns from the space of the Metsys painting:

And you—look at yourself
In the haze of centuries
In the peaceful city museum:
There reigns Quentin Metsys;
There flowers of gold
Fold into Salome's dress.

А ты—во мглу веков глядись
В спокойном городском музее:
Там царствует Квентин Массис;
Там в складки платья Саломеи
Цветы из золота вплелись.[56]

Like the Salome in San Marco, Metsys's princess is garbed in the dress of her maker's time and place. In the poet's mind, she is linked to the past ("the haze of centuries") collected in that artificial receptacle of history, the museum, but in the Belgian poem she also evokes the devastation of war, rendered by the image of "a sea of blood" and a "circling airplane." In contrast to the Venice Salome, the Flemish princess remains inside the frame. Instead of the decapitated head on a charger, she is the object of the poet's gaze and that of the citizens of Antwerp, as in "Cleopatra." On the eve of war, the decapitating muse resumes her more common position of deadly power and omen of things to come. She wields the sword as the goddess of war and the spiller of blood.

## Eurasian History

So far I have considered Blok's view of history as the site of art objects—or fetish objects—that inhabit museums and of archeological tourist locales. Retrospectivist admiration of European culture, however, does not explain his fascination with Russia as an apocalyptic Eurasia defined by an Asian substratum. In the context of Blok's Eurasian discourse, the bifurcation of his poetic voice, in this case into a lyrical first-person singular and an epic first-person plural, serves a fantastic national agenda that ruptures the European palimpsest. The epic "we," which marks the poet's sense of collectivity, gives voice to violence.

Like that of his symbolist contemporaries, Blok's master plot of Russian history is prophetic, not enlightened. It views Russian history as

Quentin Metsys, *Salome Offering the Head of St. John the Baptist to Herod* (1508; Museum of Fine Arts in Antwerp)

rupture. And like the romantic historiosophy that had informed the intelligentsia's views since the first half of the nineteenth century, it reveals a quandary regarding Russia's place in history. Romantic historiosophy gave only gifted nations such a place. What special aptitude or momentous idea could the Russian nation, considered by Peter Chaadaev as lacking history, individuality, and cultural memory, offer to European society? What concerned him and his followers was whether a backward country could have any purpose in history other than to slavishly borrow invented ideas and practices. Chaadaev, whose philosophical ideas instantiated the Slavophile-Westernizer debate, figured Russia as "a blank sheet of paper" on which Peter wrote "Europe and West."[57] Like Chaadaev, Blok claimed in "Collapse of Humanism" (1919): "We have no historical memories, but great is our elemental memory; our expanses are still fated to play an important role."[58] His response to the dilemma posed by Chaadaev and to his image of the empty slate suggests a prophetic answer.

At the turn of the twentieth century, Solov'ev and his visionary followers developed an apocalyptic discourse of Russia's historical mission of transforming the world. So far I have considered their apocalyptic vision as an expression of decadent utopianism—as a way to escape procreative nature and epochal degeneration. In more traditional historical terms, Russia's Solov'evians imagined themselves as the apocalyptic vanguard of a messianic project that offered an answer to the nagging issue of Russia's backwardness. Like the Slavophiles, they insisted on spirituality as Russia's advantage over the rational, bourgeois West, conveniently erasing progress as the obstacle to Russia's place in history. They replaced progress with prophecy, making transfiguration their goal. Solov'ev's utopian project of immortalizing humankind, as I have shown in chapter 2, substituted miracle for evolutionary change. A similar substitution characterized Fedorov's pseudoscientific project of replacing the procreative cycle with the collective resurrection of ancestors. Inverting past and future, Blok reversed the order of genealogical progression in the Venice triptych and in *Retribution* (see the Salome section of this chapter). He rejected enlightened, rational historiosophy in the introduction to the narrative poem, speaking of his "growing hatred of different theories of progress."[59]

Forecasting the end of history, based on the end of life in nature, Solov'ev prophesied the replacement of nature's body with one that miraculously triumphs over death. The prophesy represents the Solov'evian "new word" that Russia brings to the world, written on that empty page uncluttered by cultural memory. This new word rewrites Russia's conflicted identity. If we consider Solov'ev's prophesy as the nation's special gift, it represents the mystical potential for collectively transforming matter into spirit. The miraculous, if not delirious, final solution erases Russia's problematic technological and civic backwardness by bringing history to an end. How much more historical importance could a single nation hope to achieve?

Blok's Solov'evian historiosophy addresses the dilemma of Russia's place in history. Instead of contributing to European culture, Russia brings to the world the new apocalyptic word coming from the East. This violent Dionysian discourse lies just below the surface of Blok's Eurasian palimpsest, which houses impoverished, oppressed Russia. The poetic cycle *The Field of Kulikovo* (*Na pole Kulikovom*, 1908), written shortly before his Italian journey, and *Scythians* (*Skify*, 1918), written after the revolution, are Blok's most powerful representations of Eurasian rupture. But similar images are also found elsewhere. Devoted to Italy as museum and to the palimpsest as art object, *Lightning Flashes of Art* contains representations of a seething, backward Russia that frame Blok's Italian journey. After leaving home, he depicted the expanses of his homeland as the space of political executions, conspiracies, and "public houses with mad yellow eyes."[60] On his return, he described Russia as moving sluggishly in an uncertain direction along an endless, muddy surface. Taken together, the images suggest a collective national body that will soon erupt in cataclysmic violence and erase its European veneer. If we give the images a Chaadaevian twist, they elicit a blank page awaiting inscription.

*The Field of Kulikovo* renders the emblematic victory over the Mongols in 1389 as a prefiguration of Russia's apocalyptic future. Blok described the battle of Kulikovo using motifs from the book of Revelation: swords, blood, trumpets, abysses, fire, smoke, clouds, thunder, lightning, horses, including the white steed of Christ. But instead of Christ, a female warrior as the incarnation of Russia reveals herself to the poet and leads him into battle. Liberating his aggressive instincts, she inspires his plunge into the Eurasian palimpsest, and contrary to the poet who descends into Italy's historical layers, the one who turns to the Eurasian palimpsest is an active participant.

The first stanza of the first poem in the cycle opens with an image of the river Nepriadva baring the Asian layer below the yellow clay ("The river sprawls [*raskinulas'*]. It flows, grieves languidly [*lenivo*]/And washes its banks.") What is particularly striking is that Blok used the same verb and epithet to figure the river's activity and the wax body of Cleopatra ("She sprawls languidly" in the glass case). The concurrency suggests an underlying feminine layer of Russia's Eurasian landscape, from which a new Russia will emerge. The association of Eurasian Russia with the female body is underscored by the fact that "Cleopatra" and the Kulikovo cycle were written during the same year.

Based on the myth of cultural return, the Field of Kulikovo, which symbolizes the end of the Mongol yoke, evokes Russia's conflicted identity; the battle is associated with a violent Tatar aspect that penetrated the Russian national body: "Our road—with an ancient Tatar freedom's arrow / Has pierced our breast" ("Nash put'—streloi tatarskoi drevnei voli / Pronzil nam grud'"), wrote Blok in the second stanza. His turn-of-the-century Eurasian discourse invokes the trope of Mongol instinctual will, which overwhelms Russia's flimsy European veneer. The steppe hordes that lie below the Europeanized surface rupture the Eurasian palimpsest, spilling blood over the country's natural expanses with the purpose of saying the new poetic word. Like the decadent trope of blood affiliated with decollation and its fetishistic relation to language, the image represents Dionysian bloodletting, which returns the poet to health, releasing in him the voice of the epic poet. Just as does the river of the first stanza, the hordes erase what lies on the surface, flattening the grass that covers the Eurasian steppe; they herald the beginning of retribution coming from the East.

The Eurasian chronotope is another refraction of Blok's desire to break out of poetic solipsism. It transforms the suffocating Petersburg habitat of Blok's narcissistic lyric voice by dispersing it in Russia's unbounded geographic expanses. Using the first-person plural to render the poet's identification with the savage Eurasian nation, he embraces contemporary premonitions of the end and embeds them in the bloody Eurasian palimpsest. In contrast to Italy's palimpsest as petrified past, in which blood is associated with the liberation of the poet's voice, the Russian palimpsest is figured as the space of revolutionary rupture. This becomes especially evident in Blok's 1918 narrative poem *Scythians*, written during the negotiations in Brest-Litovsk for a separate peace between Bolshevik Russia and Germany. Blok's nomadic Scythians, like the Tatars of *The Field of Kulikovo*, emerge as a powerful revolutionary force that will do battle with Europe. Russia's Europeanized surface has been erased: "Yes, we are Scythians! / Yes, Asians—with slanted, greedy eyes!" ("Da, skify—my! Da, aziaty—my / S raskosymi i zhadnymi ochami!"), wrote Blok in the first stanza of *Scythians*. He went on to describe Russia as Sphinx, a hybrid figure of beast and woman, whose image also characterizes Blok's Egyptian woman in the Florentine museum.[61] The Sphinx, whose enigmatic smile suggests violence, is a common embodiment of the decadent femme fatale. Blok's revolutionary Sphinx stares into the eyes of Europe, daring it into apocalyptic battle and reversing the direction of Europe's historical gaze: Europe "has looked to the East for hundreds of years," wrote Blok; now Russia stares at Europe. Russia as Sphinxian hybrid wields the sword that brings history to an end.[62]

In "Collapse of Humanism" (1919), Blok defined the revolution as the force of antihumanism that had been growing in the world: "man is drawing closer to the elements," which Blok associated with the spirit of music and the end of the civilized world. "We listened to . . . the sounds of our cruel nature [that] always rang in the ears of Gogol, Tolstoy, and Dostoevsky." In the revolution, "a new human species [was] emerging," wrote Blok, "a race that has awakened from civilization's slumber."[63] Civilization is the decrepit top layer that the revolutionary palimpsest removes.

If we consider Blok's apocalyptic representation of Eurasian Russia in terms of the cursed question of its place in history, its new word is totalizing revolution. Blok's revolutionary Orient, unlike the Byzantine one, is instinctual, uncivilized, and bellicose. The poet enters the bloody palimpsest of Russian apocalyptic history with the purpose of becoming a man of action who will spread the new word to Europe. Unlike its decadent connotations, the blood of revolution reinvigorates the poet. Contrary to his reverence for artistic representation during the Italian journey, the Eurasian apocalyptic fantasy erases ancient historical sites. No traces of Paestum, the site of a Greek temple, which still stands today in southern Italy, would remain, wrote Blok in the *Scythians.* Willful erasure of civilization characterizes his revolutionary palimpsest, which privileges emptiness over cultural memory and recorded history. The new revolutionary word can only be written on a blank page, which the new man—*the artist,* born of the spirit of music—would inscribe on the body of Russia.

The two kinds of palimpsests represent two sides of the same coin: the Eurasian one, which reinscribes Chaadaev's image of Russia as a blank slate, instantiates the erasure of the European palimpsest in which Blok fashions himself as a passive observer of history. In the revolutionary Eurasian palimpsest, he is a man of action, the product of nature's elemental force. The image of Russia as tabula rasa offers the poet rebirth garbed in apocalyptic fire and brimstone. It gives him an opportunity to refashion himself as a Scythian warrior with a healthy body.

Blok's self-image as an emasculated degenerate allowed him to evade reproductive responsibility to the gentry class. The symbolic engagement with the historical past served the poet as an escape from the law of biology as destiny. In his descents into history, he distanced himself from it, either by entering an aestheticized European past or by imagining his place in an eschatological future. It remains open whether the substitution of his neurasthenic self with the vigorous collective body of Russia offered Blok a more lasting deliverance from solipsism. What we can conclude is that history—especially in its apocalyptic guise—subdued his fear of degeneration.

Blok's historiosophy, like Solov'ev's, was gendered female, meaning antiprogressive. Having feminized history, decadence recycled the cultural artifacts of the man-made past back into the inert soil of the graveyard. This is certainly the case of the female corpse as art object in Merezhkovsky's *Leonardo da Vinci*. Blok's woman-warrior who leads him into battle in his Eurasian apocalypse heralds the end by shedding blood and eradicating Europe's past, including its ancient art objects.

The poet's obsession with Cleopatra, Salome, and the Eurasian female warrior reveals his desire to move beyond the limitations of lyrical self-expression by becoming vox populi, which involves the spilling of blood—blood from which emerges the poem. It explains his treatment of these mythical women as facilitators of both lyrical and epic narrative, not simply as objects or subjects of conflicted erotic passion. Contra Freud, castration figured as decapitation released Blok's poetic voice instead of silencing it: the decapitated head, symbolizing the severed phallus, did not lead to poetic impotence. On the contrary! The fragmentation of the body produced poetry. The early modernist tropes of male dismemberment and of blood—whether supressed or palpable—served the dispersal of the poetic voice: the part assumes a life of its very own without longing for the lost whole. The multiple perspectives that dispersal offered include fetishism, necrophilic love of the past, poetic transcendence, and the myth of barbaric Sphinxian Eurasia by means of which Blok insinuated himself into history. The expansion of his lyrical "I" into a collective "we" in his Eurasian poems allowed him to transcend emasculation by joining his apocalyptic wife in battle against civilized Europe. He was further liberated by the revolution, which in his enigmatic essay *Katilina* is associated with self-castration.

The Roman seditionist's castration, according to Blok, turned him into the agent of revolution. This suggests that he identified castration with ecstatic power—on the order of the religious potency attributed to the sectarian self-mutilators (*skoptsy*).[64]

Finally, Blok's femme fatale represents his fetishist relationship to language. She is a figuration of the symbol, the medium of poetry. By thematizing Salome as the mediator of poetic liberation, he inscribes the veil of transparency—Salome's fixed attribute—into his representation of the femme fatale. Like Mallarmé, he associated the decollating princess with metaphor and the language of poetry, describing the poem as "a veil, stretched across the sharp tips of several words," which have a severing, dispersing function. "These words glimmer, like stars. Beyond them exists the poem."[65] We can conclude then that Blok's veiled woman represents the sphere of language that opened for him a symbolic window into poetry. The erotic body—which is beyond castration—and writing became one.

# 5

# Transcending Gender

## The Case of Zinaida Gippius

Zinaida Gippius (1869–1945) met Dmitrii Merezhkovsky (1865–1941) in the Caucasus resort town of Borzhom in 1888. A capricious, provincial young woman of eighteen, she was surrounded by local admirers and at first seemed indifferent to Merezhkovsky's attentions. If anything, their encounters were adversarial. She wrote many years later that she was not attracted to the young Petersburg author and was annoyed by the fact that he considered her uncultivated. During a local dance on July 11, Gippius and Merezhkovsky decided to get married, but not because he had proposed to her, or she to him. "There was no 'proposal' or 'declaration [of love],'" wrote Gippius. "Yet, both of us suddenly began to talk as if it had been decided long ago that we would marry" and as if "nothing unusual had happened." The decision to marry was not followed by a wedding announcement.[1]

Gippius and Merezhkovsky were married in Tiflis (Russian for Tbilisi) on January 8, 1889. They did not see eye to eye on many things, but both shared contempt for weddings: veils, white dresses, and wedding feasts. Despite their effort to minimize the amount of ritual, they had the obligatory crowns held over their heads. Gippius later complained that unfortunately they couldn't simply be worn like hats. Instead of a white gown and veil, the bride wore a dark gray suit and a hat of the same color. The bridegroom was asked to take off his greatcoat in church, because it just wasn't worn in wedding ceremonies. There was no deacon or choir. Afterward, the married couple returned to Gippius's home and had an ordinary lunch in the company of her immediate fam-

> ily and a few guests. When the guests left, their day proceeded as usual: "D. S. [Dmitrii Sergeevich] and I continued to read the book we were reading yesterday in my room. . . . Dm. S. went back to his hotel rather early, and I went to bed and forgot that I was married" (Gippius-Merezhkovskaia, 34).

Written fifty-four years after the fact, this is the only available description of Gippius's wedding. It is taken from her unfinished biography of Merezhkovsky, *He and We* (*On i my*), begun in Paris in 1943 and published under the title *Dmitrii Merezhkovsky* (1951) after her death. Like most symbolist biographies, it presents a mythologized version of the Merezhkovskys' life. This chapter focuses not on Merezhkovsky, but on Gippius, her perspective on sex, gender, marriage, and life creation, and on her image as a cultural icon of the turn of the twentieth century. The key to my examination of Gippius is not her poetry but her diaries, biographical writing, and epistolary prose. I read them as documents concealing as well as revealing her enigmatic gender in an unconventional marriage and her equally unconventional love affairs premised on Solov'ev's ideal of erotic celibacy. I consider Gippius's private writings the record of her Solov'evian project of transfiguring the body by means of erotic fusion with God in divine love.

Gippius's uncertain sexual identity and unconventional marriage helped define the Merezhkovskys' erotic utopia. Living together for fifty-two years without parting from each other except for a few days—in *Dmitrii Merezhkovsky* she claimed they never parted at all—the Merezhkovskys constructed the most celebrated turn-of-the-century celibate marriage based on a "common cause." Celibacy was not the only unconventional aspect of their marriage. It was combined with collectivity in love—the opposite of celibacy, at least on the face of it—which first took the form of multiple romantic triangles, apparently also unconsummated. Later, when the Merezhkovskys began to promote their apocalyptic vision of Christianity, a celibate triple union, a term for an ideological ménage à trois, became the vehicle of their collective erotic ideal.

Members of a generation in transition, characterized by an ideology that commingled populism, decadence, and religious utopianism, the Merezhkovskys were eclectics. They stitched together a life practice from a variety of cultural and historical sources with the purpose of reinscribing the body of Christ into a new church that sought to restructure the individual and collective body of society. Underlying the metaphoric outer garment of the project was Gippius's "deviant" body: its uncertain biological sex and gender.

## What Is to Be Done about Gippius's Marriage?

Gippius's representation of her wedding differs radically from the way relatives and friends of Alexander Blok remembered his. It was manifestly nontraditional and unromantic, as was the courtship. Although some of the dissimilarities must be attributed to personal preference, the ideological and cultural subtexts of the two weddings were different. If Blok's wedding was an ambitious mixture of apocalyptic, gentry, and folk elements, the Merezhkovskys' took its cue from the 1860s radical tradition, rejecting ceremony and frivolous display. What the two weddings did have in common was the rejection of the procreative meaning of epithalamic symbolism. As if to illustrate this point, Gippius contrasted her own wedding with a model fictional ceremony celebrating procreative marriage: the wedding of Kitty and Levin in *Anna Karenina.* In raising Tolstoy's views on marriage as a point of reference for her own, Gippius may also have been subtly alluding to his later writings, such as *The Kreutzer Sonata,* which, as we know, promulgated a radical antiprocreative position.

Most unexpected is the hidden Chernyshevskian subtext of the Merezhkovsky marriage, surprising because in the 1890s both Gippius and her husband were staunch opponents of the Chernyshevsky generation. Gippius referred derisively to *What Is to Be Done?* in the Merezhkovsky biography, although her scorn was directed at the novel's artistic merit, not its ideas. She revealed her sympathy for Russia's radical populists in her memoirs, *Living Faces* (*Zhivye litsa,* 1925), in which she described the literary critics Vissarion Belinsky, Chernyshevsky, Dmitrii Pisarev, as well as Turgenev's Bazarov as men of true chivalry and spiritual strength: "Only a thin film of unconsciousness separated them from authentic religiosity. That is why most of them were 'standard bearers of high moral values.' . . . That is also why people of amazing spiritual strength [like] Chernyshevsky, capable of great deeds and sacrifice, could have emerged at that time."[2] She preceded this passage with the comment that they were really romantic idealists who only called themselves materialists.[3]

Gippius expressed this admiration for the men of the 1860s only considerably later, not in the l890s or early 1900s, when she, together with her contemporaries, was engaged in a generational conflict with the older intelligentsia. The changing of the guard took place to the accompaniment of an ideology of rupture, not of cultural continuity. Yet Merezhkovsky's affinity with the 1860s was sensed by the younger symbolist Viacheslav Ivanov, who accused Merezhkovsky of being part of the despised nineteenth-century utilitarian literary tradition. "Still alive . . . is the heresy of social utilitarianism, which has found its last . . . champion in Russia in the person of D. S. Merezhkovsky," wrote Ivanov, accusing him of pouring new wine into the old bottles of Belinsky's time and of 1860s radicalism.[4] The philosopher Nikolai Berdiaev saw the affinity as well, although he also perceived Merezhkovsky's desire to shake off the earlier layer of his cultural identity. He claimed that Merezhkovsky actually wanted to be a Chernyshevsky with a religious twist.[5] Without naming Chernyshevsky, Vasilii Rozanov wrote that despite Merezhkovsky's religious vision, he was "a utilitarian of the highest degree, attempting to be . . . useful . . ., in a word, 'in the awareness of his duty to humanity' he is no longer 'Merezhkovsky' but Vodovozov. . . . Vodovozov is his great moral justification."[6] Vasilii Vodovozov, a radical journalist of Merezhkovsky's generation, was the son of Elizaveta Vodovozova, an 1860s activist for whom *What Is to Be Done?* was a handbook for enlightened living.

Despite her negative remarks about *What Is to Be Done?* Gippius's description of her marital life with Merezhkovsky bears a remarkable resemblance to the relationship of Chernyshevsky's utilitarian heroes Vera Pavlovna and Dmitrii Sergeevich Lopukhov. Although for Gippius, unlike for Chernyshevsky's heroine, marriage did not mean escape from a repressive family, it did mean upward mobility for her just as for the fictional Vera Pavlovna, both intellectually and socially. Uncannily, Dmitrii Sergeevich Merezhkovsky had the same name and patronymic as Lopukhov, Vera Pavlovna's mentor and husband, who saves the young woman from an undesirable marriage for profit. The similarity of names is, of course, sheer coincidence, but, as we know, the symbolic and intertextual significance of names was important in symbolist discourse, suggesting that Gippius may have noted this coincidence at the time. Like Dmitrii Sergeevich Lopukhov, Merezhkovsky played the role of mentor to the provincial young woman in the beginning of their relationship, initiating her into the "new" ideas of the European and Russian fin de siècle. Together they reenacted the 1860s version of the Pygmalion myth, which became such an important metaphor in symbolist culture.[7]

As we learn from her description of their courtship and wedding, the attraction between Gippius and Merezhkovsky was not sexual. This never changed. Rather it was an intellectual attraction, which developed into a lifelong ideological partnership devoted to a socioreligious cause. Their life together was unusual and unconventional, living as they did in an unconsummated fraternal union, one that resembled the radical institution of fictitious marriage practiced in the 1860s and 1870s.[8] Fictitious marriage was premised on a vow of chastity, whose infringement was considered a transgression of the "new people's" moral code.[9] Thus, chastity, an integral component of some forms of courtly love, was grafted onto marriage, an institution conventionally considered incompatible with the romantic courtly ideal. True, the practice of chastity in the 1860s was the result of the original premise of fictitious marriage—that, as in the case of Vera Pavlovna, a progressive young man married a young woman to liberate her from the parental yoke and society's expectations of her, not because of chaste love. Yet there is something unabashedly courtly in Lopukhov's behavior toward his young wife, with whom he has no sexual relations until the last year of their marriage. Ironically, we find out about their celibate life from their landlady, who snoops on them through one of the many transgressive keyholes riddling *What Is to Be Done?*[10] The reader learns that the two never see each other naked from a scene in which she observes Lopukhov getting dressed in order to open the door to his wife, who knocks on it unexpectedly.

There is, of course, no corresponding evidence about the Merezhkovsky marriage, although Gippius's chastity was considered public knowledge. According to Sergei Makovsky, the editor of the modernist journal *Apollon*, the young wife for several years wore her hair in a way that signified her virginity: she plaited it into a single braid as an emblem of her white marriage.[11] Virginal white was her favorite color, with her famous white dresses symbolizing her virginity.

Whether intentionally or not, Gippius evoked in the Merezhkovsky biography some of the details of the marriage of Vera Pavlovna and Lopukhov. After Chernyshevsky's hero and heroine first discuss their marriage plans, they shake hands and part as if nothing unusual has happened. When they get engaged, Vera Pavlovna tells Lopukhov that she feels as if they have been married for a long time already. After the wedding, Vera Pavlovna returns home to her parents without her husband. True, her reason is pragmatic; she is hiding her marriage to Lopukhov from them. Both couples, however, exhibited remarkable nonchalance regarding the change in their lives as well as an antibourgeois

Zinaida Gippius ca. 1901 (photograph by Otto Renar, Moscow)

Dmitrii Merezhkovsky (Museum of Alexander Blok in Solnechnogorsk)

disdain for epithalamic ritual. Most importantly, their nonchalance was a reflection of the covert fact that their wedding was not intended as sexual initiation. Quite the opposite—it revealed the asexual nature of their future marital relationship.

There is, of course, no honeymoon trip in *What Is to Be Done?* Gippius and Merezhkovsky had no choice but to embark on one and travel along the Georgian Military Highway, the archetypal locus of Russian romanticism. How else could they have made the move from the Caucasus back to Petersburg? In keeping with Chernyshevsky's debunking of traditional epithalamic custom, Gippius described their honeymoon trip over the famous pass through the Caucasus mountains just as unromantically as their wedding; their trip inverted the archetypal romantic journey to the Caucasus by representing the trip back to the imperial center. Just as she used Tolstoy to define her wedding, she used Lermontov to offset her honeymoon—in particular the first chapter of *A Hero of Our Time,* "Bela," a romantic tale framed by the narrator's trip along the

Georgian highway. Gippius invoked Lermontov's romantic descriptions of Caucasian nature, and like the narrator in "Maksim Maksimych," another of the stories comprising Lermontov's novel, she claimed not to be able to do it justice because of her literary shortcomings. She framed their patently unromantic journey by referring to Lermontov's love story involving an exotic native girl and a Byronic hero. In thus rejecting the romantic conventions that were attached to travel and weddings, Gippius set the stage for the unromantic character of her marriage and its comparison with that of the Lopukhovs in Chernyshevsky's stridently antibourgeois novel.

Even the arrangement of the Merezhkovskys' first apartment in Petersburg, which Gippius described with Chernyshevsky-like precision, resembled the Lopukhov apartment. Like the narrator in *What Is to Be Done?* Gippius highlighted the fact that they had separate bedrooms divided by a common dining room. She made the arrangement of domestic space a key element in the way she emploted her marital life. Like Vera Pavlovna before and Virginia Woolf later, Gippius considered it very important to have "a room of her own"—as an emblem of her intellectual equality with her well-known husband.[12] She also emphasized the spatial division of a woman's private life into that which she does and doesn't share with her husband, that is, into private and common space. The former was intended for her intellectual activities and intimate relations. In traditional gentry or bourgeois homes, a woman's private quarters included children's rooms and boudoirs, the latter serving as space in which the lady of the house entertained family, female friends, and lovers. Vera Pavlovna and Gippius, however, have personal rooms for intellectual exchange, not secret trysts, despite the rumors that Gippius used hers for wild nights with male admirers. Even in this respect, she can be compared to the *nigilistki,* whose lascivious reputations in most instances were the product of public fantasies inspired by their emancipated ideology, not their actual behavior. Although the domestic arrangement that Chernyshevsky and Gippius proposed promotes female privacy, it also can be seen as a byproduct of their chaste, nonprocreative agendas.

Thus Gippius's celibate marriage resembled marital practice in *What Is to Be Done?* placing the highest premium on ideological compatibility and gender equality. Like Chernyshevsky's new men and new women, Gippius considered her intellectual partnership with Merezhkovsky superior to marriage based on passionate love and genealogical

Zinaida Gippius in 1890s (State Literary Museum in Moscow)

continuity. Such an attachment, according to Gippius, has deeper spiritual meaning and greater potential for transforming society (Gippius-Merezhkovskaia, 115). The most intriguing aspect of her ambitious project is the incongruity of its constituent parts. If we consider the Merezhkovsky marriage as a cultural palimpsest, its lowest faded layer resembles fictitious marriage as developed in the 1850s and 1860s and codified in Chernyshevsky's novel. This layer is overwritten by Solov'evian erotic mysticism, which also had a powerful impact on young Blok and Andrei Bely. For all three, however, fear of degeneration tainted their heartfelt submission to erotic mysticism; in Gippius's case, Krafft-Ebing would have certainly noted egregious signs of degeneration.

## Fin-de-Siècle Cleopatra or Female Dandy

Gippius's celibate marriage contrasted sharply with her public image as decadent femme fatale. This side of her behavior reflected most vividly the fin-de-siècle provenance of her persona, one that was grounded not in "nature's" wholeness, but rather in a fetishist sensibility privileging parts instead of wholes. Instead of a singular identity, hers resembled an eclectic collage of seemingly incompatible fragments, revealing a decadent subjectivity consisting of contradictory elements. Perhaps more than any other contemporary Russian writer, Gippius approached ideal decadent subjectivity, especially in the sphere of gender. Typically decadent is the literary origin of her femme-fatale image, which she modeled on the emblematic power-wielding Cleopatra. Russian literature's prototype of Gippius's self-representation as ancient Egyptian queen was Pushkin's Cleopatra from the society tale *Egyptian Nights* (*Egipetskie nochi*), who offers one night of love in exchange for a man's life.[13] Her image was celebrated by the symbolist poets Constantine Bal'mont, Valerii Briusov, and Blok.[14] What makes Pushkin's Cleopatra particularly suitable as Gippius's prototype is that she seeks not just female power, but transcendent love, as if her yearning prefigured the poet's life-long "desire for that which does not exist in this world." Gippius first articulated this wish in "A Song" ("Pesnia," 1893), her best-known poem, which opens her first book of verse and which Blok appropriates for his vision of Cleopatra in his Italian travelogue.

Gippius's Cleopatra look included a diadem, a fashionable accessory at the turn of the century: "Zinochka . . . wore a diadem on her head arranged in such a way that a diamond fell on her forehead," wrote Briusov in his diary.[15] Reenacting the figures of both Pushkin's Cleopatra and the salon hostess of his unfinished society tales, Gippius liked to entertain guests reclining on her couch. Briusov supposedly procured a special sofa for her when the Merezhkovskys came to Moscow in 1901.[16]

Gippius's appearance also revealed a gender-bending agenda. Like

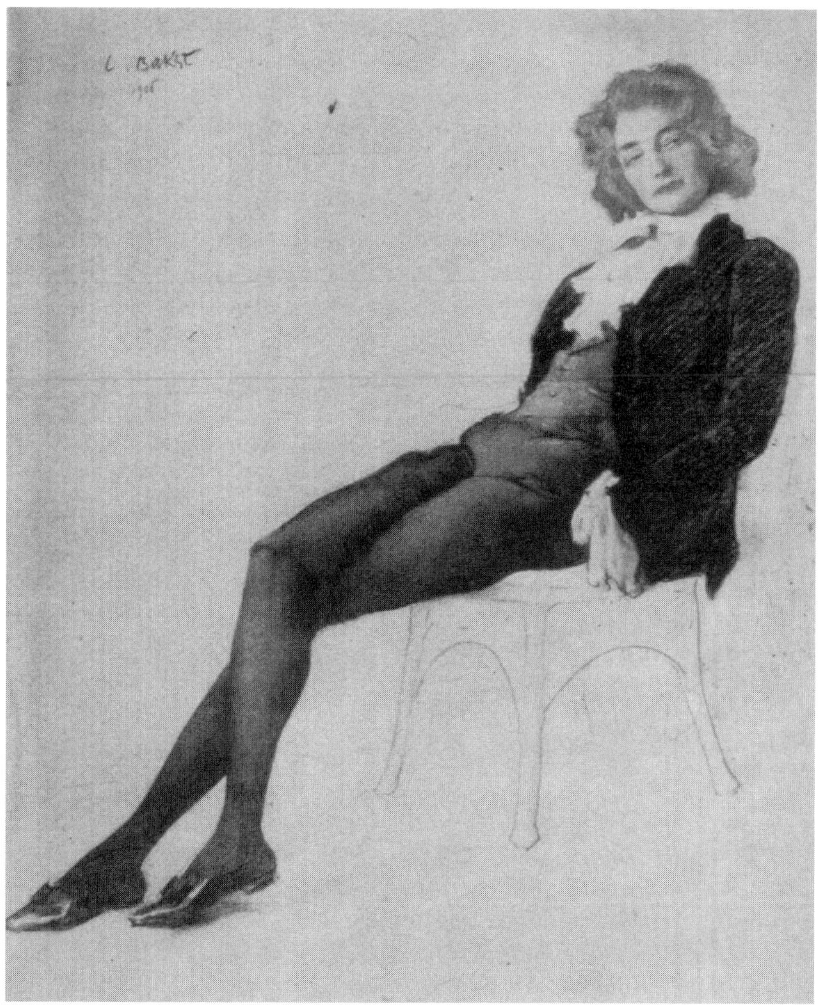

Leon Bakst, portrait of Zinaida Gippius (1906; Tretyakov Gallery in Moscow)

George Sand or Gippius's friend Poliksena Solov'eva, she was a cross-dresser. Her self-representation as a man included a male poetic persona and male pseudonyms. With very few exceptions, the "lyrical I" of her poetry was masculine in those instances where Russian grammar expresses gender, that is, in the past tense and in personal pronouns. In the desire to scramble her gender, Gippius wrote her poetry in the male voice or one that is gender neutral, yet signed it as a woman. As a critic she appeared under male pseudonyms; the best known was Anton the Extreme (Anton Krainii).

Zinaida Gippius in 1890s (State Literary Museum in Moscow)

Leon Bakst's famous 1906 portrait of her displays a tall figure reclining in a chair in the costume of a dandy in a distinctly masculine pose: long legs artfully crossed, hands in pockets, she wears tight knee-length trousers.[17] Gippius was known to sport culottes as well. (She wrote to her friend Zinaida Vengerova in 1897 that she wore culottes with a Ukrainian shirt at the dacha and that the ladies and country folk had

Leon Bakst, portrait of Zinaida Gippius (1900)

become accustomed to it.)[18] The face in the portrait, framed by a head of thick red hair and a filmy white jabot, is appropriately pale; her sensuous mouth displays an ironic smile, and her languid eyes challenge the viewer by averting disdainfully his curious gaze. Most importantly, the image reveals a Wildean dandy, a turn-of-the-century aristocratic transvestite who subverts the binary system of gender. According to

Anonymous pencil drawing of Zinaida Gippius (State Literary Museum in Moscow)

Baudelaire, the dandy was the most privileged male gender because of its artful self-construction.

Bakst's earlier portrait of Gippius, which appeared in a supplement to the journal *World of Art* (*Mir iskusstva*) in 1900 (nos. 17–18), reveals a similar dandified image; although the representation shows her only down to the waist, she is dressed in a similar costume, and her seductive gaze challenges the viewer.

Gippius smoked perfumed cigarettes using a cigarette holder. An

Caricature of Zinaida Gippius by Mitrich (1907; State Literary Museum in Moscow)

emblem of mannishness, smoking by women was a turn-of-the century sign of lesbian sexuality. The "tendency to adopt male attire" and the "taste for smoking" characterized sexually inverted women, wrote Havelock Ellis in 1895.[19] An unpublished, anonymous pencil drawing of Gippius, which shows her in profile reading, contains an ashtray with a cigarette in it. A 1907 caricature by Mitrich (Dmitrii D. Togolsky) of Gippius smoking displays her anorexic figure in profile, sheathed in a tight-fitting white dress with a fashionable train forming a flared bottom and a pocket containing a pack of cigarettes. A phallic cigarette between her lips, she holds in one hand a lorgnette, the female dandy's counterpart of the monocle. Typifying the femme fatale, a sinister spider, which captures its victims in its sticky web, hangs from the other hand like a pendant. Her large coiffure dwarfs her face. She casts a small black shadow. In other words, she is phallic—a fetish object—but not mannish. Her phallic image is enhanced by the profile representation, which, according to the philosopher Pavel Florensky, signifies power, unlike the frontal view.[20]

Gippius's contemporaries frequently emphasized her androgynous look. Sergei Makovsky depicted her as flat chested and narrow hipped, likening her to an androgyne from a canvas by the Renaissance painter Sodoma, an epigone of the master of androgynous representation, Leonardo da Vinci. Makovsky emphasized her green mermaid eyes, Gioconda-like ambiguous smile, bright red mouth—associated with the phallic woman's bloodthirstiness—and its serpentine sting, a reference to her sharp tongue.[21] Andrei Bely painted a verbal portrait of Gippius that reflects gender slippage as well as her Cleopatra look:

> Z. Gippius is just like a human-sized wasp, if she is not the skeleton of a "seductress" (the pen of Aubrey Beardsley); a lump of distended red hair (let down, it would reach her toes) concealed a small, crooked face; powder and luster from a lorgnette into which a greenish eye has been inserted; she fingered her faceted beads, staring at me, retracting the flame of her lip . . . ; from her forehead, like a beaming eye, dangled a stone; on a black cord, a black cross rattled from her breastless bosom, and the clasp of her little boot flashed; legs crossed, she tossed back the train of her close-fitting dress; the charm of her bony, hipless skeleton recalled a communicant deftly captivating Satan. And Satan, Valerii Briusov, seemed to convey to her, through a pose straight out of a Felicien Rops painting, that he had become her captive.[22]

Bely's portrait of Gippius, which may reveal as much about Bely as about his subject, resembles his earlier description of Solov'ev. Fragmented and grotesque, the representations single out typically decadent features. Perhaps the most striking similarity between the two portraits is the focus on the vampiric, bloodthirsty mouth, which in the case of Gippius ("retracting the flame of her lip") evokes the figure of the vampiric femme fatale; the color red is used both for her flaming mouth and floor-length hair. Bely reinforces the deadly image by comparing her to a human-size wasp, whose sting can be likened to a serpent's; Gippius's self-description as a snake, one of the fin-de-siècle tropes of the phallic woman, especially Cleopatra, is not uncommon in her poetry.[23] Like Briusov, Bely mentioned the fetishistic Cleopatrine jewel adorning her forehead, which is only one of many reflecting surfaces that ornament her elaborate costume, thus displacing her body. Adding an element of distortion, he compared the jewel to an eye, which forms a Picasso-like pair with her own green eye, grotesquely magnified by the lorgnette. The artist to whom Bely referred in the beginning of his visual portrait is Aubrey Beardsley, the illustrator of Oscar Wilde's gender-bending *Salome,* whose illustrations, I would suggest, serve as a subtext for Bely's representation of Gippius. It ends with a mention of the Belgian decadent Rops, who painted and drew decidedly lascivious, if not bestial, images of women. The reference to Beardsley, one of the creators of contemporary homosexual visual discourse, underscores the uncertain gender of Gippius's anorexic body and the underlying homosexual desire of its male beholder: the lack of breasts and hips, traditional markers of feminine sexuality, titillates her male observers who seek in her a fetish substitute, not the image of woman as nature.

The figuration of Gippius as an androgynous Cleopatra emerged in the early 1900s, after the symbolist generation had at least partially vanquished the utilitarian fathers in the culture wars of the time. As I have suggested, in the 1890s, a decade still intimately linked to radical populist culture, Gippius modeled her subjectivity on the radical ideals of the 1860s and 1870s. But in the sphere of erotic triangulation, which she perceived as a means of exercising and extending her power over others, Gippius evoked Dostoevsky's most memorable femme fatale of the 1860s: Nastas'ia Filippovna from *The Idiot* (1868), whose behavior also reveals characteristics associated with the new woman. Like Gippius, Nastas'ia Filippovna is linked to Cleopatra through Pushkin's *Egyptian Nights:* the words *"tsenoiu zhizni noch' moiu"* ("one night of love in exchange for your life") remind Nastas'ia Filippovna of her Pushkinian provenance and of Pushkin's queen, who utters the fatal challenge to the men gathered at her feast. In other words, Nastas'ia Filippovna, whom Mario Praz considered a prototype of the femme fatale in the French decadence, is more than an educated, vindictive kept woman: her genealogy reaches back into ancient Egypt.[24]

Besides sharing a Cleopatrine layer as the foundation of their female power, Nastas'ia Filippovna and Gippius are architects, as well as victims, of triangulated desire. They both stage numerous protean threesomes in which they play the pivotal role. They even share a bisexual orientation; Nastas'ia Filippovna falls in love with Aglaia, constructing a highly-charged erotic threesome consisting of herself, Aglaia, and Myshkin. What links them further is their celibacy, which they flaunt despite their roles as love goddesses. Refusing to have sex with their male admirers, they do not, however, release them, but instead pit them against each other by means of triangulated desire "between women." They act out the fin-de-siècle misogynist myth of female perversion, which intertwined lascivious desire and lascivious frigidity, all the while dreaming of a love not of this world.

## Erotic Triangulation in the 1890s

During the 1890s, Gippius combined celibate marriage with numerous overlapping love triangles. Her extramarital "affairs" with men were apparently also unconsummated; they were as "fictitious" as her marriage. Despite her many romantic entanglements, Gippius was reputed to be a virgin. Viacheslav Ivanov told S. P. Kablukov, the secretary of the Religious-Philosophical Society in Petersburg, as much. According to Ivanov, she was oppressed by her gender; she couldn't "give herself to a man" no matter how much she loved him. This inability, thought Ivanov, was the source of her personal tragedy.[25] Gippius herself lamented this ambivalence; she wrote in her diary that sexual desire triggered her attraction to men, which almost immediately turned to revulsion. Gippius repeated the pattern of attraction and revulsion in all her affairs of the 1890s. She generally considered the satisfaction of sexual desire in coitus reprehensible: "[I]f only I could let go . . . of the voluptuous filth, which, I know, is hidden in me and which I don't even understand," wrote Gippius in *Contes d'amour.* "I don't want a certain kind of love, that funny one about which I know."[26]

The men and women with whom Gippius had intense erotic relations in the last decade of the nineteenth century included the poets Nikolai

Minsky (Vilenkin) and Aleksei Chervinsky, the critic Akim Volynsky (Khaim L. Flekser), the critic and translator Zinaida Vengerova, and the poet Liudmila Vil'kina. Vengerova, Vil'kina, and Minsky were members of the famous Vengerov family.[27] All five, though reared in the liberal "civic" tradition, were influenced by the new sensibility of the 1890s. Volynsky wrote for *The Northern Messenger* (*Severnyi vestnik*), the first Russian journal to publish the first examples of Russian and European modernism; Gippius's first poems appeared there, as did works by Merezhkovsky, Minsky, and Vengerova. In the early 1900s, some of these men and women became involved in the religious revival inspired by the Merezhkovskys.

Gippius formed the following overlapping triangular configurations: Gippius, Minsky and Chervinsky; Gippius, Minsky, and Volynsky (the relationship with Minsky apparently began in 1891, with Volynsky in 1894); Gippius, Minsky, and Vengerova; Gippius, Minsky, and Vil'kina; Gippius, Volynsky, and Vil'kina; and Gippius, Volynsky, and Liubov' Gurevich. Minsky also formed a separate triangle with Vil'kina and Vengerova, which frustrated Gippius no end.[28] Merezhkovsky wrote love letters to Vil'kina, but this fact did not seem to disturb Gippius. Starting at the top of the list, she played off Minsky against Chervinsky and later against Volynsky, Minsky against Vengerova and Vil'kina, doing everything she could to prevent the latter's marriage to Minsky, even though she herself rejected him as a lover. Needless to say, these were tumultuous triangular relations. At least, such is the impression from Gippius's letters and diaries.

From the outside looking in, these erotic dramas resemble melodrama, if not outright farce; certainly, the exaggerated dramatic gestures characterizing the discourse of Gippius's intimate diary and love letters attest to the melodramatic atmosphere of her erotic life. It consisted of a standard cast of stock characters: the disengaged prominent husband (Merezhkovsky), the older family friends, the doctor (Nikolai Chigaev), and the husband's lesser colleagues (Chervinsky, Minsky, Volynsky), all of whom were chasing his wife. Gippius played the role of a young refined woman of the world, with a supporting female cast that included her understudy and rival (Vil'kina), a cheaper version of the heroine, who also received her guests reclining on a Cleopatrine couch (she may have been the heroine's lover too); a loyal woman friend (Vengerova), who was a patient admirer of one of the wife's lovers as well as the possible lover of the wife herself; and the obligatory downstairs maids, with whom one of the lovers (Minsky) had sexual dalliances. Playing the double role of ingénue and stage director, Gippius wreaked havoc in the play, resorting to different strategies of epistolary manipulation.

The affairs, which intertwine high drama, sexual freedom, and farce, must have tickled the nerves of all participants. Titillation was a favorite pastime of the decadent generation, which replaced Victorian bourgeois morality and family values with sexual experimentation. In psychophysiological terms, the men and women of this generation were preoccupied with their nervous systems, suffering from a condition the psychiatrists Charcot and Krafft-Ebing called neurasthenia and hysteria. If we compare the 1890s with the 1860s, we see that the younger generation rearticulated the positivist physiological discourse of their fathers and mothers into a special vocabulary of enervation. When evoking the 1860s master trope of anatomical dissection, these men and women dwelled on its degenerate, erotic subtext, not its positivist meaning. Fusing dissection and the early modernist metaphor of unveiling the body, they used the image of exposing their own nerve endings as a way of rendering neurasthenia. Alexander Emel'ianov-Kokhansky, the first Russian poet to call himself a decadent, titled his book of poems *Exposed Nerves* (*Obnazhennye nervy*, 1895) and dedicated it to himself and to "the Egyptian queen Cleopatra." The epithet *obnazhennye* also suggests nudity, which was displayed in public places in the fin de siècle.

Just as the positivist meaning of the dissection metaphor was replaced by its enervated, erotic connotations, the superimposition in real life of one erotic triangle on another resembled the modernist device of double exposure. The result was a chaotic and slippery set of erotic relationships. If we consider these tangled love lives in the context of Gippius's later ideological concerns, they can be seen as an early experiment in the construction of a collective body, a project that had occupied a central place in symbolist life creation since Solov'ev's *The Meaning of Love*. I have in mind what the philosopher and his followers called "collectivity in love," an important, though obscure concept for their utopian project.

## A Fatal Woman of Letters

Gippius's love affairs have come down to us in epistolary and diary form. The primary sources of my reconstruction of her life in the 1890s are her erotic diary *Contes d'amour* and what remains of her letters to

Minsky, Chervinsky, Volynsky, Vengerova, and Vil'kina, most of which remain unpublished. In most instances we have only some of her letters and, with the exception of the correspondence with Minsky and Volynsky, only her side of the story, which perforce offers only limited access to the actual experience of the erotic hothouse in which Gippius lived at the end of the nineteenth century.

A love letter centers on the beloved, although typically it erases the beloved's autonomy. By anticipating or projecting the other's feelings and words, the epistolary self absorbs the addressee. With a correspondent like Gippius, the degree of self-absorption impeding the later reader's access to the feelings of the addressee is particularly high. Her contemporaries considered her a masterful correspondent, which, however, had little to do with the factual reliability of her epistolary prose. The émigré poet and critic Georgii Adamovich said that "sooner or later, it will be generally recognized that the talent of Z. Gippius [was] more evident in her private letters than in her poems, short stories, and essays."[29] Personal mythmaking, which presupposes factual unreliability, also typifies her diaries, which as a genre are the most common site of discursive fantasy and unabashedly subjective discourse. What is particularly curious about her letters and diaries, which contain numerous profound insights into her artfully constructed subjectivity, is the frenetic fluctuation of feelings, which at its most extreme seems parodic, even farcical.

On the level of melodrama, the most common narrative device of Gippius's frequently manipulative love letters is an annoying oscillation, reminiscent of Nastas'ia Filippovna's novelistic behavior. Replicating the narrative strategy of a hysterical quest for power—fueled by erotic excess—her seesaw epistolary discourse was accompanied by obsessive, open-ended Dostoevskian self-analysis. In a typical example of epistolary ambivalence, or hysteria, she wrote to Minsky on January 14, 1892: "I must be in love with you. But it seems that I am not. Why does everything appear so untrue? Or perhaps that which appears—is itself the truth? . . . What does it mean that I am 'in love'? By this do I mean love, or something else? . . . One thing is true: I am talking about love, which means I do not love. . . . [S]hould I be in love with him? . . . Would I like to be . . . in love with you? No. . . . To make you not love me is impossible; I must make you love me less, if only for a moment. . . . I am taking action, subjugating myself to my new desire: that you will love me more."[30]

She could not decide whether she loved Minsky and if she wanted him to love her. Her strategy was to keep herself and the lover off balance, a state in which nothing can be finalized and emotions remain in endless turmoil. The result was a self-absorbed lover's discourse, silencing, for all intents and purposes, the voice of the beloved. It resembles the fin-de-siècle sensibility of solipsism, which questions the very existence of the empirical world. Looking at the passage through the prism of degeneration, one sees that it exemplifies a neurasthenic desire to stimulate and then bare one's nerve endings in an enervated display—the consequence of unexpended erotic energy.

The ambivalence of desire, so characteristic of her epistolary prose and diaries, is a key theme in her poetry, especially the work she produced during the 1890s. One such example is the poem "Stairway" ("Lestnitsa," 1897), which contains feelings similar to those Gippius expressed regarding Minsky in the letter quoted above. The difference between them is the distillation of feelings in the poem. While the letter is emotionally unrestrained, the poem is laconic and dry. In it Gippius staged the persona as a man and the addressee as a woman, rendering their genders grammatically. The masculine grammatical gender of the lyrical persona contributes to the poem's cold, self-restrained tone, which is lost in genderless English:

> You I did not love,
> You, recent, fortuitous, alien . . .
>
> But my heart began to ache, to feel strange,
> And a sudden thought illuminated my soul:
> O you unloved one—I know not why,
> But I expect your love! I want you to love me!

> И было ясно мне: тебя я не любил,
> Тебя, недавнюю, случайную, чужую . . .
>
> Но стало больно, странно сердцу моему,
> И мысль внезапная мне душу осветила,
> О, нелюбимая, не знаю почему,
> Но жду твоей любви! Хочу,чтоб ты любила![31]

"Stairway" is dedicated to the young musician Elizabeth von Overbek, with whom Gippius apparently had an intimate relationship that Briusov described derisively as lesbian: "[A]ttending Zinochka was Liza Overbek, a girl for lesbian caresses, gaunt, dried up, bad looking."[32] Gippius met the Baroness von Overbek in Taormina in 1898, the same year she met Wilhelm von Gloeden.[33] Taormina, located on a mountain overlooking the Ionian Sea in Sicily, had been an educated European traveler's destination since the days of the grand tour. Gloeden was a homosexual artist and photographer whose photographs of beautiful, languid ephebes posed as Grecian statues or in imitation of Caravaggio's young men were typically set in a Sicilian natural environment with architectural traces of the ancient world.[34] Gloeden knew Oscar Wilde and Gabriele d'Annunzio; his villa in Taormina was frequented by Marcel Proust, Sarah Bernhardt, Eleonora Duse, Anatole France, Richard Strauss, the American expatriate Romaine Brooks, and many others. The Merezhkovskys spent part of the summer of 1898 there, mixing with Gloeden's guests.

An interesting example of Gippius's epistolary play with gender difference is her manipulative 1894 letter to her understudy and rival Liudmila Vil'kina.[35] The letter is in English, because, as Gippius claimed in her letter, she had a "strange habit—writing letters in English." The assertion is, of course, false, but her use of English in writing to Vil'kina suggests dandyism in the manner of Algernon Swinburne or Oscar Wilde, which Gippius flaunted to her less sophisticated rival. Furthermore, English, unlike Russian, is gender neutral. Although it is a letter from one woman to another, Gippius pretended that her correspondent was male, addressing Vil'kina as "my dear boy" and signing the letter "your only beloved Z," which could have referred to a man. This is a departure from her love poetry, which when addressed to a woman follows the convention of masked lesbian desire: the lyrical voice is marked male, the object of desire, female. Gippius reminded Liudmila of their intimacies and asked her to "come quickly," addressing her as "my mate . . . in our illness." Invoking the trope of illness and physical decline, the letter started with an inquiry about Liudmila's "consumption" and a report on hers.

Despite the play with gender, pleasure in illness, Nietzschean denigration of pity ("pity is not for we [presumably for the sake of rhyme] and you must be like me"), the core of the letter is about Liudmila's relationship with Minsky.[36] Although not named, Minsky, not Liudmila, was supposedly the object of Gippius's triangular desire. In an inversion of Eve Kosofsky Sedgwick's concept of homosocial desire between men, Gippius in this instance played it out "between women." The same triangular subtext holds true for the next preserved letter, in which she made a pass at Liudmila, this time in Russian and in more straightforward lesbian terms: "There has not yet been a case in which any woman—whether pretty or ugly, kind or mean—was attracted to me. That has been the rule—one that remains unclear—for I myself like women—beautiful ones, of course, such as yourself. I knew that something of the sort would happen with you too; but I so genuinely wanted to see you that I decided all the same to endure the inevitable yet another time."[37]

Despite the erotic tone of these letters, Gippius had only the most derogatory things to say about Vil'kina, referring, for instance, to her lack of intelligence. She made anti-Semitic remarks about her, calling Liudmila "a little Jewess" (*zhidovochka*) who was undeserving of her jealousy.[38] Her condescending anti-Semitic remarks also extended to Minsky and Volynsky.[39]

Gippius's letters to Vengerova, for whom she had much greater respect, were less stylized but just as overtly erotic. There is no evidence that Gippius's relationships with Vil'kina and Vengerova were sexual. Unlike the relationship with Overbek, which was very possibly also Platonic, these "affairs" were triangulated—Minsky being the main object of the tug of war—in which Gippius placed a man between herself and another woman.

The letters to Vil'kina and Vengerova again bring to mind Nastas'ia Filippovna, whose letters to Aglaia, her rival for Myshkin's love, similarly imply a double addressee and exhibit a hysterical, discursive style. Nastas'ia Filippovna's letters reveal the entwinement of lesbian desire and female rivalry, which, as in the case of Gippius, can be read as "gynosocial desire" between women. Here is an epistolary example of the way Nastas'ia Filippovna declares her love for Aglaia: "I love you. . . . I am in love with you. . . . You know, I think you should love me. You are for me the same as you are for him: a pure spirit; an angel. . . . What does my passion for you matter to you? Now you are already mine, I shall be all my life beside you. . . . Your marriage [to Myshkin] and mine [to Rogozhin] are to take place together: thus we have arranged it."[40]

If Gippius's epistolary prose and diaries simply revealed the feelings and behavior of yet another "hysterical woman," they would not hold our interest very long. Her epistolary fainting spells, bouts of illness, and feelings of abandonment and victimization are typical symptoms of hysteria, the most common neurasthenic illness among women in the fin de siècle. The symptoms interest us because they reveal Gippius's decadent economy of desire, shedding light on her project of life creation, whose agent was what she called a higher, miraculous form of love. Since this kind of love was virtually unattainable, she at times tricked herself by replacing it with enervated, decadent alternatives. These included cerebral abstinence that stimulated the nervous system, especially in cases of erotic triangulation, and solipsistic unrequited love. In the quest for miraculous love, Gippius frequently privileged unrequited love as if it were the closest substitute for fusion with God in divine love: "There is no miraculous final love," wrote Gippius in *Contes d'amour* in 1893, "the love that comes closest to it is unrequited, that is, not the same but different on both sides. Should I myself fall in love with someone, and not know whether or not he loves me, I will do everything in my power not to know it to the very end. And should it appear to me that [he loves me] I won't want that; I will kill his love in the name of mine."[41]

The affair with Volynsky, especially during the years 1895–96, seemed to come closer to her erotic ideal than the involvements with Minsky, Chervinsky, Vil'kina, or Vengerova, even though Gippius would claim that Volynsky was just as incapable of experiencing a "miraculous" love as the others. Alienated by his Jewish faith (as he was, according to her, by her love of Christ), repelled by his Semitic features, and disheartened by his lack of aesthetic refinement, she nevertheless hoped that they would become one in a Platonic, androgynous union that would transcend gender.[42] "[I] want such a union between us as if [we were] inseparably woven together," wrote Gippius to Volynsky on November 23, 1896.[43] During those years they lived together in the hotel Palais-Royal on Pushkin Street—the meeting place of the editorial board of the *Northern Herald*—for reasons other than carrying on a sexual affair. In fact she may have placed greater hope in Volynsky because she considered him asexual. According to Gippius, he had lived ascetically for ten years and promised to be "pure" for the rest of his life![44] Although Gippius's letters to him display her characteristic possessiveness and ambivalence, the epistolary outpourings of love seem less manipulative than in her love letters to others. They contain fewer statements of the "I almost love you" variety than her other epistles of the 1890s.

The letters to Volynsky reveal the familiar configuration of overlapping multiple love affairs. In fits of jealous rage, Gippius accused Volynsky and Minsky of intentionally tormenting her. But then she accused Vengerova of the same. A masterful manipulator, she played her lovers off against each other, in letters and in poems. The 1895 poem "Follow Me" ("Idi za mnoi") was written in such a way that it could be applied to Volynsky, Minsky, or Vengerova; elsewhere Gippius wrote that it was dedicated "to no one, but each one thought that it was to him or her."[45] The poem articulates the persona's desire, formulated in the imperative mood, for the addressee to love her even after death.

It appears then that, like her novelistic predecessor Nastas'ia Filippovna, she searched for her own Prince Myshkin who would love her with a higher spiritual love, but most of these men, with the possible exception of Volynsky, wanted sex, not a Platonic love affair. In her letters to Minsky, she regularly reminded him that if he wanted her body, he should look elsewhere, that "she [would] never become his lover."[46] "I don't want human flesh (*chelovechina*)," wrote Gippius in 1892.[47] *Chelovechina,* which evokes *mertvechina* (dead flesh), also refers to human flesh as something edible (by analogy with *goviadina* [beef] and other words for meat). She likened sexual contact with Minsky to dirtying her dress.[48] "You want to kiss me and try to accomplish it by any means possible. In the same way as all roads lead to Rome, all reconciliations that you offer me lead to kissing. That won't happen," she insisted, although in one of her letters, she referred to a "tortuously ugly union" with him.[49] What becomes palpably clear from Gippius's correspondence with Minsky is her erotophobia.

Withholding her body from Minsky, she showered him with letters, sometimes up to five a day. She often described the letters in bodily terms as if they were substitutes for sexual contact. The converse of this dynamic—the body becoming a substitute for writing—emerged in Gippius's letters to Zinaida Vengerova, which are just as passionate, possessive, and ambivalent as those to Minsky. She reproached Vengerova for not loving her, writing too infrequently, and betraying her to the other members of their claustrophobic coterie, that is, to Minsky and Vil'kina. "I would like to become for you the only one. . . . I want you *separately,* you alone, loving me yourself and for yourself. . . . I made plans for you to replace . . . *Contes d'amour,*" about which nobody knows, wrote Gippius to Vengerova in 1897. Lying to Vengerova that she had burned her diary of love affairs, she expected her to take its place, becoming that body on which Gippius would secretly inscribe her passion.[50] Although only privately, like her contemporaries, she deployed the female body as a trope of writing.

In another example of domesticating this poetic trope, Gippius wrote Vengerova that on her birthday, a day she dedicated to their past together, she wore the pink blouse that Vengerova liked and fixed her hair in a special way. Gippius wrote her letters to Vengerova on thick red paper, meant only for her, and Vengerova wrote hers on gray stationery. In the birthday letter to Vengerova, Gippius fantasized about making their correspondence into a red and gray dress.[51] In a subsequent letter, she lamented that the dress would be mostly red, with only a narrow gray band at the bottom. Beyond this metaphorical rendering of a standard epistolary reproach—that the addressee didn't write enough—is a more striking message: she wanted to cover her own body with the intimate language of their correspondence. Fearing sexual intimacy in the flesh, she longed for it in the realm of discourse. Words became fetish substitutes for sex, and the exchange of letters, like the red and gray dress she was designing, became a symbolic veil, which in this case served to conceal her uncertain sex.

What we see then is a conflation of the ambivalent, melodramatic discourse of Gippius's love letters and their metaphoric embodiment. Gippius pointed to their embodiment herself in diary descriptions of her epistolary prose. Recounting her strained relations with Chervinsky, another Minsky rival, in *Contes d'amour* on September 20, 1893, Gippius described their conflict in terms of their correspondence. The entry opened with a depiction of their relations as a series of dramatic body gestures provoked by an epistolary exchange; at the end of the entry, the discourse shifted to a philosophical level: her letters became metaphors of words made flesh as she lifted the domesticated variant of the trope in her correspondence with Vengerova to a spiritual plane by invoking Christ's sacred body, which is the word made flesh.

What is most striking here is that Gippius wrote nothing of substance about her relations with Chervinsky as she overlaid one form of intimate narrative with another (diary on letter). This may be explained by the diary genre in which the letter is embedded. The genre presupposes writing for oneself, which in this instance helps explain the erasure of the letters' contents. My main point, however, is that the lovers' spat was conducted on the battlefield of gestures, not just words: "'Here is your letter, I didn't read it. Return my last letter.' He grabbed the poor letter, with the sprig of lilies of the valley, and tore it up angrily. 'Now I know, you couldn't answer; you didn't know how I needed an answer. This letter should not have been left without an answer. I will return yours. I couldn't then,' [he says]. . . . 'Now I don't need it anymore.'"[52]

Gippius spoke of the reception of Chervinsky's letter in gestural terms, as if revealing the inaccessibility of intimate experience to language. As in melodrama, she highlighted physical gestures, which effectively replace the verbal content, turning the diary into a public genre and the reader into a spectator who is given access to only part of the picture. While the reader concludes from the exchange that it marks the end of their relationship, it was not. We learn in the next breath that she had written Chervinsky another letter, perpetuating the seesaw discourse of their tangled affair, which only added fuel to her ever-growing unexpended desire.

Typically for Gippius, the diary entry in question ended on a high note, as she shifted from the hostile, open-ended exchange with Chervinsky to a philosophical plane. She attained philosophical insight in the solitary space of writing. Narrative closure took place there: rising above melodrama, she spoke about the philosophical meaning of her letters. She lifted bodily gesture from the realm of psychological vacillation to the level of philosophical metaphor. The closing comment regarding the relationship with Chervinsky raised it from the quotidian to the Platonic, whose highest form of love is "birth in beauty":

> Upon leaving, I left him a letter. Why? Oh, these letters of mine! Oh, how they burn me, each one, even the innocent ones, not with their contents, but with the very fact [of their existence]! I love my letters, I value them—and I send them off like small, helpless children, [exposing them] to people's cold, uncomprehending gaze. I never lie in letters. No one knows what a piece of raw meat my letters are! What a rare gift! Yes, rare. Even if they are poor, I give them what I have, with pain in my heart, with faith in words. I don't write letters from pride [*samoliubie*], but afterward they turn against my pride. I know this, and I sacrifice my pride to the word. And in my letter [to Chervinsky] there was truth, again the same old truth, only without hope. Lord, forgive me for these poor little children, with whom I am so cruel at times.[53]

The metaphoric embodiment of her epistolary prose has both New Testament and Platonic connotations. It evokes the image of Christ as the word made flesh; it paraphrases Socrates, who claims in *Phaedrus* that discourse "ought to be constructed like a living creature, with its own body." Discourse "veritably written in the soul of the listener," continues Socrates, "ought to be accounted a man's legitimate children."[54] Like Diotima in the *Symposium*, Gippius rendered transcendent thought and feeling by means of birthing metaphors. Rejecting the procreative function of her sex, she associated letter writing with childbirth. Her designation of her letters as "small helpless children," whom she compared to "a piece of raw meat," is echoed in a March 4, 1895, diary entry about her "good letters" to Volynsky, which she also called "my children."[55] She insisted that she could write letters only to a person "with whom she [was] linked by a bodily thread," as if by an umbilical cord.[56] Her correspondent, the one with whom she has that intimate bond, fathered the letter-child in the Platonic sense, providing the stored erotic energy for what is an epistolary immaculate conception or what Diotima calls "birth in beauty."

Gippius hoped that her letters would be received with love and understanding, although she suspected that they would be subjected to "a cold, uncomprehending gaze." She feared that the recipient of the letter would only peek into her soul without accepting the offer of intimacy. In an undated letter to Vengerova, she spoke of her letters as "helpless, submissive, unable to protect their author."[57] This again seems to refer to Socrates' statement in *Phaedrus* that "once a thing is put in writing, the composition . . . [gets] into the hands of . . . those who have no business with it. . . . [W]hen it is ill-treated and unfairly abused it always needs its parent to come to its help, being unable to defend or help itself."[58] In the diary entry regarding her correspondence with Chervinsky, Gippius made another typical flip-flop: she implied that she was a bad epistolary mother because she abandoned her children by sending them off to bad fathers. When she confirmed the father's suspected "cold, uncomprehending gaze," she became a cruel, destructive parent who asked her correspondent to destroy the epistolary offspring, despite its helplessness.[59]

In conclusion, Gippius's diary and letters from the 1890s are not just a curious mixture of self-aggrandizing, high-minded discourse and silly erotic play. They reveal her desire for transcendence, especially of the physical body, a desire that helped motivate her enervated ambivalence. They also reveal her search for abstract, Platonic motherhood. Instead of becoming a mother biologically, she acted out maternity in letters and poems—the love children of her, so to speak, immaculate conceptions. In a self-aggrandizing decadent fantasy, Gippius staged her epistolary self as the Holy Virgin bringing a child into this world to be sacrificed. This analogy, however, did not fully render her conflicted epistolary desire: the Virgin turned into a fatal Medea who sacrifices her children on the erotic battlefield of vengeance. What began as an epistolary triangle modeled on the Holy Family, in which the letter is equated with the Christ Child, became vengeful: Gippius ended up wreaking havoc in the manner of the decadent femme fatale whose desire is frequently cerebral.

## Toward a Triple Union

As early as 1895, Gippius articulated a conceptual model of triangular desire. In a letter to Minsky that year, she wrote: "A third person is needed for you to see me."[60] (The third person was Volynsky.) After 1899, when the Merezhkovskys began to think about creating their Church of the Third Testament, based on the book of Revelation and the reign of the Holy Spirit, Gippius's view of triangular desire became increasingly ideological. Describing their plans for a new church in 1900, she wrote in her diary: "We needed a third person to divide us, while uniting with us."[61]

Her initial triangular affairs, characterized by multiplicity in love, reflected an eroticized though cerebral will to power. In the early 1900s, Gippius, like Solov'ev before her, began articulating a life practice that would convert erotic energy into the transfiguration of life. A decadent utopian, she developed the view that stored erotic excess—produced by triangulation—should be channeled into a single purposeful triangle. Instead of an erotic economy in which the stored energy dissipated into the kind of frivolous rivalries and quarrels that characterized her love life of the 1890s, she began to link triangulation to a religious cause. It is as if Gippius had taken to heart the phantasmic aspect of Solov'ev's erotic utopia, which, as we learn in the culmination of *The Meaning of Love,* would be instantiated by the release of the stored sexual energy of all heretofore celibate erotic unions. As a first step, she concluded that a third person was needed to invigorate her partnership with Merezhkovsky, who would become one of the three members of such a purposeful triangle—the triple union—that would initiate the utopian task of transfiguring life.

In the early twentieth century, Gippius came to view her private life as a medium of social and religious change. Erotic, religious, and social desire became entwined; the triple union, conceived as a legitimate alternative to the procreative family, became the instrument of transfigurative desire premised on the containment and future expenditure of erotic excess. This arrangement, I suggest, had its historical roots in Chernyshevsky's appreciation of the energizing power of triangulation and its use for ideological purposes.

Just as in the case of her celibate marriage, Gippius seems to have appropriated Chernyshevsky's concept of the triple union but applied it to a different cause.[62] Chernyshevsky believed that the expansion of traditional marriage into a union of three was the agent of radical social change. So even the structure of Chernyshevsky's and Gippius's vision of the triple union was similar. Both consisted of a bond between fundamentally similar men whose efforts to transform the world are stimulated by a woman. The dedication to social revolution of Lopukhov and Alexander Kirsanov, both medical students and former roommates, is mediated by Vera Pavlovna, who, as it turns out, is unprepared for the socially unconventional role of mediatrix. Instead of forming a triple union with the two men, she wants a proper marriage—with Kirsanov—prompting the honorable Lopukhov to feign suicide! While Chernyshevsky's heroine in *What Is to Be Done?* is unready for the radical role, Gippius showed no such hesitation. In line with Kosofsky Sedgwick's view of eros, which builds on Rene Girard's theory of erotic love as mimetic or triangulated, she was ready to serve as the mediator of homosocial desire.[63] As it turns out, Gippius was more liberated than Vera Pavlovna.

The Merezhkovskys first attempted to form a triple union at the beginning of the 1890s with Ol'ga Nilova, an obscure figure, perhaps from the theatrical world. Merezhkovsky wrote her love letters. Gippius, who gave herself the name Snow Queen in this triangle, formed a playful erotic alliance with Nilova, but there is no indication that it had any ideological connotations.[64] Their relationship with Volynsky, however, had from the beginning the goal of an intellectual alliance despite the rumors that Gippius was having an affair with him. As Alexander Sobolev has pointed out, it contained an important ingredient of their later triple union: a trip abroad.[65] Like so many Russians of the time, the Merezhkovskys and Volynsky traveled to Italy together in 1896.[66] Their Italian journey resulted in two major books about Leonardo: a popular novel by Merezhkovsky and a scholarly study by Volynsky.[67]

In 1901 Gippius began actively seeking someone to form a triple union with her and Merezhkovsky; this union would function as the secret, conspiratorial nucleus of the Church of the Third Testament. Based on an apocalyptic blueprint, it was to replace the church based on the Old and New Testaments, marking the end of history and the transformation of nature.[68] In the initial phase of their plan, the Merezhkovskys looked for an appropriate third partner; the "indissoluble bond" among the three members of the union would be the secret "inner deed," which would not be disclosed "until the right time." In the meantime, it would propel and empower what they called, in accordance with esoteric Gnostic discourse, the "outer deed," a code phrase for their religious project.[69] The strikingly handsome, refined son of the well-

Zinaida Gippius, Dmitrii Filosofov, and Dmitrii Merezhkovsky

known feminist Anna Filosofova, Dmitrii Filosofov, became the third person.[70] The first and only public manifestations of their conspiratorial religious triad were the Religious-Philosophical Meetings of 1901–3 (see chapter 6). Together with his cousin Sergei Diaghilev and other childhood friends, Filosofov also helped found the journal *World of Art*, which played a key role in the revival of the Russian arts and the polemic against social utilitarianism. Like many at the turn of the century, including Gippius and Merezhkovsky, he became intensely concerned with religious questions, especially as they pertained to the social sphere.

The Merezhkovskys first met Filosofov, a confirmed homosexual, in Italy in 1892. Their acquaintance deepened at the end of the century, when all three worked on *World of Art*. Gippius and Filosofov began to correspond in 1898. In Filosofov's first surviving letter to her, written April 7/19, 1898, we learn that Gippius insisted on an epistolary relationship of complete "biographical honesty," meaning discussion of the intimate details of their personal lives. This was very much the old Gippius, who substituted discourse for physical intimacy. In this case, her immediate motive was her desire to intrude on Filosofov's on-again, off-again love affair with his cousin Diaghilev, which began when the two young men went to Italy on a grand tour after graduation in 1890. Filosofov rebuffed Gippius's request for epistolary intimacy, writing that he was not interested in her marriage, nor did he want to develop the kind of relationship that she had had with Volynsky, which ended in an ugly break-up. Most importantly, he told her that he was not in love with her.[71] To borrow Bely's image of Gippius, Filosofov initially tried to escape her "envelopment."[72]

Merezhkovsky concurred with his wife's selection of Filosofov as the third member of the triple union. In their newly discovered apocalyptic Christian zeal, the Merezhkovskys wanted to rescue him from "drowning" in Diaghilev's waters, characterized by unsublimated sex and lack of metaphysics in the erotic sphere. They tried to enlist the help of Walter Nouvel, a musician and member of Diaghilev's circle who was also in love with Filosofov. Using her old triangulating strategies, Gippius hoped to bring into play Nouvel's erotic rivalry with the more powerful Diaghilev. An object of a tug of war between the Merezhkovskys and the predominantly homosexual Diaghilev circle, Filosofov moved back and forth between them for several years. He apparently struggled against his homosexual identity, which helps to explain his reason for turning to the Merezhkovskys, but after suffering a nervous breakdown, Filosofov went back to his lover Diaghilev in late 1901–2. They again traveled to Europe and spent time in the famous clinic of Richard von Krafft-Ebing in Graz, which specialized in treating neurasthenia and sexual "degeneracy," including homosexuality. Filosofov's reason for taking Krafft-Ebing's cure may have been the result of an effort to contain homoerotic desire, which he would try to do while living with the Merezhkovskys.[73]

According to Bely, both Filosofov and Gippius were interested in psychopathology and were reading *Psychopathia Sexualis* at the end of 1906 or the beginning of 1907.[74] Her sister Tatiana wrote her at the end of 1906 that she is reading Krafft-Ebing's book and will send it to her.[75] Earlier, in 1898, Gippius had referred to Volynsky's "psychopathology," suggesting that she was familiar with degeneration theory already then.[76] In all likelihood, Gippius considered herself a "degenerate" and read psychopathological literature more extensively than she acknowledged. Yet for all intents and purposes she seems to have circumvented the discourse of psychopathology, raising the questions of sex and gender from the physiological to the metaphysical sphere and erasing thereby the palpable physical body from her writing. For that matter, we can consider her celebration of unrequited love—the best possible substitute for divine eros, according to Gippius—as a veritable screen concealing the mystery of her body and physiology. Suppressing them, at least on the page, she gave voice to a view of sexuality that promoted a utopian and metaphysical perspective on erotic love at the expense of a psychological one. By disavowing psychological insight into her own sexuality, she looked for an answer located outside her body—in the divine sphere.

As to Filosofov's seesaw relationship with the Merezhkovskys, he made a final decision in their favor in 1903, became a permanent member of their household in 1906, and lived with them for fifteen difficult years. Several years before Filosofov became a committed member of their triple union, the Merezhkovskys were the focal point of a circle, consisting of Rozanov, Filosofov, Nouvel, Alexander Benois, Bakst, Vladimir Gippius, and Petr Pertsov (later the editor of Gippius's journal *New Way* [*Novyi Put'*]), that discussed the "'unsolved' riddle of sex" in relation to God. This intertwining of religion and sex, which corresponded to the epoch's decadent focus on sex in relation to religious feelings, developed under the influence of Solov'ev's eroticized view of religion. According to Gippius, "many [in the circle] desired God as a justification for sex."[77] Rozanov in particular emphasized its divinity. According to him, Merezhkovsky remarked during those years that "'God emerged from the vulva; God had to have emerged from the vulva—precisely and only from it.' Now the scoundrel has forgotten about it," wrote Rozanov to Gippius in 1908, "but then . . . it surprised me, and I remembered it."[78]

With the exception of Rozanov, the members of the group wanted to separate sex from procreation. It appears that some tried to reinvent the sex act by creating a new form of erotic union based on a relationship of equality between partners. Genital sex, according to Gippius, made such equality impossible. In the words of Anton Kartashev, then a young docent of the Theological Academy, who in 1917 became the last procurator of the Holy Synod, Gippius preached celibacy and the abolition of childbearing to her friends, including Blok and Bely.[79] In a letter to Filosofov in 1905, she claimed that she lacked "procreative feeling" (*rodovoe chuvstvo*)—a euphemism for heterosexual desire and the will to procreate. In the same letter, she tied her disdain for heterosexual union to a polymorphous sexual sensibility, claiming that she was capable of "lusting" for anybody, that her sexuality made no gender distinctions.[80] What remains unclear in this self-disclosure, however, is whether it suggests the transcendence not only of gender but also of sex.

Several years later, in fact, Gippius proposed to abolish the sex act altogether. Her statement about denaturing sex paraphrased Solov'ev, who wrote in *The Meaning of Love* that the expenditure of sexual energy "outward," in reproduction, should be turned "inward," resulting in an androgynous collectivity in love. In Gippius's words, "the act [as it exists in nature] is directed backwards, downwards, into generation, childbirth. The abolition of procreation abolishes the [sex] act, of its own accord—not by any law, but because of its having become an unlawful state. Conversely we must . . . assert the physical transfiguration of the flesh here."[81] Although opaque, this comment on procreation reflects her grappling with the physical transfiguration of the body: whether with the end of procreation the sex organs will simply become vestigial, or will the body be transformed. Merezhkovsky, like Solov'ev, imagined an erotic union that transcends nature by transfiguring the body.

It was as if the Merezhkovskys wanted to tamper with the part of the physical body that is most intimately tied to its sex and biological origin. Around 1905 Merezhkovsky and Filosofov toyed with the possibility that the procreative sex act would be replaced by "some other common single act . . ., equally powerful in its sensation of union and corporeality." Gippius saw in this vestiges of the old animal law and old procreative psychology, which, according to her, had to be transcended.[82] As a lifelong proponent of the unfinalizability of erotic love, she felt that the "mystery of the ultimate transfiguration of sex cannot and should not be found; . . . the mystery of sex should not become clear and definitively resolved."[83]

We should not forget, however, the link between these rather delirious fantasies and the epoch's fear of sex and disease, which, if considered from such a vantage point, mediates the terror inspired by the phallic woman or, in the case of female sexuality, of penetration. Gippius's proposed substitute for sexual intercourse was the kiss containing God's spark, a nonintrusive, momentary bodily fusion drained of corporeality. Premised on the partners' equality, it represented for her Solov'ev's androgynous ideal of the "two in one," all the while preserving the uniqueness of each individual. "I like kisses. In a kiss both are equal," wrote Gippius in *Contes d'amour*.[84] In the essay "Amorousness" ("Vliublennost'," 1904), she developed a Solov'evian argument for reclaiming the kiss from carnal passion: "Desire [and] passion stole the kiss from love [*vliublennost'*] because of greed—a long time ago, when it was still asleep—adapted it [the kiss] to their own needs, altering it by dyeing it another color. In actuality [desire and passion] don't need it at all. Animals don't have it; they implement the law [of procreation] honestly."[85]

For Gippius, the kiss was an erotic union that abolishes procreation and transcends carnal lust. Replacing the sex act, it represents the kind of eroticized chastity and disembodied erotic union that she desired. She associated the kiss with Christ, who offered the hope of resurrection to humankind and freed it from nature and the prison of the body. According to Gippius, the kiss did not exist before Christ because the Old Testament worshiped nature and the procreative ideal.[86] "The entire meaning of my kiss," wrote Gippius, "is that it is not a step to that form of love. . . . A hint of possibility. It is a thought or feeling for which there are no words as yet. It is not that! It is not that! But I know: one can deepen the precipice. I can't—so be it! But it will happen. One can. To the heavens. To God. To Christ."[87]

For Rozanov, who was close to Gippius in those years, the kiss was associated with sex and procreation; in contrast to her timorous, disembodied kiss, his was bloody and physical.[88] Rozanov celebrated circumcision as the site of the Jewish God's procreative kiss, marking the male betrothal to God in a union with homosexual implications (see chapter 7).

The triple union with Filosofov, documented in Gippius's diary *About the Past* (*O byvshem*), took shape in the context of their religious project.[89] Their first secret religious service took place in the Merezhkovsky apartment on March 29, 1901; it was Holy Thursday, which commemorates the Last Supper. The diary entry in which she recorded the event was written on December 24—Christmas eve according to the new style—the same year. Gippius framed their ritual initiation into the new church with the birth, death, and resurrection of Christ, the prototype of the new man of the Third Testament. On the evening before the ritual service, Gippius fell into a long, deep sleep in the waiting room of an unfamiliar doctor. She wrote later that it was "as if I had died . . . [and] my spirit had been taken from me for five consecutive hours" (Gippius-Merezhkovskaia,107). The experience reenacted symbolically Christ's death and resurrection. After she arrived home in the middle of the night, she sewed the ritual coverlets for the cross and the chalice to cover and unveil the Eucharist. During the liturgy, which they performed the next night, they read the passage from the Gospel in which Christ enjoins his disciples to leave their fathers and mothers and follow him, signifying their severance of all past relations and the establishment of new nonbiological bonds.[90]

The number three, associated with the Holy Trinity, informed all aspects of the liturgy, which they planned in great detail. The liturgy was intended as a wedding ritual, which included the taking of the Eucharist. In subsequent years, other people took part in their Thursday services, but the number was always small.[91] In a later diary entry, Gippius described their Thursdays as "quiet 'suppers of Love,'" fusing Christian and Platonic mythology by invoking two kinds of "banquets": Christ's Last Supper and Plato's symposium.[92] During the first ceremony, the threesome removed all rings (Gippius had seven) associated with past relationships and replaced them with crosses, which they hung around one another's necks, to mark the Trinitarian wedding. The equality of each member was symbolized by each one administering the Eucharist to the others separately. Describing their relationship in another context, Gippius wrote that "Dmitrii Sergeevich . . . is equal to me; I . . . am equal to him; Filosofov . . . is equal to me; I . . . am equal to him."[93] Unlike the wedding in Tiflis, this one was filled with ritual. Gippius even wore a long white garment, not a dress but a nightgown that she had never worn before. The virginal connotation of this garb was purely symbolic since no actual defloration would take place.

In the fall of 1901, the short-lived and shaky union was dissolved, and Filosofov went back to Diaghilev. He returned to the Merezhkovsky fold in 1903. It was not till after the collapse of the Religious-Philosophical Meetings in 1903 (see chapter 6), the demise of the journal *New Way* (*Novyi put'*) in 1904, and the 1905 revolution that they began to live together as a "married" threesome. In a letter from Paris to Briusov in 1906, Gippius wrote that they felt like newlyweds, enjoying their new *marriage à trois* (*troebrachnost'*).[94]

Just as with Volynsky, this attempt to create a triple union was marked by a joint journey, first to the Crimea, then to Paris. But unlike the Italian trip with Volynsky, which had the goal of immersing them in Renaissance art, this journey reenacted Christ's forty-day sojourn in the desert and was based on the antithesis of desert and world in early Christianity.[95] In a letter to Diaghilev's stepmother on August 11, 1905, Gippius wrote that their going to Paris should not be equated with going to the monastery: it was not "permanent seclusion, but rather like a desert retreat, . . . a joint desert, the creation of a strong field camp."[96]

The description evokes Christ's sojourn in the desert for forty days. Its metaphors combine hope for purification with a note of militancy; indeed, in Paris they proselytized their religion, though without much success.

In the same letter to Diaghileva, who was also Filosofov's aunt and a potential member of their religious cult, Gippius wrote that abandoning their old life and personal ties was necessary to establish the new religious cell. Gippius used the term *iacheika,* meaning underground political cell, which unlike the English does not also denote a monk's abode or a prison compartment. The trip was necessary for the emergence of the "new man," because in their old environment they would inevitably fall back into behaviors associated with the "old man," a reference to Paul's words that Christ came to renew Adam of the Old Testament. The latter trapped them in their old ways, making the Trinitarian relationship among them impossible. Gippius also described the journey as a rearticulation of spatial relations, using an architectural metaphor to depict their desired spiritual progress. The image of the stone foundation on which their new house would stand evokes Christ's words about Peter as the rock grounding the new religion:

> There all people will be at an equal remove, at an equal distance, from each of us, and if anyone comes close, . . . it will be to us three, to our union, i.e., in a new way; here each of us has his old, previous ties; and in associating with them, with his close friends individually, each of us inevitably returns to the past, becomes for that time an "ancient man." And as a "triad," the three of us cease to exist for that time. . . . The old threads that join us . . . are what we want to break, in order to bind ourselves more tightly with new ones. And at first we will want to bind ourselves together with these new ones. . . . It seems to me that only on such a foundation, verily one of stone, can a house rest; and the communal erotic life of people can rest only on a common faith in the one God.[97]

Filosofov wrote in a similar vein to his aunt about their 1905 trial journey to Crimea before the trip to Paris. He compared Oreanda, where they lived in Crimea, to the Greek island of Patmos, on which, according to some sources, John wrote Revelation:

> Oreanda, ancient Greece. Nothing velvety or filthy, nothing Russian or quotidian. A severity of lines, the distance of the horizon, classical simplicity. We sat below, at the very sea, which splashed noisily at our feet. Dmitrii [Merezhkovsky] read a chapter of the Apocalypse. And it was good. One felt that John had written his

> mysterious book on an island, by the sea, and from time to time divine shadows rushed over the sea. Afterward, having clambered high up a mountain to a rotunda consisting of a semicircle of columns, a semicircle coinciding magically with the semicircle of the horizon, the three of us each read a psalm. It was joyous, majestic. Then Dmitrii read chapter six of Matthew. We returned home late, tired but lucid.[98]

Filosofov's Crimea resembles ancient Greece; its aesthetic austerity evokes the space of the desert fathers, a far cry from Paris. Although the underlying reason for their trip to Paris was the failure of the Merezhkovsky "cause" in Russia, the trio articulated the sojourn as leaving worldly cares behind in search of the Kingdom of God. Writing to Bely, Merezhkovsky described Paris as "a human desert" and the south of France as "God's desert," referring to their trip as "our desert wandering."[99]

From the outside, the Merezhkovsky triple union seemed to be a functional arrangement that served their religious and political cause. They even wrote a play about the 1905 revolution together called *Color of the Poppy* (*Makov tsvet*, 1908). Others began to see them as a trio, addressing letters to all three of them, as if they indeed formed a single body. Ivanov, for example, began his letters to them as "dear trio" (*dorogoe trio*).[100] Inside the triple union, however, there was friction from the very beginning. Its main source was Gippius's unrequited love for Filosofov. In describing her erotic feelings, she would tell him that they brought her closer to divine erotic experience. In a letter to Filosofov's aunt, Gippius wrote of her love for him as the most important spiritual event in her life.[101] In the summer of 1905, shortly before their trip to Paris, she tried to seduce Filosofov. He was repelled by the encounter and let her know about his feelings of disgust in no uncertain terms: "Although my spirit . . . is . . . drawn to you, there has grown in me a kind of hatred for your flesh that is rooted in something physiological. At times it is almost pathological. For example, today you used my cigarette holder, and I can no longer use it because it arouses in me a specific feeling of disgust. . . . [B]efore we were intimate that wouldn't have happened. . . . [T]here has arisen between you and me some kind of fact that causes me to feel disgust in the highest degree, to feel a purely physical nausea."[102]

Filosofov's rude rejection must have been very hurtful. Implying that Gippius fetishized his cigarette holder, he wrote that she had contaminated it, just as she had defiled, or attempted to defile, his phallus. His comments, in fact, reveal the misogynist response of a fin-de-siècle male to a masculinized woman, among whose accoutrements was smoking with the help of a phallic cigarette holder. Although he admitted his pathological aversion to her body, the female stereotype that he evoked resembles Gippius's public image, one that may have both attracted and repelled Filosofov.

Substituting physical intimacy with fetishist, epistolary discourse, Gippius wrote Filosofov about her physical ailments. In these letters, she replaced expressions of love with sniffles, coughs, pleurisy, rashes, fever, digestive problems, including irregular bowel movements, nose drops, ointments, and other medications. In employing a medical discourse and its relation to death, which in decadent sensibility was tied to sexual desire, Gippius may have been trying, perhaps unconsciously, to arouse Filosofov. In one of her letters to him, Gippius admitted to loving illness, writing that it brings one closer to death. As I noted in previous chapters, decadence glorified illness and the near-death state. For Gippius, the state of bodily decomposition in an ailing world seemed to offer the possibility of physical intimacy, one that circumvented penetration and genital sex. On an eschatological level, Gippius found in the corrupt, polluted body a readiness for purification in the resurrection. In this sense, the extensive references to ailing flesh can be read as a call for help in which Filosofov was expected to play the role of healer and savior.[103] In a limited, displaced way, the potential double meaning of Gippius's discourse of illness reflects the era's conflation of decadent and religious sensibilities, blurring the boundaries between decadence and utopianism.

During the Paris years, the Merezhkovskys became ambitious and hoped to establish more triads as well as expand theirs into a larger collective. The union of individuals into a harmonious collective symbolizing Christ's body underlay the project of the Church of the Third Testament. After the failed 1905 revolution, Gippius also spoke of their trio as a revolutionary cell. Like Nechaev and other Russian revolutionaries of the past as well as their contemporary Lenin, the Merezhkovskys tried to organize other triple unions modeled on their own to promote their cause. (Lenin, who was very much influenced by *What Is to Be Done?* lived in a triple union with his wife, Nadezhda Krupskaia, and the young revolutionary Inessa Armand.) In the course of those years, the Merezhkovsky circle grew to include Berdiaev; Bely; Poliksena Solov'eva, the philosopher's sister; Serafima P. Remizova, the writer's wife; Marietta Shaginian, who later became an official Soviet writer;

Kartashev; and Gippius's sisters Tat'iana and Natal'ia.[104] The last three formed the only other antiprocreative triple union based on the Merezhkovsky model. They performed a ritual similar to the Merezhkovskys' to initiate their *marriage à trois.* (Kartashev had wanted to become the third member of the Merezhkovsky triumvirate earlier, at the time when Filosofov abandoned them for Diaghilev, but Gippius was not interested.) After a brief period of living with Gippius's younger sisters, Kartashev reverted to more traditional ideas about love and family. He became increasingly frustrated by their "disembodied bisexuality" and "multiplicity in love," accusing all three Gippius sisters of the "heresy of celibacy." Instead of what he called "bloodless Gippiusism," Kartashev wanted an exclusive, personal love that included sex and children.[105] His return to the values of the patriarchal family, the bane of Solov'evian utopianism, marked the end of Kartashev's experiment with an eroticized celibacy, the agent of apocalyptic transfiguration.

In their search for disciples, the Merezhkovskys frequently competed with Viacheslav Ivanov and his wife, Lidiia Zinov'eva-Annibal, whose collective gathered at the Tower, the nickname for their Petersburg apartment. Some, like Bely and Berdiaev, would go there from the Merezhkovsky "field camp," angering Gippius no end. The Ivanovs hosted their meetings, dubbed Socratic symposia, on Wednesdays, and they were regularly attended by large numbers of Petersburg's cultural elite; the first Tower symposium in 1906 was devoted to the meaning of Platonic love. The Ivanovs also actively looked for a third person to join them in their radical enterprise of Dionysian collectivity in love.[106]

While in France, the trio wrote and published a collection of essays on Russia, the revolution, and the autocracy. The essays were influenced by Filosofov and by the circle of socialist revolutionaries close to Boris Savinkov and Il'ia Fondaminsky-Bunakov, whom they tried to convert to their new religion while in Paris. Although some of these socialists expressed an interest in their religious ideas, what is more significant is the Merezhkovskys' conversion to the socialist cause. In response to these new people, Gippius wrote: "We understood the soul of the old Russian revolution there and came to love it. Its truth and falsity. Internally I felt its dark bond with Christ. The possibility of enlightenment and then—of strength."[107] The revolutionary cause fit with the Merezhkovskys' growing preoccupation with social issues during those years. Savinkov, to whom Gippius was particularly close, was the terrorist leader of the secret Fighting Organization of the Socialist Revolutionary party, which carried out the most celebrated terrorist acts of the prerevolutionary period. Around the time of the February Revolution of 1917, they had close ties with Alexander Kerensky and his cohort but always felt revulsion toward the Bolsheviks.[108]

Despite their dreams of a collective union, in the end the Merezhkovskys remained alone in their utopian enterprise; even Filosofov abandoned them, especially because of Gippius's possessiveness—her claim that she and he were one person. Filosofov's break with them was also the result of the characteristic psychodrama of the Merezhkovsky ménage, which he found increasingly unbearable. He resented, for example, Gippius's insistence on making their correspondence a communal affair: "I ask you not to drag my letters through various committees and read them to others," he wrote her in 1916.[109] In 1913, on the eve of the Great War and a year of personal crisis for them, he attacked the project as a whole. Instead of the creation of a larger collective, he saw the "collective withering" of their union. "Our collective is only a symbol," wrote Filosofov to Gippius; "we have neither the strength nor the right to embody it in a popular movement." This was a big disappointment to Filosofov for personal and more general reasons; he conceded that "the only way to remain true to the bridegroom [Christ was] individually. . . . A return to 'primitive Christianity' [was] not acceptable to [them] theoretically, ideologically."[110] The trio stayed together through the war and the revolution. They emigrated together to Warsaw in 1919, where they attempted to create their own alliance with Jozef Pilsudski, the first president of Poland, against the Bolsheviks. Filosofov remained in Poland with Savinkov after Gippius and Merezhkovsky left for Paris in 1920.

Despite the failure of the Merezhkovsky triple union, it was an extraordinary attempt to create an alternative model of family life. Characteristic of early symbolist culture, it represented a palimpsest consisting of cultural layers of different origins. The main cultural sources of the Merezhkovsky experiment were the books of the New Testament (especially Revelation), *What Is to Be Done?* Solov'ev's erotic philosophy, and decadent, or degenerate, sexuality. They worshiped both the historic Christ and the Christ of Revelation. The seminal event for them was Christ's resurrection, heralding the transfiguration of man's body. They also worshiped the Holy Trinity. Like Nikolai Fedorov, Gippius was interested not only in the abstract idea of the Trinity but also in its practical, everyday connotations. Her view of the triple union resembled Fedorov's image of the "indivisible Trinity" as a close-knit friendship or union of three people.[111] During their first liturgy in 1901, a ceremony that could have resulted in their excommunication from the Russian Orthodox Church, Gippius spoke of the indestructibility of their union represented by the "trebling of 'Is'."[112]

The motif of indivisibility, so important for Gippius psychologically, reflects the concept of the collective body in whose formation she would play the key role. Collectivity in love provided her with an escape from gender and her own body. In keeping with her position between men, Gippius mediated the triple union, viewing it as the earthly reification of the Holy Trinity.[113] During the 1905 revolution, she formulated her theory of the "tripartite structure of the world" in an effort to give social meaning to their Trinitarian religion. According to her dialectical numerology, one refers to the uniqueness and indivisibility of the individual; two to divine erotic love, or the "two in one," which preserves individual uniqueness; and three to community—the "three in one"—which neither destroys the integrity of the individual nor the erotic union. Following the Hegelian triad, this deceptively simple scheme unites everyone into a collective body, ensuring egalitarianism and the satisfaction of everyone's personal, erotic, religious, and social needs.

The triple union offered Gippius a way out of procreative marriage, which in her Solov'evian view only fed the natural cycle. The desired relationship with Filosofov was supposed to enact Solov'ev's idea that the higher form of erotic love must be mediated by God, creating a divine triangle within the larger triadic family. Gippius considered divine love triangular, with Christ as the third person in the configuration: "The one I love—I love for God," proclaimed Gippius in the poem "Truth or Happiness?" ("Pravda ili schast'e," 1904). Revealing herself as a flamboyant decadent in a letter to Filosofov in 1905, she placed Christ in the position of voyeur: "[W]ith you," wrote Gippius, "I could do and feel only what I could do before Christ, under His gaze, and even of necessity in His presence."[114] As we know, Filosofov was not interested, but her justification of desire by Christ's gaze is decadently perverse.[115] The decadent, Christian, and Solov'evian layers of the Merezhkovsky triple union lay on the surface. Less obvious was the Chernyshevskian layer, which had sunk to the bottom of their palimpsest-like life practice. In this layer, Filosofov, whose surname means "son of philosopher," mirrored Merezhkovsky, considered for a time the leading thinker of his generation. This ideological reduplication characterizes the relationship of Lopukhov and Kirsanov in *What Is to Be Done?*

Last but not least was the erotic layer, enacting the romantic idea of unrequited love, which Gippius considered the closest approximation to divine love in this life. In personal terms, unrequited love may have become such an important component of the union because its participants turned out to be sexually incompatible, assuring the celibacy of the ménage a trois. Although Merezhkovsky appeared asexual, he was interested in women, and perhaps men, but wasn't sexually attracted to his wife; Gippius, it appears, was frigid, except with homosexual men and lesbian women; Filosofov seems to have practiced same-sex love only. Incompatible in their sexual preferences, the members of this unusual triangle were psychologically incapable of consummating their love for one another, although they did love one another in the higher spiritual sense. In actuality, however, Filosofov was Gippius's ideal sexual partner because he was unattainable to her. She chose him as the love of her life precisely because he made it possible for her to experience that solitary, decadent love not of this world, the only possible form of erotic love in an untransfigured life—a life defined by a fragmented whole whose parts serve as fetish objects.

## Correspondence in Letters as Bodily Fusion

Despite her many disappointments in love, Gippius continued to seek an androgynous union. Her most successful erotic fusion beyond gender was her epistolary relationship with the young student Vladimir Zlobin, who appeared on the Gippius scene during the First World War, a period of growing estrangement between the Merezhkovskys and Filosofov. During the war, Zlobin was part of a Petersburg student poetry circle patronized by Gippius. Among its members were Larisa Reisner; Mikhail Slonimsky (later one of the Serapion Brothers); the young poets Dmitrii Maizels, Georgii Maslov, and N. Iastrebov; the young Mikhail Sazonov, and Zlobin. (Gippius's relationship with them inspired her *Green Ring* [*Zelenoe kol'tso*, 1916], a play about young men and women who revitalize Russian life with new social and religious ideas.)

This is the same Zlobin who emigrated with the Merezhkovskys to Poland in 1919 and then to Paris in 1920. He was their secretary and loyal ally till Gippius's death in 1944. In *A Difficult Soul* (*Tiazhelaia dusha*), his memoirs about Gippius, Zlobin erased all references to his relationship with her in Russia. Gippius scholars generally represent him as a pale replica of Filosofov, whom he replaced as the third member of the Merezhkovsky triple union after Filosofov chose to stay in Poland. This is probably true, but there is much more to the Gippius-Zlobin story. The unpublished correspondence between Gippius and Zlobin during the war years reflects the kind of ideal love between a man and woman of which she had dreamed all her life. Twenty-five years her junior, he was a man of simple background and was flattered by Gippius's attention. She saw him as that ideal, sexually indeterminate Galatea whom she could mold in accordance with her ideas of a love mediated by Christ, a persona the pliant Zlobin adopted. Besides being flattered, Zlobin also may have been willing to take part in Gippius's erotic experiment, which served as a displaced sex act, because he wished to overcome his homosexuality. Gippius's epistolary sexual fantasy offered him a way to combat same-sex desire.

In his letters to Gippius, Zlobin described his fantasy about sleeping with her in the same bed under her blanket and waking up together. This is a typical example of the kind of epistolary discourse that served as a substitute for sexual relations in Gippius's life, with the correspondents creating physical intimacy on the page, not in life. Emblematic of their union—of the "two in one"—they corresponded by writing on each other's letters. In an undated letter, she wrote him that he was becoming an invisible part of her body and vice versa, as if that "corporeal thread" about which she dreamed in the 1890s had been established between them.[116] She implied that as a result of their epistolary reconstitution of the Platonic androgyne, she could not tell who was who.

Gippius and Zlobin emphasized the sexual indeterminacy of their love by playing gender games with each other's names and related grammatical forms, as if they were invoking Gippius's 1905 poem "You:" ("Ty:"). Alternately masculine and feminine, the poem's persona addresses the moon, which in Russian has both feminine (*luna*) and masculine (*mesiats*) forms, as his/her beloved. The alternating masculine and feminine lines reinforce the bisexual statement. The word *luna* never appears in the text; it is insinuated grammatically by such metaphors as "bridal haze" (*dymka nevestnaia* is grammatically feminine), which evokes the image of a bridal veil. Paradoxically, however, the implied feminine full moon (*luna*) has two phallic horns (*dvurogaia*), as if it were a new moon (*mesiats*). The gendered images of the moon and the alternating gender of the implied lovers, the product of carefully deployed grammatical endings, create sexual ambiguity:

> You are a bright, greedy bonfire* at the crossroads,[117]
>   And a bridal haze** above the valley.
> You are my gay and merciless one*
>   You are my near one and my unknown.**

I have awaited* and I await my clear dawn,**
  I fell in love** with you tirelessly . . .
Now rise, my silver red moon,*
  My two-horned one**—my sweet*—my sweet** . . .

Ты—на распутьи костер ярко—жадный—
  И над долиною дымка невестная . . .
Ты—мой веселый и беспощадный,—
  Ты моя близкая и неизвестная.

Ждал я и жду я зари моей ясной,
  Неутомимо тебя полюбила я . . .
Встань же, мой месяц серебряно-красный,
  Выйди, двурогая,—Милый мой—Милая . . .[118]

As in her letter to Liudmila Vil'kina and in her poetry, Gippius sometimes masqueraded as a man in her letters to Zlobin by using masculine grammatical forms for herself. Zlobin referred to her as "my brother" and "my dear boy or girl"; "I don't know who [you are]," he wrote, "but [you] are my dear little child [*detochka,* which is grammatically feminine]." Gippius, in turn, played with his name Volodia, the diminutive form of Vladimir, by addressing him as "Volia" (or "VOlia, V-Olia"). A combination of the first letter of his name and the diminutive female name Olia (from Ol'ga), *volia* means "will" in Russian; will power not to succumb to same-sex desire is the subtext of their relationship.[119]

Like Liudmila in Fedor Sologub's *Petty Demon,* who plays with the schoolboy Sasha's adolescent sexual ambiguity by dressing him up as a girl, Gippius figured Zlobin as a female concubine, describing him as her odalisque, as if to evoke Baron von Gloeden's beautifully posed images of male youths. She then went on to ask him where her Olia was hiding.[120] The implication was that he had grown up—that he had become a man—which deprived her of the male Pygmalion role, to which she responded by taking over the female role of Olia, revealing her own gender fluidity.

Reflecting her perennial need to oversee the behavior of the members of her cohort, she sometimes invoked the motif of transparency in her letters. For instance, she told Zlobin that she could see him from within: "[Y]our love sometimes makes you crystal clear to my view. . . . You must become transparent to yourself, but to accomplish that don't look into yourself but into me. . . . At yourself—through me."[121] The message is that two could become one in a refracting and reflecting mirror by making their bodies transparent to each other. Instead of uniting in the sex act, they could become one body by serving as each other's mirrors. The result would be bodily fusion without physical penetration.

The suggestion of transparency, however, also has sinister overtones, just as it did in Chernyshevsky's Crystal Palace, to refer back to *What Is to Be Done?* and Dostoevsky's scathing parody of it in *Notes from the Undeground.*[122] The underside of the idyllic union that Gippius imagined is the desire for surveillance, associated with the use of glass architecture by utopian thinkers in Russia and elsewhere. We need only think of Vera Pavlovna's fourth dream, in which she is shown a beautiful glass house. Foucault's writing on prison reform, especially on Jeremy Bentham's Panopticon, the first glass reformatory, has made us fully aware of the repressive implications of transparency, which in the case of desire serves as the agent of its containment. As with Filosofov, Gippius wanted to control Zlobin. What better way than to see directly into his body!

The purpose of their epistolary love affair, from Gippius's point of view, was to transform Zlobin: to convert him to a new kind of love, which did not yet exist but could be created by an androgynous erotic union. According to Gippius, in doing so they would solve the riddle of the Sphinx. This is what she had hoped to accomplish with Filosofov but failed to do; her epistolary affair with Zlobin overlapped with the Merezhkovsky triple union with Filosofov. Gippius and Zlobin inscribed the collective body into their correspondence, creating a playful form of gender slippage as the basis of the renewal or transformation of life. Zlobin turned out to be, at least for a time, the most pliable of her many partners.

Solov'ev, Blok, and Gippius all espoused a conflicted view of love. Placing the highest premium on erotic love because of its power to transfigure life, they insisted on celibacy for those men and women who expected to participate in life's transfiguration. While Solov'ev and Blok did not live up to the ideal, Gippius apparently did. The virginal reputation of Gippius remains intact. Ambivalence and paradox, not to say conflictedness, typified their sensibilities, characterized by enervation and cerebral stimulation of the senses rather than fulfillment of desire.

The case of Gippius is the most puzzling of the three. More than Solov'ev or Blok, Gippius had difficulty inhabiting her body. The most immediate explanation was her indeterminate gender, as she describes it in *Contes d'amour* in 1900: "I do not desire exclusive femininity, just as

I do not desire exclusive masculinity. Each time someone is insulted and dissatisfied within me; with women, my femininity is active, with men—my masculinity. In my thoughts, *my desires* [emphasis mine], in my spirit—I am more a man; in my body—I am more a woman. Yet they are so fused together that I know nothing."[123]

In a philosophical sense, her self-description resonates with Solov'ev's androgynous ideal. As he wrote in *The Meaning of Love*, "the true human being . . . cannot be merely a man or merely a woman, but must be the higher unity of the two. To realize this unity . . . is the direct task of love."[124] Gippius was attracted to androgynous homosexual men. "I like the illusion of possibility—as if [offering] a hint of bisexuality," wrote Gippius; "he [androgynous homosexual] seems to be both woman and man."[125] She also chose homosexual men who were uncomfortable with their sexual identity and for long periods of time—under Gippius's intrusive scrutiny—struggled against it. If we invoke her own mirror metaphor, which she deployed in her correspondence with Zlobin, these men may have mirrored her own struggle against lesbian desire.

Gippius's statements about bisexuality predate Otto Weininger's claim in *Sex and Character* (1903) that no individual is wholly male or wholly female. This sensational book, which had multiple Russian editions, was first translated into Russian in 1909. Gippius referred approvingly to Weininger's theory of gender, even in later years. Her statement that she is mannish intellectually and spiritually reveals the same misogynist prejudices as those expressed by Weininger, who believed that women were defined solely by the body, seeking only sexual gratification. Both misogynist and mannish in some fundamental ways, Gippius figured her desire as male in her diary of love affairs.

The indefiniteness of her psychological, perhaps even physiological, makeup may explain Gippius's celibacy, her search for a love not of this world, and her self-conscious creation of an impenetrable physical gestalt. This bodily self-image reflected, on one hand, the cult of decadent sterility, on the other, the utopianism of Russian apocalyptic thought. Like Solov'ev and Blok, Gippius was an advocate of both. A consummately theatrical personality, she staged herself as desirable but impenetrable, a woman of marble, so to speak. A follower of Solov'ev, she promoted a self-image of impermeability. Solov'ev's androgynous new men and new women would achieve immortality precisely because they had abandoned the earthly genealogical desire to penetrate each other's bodies. Rozanov spoke of Gippius's virginity playfully, addressing her in a letter as "a little she-goat whose udder [unfortunately] has no milk."

He revealed the high degree of discursive intimacy between them when he inquired about her health and well-being by asking how her "little nipples and little breasts" were doing, adding that "it would be sad if no one were caressing them."[126]

The question that remains—one that has been raised behind closed doors for years—is whether her body could be penetrated sexually. Gippius's anatomy has been the subject of much gossip. In a letter to Gippius in 1907, Rozanov wrote that even though she wore a skirt, she was a boy, explaining why he could share with her his base sexual fantasies, which he proceeded to do.[127] Makovsky claimed in 1962 that "Gippius's physiological femaleness was underdeveloped; she could not become a woman, a mother in a complete physical sense."[128] Nina Berberova, a novelist and memoirist who was intimate with Gippius, confirmed Makovsky's claim. According to her, "internally [Gippius] was not a woman." She compared her to Gertrude Stein, to whom Berberova ascribed hermaphroditism.[129] "You've been punished by Aphrodite, you've been sent as a wife a hermaphrodite," wrote an ill-wisher to Merezhkovsky.[130] In a lurid anecdote, Iurii Fel'zen, an émigré author who knew Gippius well, supposedly told another émigré writer, Vasilii Yanovsky, the following story: "[W]ell-informed people tell me that Z[inaida Nikolaevna] has some sort of anatomical defect." Chuckling condescendingly, he added, "[T]hey say that D[mitrii Sergeevich] likes to look through the keyhole."[131]

What did Merezhkovsky spy on? If Gippius indeed was a hermaphrodite, it gives a new twist to the cigarette holder that was an inseparable part of her phallic image. It also gives an ironic twist to Trotsky's tongue-in-cheek description of Gippius as a witch with a tail in *Art and Revolution.* It's a nasty joke to be sure, but his claim that he could not say anything definite "about the length of her tail" because it was hidden from sight has clear sexual connotations, especially in the Freudian 1920s.[132] The most recent reference to Gippius's anatomical abnormality that made it impossible for her to have sexual relations with men appears in Nikolai Slonimsky's memoirs of 1988. Slonimsky, the brother of the Serapion Brother Mikhail Slonimsky, was part of the group of young students, including Zlobin, whom Gippius befriended during the First World War.[133]

I raise the question of Gippius's physiology to make the point that her experiments with alternative family and erotic relationships—celibacy, unconsummated sexual love, erotic triangulation, relations with homosexual men, lesbian love—were motivated not only by utopian desire or decadent fashion but also by Gippius's profound uncertainty about her body and gender. They remain a mystery, although both Gippius and her contemporaries left numerous traces of her psychic and physiological difference. Of all the representatives of the turn of the twentieth century in Russian culture, her behavior offers the best fit for what Elaine Showalter has aptly termed "sexual anarchy."

Gippius, her predecessor Solov'ev, and her younger contemporary Blok all belonged to a period in Russian cultural history characterized by feelings of extreme personal and historical anxiety. One of the striking aspects of the fin de siècle was the production of cultural artifacts of true value from a standpoint of fear. Despite their potentially debilitating feelings of neurasthenia, sexual inadequacy, and genealogical anxiety, these early modernists possessed an extraordinary power of sublimation. Their creative energy transformed their fears by stimulating "birth in beauty" or birth to utopian projects that would transfigure life in history. Gippius was one of the boldest practitioners of utopian life creation, which attempted to reconceptualize the body and gender.[134]

# 6

# Religious-Philosophical Meetings

## Celibacy contra Marriage

On October 8, 1901, Dmitrii Merezhkovsky, Dmitrii Filosofov, Vasilii Rozanov, Vladimir Miroliubov, and Valentin Ternavtsev had a private audience with the general procurator of the Holy Synod Konstantin Pobedonostsev, at which they requested permission to have public gatherings of representatives of the clergy and the intelligentsia to discuss questions of mutual religious and social concern.[1] That same evening Zinaida Gippius and the members of her inner circle, including the artists Alexander Benois and Leon Bakst and the poet Nikolai Minsky, visited Metropolitan Antonii (Vadkovsky) of Petersburg at the Alexander Nevsky Lavra with the purpose of gaining his support.[2] The metropolitan lived in sumptuous quarters, with original eighteenth-century decor and liveried servants. "Narrow runners lay on the floor, which had been polished to a glassy sheen, and the large windows were crammed with tropical plants." They were all struck by Antonii's beautiful white cowl decorated with a diamond cross.[3] Gippius also wrote of a visit to the quarters of Bishop Sergii (Stragorodsky), rector of the Petersburg Theological Academy.[4] Rozanov whispered to her during the visit that the bishop's jam was tastier than the metropolitan's, revealing his characteristic appreciation of the everyday.[5] Permission for what came to be known as the Religious-Philosophical Meetings was granted in November, on the condition that attendance by the public remain limited.

Pobedonostsev's uncharacteristically liberal decision was in all likelihood the result of the efforts of the broad-minded metropolitan and Ternavtsev, an employee of the synod and mediator between the laity and the clergy. The editor of the *Missionary Review* (*Missionerskoe obozrenie*), Vasilii Skvortsov, also played a positive role; an official of the synod, he worked directly under Pobedonostsev. Skvortsov saw the meetings as an opportunity to proselytize Russian Orthodoxy among the intelligentsia.[6]

The first meeting was held on November 29, 1901. It took place in a long, narrow hall of the Imperial Geographic Society, housed in the building of the Ministry of Public Education on Theater Street, across from the theater school. A table covered with green cloth ran the length of the hall. At the head of the table sat Bishop Sergii, the chair of the meetings, and the vice-chair, Archimandrite Sergii (Tikhomirov), rector of the seminary. On the right sat the clergy; on the left, the intelligentsia. In one of the corners stood a "huge, terrifying statue of Buddha," covered with black calico, which Valerii Briusov described as a "Boxer idol."[7] According to Benois, it was not Buddha but a monstrous demon brought back from an expedition to Mongolia or Tibet. It reminded him of the devils "which persecuted [him] in the nightmares of [his] childhood and which were depicted on *lubok* pictures representing the 'Day of Judgment.' This reptile [*gadina*] had real hair on its head and in its beard, and its whole body was covered with dense black fur. Long, curved fangs jutted out of its gaping, blood-colored mouth, its fingers and toes were armed with sharp claws, and long horns jutted from its head. But the most terrifying part were the idol's huge, bulging eyes, with their ferocious, merciless expression."[8]

Gippius, who originated the idea of the Religious-Philosophical Meetings, had "a black, seemingly modest dress" made for the first meeting. "It was designed in such a way that with the slightest movement the pleats would part and a pale pink lining would show through. The impression was that she was naked underneath. She would often recall that dress with evident pleasure. . . . Either because of that dress or because of some of her other whimsies, the church dignitaries nicknamed her the 'white she-devil,'" a mythical demonic figure from Merezhkovsky's popular novel about Leonardo da Vinci.[9]

Gippius considered the Religious-Philosophical Meetings as the only semipublic locus of free speech in Russia during those reactionary years. The gatherings, of which there were twenty-two, were banned by Pobedonostsev in April 1903.[10] Pobedonostsev was enraged by the intelligentsia's attacks on the church and by criticism from within. The desired fusion of the two sides had not taken place. The meeting on April 5, 1903, began with the announcement of the ban.

Revised and censored versions of the transcripts were published in the *New Way* (*Novyi put'*), also the brainchild of Gippius. The expressed purpose of the meetings and the journal was to further the dialogue between those among the intelligentsia who were becoming increasingly concerned with religious questions and members of the clergy who longed for an exchange of views.[11] Despite their cultural importance, the Religious-Philosophical Meetings remain virtually unstudied. Except for Jutte Scherrer's chapter in *Die Petersburger Religiös-Philosophischen Vereinigungen* (1973), a book devoted to the later Religious-Philosophical Society, very little has been written about the earlier meetings, except by the participants themselves.

Among the topics discussed at the meetings were Christianity's relative valuation of celibacy and marriage, the role of sex and procreation in modern life, and Rozanov's criticism of the church. Ironically, the staunch supporters of monastic celibacy expressed views resembling the "antinature" strain of Russian utopian thought of the nineteenth century, as reflected in *The Kreutzer Sonata* and *The Meaning of Love.* References to these works, shaped in part by the contemporary discourse of degeneration, were made at the Religious-Philosophical Meetings. Rozanov, the key figure in these discussions, opposed all forms of antiprocreationism, asserting several years later that the antiprocreative ideal of the 1860s, including Chernyshevsky's, emerged out of "the glass [meaning 'retort'] of homosexuality."[12] At the meetings he insinuated a homosexual subtext into the Christian institution of monasticism and celibate marriages like the Merezhkovskys'.[13]

Besides the transcripts, Gippius, who was active only behind the scenes, is my primary source for the meetings, not only because she left the most extensive descriptions of the gatherings, but also because they were so closely linked to her private concerns, as described in the previous chapter. Merezhkovsky—we would have to assume that Gippius was in agreement with him—sided with Rozanov in criticizing the church for its asceticism and lack of engagement in the concerns of the everyday.

## Religious-Philosophical Meetings

The Religious-Philosophical Meetings were a major event in Russian cultural history. The meeting hall, which held some two hundred people, was usually packed. Where else between 1901 and 1903 did people of such different ideological convictions and social origins have free public discussions regarding religion, sex, and politics? Petersburg's cultural elite, whom the church viewed as dangerous libertines, confronted the ecclesiastical world, whose members differed theologically and politically not only with the intelligentsia but also among themselves. Despite this mutual distrust, both sides tried, especially in the first year, to address the issues constructively and frankly.

The Religious-Philosophical Meetings were attended by the intellectual and spiritual beau monde of Petersburg and by visitors from other cities. Among them were the philosophers N. Berdiaev and P. Florensky (who later became a monk); the poets K. Sluchevsky, V. Briusov, L. Vil'kina-Minsky, P. Solov'eva-Allegro, A. Blok, and his friend E. Ivanov; S. Makovsky, future editor of *Apollon;* S. Diaghilev and his stepmother E. Diaghileva, close friend of the Merezhkovskys; Z. Vengerova, translator and close friend of Gippius; A. P. Filosofova, well-known feminist and Filosofov's mother; composer and music critic V. Nouvel'; theater critic S. Volkonsky; editor of *New Way* P. Pertsov; originator of "mystical anarchism" G. Chulkov; renowned painter I. Repin; M. Novoselov, classicist at Petersburg University and head of a religious circle that included Nikolai Fedorov's student V. Kozhevnikov; M. Men'shikov, contributor to the *New Time;* and many others.[14]

At least in the beginning, members of the "black," or monastic, clergy dominated over the "white," or married, clergy, that is, parish priests. Some of the leading clerics in attendance, besides Bishop Sergii and Archimandrite Sergii, were Archimandrite Antonin (Granovsky), a tough, brilliant church reformer who later became a bishop; Archimandrite Feofan (Bystrov), an authority on asceticism who, ironically, introduced Rasputin to the Russian court several years later; Bishop Innokentii (Borisov) of Kherson and Tavrida; Archimandrite Mikhail (Semenov), professor of canonic law; Fathers T. Nalimov, S. Sollertinsky, and T. Iakshich; radical priest Grigorii Petrov, a socialist who worked among students and workers and later became a member of the second State Duma. Most of the radical priests of the "Group of Thirty-two," active in 1905, attended the meetings. The most prominent lay professors and docents of the Theological Academy were A. Brilliantov, P. Leporsky, N. M. Griniakin, A. Kartashev, and V. Uspensky; Kartashev and Uspensky collaborated with Gippius for a period, as did Ternavtsev. Those among the theologians who were not clerics sat with the intelligentsia.

The published transcripts of the meetings were subject to several kinds of censorship: government, ecclesiastical, and individual (participants often revised their statements themselves). Formal presentations by the clergy and theological professoriate had to be approved by Metropolitan Antonii. When the young docent Kartashev read a short response by Rozanov at one of the meetings, he was reprimanded by the metropolitan. Yet the discussions seem candid, even though they took place among people of very different life experiences. In the words of Gippius, Petersburg's clerical world lived behind an "iron curtain," which began at the Nicholas Railroad Station on Nevsky Prospect and ended at the Alexander Nevsky Lavra.[15] There appears to have been an informal spatial divide between lay and clerical Petersburg, contributing to their virtual ignorance about each other.

Gippius believed that the key result of the Religious-Philosophical Meetings was the acquaintance of the two worlds with each other, which led to the cultural enlightenment of those participants from ecclesiastical circles who were susceptible to change. The meetings helped lift the "iron curtain," wrote Gippius in her memoirs *Living Faces* (*Zhivye litsa*, 1924).[16] Even though their mission of finding supporters for the Church of the Third Testament failed, the Merezhkovskys considered themselves reformers of the "historical church" during those years. Contemporaries referred to Merezhkovsky as Russia's Martin Luther.

The most controversial "reformist" figure at the meetings was Rozanov, not Merezhkovsky. Rozanov, in fact, was the most outspoken critic of the church at the meetings, even though he had many more connections with the clergy than other participants from the intelligentsia. A close collaborator of the Merezhkovskys at the beginning of the century, Rozanov differed from the other members of their inner circle, in part because he was not a product of the fin-de-siècle hothouse with its utopian projects: he lacked the kind of archly constructed biography with mythologizing potential that was a prerequisite for symbolist life creation. Rozanov was an eccentric scion of the provinces, the son of a lowly civil servant who died when Rozanov was four years old. Like so many of his generation, he had a radical nihilist phase, which included veneration of Chernyshevsky and study of the natural sciences prior to discovering religion. Before moving to Petersburg in 1893, he worked as a provincial schoolteacher of history and geography. In Petersburg he became a journalist, publishing primarily in the conservative *New Time*, which distinguished him from the other members of the Merezhkovsky circle, whose politics were liberal.

Considered by many the most original writer of the symbolist era,

Rozanov was a paradoxicalist, whose main subject was the philosophy and physiology of sex and procreation. Nikolai Berdiaev, perhaps still the best known Russian philosopher outside Russia, characterized his ideas as "physiological," not "logical," describing his writing by means of the classical metaphor of embodiment.[17]

As Berdiaev wrote, the centerpiece of the meetings was sex and life in the body.[18] Meetings twelve through sixteen focused on church dogma regarding celibacy and married life: the key question was whether one was superior to the other. The answers were frequently ambiguous, with the shifting battle lines drawn between Rozanov, the monastic clergy, and the intelligentsia. One way that the Merezhkovskys and Rozanov countered the demonization of the body in Christianity was by ascribing metaphysical significance to the "sexual question"; the Merezhkovskys' retort to the repressive sexual regime was to declare the body's potential for godliness, which, they claimed, would take place when it united with the spirit. The union of the two—what they called "consecrated flesh"—could be accomplished only by means of erotic love. This had been Solov'ev's position as well. Like their predecessor's, the Merezhkovskys' defense of the body was essentially discursive without the engagement of its actual physicality. The elevation of physical love to the realm of philosophical discourse maintained the repressive sexual regime while at the same time offending the more conservative members of society. Rozanov's response, also discursive, was, as we will see, far more radical.

From a social perspective, the critics attributed the ambiguous relation between spirit and body in Christian dogma to the alienation of the church from the everyday and from pressing social concerns. Ternavtsev—known as "fiery Valentin"—introduced the issue at the opening meeting. He delivered an impassioned lecture on the importance of life in the here and now, what he called "the truth on earth." "The time is coming for all Christianity to show not only in words, in teachings, but also in deed, that the church holds more than an ideal of the afterlife. The time has come to reveal the Truth about the world hidden in Christianity," announced Ternavtsev, an exegete of the book of Revelation.[19] The lecture put the church on the defensive, while also encouraging the clerical reformists to speak about the need for greater church involvement in real life.

In attempting to reconstruct the history of the Religious-Philosophical Meetings, we must also consider the role played by the circle associated with Diaghilev's journal *World of Art* (*Mir iskusstva*).

The impact of the World of Art movement on Russian culture is well known, and this is not the place to discuss it. What is less known is the flirtation with religion by some of its members at the beginning of the century. Religious ferment contributed to the split of the World of Art group into those who maintained a position of radical aestheticism and others who were caught up in the Russian spiritual renaissance. The latter camp included the Merezhkovskys and Rozanov, who had earlier allied themselves with the World of Art aesthetes, as well as Filosofov, whose alienation from the circle was the result of his growing interest in religion and social issues. But even the confirmed aesthetes Benois, Bakst, and Nouvel experienced a religious crisis and participated in the Religious-Philosophical Meetings, especially in the early stages.[20]

## The Role of Gippius and the Poetics of Privacy

Gippius does not appear in the annals of the Religious-Philosophical Meetings. Only her close acquaintances knew of the important role she played in their organization. Although apparently she spoke at the meetings, her words are not recorded in the published or archival remains of the transcripts.[21] This could not be simply a matter of censorship, especially since she was responsible for the publication of the transcripts in the *New Way*. As Scherrer has pointed out, she must have erased her name herself.[22]

The tantalizing question is why Gippius, an influential figure of the time—whose provocative dress at the meetings reflected her exhibitionism—decided to efface herself on the printed page. My explanation is that Gippius chose for herself the role of ventriloquist: she wanted to be the puppeteer that pulls the strings behind the stage. She had always liked secrecy and mystification. She loved to manipulate people into positions that she had predetermined for them. The public genres of Gippius's self-expression were the lyrical poem, prose fiction, and the philosophical essay. Her private genres were the personal letter and the diary; her private setting of choice was her apartment, whose ambience Andrei Bely invariably described as brown, cinnamon-like, and enveloping.[23] Spinning invisible webs around people was one of Gippius's favorite pastimes.

As we learn from her diary *About the Past* (*O byvshem*), the personal subtext of the official meetings was the creation of an ideological triple union with Filosofov as the secret nucleus of the Church of the Third Testament. Conspiring to insinuate her erotic project into the common domain, she spoke of the meetings as the "outer task" of their "inner task." In other words, she hoped that the meetings would also serve as the catalyst for the expansion of their burgeoning new religion—quite a grandiose plan, which had the purpose of supporting her conflicted relationship with Filosofov and promoting the growth of their church. Gippius's desire, however, remained unconsummated. As she wrote in the diary, "this outer task" was already separated "from [their] inner task" at the first meeting.[24]

As I noted in the previous chapter, it was during this time that Filosofov suffered an emotional breakdown and distanced himself from the Merezhkovskys, even taking a cure in Krafft-Ebing's clinic together with Diaghilev. Having returned to his former lover Diaghilev, he attended the meetings in his company sometimes, which upset Gippius no end. The Merezhkovskys' power struggle with Diaghilev included other members of his family. Gippius succeeded in attracting Diaghilev's stepmother, who was also Filosofov's aunt, to their sect; she tried to ensnare Diaghilev's brother, Iurii, a minor writer who wrote under the pseudonym Chereda and published in *New Way*, but he managed to slip away.[25]

My explanation for Gippius's apparent silence, as I have suggested, is her desire to play ventriloquist, which reveals her task of secretly birthing ideas that her life partners would reproduce. Gippius was a confirmed Platonist, using reproductive metaphors to represent spiritual progeny, whom she affiliated with "children not of the flesh." Many of her contemporaries considered her the creative inspiration and brain power behind her husband's theory of Trinitarianism. We have seen her staging herself as the invisible third person, or mediator, of the familial trinity. Even though Filosofov had taken himself out of the budding triadic relationship at this time, Gippius continued the struggle of bringing him back to the fold. After the first meeting, she insisted that at the next one Filosofov present an essay that the two would write together. Filosofov balked but ended up working on it with Gippius. Claiming illness, he did not come to the meeting, however, and instead of Gippius, Ternavtsev read the coauthored text.[26]

Under pressure Filosofov succumbed to the idea that on January 2, 1902, they would hold a prayer meeting of their invisible inner church. The Merezhkovskys made elaborate preparations for the service. Gippius sewed red cassocks with white velvet crosses on the front, a design on which all three had agreed, and red ribbons with red buttons for the forehead. Filosofov again did not come. The following evening, at the third Religious-Philosophical Meeting, Merezhkovsky gave his lecture on Tolstoy's excommunication, despite the fiasco suffered by their "inner task" the night before. Filosofov, looking like a corpse, came to the lecture in the company of Diaghilev.[27]

Rozanov also had someone else read his prepared presentations in his presence, rarely speaking himself. The ostensible reason for Rozanov's ventriloquism was that he could only speak in his trademark intimate whisper. His interest in the meetings had a personal subtext as well, but his was quite straightforward and public. The fact that he could not divorce his first wife and marry Varvara Dmitrievna Butiagina, his common-law wife, motivated his efforts to reform Russia's antiquated divorce laws and intolerance of illegitimate children.

Unquestionably, the most interesting aspect of Rozanov's biography was his relationship with Apollinaria Suslova, Dostoevsky's dominatrix of the 1860s and prototype of his infernal women, such as Nastas'ia Filippovna in *The Idiot.* Rozanov's affair with Suslova began while he was still in high school and while Dostoevsky was still alive; the couple married in 1880. Sixteen years Rozanov's senior, Suslova, whom he described as a "sectarian Madonna" (Khlystovskaia Bogoroditsa), tormented him as she had the novelist; Rozanov wrote that she liked sex without penetration, having "disdain for semen."[28] The real difficulties began when she refused to give him a divorce, even though she had apparently left Rozanov of her own accord.

Rozanov met Varvara Dmitrievna, the daughter and widow of parish priests, in 1888, and they soon began to live together as husband and wife. Suslova's denial of a divorce to Rozanov was devastating to the devout Varvara Dmitrievna, who gave birth to their six children out of wedlock. Thus it was this "illegitimate" aspect of his private life, not a progressive social agenda, that motivated Rozanov's campaign for the liberalization of divorce laws and for the rights of unwed mothers and illegitimate children. A keenly felt private concern helped fashion Rozanov's unconventional metaphysical discourse, which intermingled religion, intimate bodily detail, and the everyday. In an age that put a premium on interior experience, intimacy became his literary trademark.

So we see that besides individual personal agendas, the Religious-Philosophical Meetings devoted to celibacy and marriage were characterized by a discourse of sexual intimacy, especially notable because of the unique ambience of the gatherings. Unlike Rozanov's rhetorical intimacy, which imitated the act of whispering in someone's ear, Gippius displayed her intimate style in a less public way. Both of their self-consciously constructed discursive masks conflated private concerns and abstract ideas, but his grew out of physiology and the everyday much more than did hers; her reasons were essentially cerebral. As I showed in the last chapter, Gippius focused on creating discursive intimacy in her love letters and diaries, which served as fetish substitutes for intimate physical relations. Inside her intimate circle, she tried to transgress the boundaries of privacy, believing, for instance, in common ownership of private correspondence and diaries.[29] Each member of her triple union, wrote Bely, had a notebook in which the others wrote their private thoughts.[30] Her notion of transparent collective intimacy, which helped drive Filosofov away, was premised on the preservation of a distinction between the public and the private in relation to the outside world, allowing her to play a manipulative role behind the scenes. This was also the case with the meetings. Their relationship to the Merezhkovskys' new religion and especially to Filosofov's role in the triple union remained hidden from public view.

Whereas Gippius's exhibitionism concealed as much as it revealed (she brandished an image of love goddess publicly), Rozanov's flaunting of discursive intimacy was primarily rhetorical, and rhetorically it was often highly unconventional, at times shocking. Some of his best writing displays intimate details of the body (which Gippius artfully concealed), including explicit, though typically unerotic, descriptions of sex organs, the sex act, pregnancy, and childbirth (see chapter 7). Unlike Gippius (and Viacheslav Ivanov, the other guru of symbolist intimacy), Rozanov made no distinction between public and private in his discourse, perhaps because he was not a sectarian and had no desire to be the leader of a conspiratorial new religion.[31] Gippius's diaries were strictly private, available only to certain members of her commune. Rozanov's diary-like books such as *Solitaria* (*Uedinennoe*) and *Fallen Leaves* (*Opavshie list'ia*) were written expressly for public consumption. "Sex in public," to borrow Eric Naiman's apt phrase describing the Soviet 1920s, was Rozanov's subject.[32]

Making sex public, which the discussions between the clergy and the intelligentsia accomplished, resulted in the conflation of private and public, which the clergy would have preferred to keep separate. Sex entered the public discursive sphere even in such an unlikely context as the Religious-Philosophical Meetings; the gatherings participated in the turn-of the-twentieth-century project of making sex discourse, becoming part of what Foucault has described as the "endlessly proliferating economy of the discourse of sex" in modern European cultures.[33]

## Marriage contra Celibacy: Rozanov and Others

In debating the superiority of celibacy or marriage at the Religious-Philosophical Meetings, some speakers invoked Tolstoy and Solov'ev, whose positions on the subject—as we know—were both ambivalent and ambiguous. Christianity's most authoritative text, the New Testament, also treats the relation between celibacy and marriage ambiguously. Fin-de-siècle theories of psychopathology, which hovered over the meetings, were conflicted on the subject as well. All this left the question of preference open to various interpretations, exacerbating the conflict between the two sides and proliferating the economy of sexual discourse.

Part of the ambiguity must be attributed to the commingling of contemporary puritanical and apocalyptic views on celibacy. The "puritans," followers of the later Tolstoy and some members of the black clergy, supported abstinence for moral reasons. The decadent utopians, who expected the new Revelation, as did Solov'ev, propagated abstinence because it was the steppingstone to the transfiguration of the body and the coming of the new man in this life. Complicating the boundaries between the participants further, the ecclesiastic members with an apocalyptic yet ascetic perspective shared some of Solov'ev's views. The underlying reason was their common expectation of the "last coming" in the manner of the early Christians. The key difference, which was at the core of the conflict between them, was that the ecclesiastical side did not consider erotic love the catalyst of apocalyptic transfiguration. Despite this difference, both groups were susceptible to the charge of degeneration, which surfaced several times at the meetings. Needless to say, marriage was discussed primarily for what it meant to men, even though women like Gippius—as we saw in the previous chapter—naturally considered it a woman's issue. Yet she never wrote about it from a woman's perspective. In a socioeconomic and ideological sense, marriage had been a woman's issue in Russia since the 1840s.

Rozanov prepared three presentations in which he championed procreative marriage, assaulting each time what he considered the morbid cult of celibacy in Christianity. He premised each lecture on the claim that the church tolerated marriage as a necessary evil, implicating Christ, especially what he perceived as his preference for death over life, in Christianity's morbidity ("In Christ the world turned rancid [including all of its earthly fruit], especially because of his sweetness," proclaimed Rozanov at a meeting of the later Petersburg Religious-

Philosophical Society.)[34] The poet V. V. Borodaevsky, one of his opponents at the meetings, illustrated Rozanov's quarrel with Christ by quoting from his *Unclear and Uncertain World* (*V mire neiasnogo i nereshennogo*, 1901): "There is the religion of Golgotha, but there is also the religion of Bethlehem. There is the religion of the 'desert' [asceticism], of 'Peter's rock,' but there is also the religion of 'animal herds' surrounding the 'manger.'" Borodaevsky's point is that Rozanov rejected the Crucifixion, the arch-symbol of Christ, and instead rejoiced in the animal body of humans.[35] In fact Rozanov's phallic religion privileged the beginning of the life cycle, not its end, which explains why he considered the manger ontologically and culturally more important than the Crucifixion, and why he made the Old Testament the cornerstone of his religion. Hence Minsky's reference to him at one of the meetings as a new Moses.[36] The monastic as well as the decadent mortification of the flesh had no appeal for Rozanov.

Despite later overt anti-Semitism, Rozanov gave clear preference to Judaism at the Religious-Philosophical Meetings because he viewed it as a life-affirming religion. In his first lecture he focused on what he considered the ancient Judaic rite of newlyweds consummating their marriage in the temple, suggesting that the Orthodox Church introduce a similar practice. In a typical instance of Rozanovian provocation, he recommended that after the wedding married couples remain in church till they have conceived, giving credence to the words of the epithalamic ritual that "marriage is honorable and the bed undefiled." Conflating Old and New Testament imagery, Rozanov described the result of such a practice as "the veil of Fata Morgana falling from the eyes of the world" and "'the church curtain being rent apart."[37] The image of the Fata Morgana, as Rozanov interpreted it, represents the veil of illusion that blinds Christians to the sexual truth, with the curtain symbolizing the hymen that must be broken: blood must be spilled so that nature is replenished. Rozanov was referring to the verse in the New Testament in which the renting apart of the temple curtain at the moment of Christ's death symbolizes the end of the old religion and the victory of the new.[38] His reading was patently polemical: contrary to the Christian meaning of the rent curtain, which is spiritual, the image, as Rozanov read it, divinizes defloration and the sex act.

Such interpretations of biblical imagery helped motivate his explicit references in the presence of the clergy to the blood of defloration, menstrual blood, maternal breasts, genitalia, and childbearing. The first two references reveal his blood fetish, which would take many forms, positive and negative, but always linked to the discursive sphere. The subsequent one reflects his breast fetish; in 1913 he again exposed the female breast in the context of his effort to reform Russian Orthodox views on procreation: "I grew nipples on [the body of] Christianity," wrote Rozanov. Eroticizing maternal breasts, he went on to say: "[T]hey were small, childlike, undeveloped. . . . I caressed them . . . ; pampered them with words. Touched them with my hand. And they became erect. Became heavy, filled with milk."[39] What is doubly striking about this typically Rozanovian image is its self-reflexive aspect: the message of his pampering the nipples with words reveals Rozanov's self-conscious discursivity, reflecting the proliferation of sex as discourse in the Russian fin de siècle.

Rozanov was not just an author who fused sex and religion; he was also a journalist with a very specific social agenda who raised various legal issues related to family life. Each of his presentations at the Religious-Philosophical Meetings dedicated to sex and marriage was organized around a specific example of the inhumanity of the church in relation to marital unions unsanctioned by it and to the plight of children born out of wedlock. At the thirteenth meeting, he focused on the story of infanticide on the Tolstoy estate, in which a woman strangled her child born out of wedlock because of the stigma of illegitimacy. At the fourteenth, he targeted the case of a Pskov civil servant in the time of Nicholas I who married his niece with whom he proceeded to have six or seven children. When church authorities learned of their close kinship, the Holy Synod annulled the marriage, declaring the children illegitimate. At the sixteenth, he told the morbid tale of Moscow's Kalitinkovo Cemetery, describing its mounds as the product of massive burials of illegitimate infants from a local foundling home.

The first of five meetings on the subject of marriage and celibacy opened with a lecture from the church side on marriage as a Christian ideal. The lecture, titled "On Marriage: Psychology of a Sacrament" ("O brake: Psikhologiia tainstva"), was given by Archimandrite Mikhail Semenov, one of the most interesting clergymen participating in the meetings (a convert from Judaism, he later became an Old Believer bishop). Prefacing his lecture with the disclaimer that he would not consider marriage in relation to celibacy, he gave marriage a glowing report in the context of Russian Orthodox canonic law. He stated repeatedly that marriage is sacred, and that contrary to some interpretations of Paul's First Epistle to the Corinthians, marriage is not "a compromise . . . [or]

an institution regulating lust." A Christian sacrament that blesses the continuation of the human race, it sanctifies marital sex.[40]

Archimandrite Mikhail's presentation was conciliatory, reflecting the desire of the church hierarchy to find common ground with secular society and to demonstrate its dedication to what Ternavtsev called "the truth on earth." He used psychological discourse to appeal to the secular side. His description of Rozanov as a potential fellow believer, whom he had called a heretic elsewhere, suggests a policy of building bridges as well as Mikhail's own growing tolerance. The underlying message was that the church is broad-minded and can embrace even Rozanov. But Archimandrite Mikhail's attempt to begin a reconciliation between the church and the intelligentsia failed. Rozanov insisted on standing alone, rejecting all "allies" from the church and from the laity. Merezhkovsky, the other key figure, was not open to compromise either, except with Rozanov. As the founder of the underground Church of the Third Testament, he had his own reason for assaulting the historical church. Criticizing what he described as Mikhail's "positivist" view of marriage, whose sanctity, according to the monk, lay in childbirth, Merezhkovsky concluded that the clergyman considered marriage not a spiritual but a fleshly life practice that served racial continuity, which, unlike Rozanov, Merezhkovsky problematized.

Archimandrite Mikhail's desire to bring the warring sides closer together was very likely sincere, but in doing so he suppressed the ambiguity of church dogma regarding marriage. He did this by simply ignoring the Christian cult of celibacy in his lecture. The canonic status of marriage in history and its relation to the celibate ideal remained uncertain, especially for Rozanov, which explains his polemic with Mikhail during the next four meetings.

One of the questions of disputed canonic history was the point at which marriage was institutionalized in Christianity. Skvortsov claimed that some apostles were married, whereas Men'shikov insisted on the opposite; Rozanov said marriage became law gradually, between the sixth and eleventh centuries, suggesting that before that time many Christians lived in "natural," not "sanctified," family unions; the conservative professor of the Theological Academy N. M. Griniakin challenged Rozanov's rendition of history, stating that the sacrament of marriage existed already in the first centuries of Christianity.[41] Professor Peter Leporsky of the Theological Academy opened the following meeting with another refutation. According to him, the early church father

Tertullian wrote that marriages outside the church were exceptions before the third century.[42] Instead of clarifying the picture, the dispute muddied it further, revealing the problematic nature of all dogma, which is, after all, the product of a complicated history of canonic disputes and of factionalism.

The canonic view regarding the hierarchical relation of celibacy and marriage debated at the meetings offered two options: lifelong virginity or observance of temporary periods of abstinence. Those who chose to dedicate themselves to God by making their body into "a temple of the Holy Spirit" (1 Corinthians 6:19) lived a life of celibacy; the others were encouraged to marry and multiply ("Be fruitful and multiply, and fill the earth." [Genesis 1:28]), subject to restrictions regulating sexual desire.

The overarching question, however, was whether celibacy, modeled on the life of Christ, was indeed superior to marriage. In this connection, it is important to keep in mind that besides suggesting moral superiority, the practice of celibacy also has political implications related to institutional power. Progress through the ranks of the church hierarchy was available only to the black clergy, whereas members of the white clergy, that is, parish priests, were for all intents and purposes obliged to marry. The decision to marry had to be made before ordination, meaning that there was intense pressure on the young graduates from the seminary to make such decisions quickly, and if affirmative, to choose a wife. This had the profound consequence of erasing the priest's influence in higher church matters, relegating his ministering to the sphere of the everyday. In other words, celibacy, which signified apartness and rejection of nature, had greater prestige in the context of worldly power.

Most clerics and theologians who spoke at the meetings were ambivalent, sometimes confused, about their ideological preferences. I believe that some simply did not reveal their true beliefs. My assumption is that most members of the monastic clergy believed in the celibate ideal but for political reasons bestowed equal honor on marriage. After all, many on the church side saw the meetings as a chance to proselytize among the intelligentsia and may have been putting their most liberal foot forward.

The black clergy's support of marriage was, of course, the obvious consequence of biological necessity. The promarriage position also emerged in the context of the general epochal fear of population decline marked by an obsession with degeneration—the *fin de race,* to quote

Max Nordau's phrase once again. Some clerics made direct reference at the meetings to European degeneration theory, which, as we know, preoccupied the decadent utopians as well as some of the politically radical social critics of the time. As I noted earlier, Nordau claimed that the Russian version of degeneration was self-castration, a reference to the *skoptsy*, an extremist religious sect whose members removed their sex organs with the purpose of dedicating themselves to God. At the turn of the century, the *skoptsy* became the object of increased persecution from the government and church. Skvortsov, one of the active participants of the meetings, did battle with the sectarians in the *Missionary Observer*.[43] The sect had long been considered heretical. Perhaps its increased persecution at the turn of the twentieth century was in part the result of a perceived decadent subtext in its religious practices.

References to the *skoptsy* came up in different contexts at the meetings. The most frequent was Christ's use of the term to describe celibacy ("there be eunuchs [skoptsy], which have made themselves eunuchs for the kingdom of heaven's sake" [Matthew 19:12]). In a 1901 essay that lambasted the cruel treatment of the sectarians by Orthodox missionaries, Rozanov compared them to monks, claiming that instead of castrating themselves psychologically, they did so physically. In actual fact, wrote Rozanov, the *skoptsy* simply embodied the Christian ideal of celibacy. It was this disparaging view of the monastic ideal that the church wanted to eradicate among the participants of the theorizing intelligentsia. Bishop Sergii condemned the sectarian practice of self-castration as a "caricature" of the celibate ideal, insisting, unlike Nordau and Rozanov, on a distinction between the containment of sexual desire and bodily intervention. It was to this end that the bishop brought up the medical procedure of castration at the fifteenth meeting, describing it as "an amputation that many sick people undergo in every hospital."[44]

While Rozanov was the fiercest defender of marriage at the meetings, some members of the white clergy did so too, raising similar questions.[45] The most courageous and unexpected criticism came from the young docent of the Theological Academy Vasilii V. Uspensky, who described celibacy as a "blank slate." For Uspensky celibacy connoted "negation" and "repression of individuality."[46] His point was that in contrast to married life, celibacy denied humankind's creative, individuating potential; like Rozanov, he believed that instinctually all people are procreators.[47]

Despite the attacks on it, celibacy—interestingly enough—was defended with far less vigor. Perhaps the church representatives did not consider a defense necessary, since from their perspective marriage and celibacy had long coexisted in Russian Orthodoxy and had come into conflict only in critiques from outside the church. But this loose coexistence was unacceptable to the most influential representatives of secular society at the meetings, Rozanov and Merezhkovsky. In conflict on some other issues, both insisted that church doctrine saw celibacy as superior to marriage. This stance was rooted in their shared rejection of Christian asceticism and distrust of the church. They were joined by Kartashev, also a docent of the Theological Academy and a friend of Uspensky; it took great courage for Kartashev to imply that the institutional church did in fact give preference to celibacy.

Rozanov went so far as to metaphorize the church hierarchy's antipathy to marriage as "wild flesh on the body," applying the fin-de-siècle focus on illness and bodily decay to the way the church viewed marriage.[48] The implication of the metaphor was that the church was an ailing institution because it problematized sex and procreation. Rozanov's first position paper opened with the comment that the church considers marriage an illness, an encapsulated tubercle bacillus: "the bearer of illness, fatal to the substance of the lungs, . . . it has become capsulated, that is, surrounded on all sides by impervious tissue."[49]

While Rozanov and Merezhkovsky were allies at the meetings, the latter was ambivalent regarding the celibate ideal. Like Solov'ev, Merezhkovsky was an apocalyptic thinker, meaning that fundamentally he opposed a procreative religion. In the discussion of Archimandrite Mikhail's keynote speech, Rozanov revealed his disagreement with Solov'ev, reminding the audience that the philosopher privileged erotic love over childbirth. Several years later, in *Solitaria* he criticized Merezhkovsky for rejecting the "'seed' and 'family' [*rod*], upon which for [Rozanov] everything [was] founded."[50] But just as some ecclesiastics may have discarded the celibate ideal for the sake of rapprochement with the intelligentsia, Rozanov overlooked his differences with Merezhkovsky in doing battle with the church.

Indeed, Merezhkovsky was in all likelihood in greater agreement with Archimandrite Antonin, who viewed procreation through the prism of the book of Revelation. Elaborating Antonin's reference to Revelation at the first meeting, Merezhkovsky said that "the absolute, although still unrevealed, but only apocalyptic ideal of Christianity—is celibacy."[51] This was at the twelfth meeting; at the sixteenth or the last meeting, he stated his disagreement with Rozanov directly: "In what lies the essence of the apocalypse? In the revelation of the end of the world. Rozanov posits the question from the point of view of the eternal continuation of the human race. And this positive, personal sense of the infinite continuation of the world is the fundamental falsehood of Rozanov, the fundamental falsehood of many."[52]

Merezhkovsky insinuated criticisms of other "procreationists" into the discussion. Turning to fiction, he attacked the nineteenth-century novelistic fixation on genealogy, specifically in Emile Zola's novel *Fecundity* (1899), without stating directly that he disagreed with Zola's negative view of those characters who refuse to populate the future. Merezhkovsky addressed the French author's concern with genealogy by criticizing his "positivist" concern with progress, based on society's commitment to procreation and the continuation of the race. Merezhkovsky brought up Zola in the context of his polemics with Archimandrite Mikhail, whom he accused of an obsession with progress.[53] *Fecundity*, however, like the Rougon-Macquart series, treats a degenerate, not a "healthy," family, one destined to suffer extinction.

Rozanov's other secular opponent at the meetings was Minsky, literary ally of the Merezhkovskys in the 1890s and Gippius's partner in erotic triangulation. Minsky countered Rozanov's Old Testament celebration of marriage with the ideal of romantic love in European literature, giving preference to Christian over biblical mysticism as one of the sources of courtly and romantic love. Minsky viewed courtly love—typically unconsummated and antiprocreative—as the secular equivalent of Christian celibacy. His view of celibacy, which he put on a secular footing, was unacceptable to the clergy because it subverted the purity of the monastic ideal. Particularly disturbing to them was the erotic subtext of chastity in the age of chivalry based on the cult of the Madonna. Minsky seemed offended by what he considered Rozanov's lack of aesthetic refinement, claiming that Rozanov may have understood the Old Testament better than anyone else, but he failed to appreciate "the mystical rose of virtue on the breast of the church." Let me add that instead of metaphorizing female breasts as roses, Rozanov chose to fetishize erect female nipples—as the source of nourishment, not beauty. Despite Rozanov's sensitivity to smells, he was unable to detect the mystical aroma of the rose, said Minsky, in perhaps an ironic reference to Rozanov's obsession with the smell of sex organs and bodily excretions.[54]

The reference to Alexander Pushkin's "Poor Knight" ("Zhil na svete rytsar' bednyi") at the Religious-Philosophical Meetings came not from Minsky but from Archimandrite Mikhail. He invoked Russian literature's best-known poem about courtly love in response to Merezhkovsky's repeated barbs against him and to Merezhkovsky's remarks about *Fecundity.* Mikhail countered them by claiming that Zola's novel is not about genealogy but about sexual depravity, lambasting the French author's representation of sex as "*psychopathic* thirst for pleasure for pleasure's sake" (emphasis mine). From Zola he turned to Pushkin's poem, saying that "nature [can also be] twisted in celibacy to the point of the sin of sodomy" (sodomy in common nineteenth-century usage referred to homosexuality). The reason for the knight's celibacy in Pushkin's poem is his erotic love of the Virgin, but for Archimandrite Mikhail this standard reading of the poem did not suffice. Here is what he had to say: "The knight, who inscribes his shield with the initials A.M.D. [Ave Mater Dei], also falls into sodomic sin. This sin is possible within the realm of marriage as well. A perversion of instinct, it has been noted in sexual psychopathology. A successful treatment is needed, and the church sees this successful treatment in the sacrament."[55]

The poem became the object of debate at the end of the twelfth and the beginning of the thirteenth meeting. Originally titled "Legend" (1829), the full version of the poem remained unpublished in Pushkin's time because of its sacrilegious content and tone. Instead of dedication to Christ, the motive for the knight's celibacy is his love of the Virgin. The penultimate stanza, which bears some similarity to Pushkin's parodic epic of the Annunciation in *Gavriliada,* is overtly sacrilegious:

To God he made ne'er a prayer,
No fasting marked his rule,
In lusting after holy *Mère,*
He lost his way, poor fool![56]

Он-де Богу не молился,
Он не ведал-де поста,
Не путем-де волочился
Он за матушкой Христа.

*Volochit'sia za* means to lust after a woman. The colloquial reference to the object of desire as *matushka Khrista* contrasts with the respectful "the mother of Christ the Lord" in an earlier stanza. The use of the enclitic particle *de,* indicating attribution of utterance to another speaker, underscores the disrespectful colloquial tone. The knight strays further from the church by not receiving Communion before death. Despite his transgressions, however, the Virgin—who by implication has sexual contact with the knight—pleads for her palatine and lets him into the eternal kingdom.

Merezhkovsky expressed shock over Mikhail's interpretation: "What? 'He traced A. M. D. on his shield with his own blood'—this is sodomy? You call this sodomy?"[57] The heated exchange continued at the next meeting. Except for Archimandrite Mikhail's first reference to the knight, the exchange was excised from the published transcript, presumably because of its focus on sexual pathology and Mikhail's apparent association of homosexuality with the knight's transgression of the celibate ideal. Bishop Sergii, chair of the meetings, intervened in the Semenov-Merezhkovsky exchange, which had crossed over into delicate territory. He did this by agreeing with Merezhkovsky that if Pushkin's knight is a "sodomite," then all of Russia's best writers, Pushkin, Dostoevsky, Solov'ev, as well as knighthood in general, must be associated with the sin of sodomy.[58]

Archimandrite Mikhail did not relent. He reiterated that the knight's religious feelings were pathological. Continuing his verbal skirmish with Merezhkovsky, he claimed that the sixteenth-century Spanish mystic St. Theresa of Avila, one of the principal Catholic saints, was possessed by demonic spirits, that her love of Christ was sexual, not chaste: "The angel pierces her heart through. She experiences pain. She tries to penetrate the depth of his eyes. This is religious *sexual psychopathology* [emphasis mine]. This is a perversion of virginity. This is also the perversion of the knight, whom Merezhkovsky champions, . . . who writes A. M. D. on his shield, goes into battle in a woman's blouse, but loves platonically, that is, with a perverted sexual love. Sexual pleasure is repressed. This is Platonic love."[59]

Mikhail's interpretation of Pushkin's knight focuses on his gender: effeminate, he goes to war wearing woman's garb; he experiences a sublimated Platonic love, which at the turn of the century connoted homoeroticism. The exegesis is certainly unconventional, as is its discourse. In fact, Pushkin's poem does not substantiate the archimandrite's claims.

Platonic homoerotic love, premised on sublimated desire, was attributed to the monastic ideal of celibacy, a conflation that inspired anxiety in the church fathers. The only way to make sense of Archimandrite Mikhail's comments is to interpret them as a case of slippage into decadent sensibility associated by the fin de siècle with monastic practice: female idealization veiling same-sex desire and the conjunction of lust and religious exaltation. Archimandrite Mikhail projected this sensibility onto Pushkin's poem, reading it through the prism of decadence and psychopathology. His reference to "Poor Knight" and unexpected emphasis on the poem's covert homoerotic meaning could be understood as an indirect response to the charge of sodomy launched at the church by Rozanov and others.

I have described this exchange, insignificant dogmatically, in such detail not simply because parts of it were excised from the published reports, but because of its link to contemporary degeneration theory. The excision of a discussion of the psychopathology of courtly love would have been a trite case of censorship had the main speaker been of the laity. Archimandrite Mikhail Semenov's reference to the term "sexual psychopathology" (*polovaia psikhopatiia*) to diagnose the knight's love of the virgin and St. Theresa's ecstatic love of Christ invoked Krafft-Ebing's *Psychopathia Sexualis,* which, as we know, was widely read at the turn of the twentieth century; its Russian title was *Polovaia psikhopatiia.* It appears that Archimandrite Mikhail, as well as other clerics in attendance, either had read Krafft-Ebing or were familiar with the premises of his study. In fact, in a footnote to the description of religious masochism, Krafft-Ebing singled out St. Theresa and the artistic representation of what he calls a "hysterical saint" in "degenerate" epochs. He quoted a description of a sculpture of the Spanish saint by Giovanni Lorenzo Bernini, in which she "sink[s] in an hysterical faint upon a marble cloud, whilst an amorous angel plunges the arrow (of divine love) into her heart."[60] Nineteenth-century psychopathologists studying perversions and their relationship to religious devotion, especially in Catholicism and in women, typically cited her as an example of religious hysteria emblematized by the Catholic stigmata, alien to Eastern Orthodoxy. Religious hysteria and sadomasochism typified the Catholic decadence, which characterized some of the French and Belgian aesthetic production in the fin de siècle.

In Mikhail's first reference to the knight, he spoke of "a cure," as if the knight's erotic idealization of the Virgin were an illness. Just as Krafft-Ebing prescribed cures for his patients—his cure for "sexual inversion" and hysteria was hypnosis and hydrotherapy—so Archimandrite Mikhail offered a therapeutic regimen for the errant knight, suggesting that he return to the church and take the sacrament.

*Psychopathia Sexualis* was actually cited by name at the fifteenth meeting. The reference again came from the church side and was censored from the published transcript. Father Timofei Iakshich, an erudite, broad-minded defender of marriage, said he wanted to quote Krafft-Ebing on the psychological benefits of marriage but was not allowed to proceed. Instead of *Psychopathia Sexualis,* he called the book *Psychopathia eksessuarov,* or at least that is the title recorded in the transcript. *Eksessuar* is a corruption of two foreign borrowings into Russian: *ekstsess* (excess) and *aksessuar* (accessory). The usage has the quality of uneducated speech, though Father Timofei was well educated. He may have mutilated the title intentionally, for effect, but no other puns by him are recorded in the transcripts. More than likely, it is the product of faulty note taking: unfamiliar with Latin, the stenographer may have heard *eksessuarov* instead of *sexualis,* both foreign words with many *s*'s; *eksessuar* also sounds like *buduar,* the private space of sexual excess in "naughty" novels. Father Timofei's comment was interrupted by general conversation and din, as if the audience disapproved of it. The chair of the meeting asked him to change the subject and return to the discussion of Christ's views.[61]

As it turns out then, the view that marriage is license for sexual excess also applied to the sphere of celibacy. The monastic clergy was suspicious not only of marriage but also of chastity. The case of the *skoptsy,* as we have seen, cast a shadow on the black clergy's celibate vow. Archimandrite Mikhail's reading of "Poor Knight" and demonization of St. Theresa as a masochist reflected the fear that chastity could be a cover for sexual perversion. These suspicions were exacerbated by contemporary sexology and masochistic decadent representation, which seem to have penetrated the church walls.

What is most astonishing about the Religious-Philosophical Meetings is not the debates regarding canonic dogma but the infusion into them of the general cultural climate of the decadence. The admixture of eroticism and religion with the purpose of sacrilegious titillation was, in the words of Jean Pierrot, "one of the most conspicuous ingredients of the decadent imagination," which typically represented erotic and religious arousal as interdependent.[62] Decadent art, especially in Catholic countries but also in Russia, offered numerous examples of the entwinement of religious and sexual desire. In contemporary Russian literature, an obvious example of such commingling was the poetry of Valerii Briusov, who had been influenced by Baudelaire's use of Catholicism for aesthetic, sensuous purposes. It is the surplus value of the discussions about celibacy and marriage—the alluring conjunction of religious exaltation and decadent discourse—that made the Religious-Philosophical Meetings so remarkable. Taken to the extreme, this conjunction helps support the intelligentsia's view of the church as a decadent institution.

The discursive strategies of Rozanov and the Merezhkovskys to bridge the gap between physical and spiritual reality at the Religious-Philosophical Meetings reflected their project of uniting spirit and flesh. In contrast to Rozanov, who infused the spiritual with the physiology of sex, the Merezhkovskys, like Solov'ev before them, shied away from messy physiology and offered instead the pristine metaphor of "sacred flesh" (*sviataia plot*). Their discourse privileged the body's spiritual potential over its physiological essence. Paul condemned the physical body as sinful, suggesting that only the ideal body was the "temple of the Holy Spirit." Sacred in essence, it becomes profane in empirical reality. Despite their project of liberating the body from Paul's ascetic teachings, the Merezhkovskys failed to do so. Consecration of the flesh remained at the level of discourse, which did not result in liberation of the body from the epoch's sexual anxiety. The main ideological difference between Rozanov and the Merezhkovskys was that the latter condemned nature's body because it feeds the life cycle, whereas Rozanov celebrated it with fearless gusto. He was much more successful in unveiling the body—even if only on paper—than were his sometimes reluctant co-conspirators, whose desire to liberate the body from its biological fetters was essentially cerebral.

Foucault's ideas about the incitement and proliferation of sexual discourse in the fin de siècle can shed light on the Religious-Philosophical Meetings devoted to sex and procreation. Describing the role of sexual discourse in modern societies, Foucault concluded that "they dedicated themselves to speaking of it *ad infinitum,* while exploiting it as *the* secret." Instead of "consign[ing] sex to a shadow existence," the language of sex became the reigning discourse, wrote Foucault.[63] It even pervaded the public discourse of such an unlikely forum as the Religious-Philosophical Meetings. In other words, no place was secure from its invasion, with the contagion spreading even to the church.

The Foucaultian perspective helps us theorize the multiple meanings of celibacy—which in decadence informed cerebral sexuality, contributing to the fascination of some of Solov'ev's younger contemporaries with the possibility that his reputed chastity concealed a sexual subtext. Similar curiosity surrounded Gippius's reputed virginity. Even though Rozanov never linked monastic celibacy and same-sex desire explicitly at the Religious-Philosophical Meetings, he did so later. In

*People of the Moonlight* (*Liudi lunnogo sveta,* 1911), he called Christian morality "sodomite." As to Solov'ev's erotic philosophy, Rozanov considered it homoerotic, describing his goddess as "Aphrodite Sodomica," who longs to "smash [the earthly Aphrodite's] children against the rock."[64]

Thus the polemics surrounding celibacy and marriage at the Religious-Philosophical Meetings had much broader implications than celibacy contra marriage. It was part of the larger debate between "naturists," who saw their life mission as replenishing nature, and utopian visionaries, who were seeking the transfiguration of the body; between practicing sensualists and cerebral sensualists; between patriarchal traditionalists and decadent utopians, who feared the exhaustion of their bloodline.

Rozanov's understanding of heredity reflected the view that it had been infected by the Christian perversion of the sexual instinct that undermined racial health. This was the ideological subtext of Rozanov's message at the Religious-Philosophical Meetings in 1901–3. His great hope at that time was the revival of Old Testament values as an antidote to degeneration. A decade later, he broadened his list of degenerate religions, adding to it Judaism and during the second decade of the twentieth century replacing Christians with Jews, as a reflection of his overarching nationalistic concern with the health of the Russian nation.

# 7

# Vasilii Rozanov

## The Case of an Amoral Procreationist

> Having sat down on a stool in front of Gippius [whom he called Zinochka,] Rozanov quietly sprayed out—together with a flying stream of spittle—brief, shaky little phrases, which leaped out of his mouth quickly in chaotic, lisping hops. . . . The conversation, which jumped from topic to topic, was a very thick physiological jam of V. V.'s [Vasilii Vasil'evich's] thinking. . . . [He would grab] the lily-white hands of Z. N. [Gippius] with the fingers of his very nervous hands; his hands twitched, while his knees danced; his devious little brown eyes seemed to be blind, fleshy morsels; [Rozanov cooked his ideas,] which he would bake somewhere (in a sacred place), where perhaps he would produce the shameless bodily function of his shameless thought. . . . Here flesh [*plot'*] . . . is not "flesh" but merely "fle" [*plo*]. It seemed to me that Rozanov was not speaking his thoughts, but rather boiling them, spurting out his bodily functions, . . . spurting and—relaxing: until—the next bodily function; because of this these functions have such an effect: Rozanov's thought would keep performing its abstract moves, while he himself would simply spurt out: bodily functions.[1]

This stylized portrait of Vasilii Rozanov was crafted by Andrei Bely long after his meeting with him in Zinaida Gippius's Petersburg apartment during the 1905 revolution. Like Bely's verbal portraits of Solov'ev and Gippius, quoted in earlier chapters, this one is grotesque, not to say vicious. Yet it captures remarkably well the physiological and culinary character of Rozanov's discourse. Employing the vocabulary of cooking, Bely figured Rozanov's production of speech as uncontrolled, unsavory, as well as unfinished bodily activity, which he rendered by truncating

Vasilii Rozanov (Andrei Bely Museum in Moscow)

the word "flesh." His most striking representation is the portrayal of Rozanov's thinking and narrative strategies as rhythmic ebbs and flows of bodily excretion, an image that he borrowed from Nikolai Berdiaev, who in 1914 described Rozanov's writings as "the biological functions of his body."[2]

Among the bodily functions that Rozanov cultivated rhetorically were coitus, breast-feeding, digestion, bloodletting, and discharge of bodily waste, which he incorporated into the act of writing. He also interlaced culinary and sexual images to depict his rhetorical practice, claiming that it was "not leavened [*zameshany*] with water and not even with human blood, but with *human semen*."[3] Semen, spittle, blood, and excrement are the main fleshly sources of his discursive power—what Bely described as "the thick physiological jam of V. V.'s thinking." The appropriation of bodily excretion for the purpose of articulating his views on religion and other important issues of the time contributed to Rozanov's controversial reputation.

Rozanov's manner of speaking and writing has been compared to whispering. The individual entries in his books, sometimes one-liners, mimic fragmentary speech whispered into someone's ear. In theoretical terms, his self-conscious stylistic trademark of whispered intimacy—accompanied by such physiological excess as spittle—seemed to erase the boundaries between body and language. Rozanov's intimate verbal gestures had the effect of bridging the gap between language and the sensible world, creating the illusion of direct access to sensible experience. Although Rozanov's strategies were uniquely his own, they mirror the turn-of-the-century desire to break down the strict boundary between language and body. They reveal the epoch's desire to penetrate the recesses of the private body and return literature to the phenomenal, "fleshly" experience from which Rozanov believed writing had been separated. Leavened by the gurgling, excreting body, it attempts to make the word flesh by engaging the sexual body, the tactile, and the everyday.

Reflecting his generation's conflicted view of eros, Rozanov's writings engaged two opposing discourses about sex—that of procreation, which underlay his love of the whole, and one based on fetishizing excess. The latter was represented by a spilling of bodily fluid (spittle, semen, blood, and their surrogate, ink) that produces fragments and fetish objects. So we see that the epoch's keeper of the procreative flame also worshiped the fetish: religious, sexual, and literary. Rozanov created a special genre to accommodate the dual trajectory—of nostalgia for the whole and of fragmenting fetishism, which he claimed characterized even the Gospels.[4] He called the genre "fallen leaves," an image that he inscribed into the title of one of his best known works (*Fallen Leaves* [*Opavshie list'ia*]). It consists of disconnected heterogeneous fragments, sometimes resembling diary entries, which are collected into a semblance of a whole, rendered by the metaphoric subtitle of *Fallen*

*Leaves: Basket One* and *Two* (*Korob pervyi* and *vtoroi*). Whether the "basket" recovered the whole is debatable, but it is certain that the new narrative genre problematized the part-whole relationship.[5] What is particularly striking in this respect is the scholarly index to *Fallen Leaves*—one that Rozanov constructed himself—which contains his favorite body fetishes as individual entries: "women's breasts," "pregnant stomach," "welcoming womb," "sex organs," and "male sex organ" (*ud*).[6]

Rozanov's obsession with the part-whole correlation resembles in

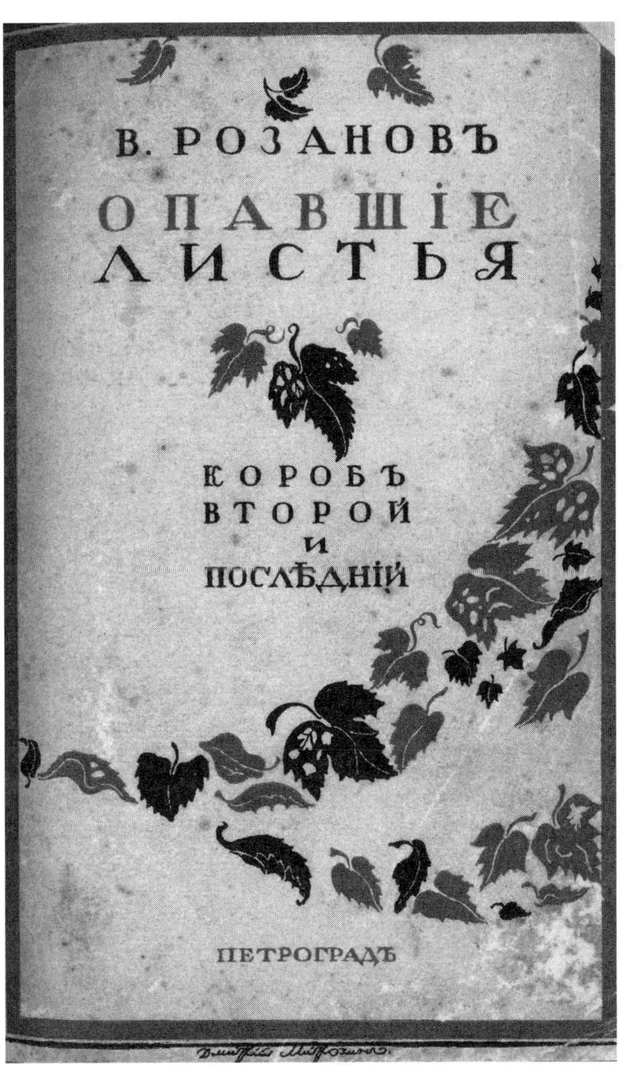


Book cover of *Fallen Leaves* by Vasilii Rozanov

444

ГРИБНАЯ ЛАВКА. **Оп. л.**, 46.
ГРИБЫ. **Коробъ 2**, 195—198.
ГРУБОСТЬ. **Оп. л.**, 408, 470.
ГРУДИ ЖЕНСКІЯ. **Оп. л.**, 287—288, 358.
ГРУДИ КОСМИЧЕСКІЯ. **Коробъ 2**, 438—439.
ГРУСТЬ. **Оп. л.**, 164—165, 303, 407, 474. **Коробъ 2**, 39.
ГРѢХЪ. **Уед.** 84, 204. **Оп. л.**, 105, 175, 261, 333, 407, 417.
ГУМАННОСТЬ. **Оп. л.**, 370.
ГУТТЕНБЕРГЪ. **Уед.**, 9, 107, 163. **Оп. л.**, 223, 262. **Коробъ 2**, 179, 334—336.

ДЕВЯТНАДЦАТЫЙ ВѢКЪ. **Коробъ 2**, 5, 6—7, 18—21, 23.
ДЕКАБРИСТЫ, 14-ое декабря. **Уед.**, 68—69. **Оп. л.**, 123. **Коробъ 2**, 28, 340.
ДЕКАДЕНТЫ. **Уед.**, 4, 286.
ДЕМОКРАТІЯ,—краты. **Уед.**, 39. **Оп. л.**, 94—97, 432—433. **Коробъ 2**, 48—51, 76—77, 222, 223.
ДЕМОНИЧЕСКОЕ начало въ мірѣ, см. БѢСОВСКОЕ н. въ м.
ДІАЛЕКТИЧЕСКІЯ вещи и процессы. **Уед.**, 62.
ДІОНИСЪ. **Оп. л.**, 59.
ДОБРОДѢТЕЛЬ. **Уед.**, 295. **Коробъ 2**, 192, 193, 362—363.
ДОБРОТА. **Коробъ 2**, 363.
ДОБЧИНСКІЙ,—нскіе. **Уед.**, 96—97, 99, 100—101. **Оп. л.**, 78.
ДОКТОРА. **Уед.**, 244—245. **Оп. л.**, 371, 383—388, 406, 496—498.
ДОЛГЪ. **Уед.**, 184, 198.
«ДРУГЪ». **Уед.**, 110, 133, 177, 179, 244—245, 249, 252, 253, 254, 256, 257, 259, 260, 261, 274, 286, 294. **Оп. л.**, 11, 22—23, 73, 176, 177, 186, 190,

Vasilii Rozanov, *Fallen Leaves*, page from index

some instances the way it functions in Tolstoy's writings. Since this last chapter circles back to the first (devoted to Tolstoy), one of the questions that it addresses is whether Rozanov was any more successful than Tolstoy in recovering the bodily whole from the fetishized part. Was he better able to resolve the problematic relation of his contemporaries to love's body? We know that Tolstoy came to renounce it, whereas Rozanov's contemporaries responded by disembodying it. Rozanov, by contrast, staged coitus in explicit detail while also spilling body fluids outside the procreative sex act. Rozanov's use of the rhetorical gesture of unveiling the private body is so radical that it evokes in this reader the image of a flasher who displays his phallus in public spaces. A public fetishist despite his insistence on intimacy, Rozanov flaunted the part, rather than hiding it in the tightly woven fabric of realist discourse, as did Tolstoy, or in an opaque, mystical discourse, as did Solov'ev and his followers. The gesture in Rozanov's case raised the question of pornography among his contemporaries.

Fetishism, which according to Foucault is "governed by the interplay of whole and part," is, as I have demonstrated, one of the master tropes of decadence. Aware of his intentions, Rozanov made frequent use of the word "fetish," calling himself a "fetishist of trifles," ostensibly referring to the beloved physical details of daily life. "'Trifles are my 'gods,'" wrote Rozanov in *Fallen Leaves* (*Opavshie list'ia,* 2:453). Whether they serve as rhetorical fetish screens for the gaping phallic void, which so terrified his contemporaries, I cannot say. My project, after all, is not a psychoanalytic one. I also do not draw conclusions regarding the reconstitutive function of the secreting female and male genitalia, of blood, and of unhygienic waste in Rozanov's poetics, whether its oozing parts have the power of making modernity's sundered body whole again. Whatever conclusions we choose to draw regarding the recuperative power of the part in Rozanov's writings, which according to Viktor Shklovsky served as the harbinger of avant-garde aesthetics, his fetishist sensibility represents the fragmented aesthetics of modernism.[7] Things fall apart in Rozanov's rhetorical economy, leaving behind messy paradox, the sort of paradox that characterized the aesthetics of Russia's decadent utopians. Let's reconsider what could be described as Solov'ev's perverse dictum that heightened erotic desire should coexist with the practice of abstinence. How much messier can paradox become? Rozanov responded to this master paradox of decadent utopianism by celebrating procreation, while also maintaining a fetishist sensibility.

No Russian writer embodied so literally the oxymoronic discourse of his time, which Tolstoy, as a member of a very different generation, could not share. There was also no other writer of the symbolist epoch whose engagement with the erotic sphere and with degeneration theory was as complex and intense. Rozanov held philosophical and sexual views that were in conflict with those of the later Tolstoy, Solov'ev, Gippius, and Blok, the main subjects of *Erotic Utopia.* Most prominently, as I have shown in the preceding chapter, he defended with persistence the values of marriage, procreative sex, and the patriarchal family—in opposition to his contemporaries' simultaneous fear and exaltation of the end of nature and history. In this regard, his views recall the procreative project of the younger Tolstoy, emblematized by the diaper with the yellow stain that crowns the novelistic edifice of *War and Peace.*[8] Speaking metaphorically, it is Rozanov's appropriation simultaneously of Tolstoy's metonymic diaper and the Tolstoyan metonym's fragmenting fetishistic power that place Rozanov at the center of the modernist project that this book examines.

My representation of Rozanov in the preceding chapter offered a portrait of someone with a consistent intellectual position based on a singular commitment to marriage and procreation. This chapter emphasizes his intellectual relativism and inconsistencies, focusing mainly on Rozanov's books that reveal his obsession with sex, degeneration, blood, and race: *People of the Moonlight: Metaphysics of Christianity* (*Liudi lunnogo sveta: Metafizika Khristianstva,* 1911/1913) and *The Jews' Olfactory and Tactile Relationship to Blood* (*Oboniatel'noe i osiazatel'noe otnoshenie evreev k krovi,* 1914). The first is a study of homosexuality, which Rozanov embedded in Christianity's demonization of sex and in degeneration theory. The second is an anti-Semitic diatribe, which contradicts his Judeophilia and reveals a racial view of degeneration. I examine the two books as exemplars of Rozanov's ideological and aesthetic slippages, not to say slipperiness, exposing the fantasies and prejudices that underlay the era's fear of tainted heredity and racial health.

## A Theory of Homosexuality

*People of the Moonlight* is classic Rozanov: it is a compilation of his responses to other texts, mostly by relatively unknown or anonymous authors. In it Rozanov typically resided on the margins, supplying the borrowed material with footnotes that are in dialogical, or polemical, relation to the text above the line typographically. Despite their marginal location, the footnotes are just as important as the text on which they comment. Sometimes Rozanov exposed this narrative strategy himself: "Certain *sharp arrows* (spearheads, lances) of my *whole world outlook* appeared only in my *footnotes* to other people's articles" (*Opavshie list'ia,* 1:284). The part supercedes the whole.

The first edition of *People of the Moonlight* appeared in 1911, the second in 1913. A polemic against the morbid cult of Christian asceticism, the book celebrates Judaism as a procreative life-affirming religion, making the claim—as did its author at the Religious-Philosophical Meetings—that Jews are better fit to maintain a healthy race. Although there are no references to Nietzsche in *People of the Moonlight*, its critique of Christianity seems to reflect the influence of *The Antichrist* (1888), a debt that Rozanov would have certainly denied.[9] (An abridged Russian version of Nietzsche's essay first appeared in 1900, a full one in 1907.)[10] Taking Nietzsche's criticism of Christianity as life denying a step further, Rozanov implied that it promoted homosexuality. As we saw in the previous chapter, he had insinuated his view of Christianity as a "sodomite" religion into his polemics with the church at the Religious-Philosophical Meetings.

Yet the main thrust of Rozanov's "sharp" polemical "arrows" in *People of the Moonlight* is Christian asceticism, not homosexuality. Like Nietzsche in *The Antichrist*, Rozanov considered Christianity thoroughly decadent, celebrating death, with Christ at its necrophilic helm. The book is an unrestrained invective against Christianity, especially its monastic tradition. "The legacy and stimulus of monasticism," wrote Rozanov in a polemical footnote, is the "destruction of the whole human race."[11] He began his history of monasticism by claiming that it originated in the Phoenician cults of Moloch, to whom children were sacrificed, and of the virginal warrior-goddess Astarte. According to Rozanov, the priests of Moloch and Astarte castrated themselves. The association of Christian monastic celibacy and self-castration (*skopchestvo*), which, of course, goes against nature, is an obsessive refrain in *People of the Moonlight*, as it had been at the Religious-Philosophical Meetings. Besides the Phoenician cults, the book's genealogy of monasticism includes Plato's ephebe Phaedrus, who, claimed Rozanov, found the female body despicable (*Liudi*, 5–7), revealing his love of men.

My assumption is that the most inflammatory aspect of *People of the Moonlight* was its inscription of monasticism into a self-castrating and homoerotic model of religion. Describing the sexual identity of Christian monks, Rozanov used interchangeably the terms "third sex," "male-female" (*muzhe-deva*), "urning," and "spiritual sodomite."[12] He compared the teachings of the church on celibacy to "arsenic with sugar" (*Liudi*, 151), sweet on the surface but poisonous in essence. Like some of his symbolist contemporaries, he emphasized Christ's male-female nature, except that he attributed negative connotations to Christ's effeminacy, making him into a degenerate male of the fin de siècle, one who lacked the necessary vigor for replenishing the race. He never went so far as to say that Christ was a sodomite—that would have never passed the censorship—but he came close. It is as if he imagined the figure of Christ in relation to the epoch's crisis of masculinity, which he identified with effeminacy. Preoccupied with the growing lack of semen everywhere, Rozanov, like his contemporaries, feared the decline of the race, with the important difference that, in contrast to Gippius and Blok, he responded to the fear by aggressively affirming nature's continuity.

In *The Antichrist*, Nietzsche represented Christ as degenerate and decadent, disputing Ernest Renan's view of him as the genius and hero of his celebrated book *The Life of Jesus*. Instead, Nietzsche called Christ an "idiot." From his discussion of Dostoevsky in *The Antichrist*, it appears that he had not read *The Idiot:* "[O]ne has to regret that no Dostoevsky lived in the neighborhood of this most interesting *decadent*," wrote Nietzsche. "I mean someone who could feel the thrilling fascination of such a combination of the sublime, the sick and the childish."[13] Christ's childishness, in Nietzsche's view, was a sign of degeneration: "{T]he occurrence of retarded puberty undeveloped in the organism [is] a consequence of degeneration . . . familiar at any rate to physiologists" (*Antichrist*, 154). Uncanny as it may seem, Dostoevsky had created a Christ figure to Nietzsche's order twenty years earlier: Prince Myshkin, who is infantile and Christlike, is a victim of sexual pathology and neuropathology, as if he had indeed been the prototype of Nietzsche's as well as Rozanov's Christ.

Nietzsche described Christ as suffering from excessive sensitivity to smell and touch, which he considered decadent symptoms (*Antichrist*, 151). His Christ, in fact, resembles Des Esseintes, the degenerate hero of Huysmans's *Against Nature* (1884), whose senses are hypertrophied. In a vitriolic attack on Christ, which surpassed Rozanov's venom, Nietzsche described him as a "hybrid product of decay, [a] mixture of zero, concept, and contradiction, in which all the instincts of decadence, all cowardices and wearinesses of the soul, find their sanction!" (*Antichrist*, xx) But like Rozanov, he did not directly impute to Christ a homosexual identity.

In a footnote in *People of the Moonlight*, Rozanov described the discussions at the Religious-Philosophical Meetings—the subject of the previous chapter—as taking place between "half-sodomites and regular people" (*Liudi*, 112n1).[14] The "half-sodomites" in all likelihood refers not only to the secular participants of uncertain gender but also to the monks, who were in Rozanov's view "sodomites" in spirit. He considered monks and sectarian self-castrators sexual deviants who sublimated their unnatural desire by directing it toward Christ instead of the natural cycle.[15]

Yet the theory of sexuality that Rozanov proposed in *People of the Moonlight* does not demonize homosexuality. If the book is homophobic, it is because Rozanov wanted to see the whole world pregnant, but it also reveals an "inverted" attraction to the fetish. Like Otto Weininger—a misogynist, self-hating homosexual, and a Jew, who had a tragic view of sexuality—Rozanov presupposed the fundamental bisexuality of all people, an assumption regarding gender that underlay the opinion of many Russian thinkers at the turn of the twentieth century, including Solov'ev and Gippius. Rozanov's emphasis on originary bisexuality in *People of the Moonlight,* symbolized by lunar light, reveals the unacknowledged influence of Weininger's *Sex and Character* (1903), translated into Russian in 1909.[16] What is so astonishing about Rozanov's assumption about bisexuality (represented by the trope of androgyny) is that it gives preference to same-sex love. Privileging the strict differentiation of the sexes most of the time, Rozanov suggested in some passages of *People of the Moonlight* the fluidity of sexual desire and gender, which he based on Weininger's theory of an infinite number of male-female combinations.

Rozanov was tolerant of homosexuality and opposed its criminalization, but in keeping with the early modernist ethos, his view of homosexuality was ambivalent, if not simply confused. Like Lombroso, for instance, Rozanov claimed that the "lunar" third sex, which he labeled "spiderlike" (not a positive epithet), has been culturally more productive than the other two: "[O]ne could almost coin an aphorism that 'all talent is hermaphroditic,'" wrote Rozanov in *People of the Moonlight* (*Liudi,* 246n1). He included the later Tolstoy and Solov'ev in his history of what he called "spiritual sodomy," or spiritual hermaphroditism, with whose antiprocreationism he polemicized throughout his life.[17] Considering homosexuals an intermediate sex, Rozanov frequently used the same term for them as the sexologist Magnus Hirschfeld (*Berlin's Third Sex,* translated into Russian in 1908–9). "Third sex" became a common synonym for the homosexual, suggesting intermediacy between male and female.

Besides offering a "metaphysics of Christianity" and a sexual theory, *People of the Moonlight* is also a study in psychopathology, which viewed homosexuality as a degenerate disorder. Its most important medical subtext is Krafft-Ebing's *Psychopathia Sexualis,* introduced to the philosophically inclined Russian readership almost two decades earlier by Solov'ev in *The Meaning of Love.*[18] A compilation of case studies, the second enlarged edition of *Psychopathia Sexualis* appeared in Russian in 1909, two years before Rozanov's book.[19] *People of the Moonlight,* a Rozanovian generic hybrid, also contains psychopathological case studies, some lifted directly from Krafft-Ebing and others that Rozanov collected himself. According to one of his students in the Bel'sk high school during the 1890s, he was a sadist who resembled Krafft-Ebing's patients and would have been of psychopathological interest to the German psychiatrist.[20]

Like Krafft-Ebing and other sexologists of the time who debated the relation of homosexuality to heredity, Rozanov considered homosexuality hereditary, without saying so explicitly. European psychopathologists generally argued that all degenerate disorders were the product of tainted heredity, of which homosexuality was one. Implying in *People of the Moonlight* that what he called sexual intermediacy was hereditary, Rozanov, however, revealed his uncertainty about its relation to nature. If bisexuality was originary, as he claimed in the beginning of the book—androgynous, in other words—then how could it also be unnatural?

The answer lies in Rozanov's attempt to naturalize same-sex desire by interlacing mythological and historical time. The entwining of myth and history is one of the signature conflations of early Russian modernism, as we saw with Solov'ev, Blok, and Gippius. Rozanov's version of the myth of origins in *People of the Moonlight* proposes the bisexuality of humans—their wholeness—in mythical time; in history they became single-sex men and women. Following Aristophanes in the *Symposium,* he claimed that sexual desire is the product of the ancestors' originary bisexuality. Premised on the idea of mythical memory, which Rozanov attributed to the soul, he asserted that the soul's sex is always different from the body's. This, according to him, is the source of sexual attraction. In contrast to his usual insistence on sexual polarity for purposes of procreation, Rozanov proposed in *People of the Moonlight*—as well as elsewhere—a sexual mythology that resembles Carl Jung's theory of the "anima" and "animus" as the basis of sexual desire; Jung's theory of sexuality was influenced by his student and patient Sabina Spielrein and other Russian patients.[21]

Thus the third sex, the product of degeneration, also appears to be an atavistic anachronism for Rozanov, representing an earlier human condition. This again resembles Lombroso, who wrote that degeneration "tends to bring the two sexes together and to confuse them, through an atavistic return to the period of hermaphroditism."[22] In other words, the effacement of sexual difference in Rozanov's myth of origins was perceived as a return to a primitive state, as if differentiation were the product of evolution. Such an interpretation of Rozanov's theory of sexual origins helps to explain his lack of nostalgia for mythical time, when the sexes were undifferentiated and therefore unable to procreate. It also explains his anti-apocalyptic vision, despite the title of his last work, *Apocalypse of Our Time (Apokalipsis nashego vremeni,* 1917–18). He rejected the utopian projections of many of his symbolist contemporaries who believed that original sexual wholeness would be reinstated after the end of history. He opted instead for regular heterosexual intercourse with the purpose of replenishing nature, which was also his way of responding to the epoch's crisis of heredity. In concert with his contemporaries, however, he remained in the realm of mythology when thinking about the origin of man, a perspective that seems to underlie the most interesting case of degeneration cited in *People of the Moonlight* (which I discuss later in this chapter).

As I mentioned, the prototype for those sections of *People of the Moonlight* that cite examples of sexual "anomaly" is *Psychopathia Sexualis,* which includes stories of sexual deviancy told to Krafft-Ebing by the deviants themselves. In *The History of Sexuality,* Foucault introduced the term *scientsia sexualis,* invoking the title of Heinrich Kaan's *Psychopathia Sexualis* (1846) as well as Krafft-Ebing's notorious book. Foucault claimed that European civilization is the only one to have developed a science of sexuality; it is a "confessional science," wrote Foucault, emphasizing the centrality of confession to the psychopathological discourse of the nineteenth century. European cultures across the centuries developed "procedures for telling the truth of sex which are geared to a form of knowledge-power opposed to . . . *ars erotica:* [He had] in mind the confession."[23] *Scientsia sexualis,* according to Foucault, combines the "procedures of [Christian] confession" and "scientific discursivity," with the practice of a listener—to whom the story is told—who takes on a "hermeneutic function."[24] A similar combination of sex, confession, and hermeneutics characterizes the discourse of *People of the Moonlight,* with the obvious exception that it is programmatically unscientific. But Rozanov's writerly practice resembles Krafft-Ebing's confessional narratives, brimming with "unsavory" physical detail, to a tee.

In *People of the Moonlight,* Rozanov claimed begrudgingly that *Psychopathia Sexualis* was the only source of knowledge about contemporary sex life. Despite this acknowledgment, similarity in genres, and long quotations of case studies from Krafft-Ebing, Rozanov spoke disparagingly of the sexologist, describing him as a "dirty medic who [dug] in all kinds of excrement, foul smells, diseases, and sewage, not feeling squeamish about anything, [although when he wrote] about diphtheria, which *kills children,* [he did not use] such a repellent tone . . . as he [did] when writing about the *life-giving* sex organs and sex life itself" (*Liudi,* 41).

He accused Krafft-Ebing of practicing "Christian medicine," which Rozanov considered hypocritical and moralistic. In a typically hyperbolic accusation, he claimed that it was more sympathetic to syphilis than to coitus, which Christian medics consider "degenerate" and "pathological" (*Liudi,* 42). As always with Rozanov, the invective is archly polemical, reflecting his extensive experience in journalism.[25] It is also dialogical in a Bakhtinian sense.[26] Rozanov has been compared to the hero of *The Notes from the Underground,* resembling especially the underground man as constructed by Bakhtin, who saw in his incessant contradictions stylistic and ideological dialogicity. Rozanov had his regular column titled *In His Own Corner* (*V svoem uglu*), a spatial underground, in Gippius's journalistic enterprise *New Way.*

If we return to Rozanov's references to the "foul smells," "excrement," "sewage," and lack of "squeamishness" in *Psychopathia Sexualis* and consider them dialogically, they seem less derogatory than at first sight. The appreciation of dirty smells and transcendence of squeamishness—inaccessible to Nietzsche's Christ—are the cornerstone of Rozanov's poetics. He fetishized the smells of home—of cooking, bodily excretions, sex organs, especially of their moistness. "A wife enters her husband with her smell, making him odorous all over with her smell just like their home," wrote Rozanov in *Fallen Leaves* (*Opavshie list'ia,* 2:569). The womblike, sexualized, sticky space of home—repulsive in the hygienic sense—was Rozanov's ideal; he flaunted publicly the organic details of intimate life.[27] So it is not Krafft-Ebing's digging in smelly excrement that offended Rozanov—quite the contrary! Rather, he accused him of bourgeois Christian revulsion by the smells of sex.

And if we reconsider Rozanov's privileging of sexual polarity in men and women in light of his self-conscious inconsistency, his support in *People of the Moonlight* of Weininger's idea that sex, or gender, is "*fluid* . . ., flowing from *positive* [mathematical] quantities to *negative* ones [from male to female]" (*Liudi,* 153) begins to make more sense. Particularly interesting in this respect is his focus on two examples from Krafft-Ebing: the cases of a transsexual male and of a transsexual female, which he cited almost word for word. The first is a long confessional autobiography of a Hungarian gynecological surgeon practicing in Germany. I will offer a close reading of this case because of its transsexual explicitness and Rozanov's astonishing "life-creating" interpretation of the story, even though he typically rejected the apocalyptic life-creation projects of his contemporaries. It is the story of a male gynecological surgeon who transformed himself gradually into a woman, to the extent that it was possible to do so without twentieth-century hormone treatment and surgical intervention. A prototypical case of gender intermediacy in the simultaneously decadent and apocalyptic fin de siècle, it is the most striking and longest narrative in the book. It may very well also be the longest case study in *Psychopathia Sexualis.*

The story, presented in Krafft-Ebing's compendium supposedly in the surgeon's own words, details the feelings and sensations of a highly intelligent "neurasthenic invert," whose transsexual identity emerged in early childhood.[28] In the doctor's own diagnosis, he was a glove fetishist. He came from a degenerate, neurasthenic bourgeois family, most of whose children died very early. In the German school that he attended after his family left Hungary, his schoolmates gave him the name of a girl they all knew because he looked like her. There are other details as well that qualify the adolescent boy as transgendered. Among other things, he was a transvestite who loved beautiful female attire.

What is most astonishing about the surgeon's first-person narrative is that he established a female identity through the power of fantasy. Were he a bachelor, wrote the surgeon, he would have castrated himself long ago. His female identity remained closeted; the man lived the public life of a successful surgeon, husband, and father. His final transformation took place during a serious attack of arthritis, accompanied by hallucinations that followed the surgeon's ingestion of cannabis and hashish. After the drug-induced hallucinations, he "became" a woman: he experienced his penis as a clitoris, his urinary tract as an entrance into the vagina, his scrotum as a vulva; his nipples developed sensitivity as if he were an adolescent girl; his stomach area assumed the shape of a woman's; he had imaginary menses every four weeks (*Liudi,* 154–73). Turn-of-the-century medical literature on male menstruation, for instance Hirschfeld's, emphasized sex as a continuum between male and female.[29] As a "woman," or as a degenerate, he also became hypersensitive to smells and to touch.

Unlike Krafft-Ebing, who treated this case as a positivist and psychopathologist, Rozanov expressed great interest in the surgeon's eroticism, which was so clearly beyond nature. In a polemical footnote, he questioned Krafft-Ebing's treatment of the surgeon's case as pathological (*Liudi,* 157n1). Particularly suggestive is his attribution of cosmic sexual significance to the case, evoking Solov'ev's vision of sex as a cosmic phenomenon that leads to resurrection, to which Rozanov normally gave little import. In his words, the story represents the "worldwide process of transition occurring in all humanity" (*Liudi,* 154). In his marginalia, he depicted the surgeon's delirium in the hospital as a fantastic emanation of cosmic activity—"during which a man, in essence, flies . . .—*internally, in an organized way*—billions of miles, through intergalactic spaces." He described the visual hallucinations as a shower of flashes from the man's eyes. "Actually having 'died' and been 'resurrected,' he heard the voice of the dead," wrote Rozanov in awe, "and experienced all kinship, including *female*" (*Liudi,* 164nn1 and 2). Commenting on Krafft-Ebing's response to the case, he criticized him for treating the surgeon's story as a curiosity instead of appreciating its cosmic bisexual meaning. Rozanov compared it to the discovery of radium (*Liudi,* 166n1), which had occurred just a few years before; the historical context in which he placed the bodily transformation of the surgeon is the excavations of Nineveh (Assyria) and Persepolis (Persia), which he considered less important than the doctor's experience of originary oneness (*Liudi,* 154).

My point is that Rozanov attributed to the surgeon's case extraordinary natural and cultural import; he interpreted it as an apocalyptic event in which the "old" man dies and is reborn in a "new," "female" body, suggesting that Rozanov privileged the latter. Even though he rejected Solov'ev's apocalyptic vision of bodily transfiguration, Rozanov's ecstatic response to the transformation of the surgeon invoked Solov'evian imagery. It is reminiscent of the conclusion of the *Meaning of Love,* in which the phallus is inverted and man receives a new androgynous body. In a footnote, Rozanov criticized the absence in medical literature of studies of androgynes (*Liudi,* 169n1). His visionary interpretation of the imaginary sex change may have been influenced by the fact that the narrator of the story was a surgeon who performed gynecological surgeries and autopsies on the dead: his power of dissection was so strong that he was able to will the reshaping of his own sex organs. On a rhetorical level, Rozanov's view that the surgeon turned the power of dissection inward reveals yet another instance of a fin-de-siècle reinterpretation of the positivist master trope. Another detail that must have endeared the surgeon to Rozanov was the overcoming of his aversion to foul odors and blood after he became a physician.

Rozanov's treatment of the surgeon evokes the figure of his bisexual ancestor who existed before the beginning of time; during his fantastic flight of fancy the surgeon experienced mythical bisexuality (all kinship, including female). In Rozanov's interpretation of the case study, the doctor emerges as a mythical androgynous ancestor. Elsewhere in *People of the Moonlight,* he described the third sex, meaning homosexuals, as "beings not of this world" who had created the "other [transcendent] world" (*Liudi,* 236n2). He concluded the analysis of the surgeon by emphasizing the latter's desire to castrate himself: since he no longer needed his procreative organs, his new life resembled the time before the onset of procreation; it also suggests that after his visionary transformation, he lacked sexual desire. Rozanov described him as "the carrier of a living miracle inside himself" (*Liudi,* 177). This may be the reason why he treated the case with such awe and suppressed Krafft-Ebing's emphasis on the man's sufferings and diagnosis of his condition as degenerate neurasthenia.[30] In the letter to Krafft-Ebing, missing in Rozanov's version, the surgeon thanked the psychiatrist for giving him courage not to think of himself as a monster.[31] It was precisely the monstrous, "unnatural" aspect that inspired Rozanov, despite his belief in procreation and patriarchal family life.[32]

Rozanov placed his commentary on the surgeon's story and on the fluidity of gender in a Russian cultural context, which resonates with his view of the radical intelligentsia of the 1860s. What makes this part of his commentary so noteworthy is that it reveals his awareness of the repressed homosexuality infused into the autobiography by the surgeon himself. But this interpretation remains at the level of subtext—in footnotes, in which Rozanov used alternately "urning" and "sodomite" to comment on the surgeon's gender; on the face of it, however, he emphasized the story's cosmic meaning, not its underlying tale of sexual repression.

Like Gippius, Rozanov wrote about the men and women of the 1860s in ambivalent terms, making Chernyshevsky the butt of his criticism while also affirming his "enormous" significance for Russian culture. Describing his portrait in a 1909 issue of *The Messenger of Europe* in a footnote to the case study of the surgeon, Rozanov compared Chernyshevsky's face to Raphael's beautiful, androgynous self-portraits. He goes on to say that Chernyshevsky was a closeted homosexual in Weininger's fluid mathematical terms: "½ urning, ¼ urning, 3/10 urning." Rozanov substantiated "the diagnosis" by claiming that desire between men is the driving force underlying Chernyshevsky's programmatic triple union in *What Is to Be Done?* In the novel Doctor Kirsanov, the best friend of Dmitrii Sergeevich Lopukhov, and Lopukhov's wife, Vera Pavlovna, fall in love with each other. Chernyshevsky represented the love triangle, or triple union, as an alternative to traditional marriage; Vera Pavlovna, however, is not ready for the reconfiguration of the adulterous paradigm into a new form of erotic relations in which triangulation would serve as the catalyst of revolutionary change. So as a liberated new man, who rejects possessiveness in love, the husband recuses himself from the marriage, freeing his wife to marry the man she loves. This is the standard interpretation of the events in the Lopukhov love triangle, whose potential energetic structure—as I suggested in the Gippius chapter—informed the Merezhkovsky ménage à trois.

According to Rozanov, however, instead of feeling liberated from possessive desire, the husband "experiences, secret pleasure, in his imagination, from the beauty and shapes of his wife's '[male] friend'" (*Liudi*, 160n1). His reading of the triple union in *What Is to Be Done?*—which eroticizes the relationship between Lopukhov and Kirsanov, not between the wife and the male suitor—is certainly very modern; it may have been influenced by the fin-de-siècle form of triangulation in the Merezhkovsky household. Whatever Rozanov's source, his original reading of the triangle can be said to prefigure Eve Kosofsky Sedgwick's theory of homosocial desire, to which I have referred on several occasions. Commenting on Krafft-Ebing's case of female transsexual desire, which Rozanov also recycled in *People of the Moonlight*, he again referred to Chernyshevsky and the 1860s, writing that "the storm of that time emerged out of the glass of homosexuality (*homosexual'nosti*)" (*Liudi*, 173n1).[33] As I noted in the introduction, the "storm" refers to the radical sexual politics of the 1860s, to which Rozanov ascribed a homoerotic and lesbian subtext; the glass refers to the retort, next to the frog the most common emblem of the positivist 1860s.

In Rozanov's list of Russian literature's sodomites, Chernyshevsky figures next to Tolstoy and Solov'ev. The inclusion of Chernyshevsky, in fact, reveals Rozanov's perception of him as the first in a series of

Russian utopian antiprocreationists who became more numerous and visible at the turn of the century.[34]

So can we say anything conclusive about Rozanov's view of same-sex desire based on his theory of bisexuality and the case of the surgeon besides labeling it as simultaneously celebratory and homophobic? We can state with some confidence that he treated individual homosexual and lesbian cases with sympathy, at times with veneration. In fact, he was more openly sympathetic to same-sex desire than were Gippius or Bely, even though he was known as the patriarchal guardian of their generation. We can also conclude that he could not envision a "third way" for the "third sex." Its male members, according to Rozanov, mimic heterosexual love, a mimicry that he described in patently physiological terms: the anus becomes the substitute for a vagina when the organ one desires is lacking. Unlike Freud, who based his psychoanalytic theory on the male fantasy of female lack, Rozanov emphasized the homosexual's lack of a vagina, not in symbolic terms but as an anatomical absence. Like Freud, however, he made multiple references in *People of the Moonlight* to castration, using both the Russian *oskoplenie* (which evokes the sect practicing physical self-castration) and the Latin *kastratsiia* (castration), which has both surgical and phantasmic connotations.[35]

I suggest then that despite the manifestly phallic aspect of Rozanov's metaphysics, he suffered from an inverted castration fear. What I have in mind is a kind of male "vagina envy" (which I discuss later in the chapter), analogous to Freudian penis envy. Such an interpretation of Rozanov's sexuality, which would certainly qualify as degenerate in Krafft-Ebing's diagnostics, sheds light on his sympathetic view of the case of the gynecological surgeon, who described the female experience of coitus in engulfing castrating terms: "[A]t that moment the woman is simply a vulva that has devoured the whole person" (*Liudi,* 168). This is, of course, the way the surgeon imagined female sexuality, with which—I would argue—Rozanov identified, despite, or maybe because, it is a textbook example of castration fear: he desired to be that woman who embraces the whole and castrates the male. In feminizing Rozanov's sexuality, I follow his own lead: he made numerous references to his "womanish" (*bab'ia*) nature: "I am not a 'man' [*muzhik*], but rather a maiden [*devushka*]," wrote Rozanov in a personal letter in 1911.[36]

But I would also suggest that Rozanov's references to the surgeon as urning and sodomite have rhetorical meaning. It seems that the homosexual is ultimately a rhetorical trope for Rozanov, one with a problematic referential function. While defending procreation and patriarchy, Rozanov's texts also have a palpable fetishistic relationship to language, represented in *People of the Moonlight* by the homosexual. From Rozanov's procreative perspective, the erotic economy of the homosexual is based on the wasteful, or excessive, spilling of semen, which, however, has a rhetorical function—it is a trope of writing, as is the blood fetish in Blok's poetics, in which the metaphor of decapitation and the bloodied head of the poet on a charger frees the persona from his body as well as from vampiric desire; it is the invigorating trope of poetry. But unlike Blok's lyrical trope in the poems that figure decollation, Rozanov's language and narratives are wildly excessive, with their excess serving as rhetorical displacement of the procreative whole.

In the end, of course, Rozanov opted for heterosexual love and the biological family. He did so in the name of what I would call reproductive immortality, which stands in sharp contrast to Solov'ev's immortalization project outlined in *Erotic Utopia.* A Marxist critic in the collection *Literary Collapse* (*Literaturnyi raspad,* 1908) offered a similar conclusion, formulating it in predictably negative terms: an immoral desire for "immortality" by means of "swinish reproduction."[37] Thus, when Rozanov idealized Krafft-Ebing's closeted homosexual, it is not inconsequential that he chose one who was not only a father but also a gynecologist who had acquired, if only phantasmically, female birth-giving organs. This allowed him to occupy the slippery position between sex that replenishes the whole and one that disperses it, thus also aligning the author with the subversion of procreation. In *People of the Moonlight,* Rozanov assigned the subversive function to the trope of homosexuality; in *The Jews' Olfactory and Tactile Relationship to Blood,* it was assigned to the Russian Jew and the trope of blood.

## Rozanov as "Pornographer"

In the addendum to the second edition of *People of the Moonlight* (1913), Rozanov offered his own Russian case studies, including the supposedly redacted diary of a homosexual novice ("Memoirs of a Novice of N Monastery"), whom the monk Pavel Florensky, a friend of Rozanov, knew. Contrary to the surgeon's story, Rozanov found no redeeming characteristics in the story of the novice, exposing it as a shockingly explicit case of sexual degeneration. (Let me remind the reader that the book is subtitled *Metaphysics of Christianity.*) Having already tried sex with women and monastic life to combat his deviant desire, the novice was attempting to purge his desire by means of confessional writing. In discussing this case, Rozanov sarcastically alluded to two of Krafft-Ebing's preferred "medical treatments" for deviancy: substitution of heterosexual for homosexual copulation and hydrotherapy, calling the latter "baths for the soul" (*Liudi,* 222). His contempt for the response of contemporary psychiatry to deviant sexuality was, as the reader may remember, shared by Solov'ev, who in *The Meaning of Love* claimed that psychiatrists sent male fetishists and sodomites to brothels and showed them pornographic images of naked women.[38]

In offering this case study of degeneration, Rozanov played with his own pornographic reputation.[39] The subject matter of same-sex desire, especially when it engages pedophilia, has always been considered obscene; moreover, literature on anatomy and sexual deviance served for many readers at the turn of the century as a substitute for pornography.[40] It was the scholarly and quasi-medical pretensions of *People of the Moonlight* as well as its use of Latin to describe some of the most explicit sexual details that not only made it an exemplar of *scientsia sexualis* but also helped it pass the censors. Krafft-Ebing had also used this device. Here is a passage from Rozanov's case study containing a virtual bouquet of degenerate thematics, with "pornographic" details in Latin:

> There turned up . . . people who took *meum phallum in orem,* and I was not frightened by this [in a footnote Rozanov noted that there are several examples of oral sex in Krafft-Ebing]. It is horrible. . . . I realized that I was threatened with the punishment of Sodom. But my passions were raised to such a pitch that I could not restrain myself. And I almost took my own life. And this passion developed to the point that I no longer felt passion for women, but only for *virum,* and in a manner that can be more simply stated as *in phallum,* or in remembering it. I conceived the goal, at whatever price, of freeing myself from this, and out of fear I decided to enter a monastery. I came home, O Lord have mercy, and made *coit. cum animali* in the full sense of the word. . . . This is nothing: I tried—although, thank God, it did not occur—but my endeavor was to commit *ac. sodomic.* With whom? With my nephew, who is moreover my godson, and five years old. Who am I and what am I to do? This happened several weeks, three or four, before I left for the monastery in 1906. (*Liudi,* 212–13)

Shocking in its explicitness, the confession of the novice is by no means Rozanov's most interesting depiction of sexual detail. Much more striking and artfully constructed are his fetishistic vignettes in which he depicted female and male private parts as if severed from the body whole. The question that arises with regard to these descriptions is whether his representation of genitalia makes use of the narrative strategies of pornography. Certainly, Rozanov regularly uncovered those parts of the body that are usually concealed, especially in polite society, but did he, like the pornographer, first stage their concealment? Rozanov attributed this action to prurient society, whose sexual squeamishness he deconstructed. The other question that arises in examining his pornographic reputation is whether his exposure of private parts is indeed sexually titillating. The answer today would in many instances be a resounding no because of the patently symbolic aspect of his discourse. Instead of representing the relation between individual private parts and their owners, Rozanov portrayed magnified images of sex organs that resemble primitive fetishes of fecundity, which are quite astonishingly physiological, but not pornographic.

Yet Rozanov's fetishist agenda was not just religious but also provocative, in a polemical as well as sexual sense. He associated his fetishist practice with Judaism—with what he perceived as the Jewish blood fetish, especially in circumcision—and other phallic religions, claiming them as the source of his religious totemism; he exposed the genitals, women's breasts, and pregnant stomachs as objects of religious worship, to which he typically affixed supplemental sexual meaning. A striking instance of Rozanov's prurient religious fetishism is the following passage from *Fallen Leaves:*

> Expansible matter embraces an unexpansible object, no matter how much larger it [unexpansible object!] *seems.* It [matter]—is always "larger." A boa constrictor as thick as an arm, at most as big as a leg at the knee, devours a small goat. This is the cause of many strange phenomena and of the appetite of the boa and goat. Yes, it hurts a little, is tight, but—it worked. . . . It is remarkable to put on a kid glove, how it lies there so narrow and "innocent" in the store box. But when it's put on, it forms a firm grip. The world gravitates metaphysically toward a "firm grip." In a "firm grip" God holds the world. (*Opavshie list'ia,* 2:563–64)

The passage first depicts the expansion of a vagina, erection of a penis (even though it is called an "unexpansible object"), and copulation, but without being anatomically concrete. It is followed by a metaphoric representation of castration fear. Rozanov embeds these aphoristic images in a fleeting reference to a woman's experience of penetration ("it hurts a little"), as if he identifies with it. He then makes an abrupt shift and locates us in a millinery shop, implicating the reader in the voyeuristic activity of watching an unknown woman put on a conventional fetish object, an activity that Krafft-Ebing's fin-de-siècle reader had come to associate with castration fear. From behind the voyeuristic shop curtain, we are then raised just as abruptly to the metaphysical level—to encounter God, whom Rozanov shockingly endowed with an expandable vagina that holds the earth in a "firm grip." This is certainly a tour de force, in which Rozanov commingles sex, religion, the everyday, and degenerate psychology in a typical decadent mix.[41]

When read against the tale of the Hungarian surgeon, who experienced his sex organs as female, Rozanov's feminization of God in this passage can be considered symptomatic of what I have described as his "vagina envy": not only women but God has a vagina. Yet Rozanov also resembles the glove fetishist, who like Krafft-Ebing's surgeon is obsessed with castration fear. However we interpret the interconnection of the sex act, the metaphoric *vagina dentata*, the glove metaphor, and God (in the shape of female genitalia), the passage reveals Rozanov's concern with the correlation of part and whole: the vignette serves as an instantiation of castration and fetishism as well as the coming together of the female and male sex organs, which reinstate the whole mediated by God.

What places Rozanov at the very heart of early modernist discourse is the simultaneity and seeming compatibility of the multiple rhetorical gestures that he used so masterfully. As to the more specific question of erotic titillation, the passage, which is remarkable in so many other ways, is unerotic, moving much too rapidly from one virtuosic sexual image to the next to be sexually arousing.

Fetishist desire also underlies Rozanov's view of other female markers of fecundity: "I was excited and attracted, rather was fascinated by breasts and a pregnant stomach. I regularly wanted to see the whole world pregnant," wrote Rozanov elsewhere in *Fallen Leaves* (*Opavshie list'ia*, 2:258).[42] The fantasy is followed by a conversation with a forty-five-year-old woman sitting next to him in the theater. Unlike the representation of God as a divine vagina—or the female fantasy of the Hungarian surgeon—the conversation, which takes place during the notorious performance of Nikolai Evreinov's production of Fedor Sologub's scandalous play *Nighttime Dances* (*Nochnye pliaski*, 1911), has an erotic charge.[43] (What critics found particularly scandalous in the play was the display of what was perceived at the time as female nudity.) Rozanov told his neighbor during intermission about his attraction to women's stomachs and breasts, adding that "there are no fewer ideas from the 'stomach' than from the 'head.'" Like a ventriloquist (ventriloquism means "speech of the stomach"), he endowed the pregnant stomach with great creative power, and in doing so, ascribed to it the status of a totemic fetish object. If we consider the fetish object in psychoanalytic rather than nature's procreative terms, we could attribute to it the function of an atypical fetish screen, on the order of the glove in the preceding example. What is more remarkable about this passage, however, is its suggestive maternal eroticism, imaginatively ventriloquized. Drawn to the eternally womanish—to reinvoke Berdiaev's epithet—Rozanov made pregnancy and motherhood sexy, taking Tolstoy's fascination with the maternal sphere several steps further. Turning our interpretive kaleidoscope one more time—with the purpose of inscribing Rozanov into the annals of psychopathology—we could diagnose him with the degenerate disorder of wanting to be a woman.

The staged figure of Rozanov confessing his intimate sexual fantasies about the maternal body to a random woman in the theater is highly transgressive, perhaps more so than the unveiling of the naked body on the stage in *Nighttime Dances*, or, for that matter, in performances of Wilde's *Salome* (to consider again Blok's female obsession). The story that Rozanov told challenges the boundaries of intimacy, a demarcation line that he loved to overstep. Making use of the characteristically Rozanovian whisper, it exposes for all to see a conversation that would normally be relegated to the private sphere. It locates us in what Bely describes as Rozanov's thick physiological jam—in which the reader may have the illusion that she has touched, if only on paper, the very private, pregnant female body. By sharing this verbal exchange with the reader, the author crossed over—between strangers—into the public sphere that censures such intimate display.

Predictably, Rozanov challenged the acceptable boundaries of intimacy in his private letters. For instance, in one of the compromising letters that he addressed to Liudmila Vil'kina (wife of Nikolai Minsky) on December 28, 1906, and which he tried very hard to retrieve, he wrote her: "[L]et your cunt stay fresh and sweet, which I caressed so often *mentally* [italics mine]. . . . I will remember it at midnight in the New Year, so black, moist, and fragrant." What is striking about this passage is that instead of remembering their intimacies, he described his sexual fantasies about her—cerebral sexual fantasies—as if their relationship had been strictly discursive. In an earlier letter in fact (May 15, 1902), he emphasized the typically cerebral enervation associated with sexual desire in the fin de siècle, writing that he would speak of his desire for her just to "excite [her] nerves for 2–3-5–8 days." Even more cerebral were his supposed fantasies about the shape and texture of Tatiana and Natal'ia Gippius's genitals. He wrote about this in a letter to Gippius, in which he told her that he was in no way attracted to either of her sisters. In an earlier letter to her, he went into great detail in describing female genitalia and the differences between kissing the genital labia and the lips of the face, interspersed between commentary regarding Merezhkovsky's writings and his thoughts about the Crucifixion.[44]

Although these samples of Rozanov's "shocking" sexual discourse are all different, what unites them is an underlying fetishistic sensibility, which is combined variously with a metaphysical vision and/or a procreative, pro-nature ideology. Fetishism and the conflation of sex and religion are generally telltale signs of decadence, as is cerebral sexuality, but the "maternal taint" that Rozanov assigned to it is uniquely his own. One way of addressing the charge of pornography against him is to consider the pornographic in his writings a self-conscious trope, one that displaces the maternal as well as the paternal body.

## The Blood Libel and Rozanov's Anti-Semitism

Both editions of *People of the Moonlight*, which praises the Old Testament at the expense of the New, came out at the height of Rozanov's anti-Semitic campaign in the press. His most virulent anti-Semitic feuilletons began to appear in 1911 and reached their peak in 1913. The occasion for the emergence of Rozanov's full-blown anti-Semitism was the accusation in 1911 of ritual murder against the Jewish shop assistant Mendel Beilis in Kiev. To repeat once again, Beilis was charged with the ritual murder of Andrei Iushchinsky, a thirteen-year old Russian Orthodox boy. The "Beilis affair" became Russia's Dreyfus case, widening further the rift between the state and the intelligentsia.[45] Not just the liberal but even some conservative members of the educated classes found the blood libel accusation against Beilis unfounded and inflammatory. Rozanov's position was made all the more shocking and controversial by his reputation as an exponent of modernist literature, whose writers were rarely anti-Semitic nationalists, at least not openly.

The two volumes of *Fallen Leaves*, which also appeared at this time (1913 and 1915), reflect Rozanov's growing anti-Semitism, whereas the coeval *People of the Moonlight* maintained his "philo-Semitic" position of the beginning of the century. But unlike his self-conscious inconsistency in matters of sex and religion—both of which are marked by the synecdoche of blood—his shift from a celebration of Judaism as a procreative religion to the "Jewish question" had overt political connotations. I have in mind his most outrageous book, *The Jews' Olfactory and Tactile Relationship to Blood* (1914), published after the exoneration of Beilis, in which the "sexual question" is subsumed by the "Jewish question." It contains feuilletons that appeared in *New Time* (*Novoe vremia)* and *Populace* (*Zemshchina),* an organ of the anti-Semitic Black Hundreds, as well as unpublished material. The published feuilletons led to a publishing boycott in the liberal press. They resulted in a "trial" by peers in the Religious-Philosophical Society in 1914. Rozanov savored his notoriety: disrepute among his former admirers and a new, reactionary readership. After the Bolshevik revolution, Rozanov revisited his outrageous anti-Semitism on the eve of the war in an apparent attempt to make amends, writing in *Apocalypse of Our Time* that "he is grateful to the Jews for everything, just as he cursed them for everything during his apostasy (the unfortunate time of Beilis)."[46]

Stylistically, the book is unremarkable. It lacks the characteristic Rozanovian whisper and paradoxical vision. His polemical voice is strident, as if he were writing political proclamations. Needless to say, the book is devoid of dialogicity: its agenda is exclusively contra Judaism and Jews. How, then, does it relate to the subject of *Erotic Utopia*?

Let me begin by recounting an episode from the beginning of the century featuring a stylized blood ritual performed at the Petersburg apartment of Nikolai Minsky and his wife, Liudmila Vil'kina, with whom Rozanov had an amorous relationship.[47] Rozanov's anti-Semitic writings on the eve of the war shed a new light on his participation in that event, which took place May 2, 1905. Evgenii Ivanov, relative, friend, and admirer of Rozanov, learned about the ceremony from Rozanov's stepdaughter. He described it in a letter to Blok, which is my main source regarding the gathering. The religious ritual, accompanied by Dionysian dancing, was modeled on the Crucifixion and symbolized divine betrothal. Viacheslav Ivanov and Minsky proposed the idea for the ritual celebration at one of Rozanov's regular Sunday gatherings. The meeting at the Minskys on the English Embankment resembled similar mystical assemblies at Ivanov's and Lidiia Zinov'eva-Annibal's Tower. The stylized ritual—a signature life-creation episode of the Russian fin de siècle—also recalls the secret initiation performed by Gippius, Merezhkovsky, and Filosofov in 1901 as the foundational rite of their new church. Like the event at the Minskys, the Merezhkovskys' ritual symbolized the Crucifixion, the Resurrection, and divine betrothal, only without bloodletting.

Among those in attendance at the 1905 gathering were Rozanov and his stepdaughter, Ivanov and his wife Zinov'eva-Annibal, who was dressed in an eccentric floor-length red shirt, Berdiaev, Aleksei Remizov and their wives, Sologub, Zinaida Vengerova (a player in Gippius's erotic triangles of the 1890s and Minsky's future wife), and her famous brother Semen Vengerov.[48] Some of them had attended the earlier Religious-Philosophical Meetings.

The long ceremony was orchestrated by Ivanov, who developed his theory of the similarity of Dionysian and Christian sacrifice during those years. The high point of the evening was the decadent blood ritual, requiring the voluntary sacrifice of one of the guests. According to Evgenii Ivanov's letter, the only outsider at the gathering, a young Jewish music student, volunteered; he was a friend of Rozanov's stepdaughter, who had invited him to the gathering. After much debate on his suitability as sacrificial victim, Ivanov and Zinov'eva-Annibal cut his wrist and let the blood flow into a goblet. It was mixed with wine and everyone drank it as if it were the Eucharist, although the vampiric subtext could not have been lost on anyone; then the sacrificial victim was placed in a crucified position. Rozanov and his stepdaughter, wrote Evgenii Ivanov, afterward felt something new resembling communal union.[49] Converting the young man into a woman, Gippius, who was not in attendance, described it secondhand as an evening "where for some reason a timid, unknown girl's finger was pricked with a pin and a drop of her blood was mixed into a glass of wine. Rozanov went there, in extreme secrecy from his wife, of course—on the sly."[50] A devout Russian Orthodox, Varvara Dmitrievna would have disapproved of the dubious activities at the Minskys; she generally disapproved of Rozanov's symbolist friends. To say the least, the gathering had the accoutrements of a decadent affair, with the symbolic expenditure of blood.

Had Rozanov not returned to it during the period of the Beilis affair, the ceremony would have been remembered as typical decadent play with religious syncretism, conflating the deaths of Christ and Dionysus. Anti-Semitic references to it, in all likelihood, would have been limited to Merezhkovsky's playful remark in absentia that quoted Pushkin's well-known poem "Hussar" (having attended a witches Sabbath, the hussar describes it as "a wedding of a Yid and a frog").[51] In an essay titled "A Telephone Reminder" ("Napominaniia po telefonu"), first published in *New Time* (1913) and then in *The Jews' Olfactory and Tactile Relationship to Blood,* Rozanov offered a new redaction of the Minsky affair; he gave it an unabashedly anti-Semitic interpretation, contrary to Evgenii Ivanov's claim that he was an enthusiastic participant in the ceremony. Like Ivanov, Rozanov described the event as an example of literary carnivalization in the hothouse world of the Petersburg artistic elite. A pin and a penknife, wrote Rozanov, were used alternately to draw blood for the Eucharist from the veins, this time of a Jewish musician and a young Jewish woman—in reverse, I would add, of the supposed bloodletting of the Russian Orthodox Andrei Iushchinsky by Beilis. Rozanov wrote: "In this event . . . it is notable that the idea of receiving communion using human blood arose not in any of the Russians, not in a Russian head and brain . . . but in a Jewish home, in predominantly Jewish company and in a Jewish brain."[52]

In the feuilleton, Rozanov claimed that the majority of the guests were Jewish, even though the Ivanovs, the Remizovs, the Berdiaevs, Sologub, and Rozanov himself—considerably more than half of those in attendance—were not! Although he mentioned it, he conveniently downplayed the fact that the sacrificial victims in this "blood ritual" were Jewish, not Russian (in his version, there were two bloodlettings), and that Viacheslav Ivanov was the main instigator. Rozanov attributed the idea to Minsky because the desire for a ritual Communion with real human blood could arise only in his "Jewish brain." Minsky and his wife were converted Jews, as were the members of the Vengerov family, and the only Jew attending the affair was the sacrificial scapegoat.

In this later replay of the blood ritual, Rozanov explained it as the product of Jewish "heredity" and Jewish "atavism," which Russian "primordial brain cells" lack; Russians, wrote Rozanov, lack the atavistic memory of "imbibing" and "ingesting human blood."[53] In the discourse of degeneration, atavism, among other characteristic features, refers to bestiality in nymphomaniacs, suggesting in this context the sexual predatoriness of the Jews; their victims by implication belong to the Russian nation.[54] Thus, Rozanov takes his admiration of what he perceived as Judaic blood worship—especially in the rite of circumcision—to its opposite extreme. The feuilleton lambasting the blood ritual performed in Minsky's apartment in 1905 interprets Jewish relation to blood as atavistic, that is, degenerate. Instead of describing the blood of circumcision and defloration in Judaism as the mark of procreative bounty, as he did before and continued to do elsewhere, Rozanov here viewed the Jewish blood fetish as vampiric and infectious.

Even if in the second decade of the twentieth century the sexual question assumed a negative correlation to the Jewish question, blood remained the binding synecdoche of Rozanov's discourse, characterized by its interchangeability with semen. This becomes especially clear when one considers his strident nationalism in response to the epoch's fear of racial decline and consequent "lack of [Russian] semen," which he associated variously with Christ's teachings and Jewish vampirism.

The two versions of the 1905 ritual are an archetypal Rozanovian palimpsest. Rozanov rewrote the earlier version as presented by Evgenii Ivanov, whose accuracy we have no reason to doubt. The new version was apparently disdainful of facts, including of Rozanov's supposedly exalted view of the ritual. Speaking metaphorically, he overwrote the combined Dionysian and Christian ritual with a crude anti-Semitic one. His later version reveals the motor that drove Rozanov's polemical style, which he took here to its shocking extreme. Unscrupulous, or immoral like Nietzsche, Rozanov ignored the potential impact of his inflammatory feuilletons. He was unconcerned that a statement such as "Andrei Iushchinsky is a Christian martyr" for whom "children should pray as about a martyred pious person" could incite pogroms.[55] His interest was discursive.

When Rozanov exhausted the polemical possibilities of a given topic, he turned to another controversial subject and proceeded to cannibalize it. Rozanov's whipping boys of the early 1900s were Christians and the historical church because they promoted a discourse that depleted the nation of its reproductive vitality; the scapegoats of the second decade of the century were increasingly the Jewish predators sucking the nation's blood.[56] The "sexual question" was displaced by the "Jewish question." Yet such a claim—of a developmental model in which one group of scapegoats replaces another—misrepresents his shifty ideology, which is considerably less linear and subject to closure, as can be ascertained by juxtaposing *The Jews' Olfactory and Tactile Relationship to Blood* and the more or less coeval *People of the Moonlight.* The only thing we can say with some certainty is that the former demonizes Jews and all forms of Judaic ritual practices, whereas the latter does not. Contrary to his positive assessment of the Jewish blood fetish, a term he used obsessively in *The Jews' Olfactory and Tactile Relationship to Blood,* he employed it here as a mark not of procreative vigor but of degeneration.

Nineteenth-century anti-Semitism was incorporated into psychopathology by its leading medical practitioners: Charcot, Krafft-Ebing, Lombroso, and others.[57] They emphasized two conflicting causes of Jewish degeneration: inbreeding and the deleterious impact of assimilation into modern, enlightened European societies. Like Weininger in *Sex and Character,* Rozanov combined two seemingly incompatible sexual stereotypes of the time: the sexually rapacious Jew who subverts the racial purity of his adopted nation, and the effeminate, inbred Jew who is the cause of its degeneration. The Jew became the living embodiment of the feared fin-de-siècle vampire, attacking the health of society from two sides; Stoker's Count Dracula was perceived by many European readers as Jewish, in part because of his foreign, East European origins. A degenerate scion of an ancient family, Dracula keeps himself alive by drinking the fresh virginal blood of women. The vampiric trope cuts both ways: bloodsucking suggests sexual rapacity; the metaphoric sex act infects future mothers with the taint of degeneration.[58]

The conflicted myth that Jews possess extraordinary heterosexual vitality yet need Christian blood to maintain their strength typified Rozanov's anti-Semitism in the second decade of the twentieth century, reflecting the views of an epoch tainted by degenerate heredity and a decadent sensibility. In a 1912 passage from *Fallen Leaves,* Rozanov wrote of the Jewish nation's blood, emphasizing its strength: "The strength of the Jews is in their extremely ancient blood. . . . Not decrepit: It has been matured well and has been getting more and more refined (struggle, effort, cunning)" (*Opavshie list'ia,* 1:220–21). On the other hand, he claimed that the Jewish nation was too old to maintain its genetic vitality: it was "a worn-out nation—ground and reground into dust."[59] Unlike other degenerate nations that lack the sexual energy to survive, Jews, according to the blood libel, revive their aging bodies by imbibing, literally and figuratively, the blood of gentile boys and virgins. Hence the vicious myth of Jewish parasitism.

So Rozanov's view of the Beilis affair inverted his oft-repeated claim that Christian blood was degenerate and Jewish blood healthy. If, as he wrote in the preceding passage from *Fallen Leaves,* the power of Jewish blood was in its "cunning" strength, then it was to blame for Russia's growing decline. After all, he figured the pale, bloodless body of Andrei Iushchinsky, ravished by Beilis, as an image of Russian degeneration that must be venerated. The young martyr, a Christ figure in *The Jews' Olfactory and Tactile Relationship to Blood,* resembles his earlier representations of male degenerates, including Christ. Having fashioned himself as a self-righteous nationalist, especially during the years of the Beilis case, Rozanov reversed his former rejection of the effeminate Christ and converted his polemical disdain for him into love, despite the abundance of images of Christian degeneration in *People of the Moonlight.* Linking the blood libel to the crucifixion of Christ in *The Jews' Olfactory and Tactile Relationship to Blood,* he blamed the Crucifixion on the Jews, in concert with the most vituperative anti-Semites.[60]

In another reversal, Rozanov attributed the conflicted anti-Semitic myth of Jewish sexual rapacity and degeneration to circumcision, which he extolled in his philo-Semitic writings as the divine rite of biological continuity celebrating childbearing and genealogy (*Liudi,* 266n1). In his philo-Semitic discourse, he described circumcision as the site of God's procreative kiss and mark of the male betrothal to God. Referring to the genitals as the "spark" of God in the body, Rozanov considered circumcision the source of the Jewish nation's sanctity. Predictably, in *The Jews' Olfactory and Tactile Relationship to Blood,* he associates the ritual with the decadent effeminacy of Jewish men, not only with their sexual vitality. As Laura Engelstein has noted, Rozanov revealed "the homosexual undertones of the blood ritual myth [which he] displaced onto his fantasy of circumcision as holy fellatio."[61] Yet he did not link circumcision and homosexuality in *People of the Moonlight,* his disquisition on same-sex love.

In *The Jews' Olfactory and Tactile Relationship to Blood,* Rozanov described the ritual of circumcision in someone else's words, a Rozanovian polemical device, but in this case he remained silent below the line and clearly expressed agreement with the cited author. The voice of the other is gratuitous here; instead of polemical dialogicity, the device gives "scholarly" value to the description. According to Viacheslav Sokolov's *Circumcision among the Jews* (1892), the source Rozanov invoked, the *mezizah,* the fourth act of the circumcision ritual, "consists in the sucking of blood from [the infant's] wound and is performed in the following way: the mohel takes a mouthful of wine into his mouth, seizes the bloody wound with his lips, holds it between his teeth, sucks blood from it, and spits it into a vessel. . . . Considering the blood of circumcision to be sacred, . . . [the mohel] during the performance of this fourth act holds the infant over a vessel containing water, so that the blood flows from the wound into the vessel, and those present . . . wash their faces with the bloody water."[62]

Looking at the passage through the lens of the fin de siècle, one recognizes Rozanov's discursive, vampiric intentions. What is curious about this description of circumcision is the similarity of the image of blood flowing from the wound into a vessel to the ritual performed by

Ivanov and Zinov'eva-Annibal in 1905. Instead of washing their faces in the bloody water, the guests attending the gathering drank the blood mixed with wine, as in the Christian Eucharist. When read through the racist filter of Rozanov's feuilleton "A Telephone Reminder" and his views on circumcision expressed in *The Jews' Olfactory and Tactile Relationship to Blood,* the ritual at the Minskys' apartment, whether intended by the participants or not, acquires increasingly shrill anti-Semitic overtones.

Whatever Rozanov's views on circumcision at a given moment, whether pro or contra, his interest in the blood fetish links him to the epoch's racial anxiety and fear of degenerate bloodlines, as in the case of Blok. It may not be fortuitous that, like Rozanov's anti-Semitic feuilletons, the writing of *Retribution,* Blok's most extensive commentary on degeneration and the blood taint, overlapped with the time period of the Beilis case. But contrary to Blok, who made no anti-Semitic references in the poem, Rozanov took racial anxiety to its extreme, accusing Jews of sacrificial violence.

And if we take the next hermeneutic step and consider the discourse of Rozanov's vituperative attack on Judaism and Russian Jewry, we discern the use of a literary strategy that reveals as much about his rhetorical concerns as about ideology. When writing about Russian Jewry and divesting it of its procreative vigor—and by extension of the power of maintaining the natural whole—he also revealed his fetishistic relationship to language. He aligned language symbolically with the Jew, who comes to inform the trope of excess and sacrificial violence in these instances instead of procreation. Hence the "excessive" nature of Rozanov's own language, which he explored with greater fascination than anything else. The same is true of Rozanov's figuration of the homosexual, as I argued earlier: when he is not an icon of primordial bisexuality, he represents a perverse, excessive relation to language. And if Rozanov's language has the function of expressing excess, then the figuration of the threat of spiritual sodomy and Judaism to the procreative economy and to the nation becomes a function of Rozanovian language.

*The Jews' Olfactory and Tactile Relationship to Blood* is certainly Rozanov's most obsessive book. So it stands to reason that the synecdoche of blood, his favorite rhetorical fetish, suffers from an embarrassment of riches in this, his most bloody book. In the mind of the anti-Semite, the most obvious locus for the blood fetish in Jewish everyday life, outside the sexual sphere, is, of course, the kosher slaughterhouse, which Rozanov described in several feuilletons dedicated to animal slaughter and sacrifice. Predictably, he disparaged the ancient preparation of meat, claiming that it is the origin of all ritual bloodletting, including of Christian children.

Like Tolstoy, who visited a slaughterhouse in 1891 (see chapter 1), Rozanov visited a kosher slaughterhouse in the southwest of the Russian Empire between 1905 and 1910.[63] And like Tolstoy, who described the slaughter of livestock in "First Step" (which Rozanov had read) with the purpose of promoting vegetarianism, Rozanov wrote a feuilleton with didactic intentions.[64] Titled "What I Happened to See There. . ." ("Chto mne sluchilos' tam uvidet'. . ."), it promotes the closing of all kosher slaughterhouses in Russia. Following in the footsteps of Tolstoy, Rozanov employed violent rhetoric to represent animal slaughter, rhetoric that dispersed the whole by dismembering the animal literally before our very eyes; the Tolstoy-like accretion of detail is accomplished by means of rhetorical vivisection, which follows the successive order used in kosher livestock slaughter. True, the description is less unrelentingly naturalistic than Tolstoy's: it does not, for instance, represent the animal's response to the butchery by showing the terrifying disintegration of its central nervous system, meaning its suffering. But it employs similar rhetorical and narrative strategies—repetition of fetishist detail that assumes a life of its own.

The narrative climax of Tolstoy's sermon on vegetarianism is a sadistic and excessively long description of the butchery of animals, whose violence the author seemed to relish rhetorically. Depicting the slaughter of many animals, one after another, piece by piece, Tolstoy implicated himself as well as the reader in the bloody rhetoric of horror. The same technique and fetishist pleasure characterize Rozanov's descriptions. He derived rhetorical pleasure from displaying the dismemberment of animals into their constituent body parts in great detail, all the while accusing the predatory Jew of the taint of the degenerate blood fetish. Tolstoy's ostensible reason for such bloodthirsty representation was to promote vegetarianism; Rozanov's reason for displaying the bloody animal parts was to implicate the whole Jewish nation in ritual murder. A master of polemical journalism, he was much more vicious than Tolstoy, interspersing visions of butchery with inflammatory anti-Semitic statements that reduplicate the horror, while simultaneously implicating himself in the rhetorical economy of bloody sacrificial excess.

Rozanov's most explicit description of slaughter is in the "scholarly" feuilleton "Ritual Sacrifice among Ancient Jews" ("Zhertvoprinoshenie u drevnikh evreev"). Based on the sacred books of Judaism, the vivisection of the lamb by the appointed kosher butcher continues until the whole lamb has been dressed for ritual sacrifice. Here is an abbreviated passage: "He (who removed the skin) did not break the hind legs, but rather pierced the knee and hung it; he flayed the skin up to the breast; having reached the breast, he cut off the head; . . . then he cut off the shins; . . . he finished flaying the skin, cut open the heart, let out its blood, cut off the front arms [*perednie ruki*]; . . . arrived at the right (hind) leg [and cut it off] . . . and with it both testicles; then he tore it [the lamb] apart and all of it appeared open before him; he took the fat and laid it on the cut of meat from the head, above it; then he took the innards [which had been washed]. He took a knife and separated the lung from the kidney; he punctured the breast [and so on]."[65]

The depiction of ritual slaughter mimics objectivity. It is informed by ostensibly "scholarly" reliance on the *Tamid*, a tractate of the Kodashim in the Talmud; the *Tamid* describes in detail the slaughter and preparation of the lamb for ritual sacrifice. Rozanov's objectivity, however, is a cover for displaced fetishist desire, in this instance satisfied by the dismemberment of a lamb in orderly succession. A self-designated fetishist of trifles, he becomes a fetishist of violent dismemberment, whose fragmenting divisive poetics—like Tolstoy's—belie a slippery inversion of his Old Testament procreative ideal.

Rozanov's view of the blood libel and of ritual slaughter of livestock demands further comment on his Judeophilia. Laura Engelstein, who has offered the most incisive interpretation of Rozanov's ambivalent relation to Judaism, aptly described his affection as an "inverted world of Judeophilia," as if it were imbricated with the epoch's homosexual desire. She also appropriately claimed that his love-hate of the Jews was the product of his essential immoralism. I would add to this the unraveling of Rozanov's faith in the rhetorical whole, whose procreative subtext had been the bringing into the world of a natural surplus—a new child—that results in racial continuity. Instead his inverted world of Judeophilia produced a relentless fetishism of parts, with blood serving as a perverse substitute for semen, of which there was not enough to maintain the health of the Russian nation. In concert with his vicious Jewish predator, Rozanov spills blood on the page himself, problematizing its vituperative message.

In the end, Rozanov's strident anti-Semitism represents racist scapegoating and paranoia that belie paradox.[66] On the eve of the war, he claimed that all Russians were a little Jewish ("all are little Beilises"), meaning that the whole national body had been infected.[67]

Rozanov's writing represents a unique early modernist palimpsest. He reversed himself frequently, but his key concerns remain visible through every new top layer. The Rozanov case study reveals typical fin-de-siècle obsessions set against the background of an exhibitionist celebration of phallic sex and what I have called vagina envy. Applying Foucault's terms to Rozanov's writings, we can say that more than the other authors whom I have examined here, he perceived "the entire social body [as having been] provided with a 'sexual body.'"[68] In his paean to procreative sex, we can see the desire to reverse the course of the epoch's degeneration and to reinfuse the nation with healthy blood; in the case of vagina envy, he revealed envy of female sexuality; his ambivalent view of same-sex desire reflected the epoch's medicalization of sexual perversion as well as a fetishizing rhetorical strategy, which had multiple layers of meaning.

Foucault's view of fetishism at the end of the nineteenth century—"governed by the interplay of whole and part, principle and lack, absence and presence, excess and deficiency"—provides an apt summary of the ways it worked in Rozanov's writings.[69] In this respect Rozanov is not unlike the other figures discussed in this study, whose sexual identities were formed by a fear of physical excess as well as of its deficiency, but he differed from them in the way he conceptualized the whole. His notion of the whole was rooted in nature—its replenishment—and Old Testament procreative discourse, whereas Solov'ev and his followers looked for it in the apocalyptic transfiguration of the bodily gestalt. Of all the authors in *Erotic Utopia*, only Rozanov remained firmly committed to sex and procreation; even Tolstoy turned against nature's procreative imperative in the end.

Yet after 1905 and especially on the eve of the war, it seems that Rozanov's cause of wresting the procreative body from life-denying Christianity was overshadowed by a crude form of Russian nationalism, whose discourse was also physiological, with particular emphasis on the disruptive synecdoche of blood. He frequently displaced the recuperative blood of circumcision, defloration, and childbirth onto the sacrificial blood of Christian boys, creating a vicious palimpsest. At his most archly anti-Semitic, Rozanov represented the national body as a corpse drained of blood by vampiric Jewish predators. An image of a degenerate, lifeless body, it reflected the fin-de-siècle anxiety about the coming end of the Russian nation. It was as if the trope of Christian sodomy, full of dispersing rhetorical power, were juxtaposed with the equally powerful dispersing metaphor of Jewish vampirism. If we apply his sinister metaphor of the Russian fly trapped in a web spun by the Jewish spider (*Fallen Leaves*) to Rozanov himself, we conclude that he was both spider and fly stuck in his own web of contradictions, garnering sticky, smelly pleasure from it.[70]

A sustained singular vision seemed to go against the grain of Rozanov's writerly style. But as he shifted in his political journalism on the eve of the war from an attack on Christianity—and former disavowal of the blood of crucifixion—to a discourse that berated Jews and the Jewish blood fetish, he proclaimed the superiority of Christianity to Judaism. Contrary to his essential paradoxicalness, Rozanov made a choice between the two religions in *People of the Moonlight* and *The Jews' Olfactory and Tactile Relationship to Blood.* It appears that the Russian and Jewish bodies could not coexist harmoniously in the same discursive space, reduplicating the state of affairs in Russian imperial society. They could only exist in totalizing conflict on the pages of these two books: the bloodless Christian corpse acquires moral superiority in one and the Jewish national body in the other, suggesting a predatory relationship between them.

Rozanov's reversals and slippery treatment of sex and Christianity were tolerated by the literary intelligentsia of modernist persuasion, because what he had to say was original. His vitriolic anti-Semitism was not, especially in the context of the Beilis trial. His former supporters at the Religious-Philosophical Meetings and its heir, the Religious-Philosophical Society, of which Rozanov was a member, were deeply shocked by his racist journalism. In 1902 the Religious-Philosophical Meetings had devoted five sessions to the "sexual question," with Rozanov prominently insisting on the sacredness of the Old Testament at the expense of the New. In late 1913 and early 1914, the Religious-Philosophical Society devoted three meetings to Rozanov's social irresponsibility, especially in his anti-Semitic writings. Rozanov's earlier radical position on marriage was overwritten by the "Rozanov question." His former literary allies, Merezhkovsky, Gippius, Filosofov, Kartashev, and others, proposed expulsion. Quoting the finale of the article "Andrei Iushchinsky"—that the boy was a new martyred saint for whom all Russia should pray—Filosofov accused Rozanov of "advocating pogroms, bloodletting, and vengeance." Filosofov made this statement at the third meeting, on January 26, 1914.[71] It reflected the liberal position for which Rozanov had a lifelong visceral dislike. As he wrote in *Solitaria*, "I am not such a scoundrel to think about morality."[72] Because they had other things in common, his symbolist contemporaries and their allies had tolerated his politics of procreation and unsavory "physiological jam," but not his racist nationalism.[73]

The other fundamental difference between Rozanov and Solov'ev's followers was the latter's commitment to life creation and immortalization of the body. Despite his fascination with the Hungarian surgeon, Rozanov had no desire to tamper with physiology in the apocalyptic sense. His view of time and history was dictated by nature, not apocalyptic ideas. He hoped instead to translate naturalistic physiology into the sphere of language. Despite his fetishist fantasies, Rozanov was a traditionalist who believed in the patriarchal family that had informed Tolstoy's great novels. He was not attracted to constructing new exclusionary forms of radical sectarianism, as were Gippius, Merezhkovsky, Bely, and Blok. On the contrary, he appealed to the nation to return to phallic sex and nature's perpetuity.

Unlike the life-creation projects of the decadent utopians, which commingled life and literature, Rozanov's program was essentially rhetorical. According to his own self-description, he had an innate "manuscript soul" (*Opavshie list'ia*, 1:250). One of the reasons for his essentially fetishist relationship to language, not to life, may have been the lack of a self-consciously mythologized biography, even though in his early youth, he had married Dostoevsky's once young femme fatale Apollinaria Suslova. This unquestionably eccentric gesture could be seen as an attempt to access the fraught relationship between the novelist and the young nihilist dominatrix. Instead of Suslova, however, he ended up celebrating the figure of his devout and sickly second wife Varvara Dmitrievna Butiagina and the Russian Orthodox patriarchal way of life practiced in their home, which housed six children. Except for Varvara Dmitrievna's illness and occasional images taken from his domestic life, including photographs of his family, his writings were not imbricated with his personal life practice, sexual or otherwise. The thick physiological jam as represented by his eccentric sexual theories and images was, in all likelihood, not the projection of personal experience, although we must admit that we know almost nothing about his actual sex life. Rozanov himself claimed a tepid libido.[74]

In fact, the only personal experience about which he wrote was his wife's mysterious degenerative disease of many years. It punctuates

Family photograph from Vasilii Rozanov's *Fallen Leaves*

*Solitaria* and both volumes of *Fallen Leaves*, as do the locations where he writes about it: his wife's bedside, hospitals, and cabs taking him there. Rozanov unabashedly displays for all to see the intimate recesses of Varvara Dmitrievna's body, such as unnatural vaginal bleeding, abscessed cervix, loss of mobility and speech. As to the squeamish "dirty medics" whom he lambasted in *People of the Moonlight*, he makes reference to a long list of Russian neurologists and psychopathologists that his wife consulted without much success: among the best known were Ivan Merzheevsky, Vladimir Bekhterev,[75] and Iakov Anfimov; among their diagnoses was cerebral palsy—then called cerebral paralysis—considered a disease of the central nervous system, the premier locus of psychosomatic illness in the degenerate age.[76]

It is ironic that of all the writers examined in this book the only one that celebrated the aesthetic power of procreation and bodily excretions, including vaginal blood, also had the most personal experience with the diseases associated with the bane of degeneration. Considered from this perspective, Rozanov's ambivalence toward the medical profession and degeneration theory makes perfect sense. So does his appropriation of their rhetorical practices to render both his aesthetic and ideological views—after all, he observed the practitioners and theorists at close hand. The unsettling experience of Varvara Butiagina's illness may help explain that which Berdiaev called Rozanov's "brilliant writerly physiology" or what we could describe as his infusion of the language of literature with the inarticulate sphere of human genitalia, bodily excretions, and smells.[77]

# Conclusion

Grand Duke Alexei, heir to the Russian throne, suffered from a hereditary blood disease. The perception was that the Romanov dynasty was doomed by hemophilia, which is transmitted through the female bloodline, but infects only men. Rhetorically, it could be described as a decadent disease, especially if we consider it in relation to the bane of degeneration and the blood trope of the decadence, not to speak of the myth of feminine evil in the fin de siècle. What could be a more eloquent symptom of degeneration than one that fits its medical, rhetorical, and ideological criteria and is found at the pinnacle of political power. The Russian monarchy manifested other symptoms of decline as well. The blood taint, however, was the Romanovs' most striking exemplar of degeneration, contributing to the downfall of the ruling house, which changed Russian life forever.

The presence of Grigorii Rasputin at the Russian court was linked to Alexei's illness. A Siberian peasant who claimed divine healing powers, Rasputin had insinuated himself into the royal family by convincing the emperor and empress that he could contain the uncontrollable flow of blood during their son's hemophilic attacks. This unseemly situation exacerbated the symbolic significance of the royal disease. Rumors were rampant that Rasputin was a member of the Khlysts, an orgiastic sect that gained attention in the decadent period, that he was having a salacious affair with the empress, and that wild orgies were taking place in the royal palace itself. Rasputin lived a life of sexual excess and was surrounded by decadent luxury, having acquired political power in court circles. His influence came to an end in 1916 when he was assassinated by a group of conspirators consisting of members of the royal family and the notorious anti-Semite Vladimir Purishkevich. In contrast to the widespread perception of the Romanov genealogy as decadent, Rasputin was seen by many as a man of the people with nothing less than superhuman strength. This was Rozanov's perspective on Rasputin in 1915.

Rozanov characterized him as a "brilliant muzhik" whose link to God was through "physiology."[1] Russian literature's agent provocateur—a religious thinker whose writing was suffused with a veneration of sex and the synecdoche of blood—was fascinated by Rasputin. His capaciousness for excess captured Rozanov's imagination, as it did that of Blok, who identified with his dark sensuality: "Grishka [still] sits inside me," wrote Blok in 1917.[2] Blok affiliated Rasputin's impact with the "exceptional atmosphere [created by] a hysterical generation" and considered him one of the causes of the revolution, which he welcomed as a cure for the degenerate body of Russia.[3] Society, according to Blok in *Katilina* (1919), "was not able to prevent that terrible illness which is the best indicator of a civilization's decrepitude: the illness of *degeneration*."[4] Describing "the condition of the body politic" in 1919, Blok wrote that "all of its body parts . . . had been struck by an illness which could neither pass on its own, nor be treated by the usual methods, requiring complex and dangerous surgery. This is how everyone with a political sense understood the state of affairs; no one doubted the necessity of surgery, but people disagreed about the degree of inevitable trauma from it and how much of it the weakened body could tolerate."[5]

Blok represented the public state of affairs in 1916 by means of the positivist cum decadent metaphor of the infected body and of surgical intervention with the purpose of healing it. In previous years, he had characterized his own condition and that of his poetic persona using similar discourse. If a Max Nordau were correlating the two bodies of Russia—the nation's, as exemplified by the Romanov blood taint and penetration of it by Rasputin, and Blok's—he would probably come to an alarming diagnosis. This is not my goal, although it is perhaps an inevitable by-product of my investigation. My purpose in this book has not been to explain the etiology of a national disease—or to ascribe the taint of degeneracy to Russian symbolist culture—but to identify the rhetorical and real-life practices associated with the self-representations, besides Blok, of Lev Tolstoy, Vladimir Solov'ev, Zinaida Gippius, and Rozanov.

If we look back at the period covered in *Erotic Utopia* and consider the book title in relation to issues of national concern, we can say that the 1890s and early 1900s, the decades when the European theory of degeneration entered the Russian cultural imaginary, brought to the fore the "sexual question." It became entwined with the "Jewish question," especially between 1905 and 1917. The first engaged fear of degeneracy and its infection of the procreative body, as revealed in the cultural debates of celibacy versus marriage. The second was exacerbated by the 1905 revolution, which reignited anti-Semitic frenzy resulting in widespread pogroms, the emergence of the Black Hundreds as an organized entity, the Beilis affair, and deportation of Jews from the Western front during the First World War. The vicious representation of the Jew as a blood-sucking spider feeding on the body of the Russian nation was a common image in the anti-Semitic press of the time. After 1911 it would be contrasted to the pale, bloodless image of Andrei Iushchinsky, the supposed victim of ritual murder in Kiev. These and other phantasmic anti-Semitic metaphors, specifically those concerned with the trope of blood, had an impact on decadent artistic representation and the epoch's obsession with the degenerate body and tainted bloodlines.

While many of the symbolists supported the 1905 and February revolutions, of those whom I examine in *Erotic Utopia*, only Blok and Bely welcomed the October Revolution, which they informed with apocalyptic meaning. Rozanov's love of excess did not extend to the Bolsheviks or to revolution, for that matter; Gippius, who had no use for the monarchy, supported the socialist revolutionaries, not the Russian Marxists. In all likelihood, the reason for Blok's enthusiasm was escapist: the revolution facilitated the erasure of his familial and personal blood taint, which linked him, if only metaphorically, to the ruling class. His utopian persona, moreover, believed that revolution would usher in the "new man," the one who would replace the imperfect "human race" with a "more perfect species."[6]

The utopian blueprint of transforming and immortalizing the body, as expressed here by Blok in 1921, underlay some of the utopian projects of the Bolsheviks as well. We need only turn to Leon Trotsky's well-known *Literature and Revolution* (1924) to realize that the Bolsheviks shared with the decadent utopians the rhetorical goal of transfiguring nature. In *Literature and Revolution*, Trotsky described the Soviet man as a "higher social biologic type," a superman who would master reproduction, subjecting it to collective experiment. The discourse of Solov'ev and his followers was, of course, different—they would not have referred to the divine androgyne as a "higher social biologic type." This was the vocabulary of Social Darwinism. But, as we have seen, the discourse of mastering reproduction with the purpose of immortalizing the body was at the very heart of their erotic utopia. Trotsky wrote in the conclusion of *Literature and Revolution* that the new man would "not submit humbly before the dark laws of heredity and blind sexual selection"; he would eliminate the fear of death, as if he were a decadent utopian motivated by the desire to transcend heredity and mortality by immortalizing the body.[7]

There were also similarities between some of the utopian projects of the Soviet avant-garde artists and the decadent utopians—as related to bodily transfiguration, family, and daily life. Contrary to what we have come to believe, there was a remarkable degree of continuity on the subjects of procreation and everyday life between the nihilist 1860s, the symbolist 1890s, and the Bolshevik 1920s.[8] As in the case of Solov'ev and his followers, who, as I have tried to show in this study, did not make a clean break with the positivist utilitarianism of the fathers, Bolsheviks, such as Trotsky, and representatives of the Soviet avant-garde, such as Vladimir Mayakovsky, Alexander Rodchenko, Konstantin Mel'nikov, and Nikolai Filonov, each in his own way, continued to pursue similar utopian goals as those of the prerevolutionary modernists. Among the unexpected lines of continuity into the Soviet epoch was Nikolai Fedorov's project of resurrecting the dead by means of universal abstinence, a notion that had captivated Solov'ev and his followers. Besides Konstantin Tsiolkovsky, the father of Soviet rocket science, Fedorov's ideas also influenced Mel'nikov and Filonov, as well as Nikolai Chekrygin, Kazimir Malevich, and Nikolai Zabolotsky.[9]

Needless to say, Trotsky would have been horrified by the comparison between his ideas and Solov'ev's, just as Gippius would have been disdainful of the claim that *What Is to Be Done?* served as a subtext of her life practice. After all, *Art and Revolution* was intended as an attack on the symbolist generation, and Gippius's project was directed against the utilitarian positivists. But as I have shown in *Erotic Utopia,* utilitarian ideas lay hidden below the top layer of the symbolist palimpsest of life creation, and there were indirect links between the symbolist and Bolshevik visions.

Historical progression characterized by continuity has been examined less intensively in Russian literary studies than historical rupture. What has happened in cataclysmic periods of Russian history—as after the October Revolution—is erasure of the past, explaining Chaadaev's trope of Russia as "blank slate." Not only revolutionaries but also the consumers of the new culture tended to neglect the historical palimpsest. Efforts to redress this reductive view of Russian history has informed the study of Soviet, as well as pre-Soviet, political history for some time. The principle of historical continuity underlying the ruptured layer in the cultural palimpsest has only recently been applied to the study of Russian post- and prerevolutionary artistic production. The best-known case of such a reversal is Boris Groys's still controversial claim that socialist realism is not just a break with the avant-garde but also its heir.[10] Although the theoretical premises and cultural contexts of my claim regarding the relation of decadent utopian culture to utilitarian utopianism are very different, I have tried to examine in this study the complex negotiation of the historical laws of continuity and change.

# Notes

# Index

# Notes

## Introduction

1. Viacheslav Ivanov, "Perepiska iz dvukh uglov: Viacheslav Ivanov i Mikhail Gershenzon," in *Sobranie sochinenii Viacheslava Ivanova* (Brussels: Foyer Oriental Chrétien, 1979), 3:396.

2. The term "Russian spiritual renaissance" is attributed to Nikolai Berdiaev, who introduced the term years later to characterize the spiritual and religious questing in Russia at the beginning of the twentieth century (Nikolai Berdiaev, "Russkii dukhovnyi renessans nachala XX v. i zhurnal 'Put'' [K desiatiletiiu 'Puti'']," *Put'* 49 [1935]: 3–22).

3. I borrow the phrase "love's body" from Norman O. Brown, *Love's Body* (New York: Random House, 1966).

4. Viktor Shklovsky, "O russkom romane i povesti," in *Povesti o proze: Razmyshleniia i razbory* (Moscow: Khudozhestvennaia literatura, 1966), 2:3–5.

5. E. N. Trubetskoy, *Mirosozertsanie Vl. S. Solov'eva* (Moscow: Put', 1913), 583.

6. Among important studies that examine Russian culture at the turn of the twentieth century and the representation of the body and of sexuality in it are: Bernice Glatzer Rosenthal, *Dmitri Sergeevich Merezhkovsky and the Silver Age* (The Hague: Martinus Nijhoff, 1975); Avril Pyman, *The Life of Alexander Blok*, 2 vols. (New York: Oxford University Press, 1978–80); Bernice Glatzer Rosenthal, *Nietzsche in Russia* (Princeton, N.J.: Princeton University Press, 1986); Peter Ulf Møller, *Postlude to The Kreutzer Sonata: Tolstoj and the Debate on Sexual Morality in Russian Literature in the 1890s*, trans. John Kendal (New York: E. J. Brill, 1988), 96; Laura Engelstein, *The Keys to Happiness: Sex and the Search for Modernity in Fin-de-Siècle Russia* (Ithaca, N.Y.: Cornell University Press, 1992); Irene Masing-Delic, *Abolishing Death: A Salvation Myth of Russian Twentieth-Century Literature* (Stanford, Calif.: Stanford University Press, 1992); Irina Paperno and Joan Delaney Grossman, eds., *Creating Life: The Aesthetic Utopia of Russian Modernism* (Stanford, Calif.: Stanford University Press, 1994); Avril Pyman, *A History of Russian Symbolism* (New York: Cambridge University Press, 1994); Igor' Smirnov,

*Psikhodiakhronologika: Psikhoistoriia russkoj literatury ot romantizma do nashikh dnei* (Moscow: Novoe literaturnoe obozrenie, 1994); Judith Deutsch Kornblatt and Richard Gustafson, eds., *Russian Religious Thought* (Madison: University of Wisconsin Press, 1996); Aleksandr Etkind, *Sodom i psikheia: ocherki intellektual'noi istorii Serebrianogo veka* (Moscow: ITs-Garant, 1996); Alexander Etkind, *Eros of the Impossible: The History of Psychoanalysis in Russia,* trans. Noah and Maria Rubins (Boulder, Colo.: Westview Press, 1997); Eric Naiman, *Sex in Public: The Incarnation of Early Soviet Ideology* (Princeton, N.J.: Princeton University Press, 1997); N. A. Bogomolov, *Russkaia literatura nachala XX veka i okkul'tizm: issledovaniia i mater'ialy* (Moscow: Novoe literaturnoe obozrenie, 1999); John E. Malmstad and Nikolay Bogomolov, *Mikhail Kuzmin: A Life in Art* (Cambridge, Mass.: Harvard University Press, 1999); and A. V. Lavrov, *Etiudy o Bloke* (St. Petersburg: Ivan Limbakh, 2000).

7. For a comprehensive discussion of life creation, see Paperno and Grossman, *Creating Life.*

8. V. F. Khodasevich, "Konets Renaty," in *Nekropol'* (Paris: YMCA-Press, 1976), 8.

9. I have borrowed the phrase "abolishing death" from the title of Irene Masing-Delic's book *Abolishing Death: A Salvation Myth of Russian Twentieth-Century Literature.*

10. Michel Foucault, *The History of Sexuality: An Introduction,* trans. Robert Hurley (New York: Random House, 1978), 1:101.

11. For a discussion of the androgyne in nineteenth-century European discourse, see A. J. L. Busst, "The Image of the Androgyne in the Nineteenth Century," in *Romantic Mythologies,* ed. Ian Fletcher (New York: Barnes & Noble, 1967), 1–96. For a discussion of androgyny in Russian literature of the fin de siècle, see Olga Matich, "Androgyny and the Russian Religious Renaissance," in *Western Philosophical Systems in Russian Literature* (Los Angeles: University of Southern California Press, 1979), 165–76.

12. See Konstantin Leont'ev, "Vizantizm i slavianstvo," *Izbrannoe* (Moscow: Rarog, Moskovskii rabochii, 1993), 19–118.

13. Slavoj Žižek, *The Puppet and the Dwarf: The Perverse Core of Christianity* (Cambridge, Mass.: MIT Press, 2003), 134.

14. The image of Russia as a "blank slate" comes from Peter Chaadaev (1794–1856), whose vision of Russian history has left an indelible mark in Russian culture.

15. Friedrich Nietzsche, *The Case of Wagner,* in *The Birth of Tragedy and The Case of Wagner,* ed. and trans. Walter Kaufmann (New York: Random House, 1967), 169.

16. Ibid., 166.

17. Foucault, *History of Sexuality,* 1:118.

18. Andrei Bely, *Mezhdu dvukh revoliutsii* (Moscow: Khudozhestvennaia literatura, 1990), 158.

19. Smirnov, *Psikhodiakhronologika,* 133.

20. "The last important representative of the persecution of Wagner," wrote Blok, "was the famous Max Nordau; . . . fifteen years ago this 'interpreter' was still an 'idol' of many members of the Russian intelligentsia, who . . . against

their will ended up in various dirty embraces" (Alexander Blok, "Iskusstvo i revoliutsiia (Po povodu tvoreniia Rikharda Vagnera)," in *Sobranie sochinenii v vos'mi tomakh* [Moscow-Leningrad: Khudozhestvennaia literatura, 1962], 6:23). In other words, Blok was familiar with Nordau's writings much earlier than 1918. Smirnov showed that Bely was already familiar with *Degeneration* when writing *Arabesques* (*Arabeski*, 1911) (Smirnov, *Psikhodiakhronologika*, 133–34n190).

21. Robert K. R. Thornton, *The Decadent Dilemma* (London: Arnold, 1983), 63.

22. For a recent discussion of Nordau's influence on Valerii Briusov and others, see Ronald Vroon, "Max Nordau and the Origin of Russian Decadence," in *Sine Arte, Nihil: Sbornik nauchnykh trudov v dar Milivoe Iovanovichu* (Belgrade and Moscow: "Piataia strana," 2002), 85–100. For an earlier discussion of Nordau's influence in Russia, see Pyman, *History of Russian Symbolism*, 5–7, and Smirnov, *Psikhodiakhronologika*, 133–36. Regarding Vengerova's influence, see Zinaida Vengerova, "Poety simvolisty vo Frantsii," *Vestnik Evropy* 9 (1892): 117; Vengerova was close to Gippius and her circle.

23. Zin. Vengerova, "Novaia kniga Maksa Nordau," *Novosti i birzhevaia* gazeta 190 (July 13, 1893).

24. "Maks Nordau, *Vyrozhdenie*. Perevod s nemetskogo, s predisloviem R. Sementkovskogo. St.-Petersburg, 1894. Maks Nordau, *Vyrozhdenie*. Perevod s nemetskogo V. Genkena, s predisloviem V. Avseenko. Kiev, 1894," *Severnyi vestnik* 1 (1894): 135. The review was anonymous, but we know that it was written by Akim Volynsky.

25. L. N. Tolstoy, *Chto takoe iskusstvo*? in *Sobranie sochinenii v dvadtsati tomakh* (Moscow: Izd. Khudozhestvennaia literatura, 1964), 15:113.

26. For a discussion of Tolstoy in relation to degeneration theory, see Olga Matich, "Pozdnii Tolstoy i Aleksandr Blok: Poputchiki po vyrozhdeniiu," in *Russkaia literatura i meditsina*, ed. K. Bogdanov and Iu. Murashov (Moscow: OGGI, 2005).

27. See Sander L. Gilman, *Difference and Pathology: Stereotypes of Sexuality, Race, and Madness* (Ithaca, N.Y.: Cornell University Press), 1985.

28. An exception is Joan Delaney Grossman, who has written about criticism of decadent writing (in Russia and elsewhere) by Russian psychiatrists. See Joan Grossman, "Genius and Madness: The Return of the Romantic Concept of the Poet in Russia at the End of the Nineteenth Century," in *American Contributions to the Seventh International Congress of Slavists*, ed. Victor Terras, 3 vols. (The Hague: Mouton, 1973), 2:247–60.

29. B. B. Glinsky, "Bolezn' ili reklama," in *Ocherki russkogo progressa* (St. Petersburg: Tovarishchestvo khudozhestvennoi pechati, 1900), 398.

30. Ibid., 399.

31. Ibid., 402–4.

32. B. B. Glinsky, "Molodezh' i ee rukovoditeli," in *Ocherki russkogo progressa*, 370.

33. B. B. Glinsky, "Literaturnaia molodezh'," in *Ocherki russkogo progressa*, 457–60. Mrs. Gurevich refers to Liubov' Gurevich, the publisher of the *Northern Messenger*.

34. Iu. Steklov, "Sotsial'no-politicheskie usloviia literaturnogo raspada," in

*Literaturnyi raspad: Kriticheskii sbornik* (St. Petersburg: Zerno, 1908), 40, 52. Steklov's essay opens the first volume of *Literary Collapse* (1908), an important anthology of Marxist critical essays that applied the discourse of degeneration to a class-oriented attack on modernist literature in Europe and Russia. For a discussion of the impact of Krafft-Ebing's discourse at the beginning of the century in Russia, see Evgenii Bershtein, "'Psychopathia Sexualis' v Rossii nachala veka: Politika i zhanr," in *Eros and Pornography in Russian Culture*, ed. M. Levitt and A. Toporkov (Moscow: Ladomir, 1999), 414–41.

35. Steklov's tone and message are venomous, not exploratory. Even though he described Nordau's *Degeneration* as "vulgarly philistine" ("Sotsial'no-politicheskie usloviia literaturnogo raspada," 20), his own commentary resembles Nordau's vituperative discourse.

36. D. S. Merezhkovsky, "Dafnis i Khloia. Povest' Longusa," in *Polnoe sobranie sochinenii* (Moscow: I. D. Sytin, 1914), 19:203.

37. Charles Bernheimer, *Figures of Decadence: Subversive Paradigms in Fin-de-Siècle Art and Literature* (Baltimore: Johns Hopkins University Press, 2002), 27.

38. Max Nordau, *Degeneration*, trans. from 2nd German ed. (New York: Howard Fertig, 1968), 14.

39. Ibid., 142.

40. Alfred Binet, "Recherche sur les altérations de la conscience chez les hystériques," *Revue philosophique* 27 (1889): 165.

41. Naomi Schor, *Reading in Detail: Aesthetics and the Feminine* (New York: Methuen, 1987), 43.

42. Nietzsche, *Case of Wagner*, 170. This passage appears to be almost a paraphrase of Paul Bourget's well-known description of decadent style in *Essays on Contemporary Psychology* (1883): "[A] decadent style is one where the unity of the book decomposes to give way to the independence of the page, where the page decomposes to give way to the independence of the word" (quoted in Schor, *Reading in Detail*, 43).

43. Foucault, *History of Sexuality*, 1:154.

44. Alfred Binet, "Le fètichisme dans l'amour: Étude dans le psychologie morbide," *Revue psychologique* 24 (1887): 164–65. For a discussion of fetishism and degeneration theory, including the French fear of population decline, see Daniel Pick, *Faces of Degeneration: A European Disorder, c. 1848–c. 1918* (Cambridge: Cambridge University Press, 1989), 37–108.

45. Sigmund Freud, "Leonardo da Vinci and a Memory of His Childhood," in *The Standard Edition of the Complete Psychological Works of Sigmund Freud* (London: Hogarth Press, 1964), 11:96–97. Regarding "screen memory," see Freud, "Fetishism," in *Standard Edition*, 21:152–57. Subsequent citations of Freud, unless otherwise indicated, refer to this edition.

46. For a psychoanalytic approach to symbolist writing, see Smirnov, *Psikhodiakhronologika*.

47. For a discussion of Freud's theories as a product of decadence, see Bernheimer, *Figures of Decadence*, 163–87.

48. For a discussion of dandyism in modernist literature, see Jessica R. Feldman, *Gender on the Divide: The Dandy in Modernist Literature* (Ithaca, N.Y.: Cornell University Press, 1993).

49. See Bernheimer, "Visions of Salome," in *Figures of Decadence*, 104–38.

50. Friedrich Nietzsche, *Ecce Homo*, in *On the Genealogy of Morals and Ecce Homo*, ed. and trans. Walter Kaufmann (New York: Random House, 1967), 327.

51. Viktor Shklovsky, *Rozanov* (Letchworth, U.K.: Prideaux Press, 1974), 16–17.

52. Masing-Delic, *Abolishing Death*, 76.

53. See Olga Matich, "Dialectics of Cultural Return: Zinaida Gippius' Personal Myth," in *Cultural Mythologies of Russian Modernism: From the Golden Age to the Silver Age*, ed. Boris Gasparov, Robert P. Hughes, and Irina Paperno (Berkeley: University of California Press, 1992), 52–72.

54. See P. S. Reifman, "Predpolagaiutsia li deti?" *Trudy po russkoi i slavianskoi filologii* 14 [=*Uchenye zapiski Tartuskogo Gosudarstvennogo Universiteta* 245] (1970): 357–63.

55. For a discussion of Chernyshevsky's conceptualization of the triple union as a political unit, see Irina Paperno, *Chernyshevsky and the Age of Realism: A Study in the Semiotics of Behavior* (Stanford, Calif.: Stanford University Press, 1988).

56. See Eve Kosofsky Sedgwick, *Between Men: English Literature and Male Homosocial Desire* (New York: Columbia University Press, 1985).

57. V. V. Rozanov, "Kogda-to znamenityi roman," in *O pisatel'stve i pisateliakh* in *Sobranie sochinenii*, ed. A. N. Nikoliukin (Moscow: Respublika, 1995), 187–88.

58. V. V. Rozanov, *Liudi lunnogo sveta: Metafizika khristianstva* (Moscow: Druzhba narodov, 1990), 173n1.

59. Renate Lachman, *Memory and Literature: Intertextuality in Russian Modernism*, trans. Roy Sellars and Anthony Wall, in *Theory and History of Literature* (Minneapolis: University of Minnesota Press, 1997), 87:22.

60. Sigmund Freud, "A Note upon the 'Mystic Writing-Pad,'" in *Standard Edition*, 19:227–34.

61. See e.g., Pick, *Faces of Degeneration*, and Gilman, *Difference and Pathology*. Both authors offer extensive investigations of the interconnectedness of degeneration and literary decadence.

62. Foucault, *History of Sexuality*, 1:32–33.

63. Shklovsky, *Rozanov*, 7.

## Chapter 1. Lev Tolstoy as Early Modernist

1. V. Shklovsky, *Lev Tolstoy* (Moscow: Molodaia Gvardiia, 1963), 7–8.

2. Ibid., 8. The reference to Tolstoy hiding his manuscripts from his family members refers to his wife, Sof'ia Andreevna, from whom he hid some of his writings in later years. Shklovsky went on to speak about a package of Tolstoy's letters to Sof'ia Andreevna that were kept in the lining of one of the chairs in the study. The inscription on the envelope says: "If there is no special decision about this letter from me, then it should be passed to S. A. after my death." Apparently, the manuscript of "The Devil," which Tolstoy hid from his wife, was also kept in the chair lining. When she decided to reupholster the furniture in 1907, the package was given to the husband of Tolstoy's daughter Maria for safekeeping. The envelope contained two letters: one that Sof'ia Andreevna destroyed and another that spoke about her husband's intent to leave Iasnaia Poliana (8).

3. For a discussion of the shape of the bed in 1920s utopian architecture and literature, see Olga Matich, "Remaking the Bed: Utopia in Daily Life," in *Laboratory of Dreams: The Russian Avant-Garde and Cultural Experiment,* ed. John Bowlt and Olga Matich (Stanford, Calif.: Stanford University Press, 1996), 59–78.

4. "Who would not prefer such fatherhood [birth in beauty] to merely human propagation, if he stopped to think of Homer, and Hesiod, and all the greatest of our poets? Who would not envy them their immortal progeny, their claim upon the admiration of posterity?" asks Diotima of Socrates (Plato, *The Symposium,* in *The Collected Dialogues of Plato,* ed. Edith Hamilton and Huntington Cairns, Bollingen Series 71 [Princeton, N.J.: Princeton University Press, 1961], 561).

5. Max Nordau, *Degeneration,* trans. from 2nd German ed. (New York: Howard Fertig, 1968), 145.

6. L. N. Tolstoy, *Chto takoe iskusstvo?* in *Sobranie sochinenii v dvadtsati tomakh* (Moscow: Khudozhestvennaia literatura, 1964), 15:193–94.

7. L. N. Tolstoy, *Dnevnik, 1847–1854: Tetrad' A.* [1847 g.], in *Polnoe sobranie sochinenii v devianosto tomakh* (Moscow: Khudozhestvennaia literatura, 1928–1958), 46:3. All further references to Tolstoy's diaries are to this edition.

8. Quoted in N. N. Gusev, *Lev Nikolaevich Tolstoi. Materialy k biografii s 1828 po 1855 god* (Moscow: Izd. Akademii Nauk SSSR, 1954), 169.

9. B. M. Eikhenbaum, *Molodoi Tolstoi* (1922; repr. as *Slavische Propylaen,* no. 53, Munich: Wilhelm Fink Verlag, 1968), 14. (Cf. Boris Eikhehnbaum, *The Young Tolstoy* tr. Albert Kaspin [Ann Arbor: Ardis, 1972], 10.)

10. Tolstoy, *Dnevnik 1847–54: Tetrad' A.* [1847 g.], 46:4.

11. Ibid., 46:30.

12. Eikhenbaum, *Molodoi Tolstoi,* 17–18.

13. Quoted in N. N. Gusev, *Lev Nikolaevich Tolstoi: Materialy k biografii s 1870 po 1881 god* (Moscow: Izd. Adademii Nauk SSSR, 1963), 253.

14. D. S. Merezhkovsky, *L. Tolstoi i Dostoevskii: Zhizn', tvorchestvo i religiia* (Moscow: Nauka, 2000), 119.

15. Levin compares the birth of his son to the death of his brother less than a year before, metaphorizing both as "openings in that usual life through which something higher became visible . . . and while watching it the soul soared, as then, to heights it had never known before, at which reason could not keep up with it" (Leo Tolstoy, *Anna Karenina,* The Maude Translation, ed. George Gibian, 2nd ed. [New York: W. W. Norton, 1995], 646). All further references to *Anna Karenina* will be to this edition.

16. Merezhkovsky, *L. Tolstoi i Dostoevskii,* 119–20.

17. Ibid., 115.

18. Ibid., 95.

19. Naomi Schor, *Reading in Detail: Aesthetics and the Feminine* (London: Methuen, 1987), 43.

20. Eikhenbaum, *Molodoi Tolstoi,* 8 (*Young Tolstoy,* 4). The nineteenth-century French physiologist Claude Bernard, who was very influential in Russia, wrote that dissection of corpses leads to vivisection: "After dissecting cadavers, then, we must necessarily dissect living beings, to uncover the inner or hidden parts of the organism and make them work; to this sort of operation we give the name

of vivisection" (Claude Bernard, *An Introduction to the Study of Experimental Medicine,* trans. Henry Copley Greene [New York: Macmillan, 1927], 99).

21. Gary Saul Morson, "The Reader as Voyeur: Tolstoy and the Poetics of Didactic Fiction," in *Modern Critical Views: Leo Tolstoy,* ed. Harold Bloom (New York: Chelsea House, 1986), 179.

22. Leo Tolstoy, "Sevastopol in December," in *Tolstoy's Short Fiction,* ed. Michael R. Katz (New York: W. W. Norton, 1991), 7.

23. Leo Tolstoy, *War and Peace,* The Maude Translation, ed. George Gibian (New York: W. W. Norton, 1966), 907–8

24. As Hugh MacLean has pointed out to me, Anatole loses the same leg with which he plays footsie with Bourienne under the table.

25. L. N. Tolstoy, "Pervaia stupen'," in *Polnoe sobranie sochinenii,* 27:81–82 (Leo Tolstoy, "First Step," in *I Cannot Be Silent,* ed. W. G. Jones [Bristol: The Bristol Press, 1989], 120). Most contemporary reviewers of "First Step" discussed it in Christian moral terms without making any references to the actual scenes of butchery. An exception was an anonymous review in the liberal newspaper *Birzhevye vedomosti* (no. 126, 1892), which contained a long quote depicting animal slaughter.

26. For an examination of the *skoptsy,* see Alexander Etkind, *Khlyst: Sekty, literatura i revoliutsiia* (Moscow: Novoe literaturnoe obozrenie, 1998); and Laura Engelstein, *Castration and the Heavenly Kingdom: A Russian Folktale* (Ithaca, N.Y.: Cornell University Press, 1999).

27. Sergei Eisenstein, "The Structure of the Film," in *Film Form: Essays in Film Theory,* ed. and trans. Jay Leyda (New York: Harcourt, Brace & Co., 1949), 155.

28. "The propagation of the human race is not left to mere accident or the caprices of the individual," wrote Krafft-Ebing, "but is guaranteed by the hidden laws of nature which are enforced by a mighty, irresistible impulse. Sensual enjoyment and physical fitness are not the only conditions for the enforcement of these laws, but higher motives and aims, such as the desire to continue the species. . . . Man puts himself at once on a level with the beast if he seeks to gratify lust alone, but he elevates his superior position when by curbing the animal desire he combines with the sexual functions ideas of morality, of the sublime, and the beautiful" (Richard von Krafft-Ebing, *Psychopathia Sexualis, with Especial Reference to the Antipathic Sexual Instinct: A Medico-Forensic Study,* trans. from the 12th German ed. by Franklin S. Klaf [New York: Stein & Day, 1978], 1).

29. Ibid., 58.

30. Tolstoy, *Anna Karenina,* 169. Further references to this work will be cited in the text.

31. Ivan Turgenev, *Fathers and Sons,* trans. Constance Garnett, ed. and rev. Ralph E. Matlaw (New York: W. W. Norton, 1966), 62.

32. S. A. Tolstaia, *Dnevniki* (Moscow: Khudozhestvennaia literatura, 1978), 1:508–9.

33. Shklovsky, *Lev Tolstoy,* 342; D. I. Pisarev, "Motivy russkoi dramy," in *Sochineniia v chetyrekh tomakh* (Moscow: Gosudarstvennoe izdatel'stvo khudozhestvennoi literatury, 1955), 2:292.

34. Shklovsky, *Lev Tolstoy,* 341.

35. Viktor Shklovsky, "*Anna Karenina*," in *Energiia zabluzhdeniia* (Moscow: Sovetskii pisatel', 1981), 216.

36. Charles Bernheimer, *Figures of Ill Repute: Representing Prostitution in Nineteenth-Century France* (Cambridge, Mass.: Harvard University Press, 1989), 214–15.

37. Émile Zola, in *Le Figaro*, December 18, 1866, quoted in Bernheimer, *Figures of Ill Repute*, 216, 308n26.

38. Quoted in Philip Walker, *Zola* (London: Routledge & Kegan Paul, 1985), 81.

39. K. Leont'ev, *Analiz, stil' i veiainie: O romanakh gr. L. N. Tolstogo*, Brown University Slavic Reprint Series, no. 3 (Providence, R.I.: Brown University Press, 1965), 40.

40. Ibid., 79, 85.

41. See Konstantin Leont'ev, "Vizantizm i slavianstvo," in *Izbrannoe* (Moscow: Rarog, Moskovskii rabochii, 1993), 19–118.

42. V. V. Rozanov, "Neotsenimyi um," in *O pisateliakh i pisatel'stve*, ed. N. A. Nikoliukin (Moscow: Respublika, 1995), 520.

43. Merezhkovsky, *L. Tolstoi i Dostoevskii*, 97–98.

44. L. N Tolstoy, *Kreitserova sonata*, in *Sobranie sochinenii v dvadtsati tomakh*, 12:192–93.

45. Tolstoy, *Chto takoe iskusstvo?* 178.

46. Quoted in Peter Ulf Møller, *Postlude to the Kreutzer Sonata: Tolstoj and the Debate on Sexual Morality in Russian Literature in the 1890s* (Leiden: E. J. Brill, 1988), 147.

47. Tolstoy, *Kreitserova sonata*, 12:157–58.

48. Fyodor Dostoevsky, *Demons*, trans. Richard Pevear and Larissa Volokhonsky (New York: Vintage, 1994), 590–91.

49. Tolstoy, *Kreitserova sonata*, 12:158.

50. Ibid., 12:217.

51. A. Skabichevsky, "Literaturnaia khronika: Nechto o '*Kreitserovoi sonate*,' o zhenskoi svobode, kursakh i tomu podobnykh interesnykh predmetakh," *Novosti i birzhevaia gazeta* 80 (March 22, 1890): 2.

52. From letters to V. I. Alekseev in 1890, quoted in Møller, *Postlude to the Kreutzer Sonata*, 124nn103, 104.

53. Tolstoy, *Kreitserova sonata*, 12:207.

54. Ibid., 12:179. The criminologist and psychopathologist Cesare Lombroso, whom Tolstoy would meet later, coauthored a book titled *Delinquent Woman* (1893) in which he linked the fat prostitute to the Hottentot woman, both of whom he considered atavistic. For a discussion of psychopathology, gender, and race, see Sander L. Gilman, *Difference and Pathology: Stereotypes of Sexuality, Race, and Madness* (Ithaca, N.Y.: Cornell University Press, 1985).

55. Rtsy, "Teksty pereputal! (Po povodu *Kreitserovoi Sonaty* L. N. Tolstogo: Pis'mo k S. F. Sharapovu," *Blagovest* 9 (December 15, 1890): 247–49. Rtsy associated Tolstoy's message in *The Kreutzer Sonata* with the sectarian practices of the self-castrators.

56. Tolstoy, diary entry of 1860, in *Sobranie sochinenii*, 19:239, and *Polnoe sobranie sochinenii*, 48:23.

57. Tolstoy, diary entry of 1884, in *Sobranie sochinenii*, 19:315–16; and *Polnoe sobranie sochinenii*, 49:77.

58. Tolstoy, diary entry of 1884, in *Polnoe sobranie sochinenii*, 32:72–74.

59. Tolstoy, *Voskresenie*, in *Sobranie sochinenii*, 13:84–86. Tolstoy also referred to Charcot on these pages as a specialist on hypnotism. Trying to understand the nature of the criminal, Nekhliudov searches among the Siberian prisoners for the atavistic criminal types described in the writings of the Italian school of psychopathology (13:350–51; 32:312–13). Lombroso visited Tolstoy at Iasnaia Poliana in 1897. He described the famous Italian as "a limited, naive old man" (Tolstoy, *Polnoe sobranie sochinenii*, 20:81). In 1900 Tolstoy referred to Lombroso's writing as intellectually mediocre.

60. Tolstoy, *Dnevniki 1847–1894 gg.*, in *Sobranie sochinenii*, 19:480; and in *Polnoe sobranie sochinenii*, 52:84.

61. Nordau, *Degeneration*, 145.

62. Ibid., 169.

63. Quoted in Nordau, *Degeneration*, 147.

64. Ibid., 162.

65. "Malen'kii fel'eton. E. Zola o grafe L. N. Tolstom," *Novoe vremia* 5198 (1890): 2.

66. Skabichevsky wrote that in *The Kreutzer Sonata* "L. Tolstoy [did] not show us any escape from [the horrors of contemporary family life] other than extreme utopianism" ("Literaturnaia khronika: Nechto o '*Kreitserovoi sonate*,' o zhenskoi svobode, kursakh i tomu podobnykh interesnykh predmetakh," *Novosti i birzhevaia gazeta* 80 [March 22, 1890]: 2).

67. Cf. Sozertsatel' [pseudonym of L. E. Obolensky], "Voprosy v noveishei belletristike," *Russkoe bogatstvo* 3 (1890): 188–200.

68. Nikolai Minsky, "14-oe religiozno-filosofskoe sobranie," *Novyi put'* 9 (1903): 319.

69. As Liza Knapp pointed out, "Dostoevsky felt that a society in a state of disintegration was one in which 'accidental families' were becoming more and more common. . . . In choosing to portray such a family [in *The Adolescent*], Dostoevsky consciously opposed himself to Tolstoy, who portrayed the 'genetic family' [*rodovoe semeistvo*], which Dostoevsky felt had become obsolete" (*The Annihilation of Inertia: Dostoevsky and Metaphysics* [Evanston, Ill.: Northwestern University Press, 1996], 167).

70. Edward W. Said, *The World, the Text, and the Critic* (Cambridge, Mass.: Harvard University Press, 1983), 19.

71. One of the few scholars to address Tolstoy's proto-modernist aesthetics is Amy Mandelker in her insightful study of *Anna Karenina* (*Framing Anna Karenina: Tolstoy, the Woman Question, and the Victorian Novel* [Columbus: Ohio State University Press, 1993]).

## Chapter 2. The Meaning of *The Meaning of Love*

1. The explanation came from the economist I. I. Ianzhul, who learned it from Kovalevsky (Konstantin Mochul'sky, *Vladimir Solov'ev*, 2nd ed. [Paris: YMCA Press, 1953], 66).

2. Vte E.-M. de Vogüé, *Sous l'horizon: Hommes et choses d'hier* (Paris: Librairie Armand Colin, 1904), 17–18.

3. Vladimir Solov'ev, *Pis'ma,* 3 vols. (St. Petersburg: Obshchestvennaia pol'za, 1908–11), 3:19.

4. V. Pypina-Liatskaia, "V. S. Solov'ev: Stranichka iz vospominanii," *Golos minuvshego* (December 1914): 12.

5. Peter Ulf Møller, *Postlude to The Kreutzer Sonata: Tolstoj and the Debate on Sexual Morality in Russian Literature in the 1890s,* trans. John Kendal (New York: E. J. Brill, 1988), 96. The first installment of *The Meaning of Love* appeared in 1892 in *Questions of Philosophy and Psychology* (*Voprosy filosofii i psikhologii*) (no. 14), the same year and same journal in which Tolstoy's feuilleton on vegetarianism, "First Step," was published. The subsequent installments of *The Meaning of Love* appeared in 1892 (no. 15), 1893 (no. 17), and 1894 (no. 21).

6. S. Solov'ev, *Vospominaniia* (Moscow: Novoe literaturnoe obozrenie, 2003), 72.

7. Irene Masing-Delic, *Abolishing Death: A Salvation Myth of Russian Twentieth-Century Literature* (Stanford, Calif.: Stanford University Press, 1992), 17.

8. Alexander Etkind, *Eros of the Impossible: The History of Psychonalysis in Russia,* tr. Noah and Maria Rubins (Boulder, Colo.: Westview Press, 1997), 151–52.

9. E. N. Trubetskoy, *Mirosozertsanie Vl. S. Solov'eva* (Moscow: Put', 1913), 583.

10. V. S. Solov'ev, "Iz literaturnykh vospominanii: N. G. Chernyshevsky," in *Sobranie sochinenii V. S. Solov'eva* (1911; Brussels: Foyer Oriental Chretien, 1966), 12:339–41. All references to Solov'ev, unless otherwise indicated, are to this edition.

11. L. M. Lopatin, *Filosofskoe mirovozzrenie V. S. Solov'eva* in *Filosofskie kharakteristiki i rechi* (Moscow: Put', 1911), 123.

12. Cited in S. M. Solov'ev, *Zhizn' i tvorcheskaia evoliutsiia Vladimira Solov'eva* (Brussels: Foyer Oriental Chretien, 1977), 69. Except when indicated otherwise, details about Solov'ev's life are taken from this biography.

13. V. S. Solov'ev, "Znachenie poezii v stikhotvoreniiakh Pushkina," 9:323.

14. V. S. Solov'ev, "Chtenie o bogochelovechestve, Chtenie desiatoe," 6:143.

15. For further discussion of this issue, see Masing-Delic, *Abolishing Death,* 121.

16. Trubetskoy, *Mirosozertsanie Vl. S. Solov'eva,* 585–86.

17. Ibid., 583.

18. Mochul'sky, *Vladimir Solov'ev,* 226.

19. An example of Solov'ev's writing on spiritism and occult experience in general is his 1894 review of A. N. Aksakov's *Animizm i spiritizm* (1893), in which Solov'ev devoted several pages to the standard spiritist apparition of the severed hand. Although he raised the question of fake mediums, he expressed his approval of the spiritist project. See V. S. Solov'ev, "Sovremennoe sostoianie voprosa o mediumizme" in *Voprosy filosofii i psikhologii* (1894).

20. V. S. Solov'ev, "Paskhal'nye *Pis'ma:* Khristos voskres," 10:34.

21. Ibid., 10:37.

22. Ibid., 10:34.

23. Mochul'sky, *Vladimir Solov'ev,* 16.

24. N. V. Davydov, "Iz vospominanii o V. S. Solov'eve," in *Kniga o Vladimire Solov'eve* (Moscow: Sovetskii pisatel', 1991), 283.

25. D. M. Tsertelev, "Iz vospominanii o Vl. S. Solov'eve," in *Kniga o Vladimire Solov'eve*, 314.

26. Cited in Mochul'sky, *Vladimir Solov'ev*, 44.

27. J.-K. Huysmans, *Against Nature*, trans. Robert Baldick (Baltimore: Penguin Books, 1959), 17.

28. After visiting the Sphinx on his trip to Egypt, Solov'ev wrote his mother that she resembled it; when he next saw his sister, he began addressing her as "Sphinx" (M. S. Bezobrazova, "Vospominaniia o brate Vladimire Solov'eve," in *Kniga o Vladimire Solov'eve*, 83–84.

29. S. M. Solov'ev, *Zhizn' i tvorcheskaia evoliutsiia Vladimira Solov'eva*, 104.

30. Solov'ev had written an introduction to an 1899 edition of Aleksei Tolstoy's narrative poem *The Vampire* [*Upyr'*], which Solov'ev greatly admired.

31. Cited in M. H. Abrams, *Natural Supernaturalism: Tradition and Revolution in Romantic Literature* (New York: W. W. Norton, 1971), 152–53 (from *De Principiis*, in *The Writings of Origen*, trans. Frederick Crombie [Edinburgh, 1869], 53–59).

32. Besides the *Symposium* and Genesis, the figure of the androgyne also appears in the kabbala and in alchemical literature.

33. Plato, *The Symposium*, trans. W. Hamilton (Baltimore: Penguin Books, 1951), 91.

34. See Vladimir Solov'ev, *Zhiznennaia drama Platona*, 9:194–241.

35. In Jung's Neoplatonic psychomythology, the syzygy is an archetypal triad that represents the experiential, archetypal, and individual presence of the self in the beloved.

36. V. S. Solov'ev, *Smysl liubvi*, 7:60.

37. Other mystics who influenced Solov'ev's view of erotic love were Erigena and Jakob Boehme, both of whom exalted erotic love while remaining celibate themselves. They believed that eros was the source of the cosmic energy that would bring about the reintegration of the sundered androgynous whole. Solov'ev wrote about Erigena in his master's thesis, *Crisis of Western Philosophy* (1874).

38. V. S. Solov'ev, *Smysl liubvi*, 7:60.

39. Trubetskoy, *Mirosozertsanie Vl. S. Solov'eva*, 583.

40. Ibid., 587–88.

41. Peter Brown noted that at the age of twenty, Origen "had discreetly gone to a doctor to have himself castrated. At the time, castration was a routine operation" (Brown, *The Body and Society: Men, Women and Sexual Renunciation in Early Christianity* [New York: Columbia University Press, 1988], 168).

42. In Plato's *Symposium*, Aristophanes claims that the androgyne is the original ancestor of biological men and women. He posits the existence of three genders (male-male, female-female, and female-male), which had been self-sufficient because they were "wholes" instead of "halves." But when these beings threatened rebellion against the gods, the gods split them in two, causing erotic longing for the sundered half. This myth, according to Aristophanes, explains the origin of love.

43. *Abolishing Death* is the title of Irene Masing-Delic's book on the Russian immortalization project of the late nineteenth and early twentieth centuries. See note 7.

44. Alexander Blok, "Rytsar'-Monakh," in *Sobranie sochinenii v vos'mi tomakh,* 5:446–54.

45. S. M. Solov'ev, *Zhizn' i tvorcheskaia evoliutsiia Vladimira Solov'eva,* 115–16.

46. "Obzor zhurnalov," *Strannik* 9 (1892): 120.

47. A. A. Nikol'sky's monograph *Russkii Origen XIX veka Vl. Solov'ev* was serialized in the journal *Vera i razum* (*Faith and Reason*) in 1902. See its publication in 2000 by Nauka in Petersburg, esp. 328–32.

48. F. F. Brokgauz and I. A. Efron, *Entsiklopedicheskii slovar'* (St. Petersburg: Tipo-Litografiia I. A. Efrona, 1897), 22:141.

49. Max Nordau, *Degeneration,* trans. from 2nd German ed. (New York: Howard Fertig, 1968), 169.

50. M. A. Kolerov, A. A. Nosov, and I. V. Borisova, "K istorii odnoi druzhby: V. S. Solov'ev i kn. S. N. Trubetskoy: Novye materialy," *De Visu* 8 (1993): 5–23. My subsequent discussion of Solov'ev's sexual experience is based on the letters and the poems published in this article.

51. Ibid., 15 (*kh—ia* [*khuia,* i.e., cock], *m—de* [*mude,* i.e., balls], and *p—de* [*pizde,* i.e., cunt]).

52. In an 1897 letter to M. M. Stasiulevich, founder and editor of *Vestnik Evropy,* Solov'ev referred to his last meeting with Martynova, writing that five years ago he had broken the seventh commandment (against adultery) at a suburban Moscow railroad station. Since then, claimed Solov'ev, he had led a celibate life (ibid., 20n16).

53. In *The Meaning of Love,* Solov'ev treated the great unrequited lovers of history as experiencing the kind of erotic desire that has the power to transform life.

54. Sigmund Freud, "The Sexual Theories of Children," in *The Standard Edition of the Complete Psychological Works of Sigmund Freud* (London: Hogarth Press, 1959), 9:215–16. All subsequent references to Freud are from *The Standard Edition.*

55. Nordau, *Degeneration,* 2.

56. V. S. Solov'ev, "Rossia cherez sto let," 10:73–4.

57. The book of the time that entwined the two in a thoroughly irresponsible way was Max Nordau's *Degeneration.* For a discussion of the commingling of decadence and psychopathology, see, e.g., Sandra Siegel, "Literature: The Representation of 'Decadence,'" in *Degeneration: The Dark Side of Progress,* ed. J. Edward Chamberlin and Sander L. Gilman (New York: Columbia University Press, 1985), 206–9. On sexual perversion and the medical establishment of the 1880s and 1890s, see Robert A. Nye, "The Medical Origins of Sexual Fetishism," in *Fetishism as Cultural Discourse,* ed. Emily Apter and William Pietz (Ithaca, N.Y.: Cornell University Press, 1993) 13–30.

58. V. S. Solov'ev, *Smysl liubvi,* 7:19.

59. Viacheslav Ivanov and Mikhail Gershenzon, *Perepiska iz dvukh uglov,* in Viacheslav Ivanov, *Sobranie sochinenii,* 4 vols. (Brussels: Foyer Oriental Chrétien, 1979), 3:396. Solov'ev never married and was considered "neurasthenic," representing the end of his immediate family line.

60. R. v. Krafft-Ebing, *Psychopathia sexualis: Eine Klinishch-Forensische Studie* (Stuttgart: Verlag von Ferdinand Enke, 1886), 50; published in English as *Psy-*

*chopathia Sexualis, with Especial Reference to the Antipathic Sexual Instinct: A Medico-Forensic Study,* trans. from the 12th German ed. by Franklin S. Klaf (New York: Stein & Day, 1978), 166 (case 108).

61. V. S. Solov'ev, *Smysl liubvi,* 7:36.

62. Ibid., 7:35.

63. L. N. Tolstoy, *Kreitserova sonata,* in *Sobranie sochinenii v dvadtsati tomakh* (Moscow: Khudozhestvennaia literatura, 1963), 12:145.

64. Solov'ev, *Smysl liubvi,* 7:36. For a discussion of the subject in nineteenth-century French literature, see Charles Bernheimer, *Figures of Ill Repute: Representing Prostitution in Nineteenth-Century France* (Cambridge, Mass.: Harvard University Press, 1989).

65. He wrote in *The Meaning of Love* that psychiatrists whose foremost goal was to battle homosexuality would show patients pornographic pictures of the naked female body, suggesting that the doctors would consider their cure complete when the patient moved on to the brothel.

66. V. S. Solov'ev, *Smysl liubvi,* 7:35.

67. Michel Foucault, *The History of Sexuality,* trans. Robert Hurley (New York: Vintage, 1980), 1:154.

68. S. M. Solov'ev, *Zhizn' i tvorcheskaia evoliutsiia Vladimira Solov'eva,* 207.

69. Mochul'sky, *Vladimir Solov'ev,* 158.

70. Freud, "Fetishism," in *Standard Edition,* 21:154.

71. S. M. Solov'ev, *Zhizn' i tvorcheskaia evoliutsiia Vladimira Solov'eva,* 314. Of his philosopher friends, Grot considered Solov'ev's position on procreation in *The Meaning of Love* inconsistent. In a letter to Grot, Solov'ev appeared to agree with him, claiming that he chose the word "procreation" as a substitute for "coitus" because the latter was inappropriate in philosophical discourse (V. S. Solov'ev, *Pis'ma,* 3:211). There is a problem with this explanation, however: if procreation is merely a synonym for coitus, then procreation is a justification for it, which is the Christian view of sex. The implication then is that contrary to his derisive comments about asceticism in *The Meaning of Love,* directed in large measure against Tolstoy, Solov'ev considered the sex act sinful and not just the instrument of death, as is procreation.

72. V. S. Solov'ev, *Smysl liubvi,* 7:20.

73. As I noted in the introduction, the concern that utopian projects endangered the family as an institution stretched back to an earlier generation: the publication of *What Is to Be Done?* in 1863 was greeted with a similar concern by Afanasii Fet and Vasilii Botkin, who asked "whether children were intended" in Chernyshevsky's utopia, implying that his project heralded the end of the human race. See P. S. Reifman, "Predpolagaiutsia li deti?" *Trudy po russkoi i slavianskoi filologii* 14 [=*Uchenye zapiski Tartuskogo Gosudarstvennogo Universiteta,* 245] (1970): 357–63.

74. V. S. Solov'ev, *Opravdanie dobra,* 8:80.

75. Ibid., 146–48.

76. Solov'ev wrote, "[T]he genital act incarnates the infiniteness of the natural process, and man, taking shame in this act, rejects this very infiniteness as unworthy of himself. . . . Man as a moral being does not want to obey this

natural law of the displacement of generations, the law of eternal death; he does not want to displace or be displaced; he senses, vaguely at first, both his need and his ability to contain within himself all the fullness of eternal life" (ibid., 167).

## Chapter 3. The Case of Alexander Blok

1. See letter written April 28, 1903, in *Andrei Bely i Aleksandr Blok: Perepiska 1903–1919,* ed. A. V. Lavrov (Moscow: Progress, 2001), 61. On May 9, Bely thanked Blok for the "honor" and wrote that he hoped to be back from his trip with his father to the Caucasus in time for the wedding, but that Blok should make other plans too (62).

2. Bely was replaced by a friend of one of Liubov' Dmitrievna's brothers, Count Alexander Rozvadovsky, a young Catholic mystic who later became a monk.

3. In *Na rubezhe dvukh stoletii* (Moscow: Khudozhestvennaia literatura, 1989), Bely described at length the intersection of his and Blok's life in the gentry nests of the Klin countryside. The connection between them included the Nicholas railway line: "The region of the Nicholas rail line—Many of the children of the 'border,' who would later be acquainted, spent their childhoods nearby: my friend S. M Solov'ev grew up by Kriukovy; another friend A. S. Petrovsky, in the vicinity of Povorovka; Blok in the vicinity of Podsolnechnoe; and I was around Klin" (163).

4. Sergei Solov'ev's parents died virtually at the same time while he was still in high school. Several years afterwards he began to suffer from bouts of serious mental illness, which continued till the end of his life and for which he would be hospitalized. In the 1930s, his doctor gave a paper about Sergei Mikhailovich at a psychiatric conference in which she demonstrated him in person as an exemplar of hereditary mental illness, presenting his family genealogy and dividing the family members into those who had suffered from mental illnesses and those who had not (cited in A. V. Lavrov, "'Prodolzhatel' roda'—Sergei Solov'ev," in S. Solov'ev, *Vospominaniia* [Moscow: Novoe literaturnoe obozrenie, 2003], 30). Solov'ev himself wrote in his memoirs that sickliness and degeneration of some members of his family compensated for the talent of others (73), as if the two had to exist in complementary distribution. In 1916, Solov'ev became a Russian Orthodox priest and a few years later converted to Catholicism.

5. The bouquet ordered from Moscow did not arrive on time (M. A. Beketova, *Vospominaniia ob Aleksandre Bloke* [Moscow: Izdatel'stvo Pravda, 1990] 63).

6. Beketova, *Vospominaniia ob Aleksandre Bloke,* 63–65. Also see S. Solov'ev, *Vospominaniia ob Aleksandre Bloke,* in *Vospominaniia,* 388–89.

7. If we consider Sergei's mythologized view of the wedding as described in Bely's memoirs and Blok's sexual anxieties about it, based on his diary entries, they both seem to invoke the power of the father. Can the young bridegroom muster the necessary phallic power to slay the patriarchal dragon? Serezha's mythical vision extended to Liubov Dmitrievna's father, Dmitrii Mendeleev, whom he described to Bely using a line of verse out of Solov'ev's poetry. Mendeleev appeared to him as "dark chaos accompanying his radiant daugh-

ter" to the altar (Andrei Bely, *Vospominaniia o Bloke,* in *O Bloke,* ed. A. V. Lavrov [Moscow: Avtograf, 1997] 53. All references to this edition unless otherwise indicated will henceforth be cited in the text). Bely embroidered on his friend's image by portraying the renowned chemist as "having overheard matter's rhythms and sketching before the world a symphony consisting of atomic weights." He deflated the father's "chtonic" phallic power by describing the tears that he shed at his daughter's wedding. This detail revealed his reluctance to relinquish his most prized possession. Such a figure as Mendeleev, wrote Bely, had to be present at Blok's wedding (53). The plot of the captive virgin imprisoned by the earthbound dragon serves as the mythical subtext of this triangulated tale of father, daughter, and bridegroom. In the myth, the young dragon slayer liberates her from the clutches of the earth father with the purpose of taking her to his fairytale kingdom, where he in turn takes possession of her.

8. The death of Blok led to the publication of numerous reminiscences by family members and contemporaries. The most extensive and valuable family memoirs were by his aunt, M. A. Beketova, also published in 1922. S. M. Solov'ev's memoir appeared in 1925. Z. N. Gippius, Vl. Piast, G. I. Chulkov, V. A. Zorgenfrei, and others also published their recollections in the first half of the 1920s.

9. For a discussion of Bely's memoirs, including those about Blok, see Lazar Fleishman, "Bely's Memoirs," in *Andrey Bely: Spirit of Symbolism,* ed. John E. Malmstad (Ithaca, N.Y.: Cornell University Press, 1987), 216–41. Bely's famous memoiristic trilogy, especially the third volume *Between Two Revolutions* (*Mezhdu dvukh revoliutsii,* 1935), paints the Bloks in dark, grotesque colors.

10. On the Argonauts, see Alexander Lavrov, "Andrei Bely and the Argonauts' Mythmaking," in *Creating Life: The Aesthetic Utopia of Russian Modernism,* ed. Irina Paperno and Joan Delaney Grossman (Stanford, Calif.: Stanford University Press, 1994), 83–121.

11. Bely, *Na rubezhe dvukh stoletii,* 358.

12. Alexander Blok, "Iskusstvo i revoliutsiia (Po povodu tvoreniia Rikharda Vagnera)," in *Sobranie sochinenii v vos'mi tomakh* (Moscow-Leningrad: Khudozhestvennaia literatura, 1960–63), 6:23. All subsequent references to Blok's writings, unless otherwise indicated, are to this edition. Regarding *fin de race,* see Max Nordau, *Degeneration* (New York: Howard Fertig, 1968), 2.

13. Bely reads the imitation of Solov'ev's life into the behavior of the young Blokists. For instance, he interpreted Sergei's disappearance from Shakhmatovo one evening in the summer of 1905—when he simply wandered away—as a reenactment of Vladimir Solov'ev's journey to the Egyptian desert to meet Sophia (Bely, *Mezhdu dvukh revoliutsii,* ed. A. V. Lavrov [Moscow: Khudozhestvennaia literatura, 1990], 454).

14. Andrei Bely, "Sviashchennye tsveta," in *Arabeski* (Moscow: Iskusstvo, 1994), 120.

15. Ibid., 119.

16. Alexander Blok and Andrei Bely, *Perepiska* (Moscow: Izdatel'stvo gosudarstvennogo literaturnogo muzeia, 1940; repr., Munich: Wilhelm Fink Verlag, 1969), 123n4.

17. Ibid., 121.

18. Their marriage was expected to enact the kind of Christian vision reflected in a sermon attributed to Augustine, in which the marriage bed is likened to Christ's martyrdom: "Like a bridegroom Christ went forth from His chamber. He went out with a presage of His nuptials into the field of the world. . . . He came to the marriage bed of the cross, and there, in mounting it, He consummated his marriage. And when He perceived the sighs of the creature, He lovingly gave himself up to the torment in the place of His bride . . . and He joined the woman to Himself for ever" (*Sermo suppositus,* 120.8, in Migne *PL* 39:1986, quoted in M. H. Abrams, *Natural Supernaturalism: Tradition and Revolution in Romantic Literature* [New York: Norton, 1971], 45).

19. Bely, *Mezhdu dvukh revoliutsii,* 13.

20. Beketova, *Vospominaniia ob Aleksandre Bloke,* 66.

21. A. Blok, "Dnevnik 1901–1902 goda," 7:46. He saw the painting in the Uffizi in 1909.

22. For a discussion of Bely's love for Liubov' Dmitrievna and his relationship with Blok, see Alexander Lavrov, *Andrei Bely v 1900-e gody: Zhizn' i deiatel'nost'* (Moscow: Novoe literaturnoe obozrenie, 1995), 196–206.

23. Bely, *Mezhdu dvukh revoliutsii,* 26.

24. Alexander Blok, *Zapisnye knizhki: 1901–1920* (Moscow: Khudozhestvennaia literatura, 1965), 50–51, 53.

25. A. Blok, "Dnevnik 1901–1902 goda," 7:50.

26. Ibid., 7:53.

27. Ibid., 7:52–53.

28. In 1908 Liubov' Dmitrievna began her theatrical career, of which she had dreamed since early youth.

29. See Liubov' Blok, *Klassicheskii tanets: Istoriia i sovremennost'* (Moscow: Iskusstvo, 1987).

30. L. D. Blok, *I byl', i nebylitsy o Bloke i o sebe,* ed. L. Fleishman and I. Paulmann (Bremen: Verlag K-Presse, 1977), 32.

31. Ibid., 62.

32. A. Blok, "Dnevnik 1918 goda," 7:339–41.

33. *Dnevnik M. A. Beketovoi,* IRLI, f. 462, ed. khr. 2, 1.34. The symbolist scholar A. V. Lavrov related to G. A. Levinton a story told him by Dmitrii S. Likhachev about Blok's venereal illness. According to Likhachev, Blok's close friend Evgenii Ivanov showed him the house in which young Blok contracted the disease. It was on Bol'shoi Prospect in Petersburg, kitty-corner from his high school (oral communication).

34. L. D. Blok, *I byl', i nebylitsy o Bloke i o sebe,* 49–50.

35. Nikolai Valentinov, *Dva goda s simvolistami* (Stanford, Calif.: Hoover Institution on War, Revolution and Peace, Stanford University, 1969), 74.

36. L. D. Blok, *I byl', i nebylitsy o Bloke i o sebe,* 51–52.

37. Avril Pyman, *The Life of Alexander Blok,* 2 vols. (Oxford: Oxford University Press, 1979, 1980), 1:58.

38. A. Blok, *Zapisnye knizhki,* 149.

39. L. D. Blok, *I byl', i nebylitsy o Bloke i o sebe,* 50.

40. Sergei Nebol'sin, "Iskazhennyi i zapreshchennyi Aleksandr Blok," *Nash sovremennik* 8 (1991): 179–84.

41. Eve Kosofsky Sedgwick, *Between Men: English Literature and Male Homosocial Desire* (New York: Columbia University Press, 1985).

42. Alexander Etkind referred to Blok's venereal disease only by analogy, writing that he died from the same illness as Nietzsche and the Russian fin-de-siècle artist Mikhail Vrubel, both of whom supposedly died from syphilis (Etkind, *Sodom i Psikheia: Ocherki intellektual'noi istorii Serebrianogo veka* [Moscow: ITS-Garant, 1996], 71).

43. M. M. Shcherba and L. A. Baturina, "Istoriia bolezni Bloka," in *Aleksandr Blok: Novye materialy i issledovaniia,* book 4, *Literaturnoe nasledstvo,* vol. 92 (Moscow: Nauka, 1987), 728–35.

44. L. D. Blok, *I byl', i nebylitsy o Bloke i o sebe,* 64.

45. Elaine Showalter, "Syphilis, Sexuality, and the Fiction of the Fin de Siècle," in *Sex, Politics, and Science in the Nineteenth-Century Novel,* ed. Ruth Bernard Yeazell (Baltimore: Johns Hopkins University Press, 1986), 95.

46. A. Blok, "Dnevnik 1918 goda," 7:343. The diary entry was written on the anniversary of his wedding; it is marked 30 (17) August.

47. K. Mochul'sky, *Aleksandr Blok* (Paris: YMCA Press, 1948), 32.

48. A. N. Apukhtin, "Sumasshedshii," *Polnoe sobranie stikhotvorenii* (St. Petersburg: Sovetskii pisatel', 1991), 250.

49. A. Blok, "Religio: Bezmolvnyi prizrak v teremu," 1:230.

50. Alexander Blok, *Pis'ma k zhene,* in *Literaturnoe nasledstvo,* vol. 89 (Moscow: Nauka, 1978), 54.

51. Andrei Bely, *Nachalo veka,* ed. A. V. Lavrov (Moscow: Khudozhestvennaia literatura, 1990), 374.

52. *Literaturnaia entsiklopediia* (Moscow: Izdatel'stvo Kommunisticheskaia adademiia, 1930), 1:507.

53. L. D. Blok, *I byl', i nebylitsy o Bloke i o sebe,* 80–81.

54. A. Blok, "E. P. Ivanovu," 8:251. Blok also records Dracula's impact on him in his notebooks (*Zapisnye knizhki,* 115). The Russian title of Stoker's novel is *Vampir—graf Drakula* (*The Vampire—Count Dracula*).

55. A. Blok, "Solntse nad Rossiei (Vos'midesiatiletie L'va Nikolaevicha Tolstogo)," 5:302. Blok ended the essay with a suckling image, saying that Russian literature absorbed Tolstoy's remarkable vitality together with its mother's milk (5:303).

56. A friend of Blok, Mikhail Tereshchenko was a wealthy industrialist and politician who served as minister of both finance and foreign affairs in the provisional government in 1917.

57. Blok wrote in his diary that Tereshchenko's sister reported that after reading *Dracula,* she noticed that the eyes of the crow in the nest outside her bedroom began to rotate. Having used one of the advertised creams at night, she also claimed that she was not able to open her eyes the next morning; all the skin on her face had peeled off (April 16, 1913, in "Dnevnik 1913 goda," 7:237).

58. A. Blok, *Pis'ma k zhene,* 139.

59. The amethyst ring had symbolic meaning for Blok: his first love, Kseniia Sadovskaia, had given him an amethyst ring in 1897, which he described in the poem "Amethyst" in 1900.

60. A. Blok, "Pesn' Ada," 3:502.

61. Another source for Blok's vampirism was Przybyszewski's prose. Here is a typical example from *Requiem Aeternum:* "I embrace your neck and bite your youthful breast and drink from your veins maternal milk mixed with blood" (*Zaupokoinaia messa,* trans. M. N. Semenov, in *Zaupokoinaia messa, V chas chuda, Gorod smerti, Stikhotvoreniia v proze* [Moscow: Skorpion, 1906], 38).

62. Bram Stoker, *The Essential Dracula* (New York: Penguin, 1993), 28.

63. Regarding the probable cause of Stoker's death, see Alexandra Warwick, "Vampires and the Empire: Fears and Fictions of the 1890s," in *Cultural Politics at the Fin de Siècle,* ed. Sally Ledger and Scott McCracken (Cambridge: Cambridge University Press, 1995), 202–20. Warwick noted that "vampirism is likened far more closely to disease than to possession, which might be the immediate religious comparison, and the disease that has already been observed as the equivalent to vampirism is syphilis" (209).

64. A. Blok, "Dnevnik 1912 goda," 7:117–18.

65. See Judith Halberstam, "Technologies of Monstrosity: Bram Stoker's Dracula," in *Cultural Politics at the Fin de Siècle,* 248, 263–64nn1 and 2. The book includes a discussion of the figure of Dracula in relation to anti-Semitic stereotypes. According to Halberstam, "the anti-Semite's Jew and Stoker's vampire bore more than a family resemblance" (248). Stoker's friendship with Richard Burton, the fin-de-siècle author who revived the blood libel against the Jews, thus assumes special significance.

66. A. Blok, introduction to *Vozmezdie,* 3:296.

67. The appeal appeared in *Rech',* no. 329 (November 30, 1911) (A. Blok, *Polnoe sobranie sochinenii i pisem v dvadtsati tomakh* [Moscow: Nauka, 1999] 5:430). Blok mentioned signing the petition in his 1911 diary (7:97). In his notebook from 1917, in which he made occasional anti-Semitic remarks, he noted that he had written a brief piece for the newspaper welcoming Beilis's acquittal, but he also wrote retrospectively that the Beilis affair had a sleep-inducing effect on him (*Zapisnye knizhki,* 330–31).

68. According to Sergei Nebol'sin, Blok's published diaries and notebooks have been purged of anti-Semitic remarks, examples of which he cited in his publication (Nebol'sin, "Iskazhennyi i zapreshchennyi Aleksandr Blok," 179, 181–88. See also Mikhail Bezrodny, "O 'iudoboiazni' Andreia Belogo," *Novoe literaturnoe obozrenie* 28 (1997): 101–2.

69. A. Blok, *Vozmezdie,* 3:297.

70. Ibid., 3:298.

71. The Polish motif is important for the poem, but not to my interpretation of it.

72. A. Blok, *Vozmezdie,* 3:323 ("Kak budto trup khotel nalit' / Zhivoi, igraiushcheiu krov'iu" [As if he wanted to fill his corpse / With living, sparkling blood]).

73. Ibid., 3:325.

74. Further examples of vampiric images from *Retribution:* "I chernaia, zemnaia krov' / Sulit nam, razduvaia veny, . . . Nevidannye miatezhi . . ." (306 [And black, earthly blood / Augers to us, swelling our veins, . . . Unprecedented changes . . .]); "No im naveki ne poniat' / Tekh, s *obrechennymi glazami:* / Dru-

gaia stat', drugaia krov'" (319 [But they will never understand / Those *with doomed eyes:* / They are of a different kind, of different blood]); "Tak / Vrashchaet khishchnik mutnyi zrak, / Bol'nye raspravliaia kryl'ia" (322 [So / Spins the beast of prey its dull pupil, / Spreading its sickly wings]); "On chuvstvoval, kak stynet krov'" (336 [He felt the cooling of his blood]); "I on stremglav ottsu vonzaet / Bulavku okolo loktia" (337 [And he swiftly plunges a pin / Into his father near the elbow])."

75. A. Blok, *Vozmezdie,* 3:297.

76. See Sander L. Gilman, *Difference and Pathology: Stereotypes of Sexuality, Race, and Madness* (Ithaca, N.Y.: Cornell University Press, 1985), 157.

77. Quoted in Pyman, *Life of Alexander Blok,* 2:109.

78. A. Blok, "Materi," 8:331–32.

79. Lidiia Ginzburg, *O psikhologicheskoi proze* (Leningrad: Sovetskii Pisatel', 1971), 51; translated by Judson Rosengrant as *On Psychological Prose* (Princeton, N.J.: Princeton University Press, 1991).

80. Quoted in M. O. Gershenzon, "Liubov' N. P. Ogareva," in *Obrazy proshlogo* (Moscow: Levenson, 1912), 341.

81. Quoted by A. L. Lavrov in Bely, *Na rubezhe dvukh stoletii,* 6.

82. Martin Malia, *Alexander Herzen and the Birth of Russian Socialism* (Cambridge, Mass.: Harvard University Press, 1961; New York: Grosset & Dunlap, 1971), 176.

83. Ibid., 179.

84. A. Blok, "Dnevnik 1921 goda," 7:406.

85. Viacheslav Ivanov, *Perepiska iz dvukh uglov: Viacheslav Ivanov i Mikhail Gershenzon* in *Sobranie sochinenii,* 4 vols. (Brussels: Foyer Oriental Chrétien, 1979), 3:396.

## Chapter 4. Blok's Femme Fatale

1. Dmitrii Merezhkovsky, *Khristos i Antikhrist: Voskresshie Bogi: Leonardo da Vinci* (Moscow: Kniga, 1990). *Resurrection of the Gods: Leonardo da Vinci* was the second volume of Merezhkovsky's historical trilogy; the first was *Death of the Gods: Julian the Apostate* (1896), the third, *Antichrist: Peter and Alexei* (1905). Regarding the influence on Freud, see Sigmund Freud, "Leonardo da Vinci and a Memory of His Childhood," in *The Standard Edition of the Complete Psychological Works of Sigmund Freud* (London: Hogarth Press, 1964), 11:63–137. In a questionnaire in 1907 regarding his favorite books, Freud mentioned Merezhkovsky's novel (James Strachey, "Editor's Note to 'Leonardo da Vinci,'" in *Standard Edition,* 11:59).

2. Lidiia Zinov'eva-Annibal published an essay on André Gide that included references to *The Immoralist.* See "V raiu otchaianiia," *Vesy* 10 (1904): 16–38.

3. André Gide, *The Immoralist,* trans. Richard Howard (New York: Vintage International, 1996), 51–52.

4. Travel to the continent, referred to as the grand tour for the first time in 1670, was considered an obligatory aspect of the construction of the English gentleman's identity since Shakespearean times.

5. A Russian traveler's response to Europe soon became an important component of cultural identity and a barometer of Slavophile and Westernizer affiliation.

6. Cf. also Mikhail Kuzmin (*Kryl'ia*, 1906), Vasilii Rozanov (*Ital'ianskie vpechatleniia*, 1909), and Pavel Muratov (*Obrazy Italii*, 1911–12). Viacheslav Ivanov met Lidiia Zinov'eva-Annibal, his future wife, in Rome in 1893. She was later nicknamed "Diotima" (from Plato's *Symposium*) and was frequently called the "soul" of the Tower symposia. The Ivanov marriage became one of the most influential erotic unions of the silver age, rivaled only by the Merezhkovskys and the Bloks. The role of Italy as cultural and erotic catalyst in the Ivanov love affair was substantial. Ivanov's *Italian Sonnets* (part of *Lodestars* [*Kormchie zvezdy*], 1903) reflect his erotic awakening to Dionysian experience in an Italy characterized by a rich synthesis of diverse cultural layers.

7. Although it is only a conjecture, Merezhkovsky may have intended to collaborate on a study of Leonardo with Volynsky, who at the time was having what I would describe as a cerebral love affair with Gippius to which Merezhkovsky was privy. The Leonardo project resulted in mutual accusations of plagiarism and a total rupture between them. In the Merezhkovskys' subsequent triple union with Dmitrii Filosofov, the three members of the *ménage* did write a play *à trois* while living in Paris titled *Red Poppy* (*Makov tsvet*, 1907). Gippius described their living experiment as a *marriage à trois* (*troebrachnost'*, see chap. 5).

8. Alexander Blok, "Nemye svideteli," in *Molnii iskusstva*, 5:390.

9. In the poem "Song of Hell" ("Pesn' Ada," 1909), written shortly after the Italian journey, Blok searches for Beatrice in the circles of hell that he traverses without finding her. Instead, he has a vampiric encounter with his dark muse.

10. A. Blok, "Nemye svideteli," 5:390–91.

11. Galla Placidia, of Visigoth origin, was the empress of the Western Roman Empire, whose capital was Ravenna. Later Ravenna became part of Byzantium. For Blok, Galla Placidia represented a synthetic historical figure that linked different cultural histories.

12. A steep flight of steps leads down to the burial site, which resembles a Roman house. The family name Velimna (Volumni in Latin) is inscribed on a funerary urn. The vault consists of several rooms, which contain magnificent Etruscan tombs.

13. A. Blok, "Nemye svideteli," 5:390.

14. Blok criticized all expressions and examples of contemporary mass culture in his Italian writings, including cinema and the modern tourist trade. He was, however, an avid filmgoer.

15. A. Blok, "Nemye svideteli," 5:391.

16. Ibid., 5:754n18.

17. Alexander Blok, "Vzgliad egiptianki," in *Molnii iskusstva*, 5:399.

18. One of the best-known emaciated new women on the Paris scene at the beginning of the century was Ida Rubinstein, whose reputation as a dancer and mime was made outside Russia. Her best-known roles were those of Salome and Cleopatra. See Olga Matich, "Gender Trouble in the Amazonian Kingdom: Turn-of-the-Century Representations of Women in Russia," in *Amazons of the*

*Avant-Garde: Alexandra Exter, Natalia Goncharova, Liubov Popova, Olga Rozanova, Varvara Stepanova, and Nadezhda Udaltsova,* ed. John E. Bowlt and Matthew Drutt (Berlin: Deutsche Guggenheim, 1999), 82–87.

19. A. Blok, "Neznakomka," 2:186.

20. A. Blok, "Vzgliad egiptianki," 5:398.

21. A. Blok, "Nemye svideteli," 5:387.

22. A. Blok, "Kleopatra," 2:207–8.

23. N. F. Fedorov, *Muzei, ego smysl i naznachenie,* in *Sobranie sochinenii v chetyrekh tomakh* (Moscow: Progress, 1995), 2:377. In another place he described the museum as the "highest level of authority, which must and can return life, and not take it away" (2:372).

24. Kornei Chukovsky, *Iz vospominanii* (Moscow: Sovetskii pisatel', 1959), 369–70.

25. The best known association of poet and tsar is Pushkin's famous poetic statement "Ty tsar': / Zhivi odin" (You are the tsar: / Then live alone) in "To the Poet" ("Poetu").

26. Andrei Bely wrote in *Arabesques* that Przybyszewski's heroes associate culture with the wax museum ("Tvorchestvo zhizni," in *Arabeski,* in *Kritika, estetika, teoriia simvolizma* [Moscow: Iskusstvo, 1994], 16). Later in the same essay, Bely wrote that "history [had] been given up to the wax museum" (54).

27. Describing the practice of anatomizing wax female figures, Ludmila Jordanova noted that even though they were already naked, they "gave an added, anatomical dimension to the erotic charge of unclothing by containing removable layers that permit ever deeper looking into the chest and abdomen. It is certainly possible to speak of shared metaphors at work here, such as penetration and unveiling, which are equally apt in a sexual and in an intellectual context" (*Sexual Visions: Images of Gender in Science and Medicine between the Eighteenth and Twentieth Centuries* [New York: Harvester Wheatsheaf, 1989], 55). Unveiling or peeling off layers of clothing to penetrate the hidden mysteries of being can be interpreted as a variation on the dissection metaphor. The comparison between dissection and unveiling was made as early as the beginning of the nineteenth century by a French surgeon (P. N. Gerdy, *Anatomie des formes exterieures,* 1829), who described skin as a veil covering the inner morphology of the body. Jordanova, who linked dissection and unveiling, borrowed the metaphor to describe J. H. Hasselhorst's 1864 painting of dissecting a female cadaver; she described dissection as a form of undressing: "One of the men . . . is holding up a sheet of skin, the part which covers her breast, as if it were a thin article of clothing, so delicate and fine is its texture" (57). Thus the sexual connotations of undressing are attributed to dissection; the conflation of the two commonly appears in decadent literature.

28. Rachilde, *Monsieur Venus,* trans. Liz Heron (Sawtry, U.K.: Dedalus, 1992), 143–44.

29. Théophile Gautier, *Mademoiselle de Maupin,* trans. Joanna Richardson (New York: Penguin Books, 1981), 205.

30. Stanislav Pshibyshevsky, *Zaupokoinaia messa,* trans. M. N. Semenov, in *Zaupokoinaia messa, V chas chuda, Gorod smerti, Stikhotvoreniia v proze* (Moscow: Skorpion, 1906), 29–30.

31. Janet Beizer, *Ventriloquizing Bodies: Narratives of Hysteria in Nineteenth-Century France* (Ithaca, N.Y.: Cornell University Press, 1994), 353.

32. A. Blok, "O sovremennom sostoianii russkogo simvolizma," 5:429.

33. Winged eyes were one of Blok's fixed epithets in describing Volokhova, his Russian femme fatale.

34. A. Blok, "O sovremennom sostoianii russkogo simvolizma," 5:429.

35. A. Blok, "Kholodnyi veter ot laguny," in "Venetsiia," 3:102–3.

36. Alexander Blok, *Zapisnye knizhki: 1901–1920* (Moscow: Khudozhestvennaia literatura, 1965), 140–41. Until recently, Blok scholars have claimed that the Salome poem had been inspired, in all likelihood, by the Dolci painting. See, for example, the commentary to the poem by Vladimir Orlov (*Sobranie sochinenii,* 3:531) and Lucy E. Vogel in *Aleksandr Blok: The Journey to Italy* (Ithaca, N.Y.: Cornell University Press, 1973), 65–67. For Vogel's discussion of the Venice poem, see 64–73.

37. See, for instance, *Salomé dans les Collections Françaises* (Saint-Denis: Musée d'Art et d'Histoire, 1988).

38. John Unrau, *Ruskin and St. Mark's* (New York: Thames & Hudson, 1984), 182. The sister of Blok's mother, who was also Sergei Solov'ev's mother, O. M. Solov'eva, translated Ruskin into Russian. Blok's library contained several books by Ruskin in Russian and French translation, including the much celebrated *Stones of Venice.*

39. See, e.g., Bely, "Tvorchestvo zhizni," 52.

40. O. V. Miller et al, *Biblioteka A. A. Bloka: Opisanie* (Leningrad: BAN, 1986), 3:171.

41. Gustave Geffroy, "Sovremmeniki o Redone," *Vesy* 4 (1904): 12–14. In the essay "Contemporaries on Redon," the French decadent Jean Lorrain described the artist's recurring severed heads of "superhuman suffering" as symbolizing "the fatal agony of the human brain in search of an ideal, of truth, understood by madness—the mother of ecstasy" (14). The eccentric artist and poet Maks Voloshin, a regular correspondent for *Balance* from Paris, knew Redon and admired his work. Voloshin served both as the go-between in *Balance*'s publication project and as author or editor of the three Redon articles that opened the fourth issue (Maksimilian Voloshin, "Odilon Redon," in *Liki tvorchestva,* ed. V. A. Manuilov, V. P. Kupchenko, and A. V. Lavrov, commentary by K. M. Azadovsky, 2nd ed. [Leningrad: Nauka, 1989], 653–55). Redon's work was first exhibited in Russia in 1906 at the thirteenth exhibit of the Moscow Union of Artists.

42. Unrau, *Ruskin and St. Mark's,* 182.

43. Oscar Wilde's *Salome* was scheduled to appear in the Theater of Vera Kommissarzhevskaia in 1909. The play's director was Nikolai Evreinov, a major figure of the Russian theater; like others, he failed to bring *Salome* to a major Russian stage. In a preemptive attempt to avoid the outrage of Russian Orthodox institutions, Evreinov removed the biblical names from the play and replaced them with generic ones (Jokanaan was called "prophet"; even the title was changed from *Salome* to *Princess* [*Tsarevna*]). The play's most provocative scene, which fetishizes the phallus—the erotic monologue that Salome addresses to the head of the Baptist—was excised. Instead, she speaks her words into the open-

ing of a cistern, at the bottom of which lies the saint's corpse. The dress rehearsal, attended by Petersburg's political and cultural elite, including Blok, was on October 27, after which the play was closed. The event became legend. For further discussion, see Olga Matich, "Gender Trouble in the Amazonian Kingdom," and Olga Matich, "Pokrovy Salomei: Eros, smert', istoriia," in *Erotizm bez beregov,* ed. M. M. Pavlova (Moscow: Novoe literaturnoe obozrenie, 2004), 90–121.

44. A. Blok, "Primechaniia," 3:530.

45. Oscar Wilde, *Salome* (London: John Lane, 1912), 78.

46. A. Blok, "Pis'ma o poezii," 5:278.

47. Stephane Mallarme, "Ballets," in *Mallarme in Prose,* ed. Mary Ann Caws, trans. Mary Ann Caws and Rosemary Lloyd (New York: New Directions Press, 2001), 109.

48. A. Blok, "Pis'ma o poezii," 5:278.

49. The Lion's Column on the Piazzetta was the old site of executions in Venice. Evreinov, who had tried to bring *Salome* to the Russian stage, was fascinated by corporal punishment and by the affiliation of the theater and the scaffold, about which he delivered a series of lectures between 1918 and 1924. His monograph on the topic—*Teatr i eshafot*—remains unpublished. He did write and publish a quasi-scholarly monograph on the history of corporal punishment in Russia: N. Evreinov, *Istoriia telesnykh nakazanii v Rossii* (St. Petersburg: V. K. Il'inchik, 1924).

50. Emphasis mine.

51. A. Blok, *Vozmezdie,* 3:301. The prologue to *Retribution,* which contains the reference to Salome, was first published in 1917, the year of the revolution. The reference to the poet's head on the scaffold carried revolutionary meaning in 1917. The ban on Wilde's *Salome* was lifted shortly after the February revolution. The best-known of the postrevolutionary performances was Alexander Tairov's production in the Kamernyi Theater in Petrograd in 1917, with Futurist set and costume design by the avant-garde artist Alexandra Exter, and with the tragic actress Alisa Koonen, of subsequent fame, as Salome.

52. A. Blok, *Vozmezdie,* 3:303.

53. A. Blok, "Slabeet zhizni gul upornyi," in "Venetsiia," 3:104.

54. The fragmentary prose piece "Neither Dreams nor Waking" ("Ni sny ni iav'," 1921), on which Blok worked for almost two decades, starting in 1902, again contains the figure of Salome and the image of the soul separated from the body. These images first appear in a draft called "Fragments of a Shakhmatovo Dream," which Blok recorded on September 13, 1909, several months after his return from Italy. In the dream, Salome passes by him carrying his proverbial head. As in the Venice poem and in *Retribution,* the lyrical subject is bifurcated: the body has been separated from the soul, and as in Blok's review of Minsky, the severed head *is* the soul, the Orphic source of poetry. What is curious about the final version of "Neither Dreams nor Waking" is Blok's new representation of Salome. She is no longer just a trace in Blok's poetic palimpsest. Although the reference to her is brief, she is sumptuously attired in "a purple and gold dress, which is so wide and heavy that she has to push it aside with her foot" (A. Blok, "Ni sny, ni iav'," 6:171). This certainly differs from the representation of Salome

in the Venetian poem, in which she is merely a phantomlike trace in the palace arcade.

55. M. V. Babenchikov, "Otvazhnaia krasota," in *Aleksandr Blok v vospominaniiakh sovremennikov,* ed. Vl. Orlov, 2 vols. (Moscow: Khudozhestvennaia literatura, 1980), 2:159.

56. A. Blok, "Antverpen," 3:153. The Antwerp poem resembles the earlier Venice one in a number of ways. Besides the figure of Salome, it contains water images, ships, bloodshed, and peering into the darkness, which in the later poem are a foreboding of war, symbolized by the headhunting princess.

57. Peter Chaadaev, "The Apologia of a Madman," in *The Major Works of Peter Chaadaev,* trans. Raymond T. McNally (Notre Dame, Ind.: University of Notre Dame Press, 1969), 205. Chaadaev, a brilliant and wealthy nobleman, was a member of Alexander I's honor guard when the Russians occupied Paris after the fall of Napoleon. Although he wrote but little, he left an indelible mark on Russian literature and intellectual history. The critical discussion of Russian national identity initiated by Chaadaev continues today. Nicholas I placed him under house arrest in response to his *First Philosophical Letter,* written in 1829 and published in 1836. An isolated existence marked the rest of his life.

58. A. Blok, "Krushenie gumanizma," 6:114.

59. A. Blok, "Predislovie," in *Vozmezdie,* 5:298.

60. The line is taken from Bely's poem "Despair" ("Otchaian'e," 1908).

61. For a discussion of "Rossiia—Sfinks," see Omry Ronen, "'Rossiia Sfinks': K istorii krylatogo upodobleniia," *Novoe literaturnoe obozrenie* 17 (1996): 420–31.

62. The image of Russia as Sphinx has become an indelible part of the European myth of Russia since Winston Churchill's famous statement that Russia "is a riddle wrapped in a mystery inside an enigma."

63. A. Blok, "Krizis gumanizma," 6:114–15.

64. For a discussion of *Katilina* and revolution as castration in Blok's late writing, see Alexander Etkind, *Sodom i Psikheia: Ocherki intellektual'noi istorii Serebrianogo veka* (Moscow: Its-Garant, 1996), 59–139.

65. A. Blok, *Zapisnye knizhki,* 84.

## Chapter 5. Transcending Gender

1. Z. Gippius-Merezhkovskaia, *Dmitrii Merezhkovsky* (Paris: YMCA-Press, 1951), 25. Subsequent references are given in the text.

2. "Blagoukhanie sedin," in Z. N. Gippius, *Stikhotvoreniia. Zhivye litsa,* ed. N. A. Bogomolov (Moscow: Khudozhestvennaia literatura, 1991), 396.

3. Ibid, 395.

4. Viacheslav Ivanov, *Iskusstvo i simvolizm,* in *Sobranie sochinenii* (Brussels: Foyer Oriental Chretien, 1971–87), 2:614.

5. N. Berdiaev, "Novoe khristianstvo," *Russkaia mysl'* (July 1916): 66.

6. V. V. Rozanov, "*I shutia i ser'ezno,*" in *O pisatel'stve i pisateliakh,* ed. A. N. Nikoliukin (Moscow: Respublika, 1995), 500. Rozanov's essay first appeared in *Novoe vremia,* no. 12, 590 (March 31, 1911).

7. See Irene Masing-Delic, "Creating the Living Work of Art: The Symbolist Pygmalion and His Antecedents," in *Creating Life: The Aesthetic Utopia of Russian*

*Modernism*, ed. Irina Paperno and Joan Delaney Grossman (Stanford, Calif.: Stanford University Press, 1994), 51–82.

8. Like the Merezhkovskys, the Russian philosopher Nikolai Berdiaev apparently lived in a celibate marriage with his wife, Lidiia Trusheva. It was an antiprocreative spiritual union without a traditional family life. Lidiia's sister Eugenie was a member of their household for forty years, living with the Berdiaevs in a platonic ménage à trois. She may have been closer to the philosopher than was his wife. The artistic and politically radical Trushev sisters shared everything, including prison and falling in love with the young philosopher. Berdiaev lived for his ideas, which Eugenie and Lidiia also shared. (See Donald Lowrie, *A Rebellious Prophet: A Life of Nicolai Berdyaev* [New York: Harper, 1960]).

9. For a discussion of fictitious marriage, see Irina Paperno, *Chernyshevsky and the Age of Realism: A Study in the Semiotics of Behavior* (Stanford, Calif.: Stanford University Press, 1988), 24–26, 29–36, 133–41.

10. For a discussion of transgressive vision in *What Is to Be Done*? see Olga Matich, "Černyševskij's *What Is to Be Done?* Transgressive Vision and Narrative Omniscience," *International Journal of Slavic Linguistics and Poetics* 44/45 (2005).

11. Sergei Makovsky, *Na parnase "Serebrianogo veka"* (Munich: Izd. Tsentr. ob'edineniia polit. emigrantov iz SSSR, 1962), 89.

12. Almost seventy years before Virginia Woolf's *A Room of One's Own* (1929), Chernyshevsky, through Lopukhov, offered a long disquisition on "one's special room" in *What Is to Be Done?* The disquisition focuses on women's lack of privacy in the patriarchal household, suggesting, however, that a private room is the right of all women (and not just women writers, as is the case in Woolf's essay). Although the phrase "one's special room" is Lopukhov's, Vera Pavlovna thinks of it first. Woolf's views on sex and its role in marriage have a great deal in common with the ideas of Gippius, who was Woolf's older contemporary. A comparative study of Bloomsbury and Russian symbolist experimental sexual practices awaits its author.

13. See Olga Matich, "Dialectics of Cultural Return: Zinaida Gippius' Personal Myth," in *Cultural Mythologies of Russian Modernism: From the Golden Age to the Silver Age*, ed. Boris Gasparov, Robert P. Hughes, and Irina Paperno (Berkeley: University of California Press, 1992), 57–60.

14. The Cleopatra theme was popular in Russia at the turn of the century. In 1895 A. N. Emel'ianov-Kokhanovsky published a collection of campy, decadent poems titled *Exposed Nerves* (*Obnazhennye nervy*), which he dedicated to "Himself" and the "Egyptian Queen Cleopatra." A collaborator of Briusov during the 1890s, he was the first Russian poet to call himself a decadent. In 1897 he published a novel called *Cleopatra*. In the early 1890s, Mikhail Kuzmin began working on an opera titled *Cleopatra*, which he never finished. The circle that formed around Diaghilev's World of Art movement was fascinated by ancient Egypt, as would be the case with artists and choreographers a decade later; the artist Alexander Benois described Cleopatra as the "most beautiful woman in antiquity" (Charles Spencer, *Leon Bakst* [London: Academy Publishers, 1973], 59). *Une Nuit de Cléopatre* was the hit of the first Paris season (1909) of Diaghilev's Ballets Russes. Briusov expanded Pushkin's short Cleopatra poem in *Egyptian Nights*

into a long narrative poem, also titled *Egyptian Nights.* Briusov, Bal'mont, and Blok all wrote their own Cleopatra poems; Blok identified her effigy with the dark female spirit of Russian symbolism (see chapter 4).

15. V. Bryusov, *The Diary of Valery Bryusov,* ed. and trans. Joan Grossman (Berkeley: University of California Press, 1980), 118.

16. Ibid., 120.

17. The portrait was displayed in Paris and London and at the controversial 1910 exhibit of women's portraits sponsored in Petersburg by *Apollon.* The portrait had been commissioned by the publisher of the symbolist journal *Golden Fleece* (*Zolotoe runo*), Nikolai Riabushinsky.

18. Gippius letter to Zinaida Vengerova, 1897, undated, IRLI, f. 39, op. 2, ed. khr. 542.

19. Havelock Ellis, "Sexual Inversion in Women," *Alienist and Neurologist* 18, no. 2 (1895): 152–54.

20. P. A. Florensky, *Analiz prostranstvennosti i vremeni v khudozhestvenno-izobrazitel'nykh proizvedeniiakh* (Moscow: Izdatel'skaia gruppa "Progress," 1993), 146–71.

21. Makovsky, *Na parnase,* 89.

22. Andrei Bely, *Nachalo veka,* ed. A. V. Lavrov (Moscow: Khudozhestvennaia literatura, 1990), 194.

23. See "Merezhi" (1902) and "Strany unyniia" (1902), in *Sobranie stikhov: 1889–1903;* "Sviatoe" (1905), "Ona" ("V svoei bessovestnoi i zhalkoi nizosti," 1905), and "Bol'" (1906) in *Sobranie stikhov: Kniga vtoraia. 1903–1909.*

24. The femme fatale is "a type," wrote Praz, that "ends by modelling itself on the women of Dostoievsky, among whom Nastasia Filippovna is the most characteristic example" (*The Romantic Agony,* trans. Angus Davidson, 2nd ed. [London: Oxford University Press, 1970], 209).

25. Diary of S. P. Kablukov, June 5, 1909, RPB, f. 322, ed. khr. 4.

26. Zinaida Gippius, *Contes d'Amour,* in *Dnevniki,* ed. A. N. Nikoliukin (Moscow: NPK "Intelvak," 1999), 1:56.

27. Its best-known member was the famous Pushkin scholar Semen Vengerov, Zinaida's brother; Zinaida was also Liudmila Vil'kina's aunt.

28. Liudmila Vil'kina was Minsky's second wife, although they were married officially only in 1905. Zinaida Vengerova was his third wife, who married Minsky in emigration in 1925.

29. Quoted in Mark Vishniak, "Z. N. Gippius v pis'makh," *Novyi Zhurnal* 37 (1954): 183.

30. Gippius to Minsky, January 14, 1892, IRLI, f. 39, op. 1, ed. khr. 205.

31. From "Lestnitsa" (Z. N. Gippius, *Stikhotvoreniia,* in *Novaia biblioteka poeta,* ed. A. V. Lavrov (St. Petersburg: Akademicheskii proekt, 1999), 100.

32. Quoted in Gippius, *Stikhotvoreniia: Zhivye litsa,* 465.

33. Temira Pachmuss confused the first name of Gloeden, calling him Franz instead of Wilhelm in a note to *Contes d'amour,* in *Between Paris and St. Petersburg: Selected Diaries of Zinaida Hippius* (Urbana: University of Illinois Press, 1975), 98n22; the mistake was repeated in all subsequent commentary regarding Gippius's reference to Gloeden and her visit to his villa. As to Elizabeth von Overbek, Gippius wrote to V. D. Komarova in 1898 that although Overbek had grown

up and lived in England, where her parents had taken her at a young age, she was Russian. Her parents died shortly after their arrival there. A "proper" Englishwoman, she graduated from the London conservatory, published many of her compositions, and conducted an orchestra (Gippius, *Stikhotvoreniia. Zhivye litsa,* 417).

34. In the summer of 2003, I visited Taormina, looking for traces of Gloeden's presence. I was told that his villa now houses the local police department, although efforts are under way to establish a small museum dedicated to the artist. Postcards with his homoerotic photographs are sold in a few tourist shops, including a toy store.

35. Liudmila Vil'kina-Minskaia was a poet whose volume of poetry and prose *My Garden* (*Moi sad,* 1906) includes representations of lesbian eroticism. Rozanov, the author of *People of the Moonlight* (*Liudi lunnogo sveta*)—an idiosyncratic history of same-sex love—wrote the introduction to the volume. He, like Merezhkovsky, was attracted to Liudmila.

36. Gippius to Liudmila Vil'kina, September 5, 1894, IRLI, f. 39, op. 3, ed. khr. 847.

37. Gippius to Liudmila Vil'kina, September 9, 1894, IRLI, f. 39, op. 3, ed. khr. 847.

38. Gippius to Minsky, October 24, 1894, IRLI, f. 39, op. 1, ed. khr. 205.

39. Merezhkovsky wrote to Volynsky about their religious and ethnic differences: "I am deeply Russian, you are deeply Jewish. There exists some kind of strange, inexplicable, and, as Vl. Solov'ev says correctly, 'zoological' power, which mutually alienates the Semitic and Aryan races and simultaneously attracts them to each other" (Merezhkovsky to Volynsky, October 19, 1891, GLM, f. 4, op. 1, ed. khr. 43).

40. Fedor Dostoevsky, *Idiot,* in *Polnoe sobranie sochinenii v tridtsati tomakh* (Leningrad: Nauka, 1973), 9:379–80.

41. Gippius, *Contes d'amour,* 43.

42. Ibid., 54–55.

43. Gippius to Volynsky, November 23, 1896, GLM, f. 9, ROF. 1357.

44. Gippius, *Contes d'amour,* 52–53.

45. Quoted in Gippius, *Stikhotvoreniia,* 461.

46. Gippius to Minsky, December 22, 1894, IRLI, op. 1, f. 39 ed. khr. 205; Gippius to Minsky, January 26, 1894, IRLI, op. 1, f. 39, ed. khr. 205.

47. Gippius to Minsky, September 26, 1892, IRLI, op. 1, f. 39, ed. khr. 205.

48. Gippius to Minsky, December 9, 1892, IRLI, op. 1, f. 39, ed. khr. 205.

49. Gippius to Minsky, January 25, 1893, IRLI, op. 1, f. 39 ed. khr. 205; Gippius to Minsky, October 2, 1892, IRLI, f. 39, op. 1, ed. khr. 205.

50. Gippius to Vengerova, July 2, 1897, IRLI, f. 39, op. 2, ed. khr. 542.

51. Gippius to Vengerova, April 8, 1897, IRLI, f. 39, op. 2, ed. khr. 542.

52. Gippius, *Contes d'amour,* 47.

53. Ibid., 47–48.

54. Plato, *The Collected Dialogues of Plato Including the Letters,* ed. Edith Hamilton and Huntington Cairns, Bollingen Series (Princeton, N.J.: Princeton University Press, 1961), 510, 523.

55. Gippius, *Contes d'amour,* 53.

56. Ibid.

57. Gippius to Vengerova, undated, IRLI, f. 39, op. 2, ed. khr. 542 (folio).

58. Plato, *Collected Dialogues*, 521. Merezhkovsky compared the Platonic metaphor of sprouting wings to teething in *L. Tolstoy and Dostoevsky: Life, Work, and Religion*.

59. Representing Gippius's attempts to manipulate the addressee, her letters resemble the behavior of a possessive mother who has the need to control her children even after she has let them out into the world.

60. Gippius to Volynsky, February 14, 1895, IRLI, f. 39, op. 2, ed. khr. 205.

61. Zinaida Gippius, *O byvshem* (1899–1914), in *Dnevniki*, 1:91.

62. The subtitle of *What Is to Be Done?* is *From Tales about New People*, whose prototype is the new man of the New Testament. In her biography of Merezhkovsky, Gippius referred to Solov'ev, Briusov, Blok, and Rozanov as "new people" (*Dmitrii Merezhkovsky*, 79). Irina Paperno uncovered a multiplicity of Christian symbols in *What Is to Be Done?* In *Chernyshevsky and the Age of Realism*, she described it as a socialist gospel and a new religion (333) and noted the apocalyptic character of Chernyshevsky's utopian socialism (353) and his concern with the heavenly kingdom on earth (341). Although at the beginning of the twentieth century the term "new man" evoked Nietzsche's superman, in Russia it maintained both its Christian and Chernyshevskian, 1860s connotations. Gippius titled her first book of short stories *New People* (*Novye liudi*, 1896). Like their predecessors in Russian utopian fiction, her heroes indulge in long debates about universal harmony, God, the meaning of love, and the transformation of life. In a typical instance of cultural layering, the title of Gippius's book and its contents were informed by three competing ideologies: Christianity, Nietzscheanism, and 1860s radical utopianism. Commenting on Merezhkovsky's study of Tolstoy and Dostoevsky, Bely emphasized the multiple referentiality of the phrase "new people" at the turn of the twentieth century. He wrote that "Merezhkovsky's task was to reveal a commune of new men who have transformed the consciousness of Tolstoy and Dostoevsky into a creative lifestyle [*byt*]; this commune would be informed by the third testament, fusing the New and the Old Testament into one." In speaking of the "new men," Bely emphasized literature as a stimulus to action (Bely, *Nachalo veka*, 188–89), which was the purpose of Chernyshevsky's novel.

63. Rene Girard, *Deceit, Desire, and the Novel: Self and Other in Literary Structure*, trans. Yvonne Freccero (Baltimore: Johns Hopkins University Press, 1965), 1–3; for a description of "homosocial desire," see the "Russian Precursors" section of my introduction.

64. I first learned of this relationship from Alexander Sobolev, who spoke about it at the first Merezhkovsky conference in Russia in 1991. The only preserved letter from Gippius to Nilova (RGALI, f. 154, op. 2, ed. khr. 320) resembles her other erotically playful letters from the 1890s to other women. Like these letters, it is "between women," with a man in between. What is unusual, however, is that the object of mimetic desire is Merezhkovsky himself. Gippius established her position in the triangle as one of mystification; she was the mysterious "Snow Queen," an image that she had invented herself. Nilova was curious

about the Snow Queen, who supposedly corresponded with Merezhkovsky, and wanted to see her letters.

65. Unpublished paper by Alexander Sobolev delivered at the conference on Merezhkovsky at the Institute of World Literature in 1991. An expanded version of part of that paper appeared in A. L. Sobolev's "Merezhkovskie v Parizhe (1906–1908)," in *Litsa: Biograficheskii al'manakh* (Moscow and St. Petersburg: Feniks-Atheneum, 1992), 1:319–71.

66. This was one of many trips to Italy by Russia's early modernists, reflecting, in part, the revived interest in classical and Renaissance culture at the turn of the century. Such trips were also made by Briusov; Viacheslav Ivanov, who met Lidiia Zinov'eva-Annibal in Italy (the Merezhkovskys met Filosofov on one of their Italian trips); Blok and Liubov' Mendeleeva (see chapter 4); Akhmatova and Gumilev; the Muratovs and Khodasevich, and many others.

67. Gippius's unpublished Italian diary (March 1–May 26, 1896) is in the archive at IRLI, f. 39, op. 6, ed. khr. 1187. From the perspective of the Merezhkovskys' model of life creation, the novel *Leonardo da Vinci* offered a failed Solov'evian androgynous union; Leonardo and Mona Lisa become one in a single, androgynous body in the space of the painting but not in life. The lesser known of the two, Volynsky's study represents Leonardo's paintings, including the Mona Lisa, as expressions of an enervated, sickly, cerebral, even immoral sensibility, as if the critic were projecting onto them contemporary decadent aesthetics (A. Volynsky, *Zhizn' Leonardo da Vinchi* [Moscow: Algoritm, 1997], 21, 150–52).

68. The best study of Merezhkovsky's religious ideas is Bernice Glatzer Rosenthal, *Dmitri Sergeevich Merezhkovsky and the Silver Age* (The Hague: Martinus Nijhoff, 1975). The Christianity of the Third Testament was based on a triadic, or Trinitarian, principle. Originally presented by Joachim Fiore, an Italian mystic of the third century, the Covenant of the Third Testament formulated a prophetic theology of history, according to which history was divided into three ages: that of God the Father, of God the Son, and of God the Holy Ghost. In the third and final stage, humankind would be ruled by an intelligentsia spiritualis, resembling the symbolist chiliastic kingdom. The actual evidence of Joachim's direct influence on modern European thought is problematic (cf. Marjorie Reeves and Warwick Gould, *Joachim of Fiore and the Myth of the Eternal Evangel in the Nineteenth Century* [Oxford: Clarendon Press, 1987], esp. 1–5); yet some contemporary historians associate nineteenth-century utopian radicalism with his Trinitarian theology. ("When translated into secular terminology the 'three states' of Joachimism became, in the nineteenth century, the dominant philosophy of history ending in a utopia" [Frank E. Manuel and Fritzie P. Manuel, *Utopian Thought in the Western World* (Cambridge, Mass: Harvard University Press, Belknap Press, 1979), 33–34].) Solov'ev's Trinitarian view of history and Berdiaev's religious philosophy have also been linked to Joachim's ideas and to Johannine Christianity (Ernst Benz, *Evolution and Christian Hope: Man's Concept of the Future from the Early Fathers to Teilhard de Chardin,* trans. Heinz Frank [Garden City, N.J.: Doubleday, 1966], 46). Also cf. Olga Matich, "The Merezhkovskys' Third Testament and the Russian Utopian Tradition," in *Christianity and the East-*

*ern Slavs*, ed. Robert P. Hughes and Irina Paperno (Berkeley: University of California Press), 2:158–71.

69. Gippius, *O byvshem*, 109.

70. Anna Filosofova (b. Diaghileva) was the wife of a high-ranking official. She was also a gentry feminist of the 1860s, meaning that she espoused liberal feminist ideas with a populist flair. She remained an active feminist and philanthropist till the early twentieth century. What she could not accept was the rise of Marxist feminism. In the twentieth century, she joined the Kadet Party, reflecting her moderate, "bourgeois" political affiliation.

71. Filosofov to Gippius, April 7/19, 1898, RPB, f. 481, ed. khr. 94.

72. Bely, *Nachalo veka*, 212.

73. On August 28, 1902, Diaghilev wrote to Alexander Benois: "We spent 1½ months in Venice, and now we are staying in Graz, in Krafft-Ebing's renowned sanatorium. Please don't think we've lost our minds; it's just that our damned nerves are demanding treatment. We'll talk about us [Diaghilev and Filosofov] when we meet; how soon this will be I cannot say. Dima [Filosofov] will return in three weeks, but I might still be held up here, for I am still considered ill" (*Sergei Diagilev i russkoe iskusstvo: Stat'i, otkrytye pis'ma, interv'iu. Perepiska: Sovremenniki o Diagileve v 2-kh tomakh* [Moscow: Izobrazitel'noe iskusstvo, 1982], 1:76).

74. Andrei Bely, *Mezhdu dvukh revoliutsii*, ed. A. V. Lavrov, (Moscow: Khudozhestvennaia literatura, 1990), 158. In the same context, Bely described Gippius's visit to a homosexual bar (Bar-Morris) in the Pigalle district of Paris together with Minsky and himself (158–59).

75. Under the influence of Krafft-Ebing's study, Tatiana wrote: "I look for pathology in myself and in others" (Tatiana Gippius, "Letter to Zinaida Gippius," December 28, 1906, Amherst Center of Russian Culture [Merezhkovsky Archive, Box 2, Folder 27]).

76. Gippius, *Contes d'amour*, 58.

77. Gippius, *O byvshem*, 93.

78. "'Raspoiasannye pis'ma' V. Rozanova" (published by M. Pavlova), *Literaturnoe obozrenie* (special issue on *Eroticheskaia traditsiia v russkoi literature*) 11 (1991): 71.

79. Temira Pachmuss, *Zinaida Hippius: An Intellectual Profile* (Carbondale: Southern Illinois University Press, 1971), 90.

80. Temira Pachmuss, *Intellect and Ideas in Action: Selected Correspondence of Zinaida Hippius* (Munich: Fink Verlag, 1972), 72.

81. Ibid., 67.

82. Ibid., 64.

83. Anton Krainii (Z. Gippius), "Vliublennost'," in *Literaturnyi dnevnik (1899–1907)* (St. Petersburg: Izd. M. V. Pirozhkova, 1908), 208.

84. Gippius, *Contes d'amour*, 59.

85. Krainii (Gippius), "Vliublennost'," 203–4.

86. Ibid., 202–5

87. Gippius, *Contes d'amour*, 68.

88. Gippius's examination of the kiss in "Vliublennost'" contextualizes the 1904 kissing episode with Kartashev. She wrote in *Contes d'amour* that their kiss

contained the potential for the transcendent erotic love that she sought, but, as usual, she suffered disappointment. The poem "Kiss" (1903), addressed to the invented woman An'es, offers a fleeting trace of the androgynous "two in one" in a playful disquisition in verse on the ambiguity of kissing. In a letter to Briusov, Gippius described the poem as "gaily perverse" (quoted in Gippius, *Stikhotvoreniia. Zhivye litsa,* 421).

89. Temira Pachmuss translated "O byvshem," which literally means "about the past," as *About the Cause* in her book *Between Paris and St. Petersburg.*

90. In the period of Filosofov's estrangement from the Merezhkovskys in 1902, they reminded him of Christ's words that "he who loves his father, or his mother, or his wife more than me—is unworthy of me" (Gippius, *O byvshem,* 113).

91. Among the participants were Gippius's sisters, Bely, Berdiaev, and Kartashev.

92. Gippius, *O byvshem,* 132.

93. Ibid., 108.

94. Gippius to Briusov, May 11, 1906, RGB, f. 386, ed. khr. 38.

95. Peter Brown, *The Body and Society: Men, Women, and Sexual Renunciation in Early Christianity* (New York: Columbia University Press, 1988), 42.

96. Gippius to E. Diaghileva, August 11, 1905, IRLI, f. 102, ed. khr. 118.

97. Ibid.

98. Filosofov to E. Diaghileva, April 30, 1905, IRLI, f. 102, ed. khr. 189.

99. Quoted in Sobolev, "Merezhkovskie v Parizhe," 342–43.

100. Bely referred to them as "trio" in *Mezhdu dvukh revoliutsii,* 146.

101. Gippius to E. Diaghileva, July 8, 1905, IRLI, f. 102, ed. khr. 118.

102. Quoted in V. Zlobin, *A Difficult Soul,* ed. and trans. Simon Karlinsky (Berkeley: University of California Press, 1980), 86–87.

103. Gippius's letters to Filosofov in Esentuki, a Caucasus spa where he was taking the cure in 1913, reflect her particularly intense interest in his ailing body. In a letter from August 5/6, 1913, she asked him to write her about each and every mud bath, the waters, whether they are hot and repulsive, and so on (RPB, f. 481, ed. khr. 160). The female discourse of illness at the turn of the twentieth century was the product of the European cult of female invalidism of the second half of the nineteenth century. It reflected the effort of Victorian women to become the suffering, fragile angels they were expected to be. Their escape into illness and even death could be seen as decadent paths to aesthetic epiphany. The fin-de-siècle fashion for consumption and wan, hollow-eyed female beauty was part of this discourse. Even though Gippius's discourse of illness has roots in the Victorian paradigm, it also has Russian literary associations. The affiliation of sickliness and female sexuality occupies an important place in *The Brothers Karamazov,* for instance. Liza Khokhlakova's paralyzed body functions as a double metaphor: it is an emblem of sexual repression and of sexual perversion, with her desire perversely entwined with the image of Christ's crucifixion.

104. See chapter 3 for a discussion of the tumultuous triple union comprised of Bely, Blok, and Liubov' Dmitrievna Mendeleeva-Blok. Poliksena Solov'eva, who wrote under the pseudonym Allegro, was a poet and prose writer. She frequently wore trousers, touting a mannish, lesbian persona.

105. See Kartashev's letters to Gippius in Pachmuss, *Intellect and Ideas,* 652–53, 659–62.

106. One of the candidates for their triple union was Margarita Sabashnikova-Voloshina, herself an artist, who lived in a celibate marriage with the poet Maksimil'ian Voloshin. Before the unsuccessful experiment with Sabashnikova, Ivanov's choice fell on the young poet Sergei Gorodetsky, who was expected to become the third person in the triple union as well as Ivanov's Platonic lover. This experiment was also a failure. For a discussion of the Tower, see Andrej Shishkin, "Le Banquet platonicien et soufi a la 'Tour' petersbourgeoise: Berdjaev et Vjačeslav Ivanov," *Cahier du Monde russe* 35, nos. 1–2 (1994): 15–80.

107. Gippius, *O byvshem,* 139.

108. See Margarita Pavlova's annotated publication of Gippius's diary, titled *Vtoraia chernaia tetrad',* in which she describes her relations with socialist revolutionaries, including terrorists, in 1918. Needless to say, she was not involved in any terrorist activities, but the Merezhkovskys' association with Savinkov and other political terrorists may have made them privy to secret political information. This part of the Merezhkovsky story is only beginning to be told (Zinaida Gippius, *Vtoraia chernaia tetrad',* introduction and commentary by Margarita Pavlova, *Nashe nasledie* 6 [1990]: 87–102).

109. Letter from Filosofov to Gippius, August 4, 1916, RPB, f. 481, ed. khr. 95.

110. Letter from Filosofov to Gippius, 1913 undated, RPB, f. 481, ed. khr. 95.

111. Nikolai Fedorov, *Sochineniia,* ed. S. G. Semenova (Moscow: Mysl' 1982), 129. Like Fedorov, Gippius also described her utopian project as a "common cause."

112. Gippius, *O byvshem,* 100.

113. In the role of mediator, she imagined herself as the Virgin Mary, Gnostic Sophia, and Holy Spirit, who were interchangeable in her syncretic Solov'evian mysticism. The figure of the Virgin invoked the celibate ideal; Sophia, the teachings of Solov'ev; and the Holy Spirit, the book of Revelation (the Merezhkovskys read regularly from Revelation during their prayer meetings).

114. Pachmuss, *Intellect and Ideas in Action,* 71.

115. The Merezhkovsky triple union also had a nonprocreative Oedipal subtext, based on sexual rivalry without generational difference. Playing the classic role of the third member in a ménage à trois, Filosofov was closer to Gippius than to Merezhkovsky. And even though he was not in love with her, he was jealous of her husband, which created friction in the triangular family. Her possessiveness revealed Gippius as a controlling mother, making Filosofov very resentful. She tried to take care of him, which included efforts to save him from bad influences. The correspondence between them reflects a mother-child relationship, although the roles are sometimes reversed. She frequently addressed him with pet names, especially *detochka* [little child], that reflected his childlike position in the "family." While this form of address was an epistolary convention, it also had clear Oedipal connotations. Filosofov addressed her in similar terms, especially when she was despondent and sick.

116. Gippius letter to Zlobin, undated, RPB, f. 481, ed. khr. 44.

117. A single asterisk (*) marks masculine nouns, pronouns, and adjectives; double asterisks (**) mark feminine ones.

118. Gippius, *Stikhotvoreniia,* 159.

119. As in her relationship with Filosofov some years earlier, Gippius's rival was a man; she considered it her task to rescue Zlobin from homosexual encounters. (We learn from the correspondence that his homosexual encounter with Mikhail Sazonov, a member of the student group that Gippius befriended, created tension between them.) As to the feminine forms of address directed to Zlobin, Gippius also used them in her letters to Filosofov. She addressed him as "my dear little girl/little boy," *rodnen'kaia moia* (the feminine form of "my dear little one"), which refers to a woman, and the grammatically feminine but gender neutral *milen'kaia moia khoroshaia detochka* ("my dear good little child").

120. Gippius to Zlobin, February 15, 1919, RPB, f. 481, ed. khr. 45.

121. Gippius to Zlobin, December 10, 1918, RPB, f. 481, ed. khr. 44.

122. See Matich, "Černyševskij's *What Is to Be Done?* Transgressive Vision and Narrative Omniscience."

123. Temira Pachmuss, *Contes d'amour,* in *Between Paris and St. Petersburg,* 77. Pachmuss, who has the diary *Contes d'amour* in her possession, excised this key self-description by Gippius from the first Russian publication of the diary in *Vozrozhdenie,* which Pachmuss published before the English version; the Russian version is the source of the recent publication of Gippius's diaries in Russia. It is important to note that Pachmuss made different excisions in the Russian and English versions. Pachmuss received Gippius's and Merezhkovsky's Parisian archives directly from Zlobin.

124. Vladimir Solov'ev, *Sobranie sochinenii* (St. Petersburg: Prosveshchenie, 1911–14), 7, 24.

125. Gippius, *Contes d'amour,* 62.

126. "'Raspoiasannye pis'ma' V. Rozanova," 70.

127. Ibid.

128. Makovsky, *Na parnase,* 115.

129. N. Berberova, *Kursiv moi: Avtobiografiia,* 2nd ed. (New York: Russica Publishers, 1983), 1:278, 282.

130. Undated anonymous letter to Dmitrii Merezhkovsky, RPB, f. 322, ed. khr. 10.

131. Vasilii Yanovsky, *Elysian Fields: A Book of Memory,* trans. Vasilii Yanovsky and Isabella Yanovsky (DeKalb: Northern Illinois University Press, 1987), 114.

132. Leon Trotsky, *Literature and Revolution* (New York: Russell & Russell, 1957), 51.

133. Nicolas Slonimsky, *Perfect Pitch: A Life Story* (Oxford: Oxford University Press, 1988), 42. A musicologist and conductor, Slonimsky was the son of Leonid Slonimsky, foreign affairs editor of the liberal monthly *The Messenger of Europe* (*Vestnik Evropy*) and author of the first book in Russian on Karl Marx (1880). On his mother's side, Nikolai came from the Vengerov family. Semen Vengerov was his uncle; Zinaida Vengerova was his aunt, as was the well-known pianist and pedagogue Isabella Vengerova. Minsky, whose wife Liudmila was a distant cousin, was either his uncle or cousin. Thus Slonimsky's many relatives were part of Gippius's tangled erotic life of the 1890s. In a private conversation in his Los Angeles home in 1992, at the age of ninety-eight, he repeated his family genealogy and what he had written about his relations with Gippius in *Perfect*

*Pitch.* He was particularly proud that he had composed the music for the *Marseillaise* for Gippius's play *The Green Ring.* Slonimsky spoke extensively about his mother's sexual fears and her preposterous ideas about how syphilis is contracted. She told him that being kissed on the nape of the neck by a woman or kissing her in the hollow of the elbow could result in syphilis. This story figures in his memoirs. What is not in his memoirs is the story of his stay at the Merezhkovsky dacha—that he found a bloodied towel in the bathroom one morning and told Filosofov about it, thinking that somebody had been wounded or even killed. Filosofov responded with some humor and said that it was female blood, which frightened the young man even more. In telling me this story, he commented with some satisfaction that he was a very naive youth. To my repeated queries regarding Zlobin, he claimed not to know who he was, which seems unlikely, since they were part of the same group at one point; rumor has it that they had a homosexual affair. In any case, Slonimsky's writing about Gippius shows familiarity with her letters and diaries published during the 1970s, in which Zlobin figures prominently. His brother Mikhail apparently had helped the Merezhkovskys get their archive out of the Soviet Union.

134. In describing the relationship between Gippius and her husband, Zlobin wrote that "she fertilized, while he gestated and gave birth. She was the seed, and he the soil, the most fertile of all black earths" (*Difficult Soul,* 42–43).

## Chapter 6. Religious-Philosophical Meetings

1. Miroliubov was the editor of a popular illustrated monthly *Zhurnal dlia vsekh* (*Journal for Everyone*). Regarding the private audience, see Z. Gippius-Merezhkovskaia, *Dmitrii Merezhkovsky* (Paris: YMCA-Press, 1951), 92.

2. Z. N. Gippius, "Pervaia vstrecha," *Poslednie Novosti,* no. 3,786 (August 4, 1931): 2. Gippius made no reference in the article to Benois, Bakst, or Minsky.

3. Alexander Benois, *Moi vospominaniia v piati knigakh,* bks. 4–5 (Moscow: Nauka, 1990), 288–89.

4. Bishop Sergii of Iamburg, later of Finland, became the patriarch of the Russian Orthodox Church in the Soviet Union during Stalin's time.

5. Gippius, "Pervaia vstrecha," 2.

6. Skvortsov longed to vindicate his bad reputation, the product of his cruel "missionary" work among sectarians. See Zinaida Gippius, *O byvshem,* in *Dnevniki* (Moscow: NPK "Intelvak," 1999), 111.

7. Gippius-Merezhkovskaia, *Dmitrii Merezhkovsky,* 97; Valerii Briusov, *Dnevniki 1891–1910* (Moscow: Sabashnikov, 1927), 117.

8. Benois, *Moi vospominaniia v piati knigakh,* 290.

9. Vladimir Zlobin, *A Difficult Soul: Zinaida Gippius,* ed. Simon Karlinsky (Berkeley: University of California Press, 1980), 46–47. Irina Odoevtseva wrote in her memoirs that Gippius had told her that she was known as the White She-Devil (Irina Odoevtseva, *Na beregakh Seny* [Moscow: Khudozhestvennaia literatura, 1989], 56).

10. One of the participants who may have pressured Pobedonostsev to put an end to the meetings was Mikhail Men'shikov, a former radical Tolstoyan who

now wrote for the conservative daily *New Time,* to which Rozanov was a regular contributor.

11. The *New Way* also published Russian and Western literature with a mystical bent. Blok's poetry first appeared there.

12. V. V. Rozanov, *Liudi lunnogo sveta: Metafizika khristianstva* (Moscow: Druzhba narodov, 1990), 173n1.

13. In *People of the Moonlight,* Rozanov described an example of a celibate triple union consisting of a schoolteacher and two sisters. The teacher lived in a "spiritual marriage" with one of them. Rozanov called the other sister an urning, a term used at the end of the century for practitioners of same-sex love. The couple had no children because they lacked procreative and sexual desire, at least for each other. Like Vera Pavlovna and Lopukhov in *What Is to Be Done?* they slept in separate bedrooms. Rozanov offered another example of unconsummated marriage resembling the practice of fictitious marriages in the 1860s: a young man married a young woman to save her from an intolerable home life; they lived with each other as brother and sister, even though she had wanted a family. Rozanov compared both to spiritual marriage among early Christians. According to him, the subtext of both unions was the homosexual or lesbian disposition of one or both partners (*Liudi lunnogo sveta,* 278–80).

14. Among the lesser known poets attending the meetings were V. Borodaevsky, D. Fridberg, A. Kondrat'ev, and L. Semenov-Tian-shansky.

15. Even though in recent history, the term "iron curtain" referred to the ideological divide between the Soviet Union and the West (Churchill used the term in 1946), originally it referred to a fire-proof iron theatrical curtain used, e.g., in Germany. In the days when fires were of real concern in theaters, iron safety curtains were lowered between the stage and the public hall after performances. But Rozanov—as early as 1918—used the term to describe the Bolshevik revolution: "an iron curtain is falling over Russian history with a terrible gnashing, creaking, and whistle. The performance is finished" (V. V. Rozanov, *Apokalipsis nashego vremeni,* in *O sebe i zhizni svoei* [Moscow: Moskovskii rabochii, 1990], 627).

16. Zinaida Gippius, "Zadumchivyi strannik," in *Stikhotvoreniia. Zhivye litsa,* ed. N. A. Bogomolov (Moscow: Khudozhestvennaia literatura, 1991), 322. Also see Gippius, "Pervaia vstrecha," *Poslednie novosti,* no. 3,784 (August 2, 1931): 2.

17. N. A. Berdiaev, *Samopoznanie (Opyt filosofskoi avtobiografii),* 2nd ed., vol. 1 of *Sobranie sochinenii* (Paris: YMCA-Press, 1983) 170.

18. Ibid., 167.

19. "1-oe religiozno-filosofskoe sobranie," *Novyi put'* 1 (1903): 1–38.

20. Benois, Bakst, and Nouvel eventually parted ways with the Merezhkovskys, which may explain Gippius's silence regarding Benois's and Bakst's role in the initial efforts to organize the Religious-Philosophical Meetings.

21. Efim Egorov referred to Gippius's comment at the third meeting that despite their limitations, monastic communes were communities of sorts (see *Novyi put'* 1 [1903]: 84).

22. Jutte Scherrer, *Forschungen zur Osteuropäischen Geschichte: Die Petersburger Religiös-Philosophischen Vereinigungen,* Osteuropa-Institut an der Freien Univer-

sität Berlin: Historische Veröffentlichungen (Berlin and Wiesbaden: Otto Harrassowitz, 1973), 102n32.

23. Andrei Bely, *Nachalo veka*, 211–13.

24. Gippius, *O byvshem*, 111.

25. In 1905, the year that Filosofov was in the process of making his final commitment to the Merezhkovskys, Gippius wrote to his aunt, E. Diaghileva, "[W]hen I love, it is absolutely communal-individual and God manlike" (IRLI, f. 102, ed. khr. 118). The letter was prompted by Filosofov's fear that Diaghilev would perish without him. Needless to say, these peripeties put Diaghileva in an awkward position in relation to her stepson, her nephew, whom she loved, and Gippius. Gippius's diary reveals her efforts to work on other members of the Diaghilev circle: Alexander Benois, Walter Nouvel, and Alfred Nurok.

26. Gippius, *O byvshem*, 112–14.

27. Gippius's personal turmoil during 1901 was further exacerbated by Merezhkovsky's passionate affair with Elena Obraztsova, who lived in Moscow and whom he visited there alone. This episode was unique in the Merezhkovsky marriage. Apparently it was the only time they were apart in the course of their life together. Obraztsova had given Merezhkovsky three thousand rubles for the *New Way* project. After Merezhkovsky broke off the affair, she accused him of not returning the money. In 1908 she wrote to Briusov, asking him to tell Merezhkovsky that she was ill and needed her money back (Evgeniia Ivanovna Obraztsova's letters to Briusov, see letter from April 8, 1908, in RGB, f. 386, ed. khr. 33). Obraztsova may have also had an affair with Briusov. In 1905 Briusov told Bely about the money, adding that Merezhkovsky was selling his body to Obraztsova. Bely was incensed and challenged Briusov to a duel, which, however, did not take place (Bely, *Nachalo veka*, 680n251).

28. V. V. Rozanov, letter to A. S. Glinka-Volzhsky, in Liudmila Saraskina, *Vozliublennaia Dostoevskogo: Apollinariia Suslova* (Moscow: Soglasie, 1994), 358–59. The *khlysty* were a persecuted Russian Orthodox sect whose ecstatic erotic practices fascinated fin-de-siècle Russians like Gippius and Rozanov.

29. In his first known letter to Gippius (1898), Filosofov rejected her suggestion that they develop an open epistolary relationship—that they read each other's correspondence with others—as an invasion of his privacy. Later, when he had become part of her commune, Filosofov asked Gippius not to circulate his letters among its members (see chapter 5, note 109, and the associated text).

30. Gippius had given Bely such a diary (Bely, *Nachalo veka*, 461).

31. Ivanov, who believed that metaphysical ideas must be rooted in the intimate sphere, also indulged in trying to snare his unsuspecting interlocutors in his sticky webs. Bely described the protean and charismatic Ivanov as a "singing spider that hung over the Duma, collecting little flies" in his web (Bely, *Nachalo veka*, 345). The reference is to the Ivanovs' Tower, an important gathering place for the cultural elite between 1905 and 1907. With a large bay window, it was located in an apartment building next to the Tavrida Palace, which housed the State Duma between 1905 and 1917. Ivanov's disarming and seductive technique based on intimacy was very effective in procuring followers. Bely described Ivanov's seduction of the Bloks as that of a cat sneaking up on its prey (347). Like Gippius, Ivanov was anxious to create his own sect, interlacing communalism

(*sobornost'*) with his brand of intimacy. The Hafiz Society, the secret inner circle of the Tower, also believed in communal diaries to be shared with one another. The homosexual poet Mikhail Kuzmin, who lived at the Tower, was the author of its most celebrated diary, which may be considered the most important intimate diary of the epoch (see M. Kuzmin, *Dnevnik 1905–1907,* ed. N. A. Bogomolov and S. V. Shumikhin [St. Petersburg: Izd. Ivana Limbakha, 2000]. Also see N. A. Bogomolov, "Peterburgskie Gafizity," in *Serebrianyi vek v Rossii* [Moscow: Radiks, 1993], 167–204).

32. Eric Naiman, *Sex in Public: The Incarnation of Early Soviet Ideology* (Princeton, N.J.: Princeton University Press, 1997).

33. Michel Foucault, *The History of Sexuality: An Introduction,* trans. Robert Hurley (New York: Vintage Books, 1990), 1:35.

34. V. V. Rozanov, "O sladchaishem Iisuse," in *Nesovmestimye kontrasty zhitiia: Literaturno-esteticheskie raboty razhnykh let* (Moscow: Iskusstvo, 1990), 426. The lecture titled "O sladchaishem Iisuse i gor'kikh plodakh mira" appeared in *Russkaia Mysl'* 1 (1908): 33–42. In 1911 it was published as part of *Temnyi lik* (1911).

35. "16-oe religiozno-filosofskoe sobranie," *Novyi put'* 10 (1903): 385–87. The transcripts of the meetings were all published in *Novyi put'*. (The Rozanov passage comes from V. V. Rozanov, "Sem'ia kak religiia," in *V mire neiasnogo i nereshennogo,* ed. A. N. Nikoliukin [Moscow: Respublika, 1995], 71.) Rozanov's essay was originally published in 1898, partially in response to *The Kreutzer Sonata.* In the essay, he associated Bethlehem and Golgotha with Christianity's conflicted view of sex and procreation.

36. "14-oe religiozno-filosofskoe sobranie," *Novyi put'* 9 (1903): 323.

37. "13-oe sobranie," *Novyi put'* 8 (1903): 296.

38. In Oscar Wilde's *Salome,* Salome's veiled dance is also linked to the temple curtain. As in Rozanov's metaphor, the veil has clear erotic connotations, emphasized by the substitution of veil for curtain. But Wilde's eroticism, which is antiprocreative and decadent, is very different from Rozanov's. Wilde's Herod speaks of the "veil of the Sanctuary," which had disappeared; Herodias accuses him of having stolen it. This exchange takes place shortly before the unveiling of Salome, metaphorizing Herod's lascivious desire to deflower the virgin.

39. V. V. Rozanov, *Pered Sakharnoi,* in *Sakharna* (Moscow: Respublika, 1998) 39.

40. "12-oe religiozno-filosofskoe sobranie," *Novyi put'* 6 (1903): 249.

41. "14-oe religiozno-filosofskoe sobranie," *Novyi put'* 9 (1903): 329.

42. Tertullian (ca. 160–ca. 220) was a Christian theologian who eventually joined the apocalyptic ascetic sect of Montanists. Leporsky's argument appeared in "15-oe religozno-filosofskoe sobranie," *Novyi put'* 9 (1903): 332.

43. For a discussion of the *skoptsy,* see note 26 in chapter 1.

44. "15-oe religiozno-filosofskoe sobranie," *Novyi put'* 9 (1903): 362.

45. Fathers Ioann Filevsky of Kharkov, D. Iakshich (author of *O nravstvennom dostoinstve devstva i braka po ucheniiu Pravoslavnoi tserkvi* [St. Petersburg, 1903]), and Ioann Slobodskoi endorsed marriage as "holy." Only Father T. A. Nalimov and the ex-Tolstoyan journalist of *New Time* Mikhail Men'shikov gave unambiguous preference to celibacy.

46. "15-oe religiozno-filosofskoe sobranie," *Novyi put'* 9 (1903): 345.

47. In his defense of procreation, Uspensky challenged Solov'ev's belief that sexual shame is the source of morality, differentiating man from the animal kingdom. For Solov'ev's discussion of shame, see V. S. Solov'ev, *Opravdanie dobra,* in *Sobranie sochinenii V. S. Solov'eva* (1911; Brussels: Foyer Oriental Chretien, 1966), 8:49–66, 163–89.

48. "14-oe religiozno-filosofskoe sobranie," *Novyi put'* 9 (1903): 316.

49. "13-oe religiozno-filosofskoe sobranie," *Novyi put'* 8 (1903): 295. In *People of the Moonlight,* Rozanov wrote that Tolstoy considered pregnancy "an infectious illness": "Every time [Nekhliudov] learned that [his sister] is preparing herself to be a mother, he experienced a feeling resembling sympathy that she had been infected again with venereal disease" (Rozanov, *Liudi lunnogo sveta,* 105). Even though Rozanov claimed that the quote is in chapter 29 of *Resurrection,* it is not!

50. V. V. Rozanov, *Uedinennoe,* in *O sebe i zhizni svoei,* 88. In *Fallen Leaves,* Rozanov questioned Merezhkovsky's virility ("if he only can have sex" [of which I am doubtful]), suggesting that his antiprocreative ideology is the product of impotence (V. V. Rozanov, *Opavshie list'ia: Korob vtoroi,* in *O sebe i zhizni svoei,* 567).

51. "12-oe religiozno-filosofskoe sobranie," *Novyi put'* 6 (1903): 257.

52. "16-oe religiozno-filosofskoe sobranie," *Novyi put'* 10 (1903): 384.

53. "12-oe religiozno-filosofskoe sobranie," *Novyi put'* 6 (1903): 258–59.

54. "14-oe religiozno-filosofskoe sobranie," *Novyi put'* 9 (1903): 323–24.

55. "12-oe religiozno-filosofskoe sobranie," *Novyi put'* 6 (1903): 270.

56. I would like to thank Andrew Kahn for the English translation of "Poor Knight." A. S. Pushkin, *Polnoe sobranie sochinenii* (Moscow: ANSSSR, 1957), 3:118.

57. RGALI, f. 2176 (*Religiozno-filosofskoe obshchestvo*), op. 1, ed. khr. 4, p. 25 (meeting 13).

58. Ibid.

59. Ibid., 27–28.

60. Richard von Krafft-Ebing, *Psychopathia Sexualis* (New York: G. P. Putnam's Sons, 1965), 31n1.

61. RGALI, f. 2176, op. 1, ed. khr. 5, pp. 15–17.

62. Jean Pierrot, *The Decadent Imagination: 1880–1900,* trans. Derek Coltman (Chicago: University of Chicago Press, 1981), 89.

63. Foucault, *History of Sexuality,* 1:35.

64. V. V. Rozanov, *Liudi lunnogo sveta,* 111.

## Chapter 7. Vasilii Razonov

1. Andrei Bely, *O Bloke: Vospominaniia, stat'i, dnevniki, rechi,* ed. A. V. Lavrov (Moscow: Avtograf, 1997), 144–45. Cf. a similar description of Rozanov in Andrei Bely, *Nachalo veka,* ed. A. V. Lavrov (Moscow: Khudozhestvennaia literatura, 1990), 476–79.

2. Bely's Rozanov, whom the author viewed as a self-consciously constructed, vulgar petit bourgeois, resembles the disgusting double-agent Lippanchenko in *Petersburg;* like Bely's character, Rozanov savored his own uncouthness. For Nikolai Berdiaev's description of Rozanov, see his "O 'vechno bab'em' v russkoi dushe," in *V. V. Rozanov: Pro et Contra. Lichnost' i tvorchestvo*

*Vasiliia Rozanova v otsenke russkikh myslitelei i issledovatelei*, 2 vols. (St. Petersburg: Izd. Russkogo Khristianskogo gumanitarnogo instituta, 1995), 2:41.

3. V. V. Rozanov, *Opavshie list'ia: Korob pervyi*, in *O sebe i zhizni svoei* (Moscow: Moskovskii rabochii, 1990), 273. References to *Korob vtoroi* come from the same edition. All subsequent references to *Opavshie list'ia*, vols. 1 and 2, are noted in the text.

4. V. V. Rozanov, "O sladchaishem Iisuse i gor'kikh plodakh mira," in V. V. Rozanov, *V temnykh religioznykh luchakh*, ed. A. N. Nikoliuk (Moscow: Respublika, 1994), 423.

5. Instead of recording the entries in a diary book, as did Gippius, for instance, Rozanov emphasized the ostensible randomness of his thoughts, writing them on scraps of paper, frequently on the back of something else. Characteristic of his diary genre was the recycling of the everyday objects on which he wrote. Sometimes the used paper or other recycled object (envelope, private letter, poster, shoe sole, etc.) was identified; sometimes he recorded the time, location, and occasion of the writing. Besides revealing his fragmenting, or fetishizing, strategies, Rozanov also described the physical process of making the book whole: first, he removed the "leaves" from the basket where he had put them; then he stacked the snatches and scribbles into a pile that resembled a whole; and finally the stack appeared in book form. Unlike the abstract word "volume" [*tom*], the metaphoric bast basket [*korob*] suggests a messy container (Russian has a separate word—*korzina*—for a neat, woven basket), providing a "natural" semblance of order for the book's disparate parts.

6. These entries were interspersed among such standard index items as personal names and abstract notions. It is surprising that the recent editions of *Fallen Leaves* have not kept this index intact.

7. Some constructivists conflated sign and object, based on the assumption that the sign, or design of an object, is the object. The rupture between sign and object in symbolist poetry revealed the gap between empirical reality and the world that exists beyond it. One way that Rozanov attempted to bridge the gap between the abstract and the palpable was by turning to a metonymic poetics. He anchored the metonymic principle of contiguity in the physical world, claiming, e.g., that "the seed of the apple is the apple, a kernel of wheat is wheat; and the seed of man is apparently man" (*Opavshie list'ia*, 2:284).

8. Polemicizing with Rozanov's controversial 1907 lecture at the Religious-Philosophical Society ("Of the Sweetest Christ and the World's Bitter Fruit") in which he called Christianity a religion of death, Berdiaev compared him to "Tolstoy [who] unfurled before the world 'the green and yellow diaper' with which he wanted to be victorious over death." *The Kreutzer Sonata*, continued Berdiaev, "was only the seamy side of this diaper" (N. A. Berdiaev, "Khristos i mir: Otvet V. V. Rozanovu" in *V. V. Rozanov: Pro et Contra*, 2:30).

9. Rozanov insisted that there was no affinity between him and Nietzsche (*Opavshie list'ia*, 2:379). As early as 1896, he wrote that Nietzsche's writing is interesting but untrue. The reason he offered for this view was Nietzsche's hereditary mental illness over a period of fourteen years, during which he wrote his compositions (V. V. Rozanov, "Eshche o gr. L. N. Tolstom i ego uchenii o neso-

protivlenii zlu," in *O pisatel'stve i pisateliakh,* ed. A. N. Nikoliukin [Moscow: Respublika, 1995], 19). Rozanov wrote this right after he had read Lou Andreas Salome's article on Nietzsche in *The New Way* (1896), the first Russian publication about the new philosopher.

10. See Richard D. Davies, "Nietzsche in Russia, 1892–1919: A Chronological Checklist," in *Nietzsche in Russia,* ed. Bernice Glatzer Rosenthal (Princeton, N.J.: Princeton University Press, 1986), 355–92.

11. V. V. Rozanov, *Liudi lunnogo sveta: Metafizika khristianstva* (Moscow: Druzhba narodov, 1990), 146n1. Further references cited in the text, under the abbreviated title *Liudi.*

12. The term "urning" was introduced in the 1860s by one of the early sexologists, Karl Heinrich Ulrichs. A homosexual, he defined the urning as a man whose psychological makeup is female. The term is derived from the Greek god Uranus, who, according to Pausanias in the *Symposium,* is the parent of the heavenly Aphrodite, the goddess of same-sex love. Solov'ev celebrates this Aphrodite over the earthly one in *The Meaning of Love.*

13. Friedrich Nietzsche, *The Antichrist,* in *Twilight of the Idols and the Antichrist,* trans. R. J. Hollingdale (New York: Penguin, 1990), 153). Subsequent citations are noted in the text.

14. Elsewhere in *People of the Moonlight*, he wrote that "self-castration (*skopchestvo*) is the parent of the dry, vain intelligentsia" (*Liudi,* 138n1).

15. Such a conflation of Christian religious practice and sexual inversion resembles the ideas of the German sexologist Iwan Bloch, whose history of ancient religious cults subsumes all known sexual practices, from phallic worship and sacred prostitution, to fetishism, sadism, masochism, and homosexuality. A Russian translation of Bloch's *Sexual Life of Our Time and Its Relations to Modern Culture* appeared in 1910–11, at the time when Rozanov was writing *People of the Moonlight.*

16. Rozanov wrote about Weininger elsewhere, however, for instance in *Fallen Leaves* (*Opavshie, list'ia,* 1:181). For a discussion of the impact of Otto Weininger's *Sex and Character* in Russia, see Evgenii Bershtein, "Tragediia pola: dve zametki o russkom veininigerianstve," *Novoe literaturnoe obozrenie* 65 (2004): 208–28.

17. Merezhkovsky's name could be added to this list, especially his representation of Leonardo da Vinci in an eponymous novel.

18. Besides Krafft-Ebing, Rozanov also made references in *People of the Moonlight* to Charcot and Auguste Forel. Forel, a Swiss neuropathologist, wrote *The Sexual Question* in 1905. It was translated into Russian in 1908. Rozanov also wrote about Forel in "Germes i Afrodita," *Vesy* 5 (1905): 44–52.

19. The 1909 translation was based on the twelfth, and final, edition of Krafft-Ebing's book. The first postrevolutionary edition appeared in 1996 (R. Krafft-Ebing, *Polovaia psikhopatiia* [Moscow: Izd. "Respublika," 1996]).

20. V. V. Obol'ianinov, "Shtrikhi vospominanii," in *V. V. Rozanov: Pro et Contra,* 1:248.

21. See Alexander Etkind, *Eros of the Impossible: The History of Psychoanalysis in Russia,* trans. Noah and Maria Rubins (Boulder, Colo.: Westview Press, 1997), esp. 54–55, 59–63, 133–34.

22. Cesare Lombroso and G. Ferrero, *La femme criminelle et la prostituée,* trans. Louise Meille (Paris: Alcan, 1896), 409.

23. Michel Foucault, *The History of Sexuality,* trans. Robert Hurley (New York: Vintage, 1980), 1:58.

24. Ibid., 1:63–67.

25. For a discussion of Rozanov's journalistic practice, see the chapter on Rozanov in Konstantine Klioutchkine's dissertation, "Russian Literature and the Media" (University of California, Berkeley, 2002).

26. Anna Lisa Crone has argued convincingly for Rozanov's polyphonic style as defined by Bakhtin (*Rozanov and the End of Literature: Polyphony and the Dissolution of Genre in Solitaria and Fallen Leaves* [Wurzburg: Jal-Verlag, 1978], 126).

27. "Close the doors of your house more tightly to prevent a draft. . . . Do not open them often. And do not go outside. Do not go down the steps of your house—it is evil there," wrote Rozanov in *Fallen Leaves* (*Opavshie list'ia,* 2:453).

28. In the twelfth edition of *Psychopathia Sexualis,* it appears as case 129. See Richard von Krafft-Ebing, *Psychopathia Sexualis, with Especial Reference to the Antipathic Sexual Instinct: A Medico-Forensic Study,* trans. from the 12th German ed. by Franklin S. Klaf (New York: Stein & Day, 1965), 200–214.

29. See Sander L. Gilman, *Disease and Representation: Images of Illness from Madness to AIDS* (Ithaca, N.Y.: Cornell University Press, 1988), 187–91. According to Gilman, the attribution of menstruation to men stems from the myth of Jewish male menstruation.

30. In Rozanov's remarks about the case, he associated the surgeon's story with instances of self-castration by Christian ascetics (*Liudi,* 177).

31. Krafft-Ebing, *Psychopathia Sexualis,* 213.

32. If we consider Gippius's self-description as an androgynous fusion of male and female in the context of Rozanov's reading of the surgeon's story, we could claim that she experienced something similar to Rozanov's surgeon at those moments when she was content with her uncertain bodily gestalt. At other times, she could be said to experience the neurasthenic predicament of some of Krafft-Ebing's patients, especially those who suffered from what the psychiatrist labeled as sexual inversion.

33. Rozanov uses Latin script, spelling the word *homosexual'nosti* with an *x.*

34. Rozanov referred to Chernyshevsky frequently. Like Gippius, he felt profound ambivalence toward Chernyshevsky and the men and women of the 1860s. Mostly, he wrote disparagingly about them—for religious, political, and aesthetic reasons. Yet he expressed admiration for the "new men." On one hand, he perceived Chernyshevsky as "a fly filled with puss," biting the bull on its back (*Opavshie list'ia,* 2:455), but he also extolled him as a man of great energy and moral resolve whom the state should have placed at the helm, instead of the less capable or less resolute government officials appointed by Russian tsars. For a discussion of the 1860s and Chernyshevsky's talent, see Rozanov's column "In His Corner" in *New Path* ("V svoem uglu," *Novyi put'* 2 [1903]: 136–41, and no. 3 [1903]: 171–72). See also V. V. Rozanov, *Uedinennoe,* in *O sebe i zhizni svoei,* 50–52. A personal instance of Rozanov's fascination with the 1860s and erotic triangulation was his marriage to Apollinariia Suslova, a lover of Dostoevsky and a woman of the 1860s.

35. The term *oskoplenie* allowed Rozanov to discuss the case of the surgeon in the context of the Russian sect of self-castrators (*skoptsy*), who, he claimed, castrated themselves not for religious reasons but because their sense of gender went against nature: instead of harmony between their anatomy and their sexual instinct, which according to Rozanov was in the soul, they experienced their bodies as contrary to their gender identity.

36. Letter to B. A. Griftsov from April 24, 1911. Quoted in the commentary to Z. N. Gippius, "Zadumchivyi strannik (o V. V. Rozanove)," in *V. V Rozanov: Pro et Contra,* 1:478n31.

37. St. Ivanovich, "Pressa-modern," in *Literaturnyi raspad: Kriticheskii sbornik* (St. Petersburg: Zerno, 1908), 160.

38. See the section titled "Fetishist?" in chapter 2.

39. G. S. Novopolin's *Pornograficheskii element v russkoi literature* (St. Petersburg: Stasiulevich, 1909) treats Rozanov as a pornographic writer.

40. Conducting a study of Moscow university students' reading habits in 1909, Mikhail Chlenov reported that while one-third of them admitted to reading pornographic texts, the other two-thirds read popular medical texts as substitutes for pornography (*Polovaia perepis' moskovskogo studenchestva i ee obshchestvennoe znachenie* [Moscow, 1909], 49–52, cited in Laura Engelstein, *The Keys to Happiness: Sex and the Search for Modernity in Fin-de-siècle Russia* [Ithaca, N.Y.: Cornell University Press, 1992], 373n23).

41. The claim that God has a vagina may have come from a supposed comment by Merezhkovsky about which Rozanov wrote in a letter to Gippius from 1908: "Dm. Serg. said once 'Yes . . . God emerged from the vulva; God had to emerge from the vulva—precisely and only from it'" ("'Raspoiasannye pis'ma' V. Rozanova" [published by M. Pavlova], *Literaturnoe obozrenie* [special issue on *Eroticheskaia traditsiia v russkoi literature*] 11 [1991]: 71).

42. In a letter to Gippius from 1908, whom he addresses as "Little goat whose udder is milkless (oh, if only it had milk)," he asks her "how are your little nipples? Your little breasts? How sad it is if no one is caressing them" ("'Raspoiasannye pis'ma' V. Rozanova," 70).

43. The play was staged by Nikolai Evreinov, the symbolist director of the ill-fated *Salome* of 1908 and author-editor of the controversial book *Nudity on the Stage* (*Nagota na stsene*, 1912).

44. "'Raspoiasannye pis'ma' V. Rozanova," 69–70.

45. Rozanov wrote one of his first anti-Semitic articles in 1899 in response to the Dreyfus affair; Dreyfus's innocence or guilt did not seem to concern Rozanov at the time. At stake was the loyalty of French Jews to France. Instead of identifying with the French nation, French Jews, wrote Rozanov, sided with Dreyfus, right or wrong. He concluded that the power of the Jews lay in their tenacious solidarity with one another, not in integration into the larger society. The article ends with a warning: "Beware, Europe, your ice is brittle, strengthen your ice!" (V. V. Rozanov, "Evropa i evrei," in *Taina Izrailia: "Evreiskii vopros" v russkoi religioznoi mysli kontsa XIX—pervoi poloviny XX v. v.,* ed. V. F. Boikova [St. Petersburg: Sofiia, 1993], 274.)

46. V. V. Rozanov, *Apokalipsis nashego vremeni*, in *O sebe i zhizni svoei*, 644. He wrote in this passage that the Jews "represent the essence of world history, . . .

the 'seed' of the world. . . . I don't believe in the enmity of the Jews toward all nations. In the dark, at night, . . . I frequently observed a remarkable, assiduous love by Jews for Russians and for the Russian land. So may the Jew be blest. So may also the Russian be blest."

47. Rozanov had an amorous correspondence with Liudmila Vil'kina. He spent many years trying to retrieve his letters from her, fearing that she would make them public, but to no avail. He was particularly afraid that his wife, who was very sick, would learn about these letters. In the period of their closeness, he had written an introduction to her book of poetry *My Garden* (*Moi sad,* 1906). For samples of these letters, see "'Raspoiasannye pis'ma' V. Rozanova," 69.

48. Many in the circles of Ivanov, Minsky, Gippius, and Blok knew about this gathering. Describing the event, Bely wrote that "in some salon [the guests] were sticking someone with a pin and squeezing the blood into wine, calling this idiocy 'co-communion' (Ivanov's word)" (Andrei Bely, *Mezhdu dvukh revoliutsii,* ed. Alexander Lavrov [Moscow: Khudozhestvennaia literatura, 1990], 176).

49. For more detail about the evening, see E. P. Ivanov's letter in "Shtrikhi vospominanii," in *V. V. Rozanov: Pro et Contra,* 1:250–53.

50. Gippius, "Zadumchivyi strannik," in *V. V. Rozanov: Pro et Contra,* 1:170.

51. V. V. Rozanov, "Napominaniia po telefonu," in *Oboniatel'noe i osiazatel'noe otnoshenie evreev k krovi,* in *Sakharna,* ed. A. N. Nikoliukin (Moscow: Izd. "Respublika," 1998), 337. The figure of the young Jewish student as the object of sacrifice may have reminded some participants of the crucified Jewish child in Liza Khokhlakova's decadent anti-Semitic fantasy in *The Brothers Karamazov,* in which the hysterical Liza imagines herself eating pineapple compote as she watches the child's torment.

52. Ibid. In a footnote to the reprinted feuilleton, Rozanov offered a postscript in which he revealed his anti-Semitism and the intelligentsia's reaction to it: his stepdaughter, who had attended the meeting with him, was outraged by the article, calling it a betrayal and denunciation of his old friends to the authorities, who could charge them with performing ritual sacrifice. She demanded that he write a letter of recantation to the editor, which he did, making himself the laughing stock of the press. Yet his concluding remarks in the note stated that the blood of Iushchinsky was worth more than "literary etiquette" (338).

53. Ibid., 337–38.

54. Lombroso identified atavism with reproductive sterility, which, according to him, also characterized the physiology of geniuses.

55. V. V. Rozanov, "Andriusha Iushchinsky," in *Oboniatel'noe i osiazatel'noe otnoshenie evreev k krovi,* in *Sakharna,* 304.

56. Besides tainting the nation's biological bloodline, Rozanov's predatory Jew insinuates himself into the economic and cultural life of the nation: Jews control banks, business, press, literature, etc. Rozanov chose some of the most stereotypical anti-Semitic metaphors to describe them, to which he added his own characteristically vituperative, fleshy discourse: "[O]ne spider, but he has ten flies in his web," wrote Rozanov in *Fallen Leaves.* "And they had wings, flight. He just crawls. And their sight is broader, horizon. But they are dead, and he is alive. Like Russians and Jews. 100 million Russians and 7 million Jews." Rozanov went on to claim that the pogroms were the result of the spider's sin-

ister activity: "The spider suckles the fly. The fly buzzes. Its wings flutter convulsively—and graze the spider, helplessly tear the web in one place." In the next entry he suggested a solution: "[W]e should cut the web around the borders, and throw it down and trample it. We must free ourselves from the web and sweep all webs out of the room" (*Opavshie list'ia,* 2:428). The repellent anti-Semitic message, which Rozanov imbricated with his favorite images of the stickiness of home and suckling, is obvious. For a discussion of this passage in the context of Russian anti-Semitism in the twentieth century, see Mikhail Zolotonosov, "Akhutokost-Akhum: Opyt rasshifrovki skazki K. Chukovskogo o mukhe," *Novoe literaturnoe obozrenie* 2 (1993): 262–82.

57. See J. M. Charcot, *Leçons du Mardi à la Salpêtriere* (Paris: Progrès médical, 1889); Richard Krafft-Ebing, *Text-Book of Insanity,* trans. Charles Gilbert Chaddock (Philadelphia: F. A. Davis, 1905); and Cesare Lombroso, *L'antisemitismo e la scienze moderne* (Turin: L. Roux, 1894).

58. For a discussion of anti-Semitic propaganda that Jews were the cause of the decline of the Russian birth rate, see Engelstein, *Keys to Happiness,* 305.

59. V. V. Rozanov, "Zapisi, ne voshedshie v osnovnoi tekst "Sakharny," in *Sakharna,* 264.

60. Rozanov's 1903 monograph *Judaism* is a "scholarly" study of Judaic religion from a philo-Semitic point of view; it was published in Gippius's *New Path.* Typically, he cites in it sacred books and recycles other written texts, offering his responses in footnotes. If it contains an underlying anti-Semitic agenda, it is expressed in the words of someone else, for instance of a Russian Jew who rationalized Russian anti-Semitism, claiming that had he not been Jewish, he would have been considered an unsavory anti-Semite. Rozanov writes that the anti-Semitic Russian peasant is a firm believer in the myth that the Jews killed Christ, adding to this a supposedly ancient peasant belief according to which the eyes of Jewish infants, like those of puppies, open only after they have been "smeared with Christian blood obtained from a slaughtered . . . [Christian] infant" (V. V. Rozanov, *Iudaizm,* in *Taina Izrailia,* 167). As a slippery immoralist, who first and foremost subverted liberal values, Rozanov did not comment on these anecdotes of Russian anti-Semitism, but his responses to the Judaic religion, its rituals, and Jewish daily life in *Judaism* were exclusively positive. He celebrated circumcision and other blood rituals as having great religious power.

61. Engelstein, *Keys to Happiness,* 327.

62. V. Sokolov's *Obrezanie u evreev: Istoriko-bogoslovskoe issledovanie* appeared in *Pravoslavnyi Sobesednik,* a Kazan' theological journal, in 1890–91. A separate publication of it also appeared in Kazan'. The quotation is taken from V. V. Rozanov, "Vazhnyi istoricheskii vopros," *Oboniatel'noe i osiazatel'noe otnoshenie evreev k krovi,* in *Sakharna,* 297.

63. V. V. Rozanov, "Chto mne sluchilos' uvidet'. . .," in *Oboniatel'noe i osiazatel'noe otnoshenie evreev k krovi,* in *Sakharna,* 394.

64. V. V. Rozanov, "Sem'ia kak religiia," in *V mire neiasnogo i nereshennogo,* ed. A. N. Nikoliukin (Moscow: Respublika, 1995), 71.

65. V. V. Rozanov, "Zhertvoprinosheniia u drevnikh evreev," in *Oboniatel'noe i osiazatel'noe otnoshenie evreev k krovi,* in *Sakharna,* 354–55.

66. Rozanov's anti-Semitism in the second decade of the twentieth century

included many standard anti-Semitic obsessions, such as identifying the Jewish origins of political radicals, social activists, writers, and artists, with the purpose of revealing how their tainted blood infected contemporary Russian culture. In his paranoia, he sometimes included in his list of "disclosures" writers who were not Jewish. He listed among others the populist writer Vladimir Korolenko; as "proof" he referred to a portrait by Repin in which Korolenko, claimed Rozanov, looks Jewish (V. V. Rozanov, "V Sakharne," in *Sakharna*, 71). When he could not locate Jewish origins, he imputed them by association: he accused Merezhkovsky of being a "secret Jew" (V. V. Rozanov, "Posle Sakharny," in *Sakharna*, 227) and Tolstoy and Solov'ev of having been "tainted" by Jewishness.

67. Ibid., 178. Many critics present a one-sided view of Rozanov's anti-Semitism, either avoiding it altogether or focusing only on it. For instance, Victor Shklovsky's groundbreaking essay on Rozanov makes no references to his anti-Semitism. It deals with rhetorical strategies, not ideology. Yet Rozanov's anti-Semitism was one of the keys to his use of the oxymoron, which Shklovsky considered Rozanov's master trope. But then Shklovsky was a formalist. Andrei Siniavsky, on the other hand, referred to Rozanov's anti-Semitism but subordinated it to his fascination with Judaism and envy of the organic Jewish relation to physiology and sexuality (A. Siniavsky, *"Opavshie list'ia" V. V. Rozanova* [Paris: Sintaksis, 1982]). This despite the fact that Siniavsky was a Rozanovian paradoxicalist who chose for himself the Jewish pseudonym Abram Tertz. *The Jews' Olfactory and Tactile Relationship to Blood* was reprinted only once before the recent Russian publication (1998); it appeared in emigration in 1932 (Stockholm reprint). All of Rozanov's writing was suppressed in the Soviet Union. This makes the 1998 publication, edited by A. N. Nikoliukin, a Rozanov scholar, an important event in the history of Rozanov publishing. The book's title, however, does not appear on the book cover. It is part of a volume titled *Sakharna* (a place name), one of the volumes in the first *Collected Works* of Rozanov. Almost half of the volume is taken up by *Sakharna*, an unpublished anti-Semitic "bundle" of "fallen leaves" from 1913, which is much less interesting than Rozanov's earlier books in this genre. The commentary to it is fifteen pages long; the commentary to *The Jews' Olfactory and Tactile Relationship to Blood* is only two and a half, even though it is much more important than *Sakharna*. It is unfortunate that such a key work continues to exist with a deficient scholarly apparatus. This is not the place to consider the possible reasons for the disproportionally meager commentary on *The Jews' Olfactory and Tactile Relationship to Blood*. What can be said with certainty is that Nikoliukin has chosen not to highlight Rozanov's most controversial book.

68. Foucault, *History of Sexuality*, 1:127.

69. Ibid., 1:154.

70. See note 56.

71. "'Sud' nad Rozanovym: Zapiski S.-Peterburskogo Religiozno-filosofskogo obshchestva" in *V. V. Rozanov: Pro et Contra*, 2:192.

72. V. V. Rozanov, *Uedinennoe*, in *O sebe i zhizni svoei*, 86.

73. In the end, however, the majority of the members of the Religious-Philosophical Society did not vote for expulsion. One reason was that people

such as Viacheslav Ivanov, who believed in literary freedom above all else, refused to consider the Religious-Philosophical Society a political party. Viacheslav Ivanov, Peter Struve, and Anastasiia Chebotarevskaia were among those who spoke out against the resolution to expel Rozanov. The resolution to expel was replaced by a harshly worded reprimand. Rozanov responded by canceling his membership.

74. In an undated letter to Metropolitan Antonii of St. Petersburg and Ladoga from the turn of the twentieth century, in which Rozanov asked him to reconsider his request for divorce, he wrote that "the physical life of a man was never hot in him" (V. V. Rozanov, "Proshenie Antoniiu, Mitropolitu Sankt-Peterburgskomu i Ladozhskomu," in *O sebe i zhizni svoei,* 696).

75. Vladimir Bekhterev, student of Ivan Merzheevsky, was an internationally renowned neurologist and psychiatrist who studied the anatomy and physiology of the brain and central nervous system. It may be worthwhile to note that Bekhterev was one of the medical specialists to testify for the defense—and against the blood libel—in the Beilis case.

76. Rozanov writes that the gynecological surgery was recommended by Dr. Karl Rentel'n (V. V. Rozanov, *Uedinennoe,* in *O sebe i zhizni svoei,* 115). The diagnosis of cerebral palsy was made either in 1896 or 1897; Varvara Dmitrievna was already in ill health. Diagnosed later with heart disease and other dispersed medical symptoms, she suffered a stroke in 1910 from which she never fully recovered. Among lesser known Petersburg doctors that she and Rozanov consulted during those years were Vera Gedroits (also a poet), Gustav Tilling, Mikhail Grinberg, (?) Kukovenov, Vol'f Raivid, and of course their personal physician Alexander Karpinsky. (According to Laura Engelstein, an Alexander Karpinsky appeared as a medical expert for the defense at the Beilis trial [*Keys to Happiness,* 326n122]; I have not been able to establish whether this was the same Dr. Karpinsky or not.) In any case, Varvara Dmitrievna's chronic degenerative illness and related depressions certainly put a pall on their lives.

77. Berdiaev, "O 'vechno bab'em' v russkoi dushe" in *V. V. Rozanov: Pro et Contra,* 2:41.

## Conclusion

1. Vasilii Rozanov, "Mimoletnoe: 1915," in *Mimoletnoe,* ed. A. N. Nikoliukin (Moscow: Respublika, 1994), 60, 66.

2. Alexander Blok, *Dnevnik 1917 goda,* in *Sobranie sochinenii v vos'mi tomakh* (Moscow: Khudozhestvennaia literatura, 1963), 7:281.

3. A. Blok, *Poslednie dni imperatorskoi vlasti,* 6:190.

4. A. Blok, *Katilina,* 6:66.

5. A. Blok, *Poslednie dni imperatorskoi vlasti,* 6:188.

6. A. Blok, *Dnevnik 1921 goda,* 6:405–6.

7. Leon Trotsky, *Literature and Revolution* (New York: Russell & Russell, 1957), 254.

8. For a discussion of antiprocreationism in the Soviet 1920s, see Olga Matich, "Remaking the Bed: Utopia in Daily Life," in *Laboratory of Dreams: The*

*Russian Avant-Garde and Cultural Experiment,* ed. John Bowlt and Olga Matich (Stanford, Calif.: Stanford University Press, 1996), 59–78.

9. Michael Holquist, "Tsiolkovsky in the Prehistory of the Avant-Garde," in *Laboratory of Dreams,* 107–9. For a discussion of Fedorov's influence on the Soviet avant-garde, see Irene Masing-Delic, "The Transfiguration of Cannibals: Fedorov and the Avant-Garde," in *Laboratory of Dreams,* 17–36.

10. See Boris Groys, *The Total Art of Stalinism: Avant-Garde, Aesthetic Dictatorship, and Beyond,* trans. Charles Rougle (Princeton, N.J.: Princeton University Press, 1992).

# Index